Praise for *Come of Age*

"Stephen Jenkinson has a way of reaching right into the heart of Western culture's dis-ease, all the while deftly rupturing and turning the English language inside out in order to do so. He traces the roots of the word elder to 'coming to fullness' or 'fully realized,' to one who may take their place among us only when the ebbing and failure of growth is admitted."

—RUTH JONES,
founder of Holy Hiatus, Wales, UK

"Jenkinson does not blame, indict, nor traffic in solution, rather he elders—with an immense love of life and the world—the long redemptive road where young and old might yet recognize each other and decide to take a little walk. *Come of Age* has so much respect for your willingness to pick it up that it will ask more of you than you ever thought possible; an unlikely and precious gift that may just change everything."

—SEAN AIKEN,
author of *The One-Week Job Project*

"Be you young, middle-aged, or in your time of greying, Stephen Jenkinson's scrying into the daunting crater of what has happened to us historically, mythically, spiritually to forge today's dominant culture with its signature malignant appetite for progress and novelty, is a much-needed missive from an uncommonly rare voice in the clamouring marketplace of protest, self-help, and innovative solutions. *Come of Age* attests to the tragic dearth of deep abiding regard for elderhood once traditionally recognized and prized as a sign of health and sanity in cultures that knew something of the artful ways of the world, of the Gods and of human making, a regard without which a culture goes bankrupt and becomes a menace to life and to itself. With a lucidity that is at once beautifully poetic and arresting, and with an astounding deftness tracing the signs available to us in both their unmistakable presences and absences, Jenkinson invites us to gather around the crackling fire of wonder and heartbreak where, without recourse to clever fixes, we might properly give ourselves to being awed, bewildered, and sorrowed, perhaps the preferred ground of real humility and courage. For the sake of the world, for the sake of the young, for the sake of elderhood, let this prescient book wreck you."

—RACHELLE LAMB, Nonviolent
Communications (NVC) Trainer

"This book transcends ideology and platitudes and takes you deep into ancestral roots and wisdom. Jenkinson is a treasure—a raspy, nonconforming sage who has the rare ability to sneak up behind you with masterful storytelling that compels you to be troubled enough and to wonder (barely in the nick of time) if you are ready to begin to live your life as if you matter. This book brings a deeply learned, insightful, and rare perspective on navigating these troubled modern times."

—DANA BASS SOLOMON,
Graduated CEO, Hollyhock Centre,
British Columbia, Canada

"If you have ever been fortunate enough to be standing by a frozen river on the days when the slightly warming temperature over the previous days has made the ice just fragile enough to finally give way to the urgent water that had been dammed upstream, you might have witnessed an analogue to this book. The cracking and groaning of the ice as the water goes from trickle to gushing flood and finding the boundaries of the banks is a marvel to see and hear. Jenkinson's words in his newest book are that bracing, urgent, and ancient water pushing through the frozen times we might find ourselves living in. This encomium to elderhood is a slow and winding affair that gathers power and purpose and new influences as the waters roll down from an altitude to and through our lives down here."

—MATTHEW STILLMAN,
author of *Genesis Deflowered*

"*Come of Age* is a timely, powerful exploration of the loss of elderhood in our society. Stephen has gifted us with a compelling, poetic appraisal of the loss of and need for elderhood, interwoven with poignant and sometimes painful stories and lessons. An invaluable contribution to our society that will inspire generations to come."

—RAMONA BOLTON, director,
Institute of Traditional Medicine

"In *Come of Age*, Stephen Jenkinson invites the reader to join him in a lyrical journey as he makes the case for elderhood. His luminous and erudite prose unravels the metanarrative of Western culture as it ponders time, the deep contours of Christianity, the implications of *civis Romanus sum* for the creation of the entity known as The West, the forgetting of place or as he puts it 'place literacy,' and the joy of poetry. In these wide-ranging musings, Jenkinson reveals the poverty of a culture in which people are old but not elders while breathing life into the possibility of an elder, forged by the calamities of time, who proceeds with deep courtesy as if he or she is needed."

—SIKATA BANERJEE, PhD,
professor of gender studies,
University of Victoria

"Many of us in this modern, dominant culture of North America walk around with a deep 'elder hunger' but we don't recognize it as such until we meet someone willing to elder. Jenkinson makes the case that waking up to this hunger and learning how to contend with it well might be one of the most needed things in this time and place we live in. I look around me and see the hunger for convenience, efficiency, ease, freedom. and more, but perhaps we might be better served to open the pages of this book and see if a certain relationship to this old, human hunger might help us conjure the food that the soul of our culture so desperately needs."

—TAD HARGRAVE,
founder, Marketing for Hippies

"We live in deeply troubled times. The biosphere is collapsing, the economy sputtering, and the mania for the ever-new continues its siren song. To whom and to what can young people turn that might still yet stand in the face of the storm? Enter *Come of Age*—a raucous and grief-soaked tangle through the annals of history, language, etymology, and, above all, a deep love of life. With fierce prose and unrelenting compassion, Stephen Jenkinson makes the case for elderhood in a time desperate for the wisdom that accrues to those willing to be aged, who are willing to know limitation and deep service to the ending of days."

—IAN MACKENZIE, filmmaker,
Occupy Love and *Amplify Her*

COME OF AGE

COME OF AGE

The Case for Elderhood in a Time of Trouble

Stephen Jenkinson, MTS, MSW

Foreword by Charles Eisenstein

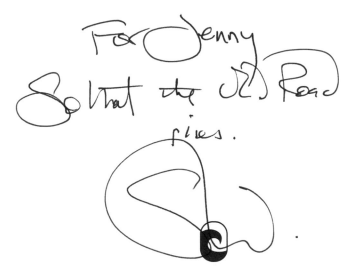

For Jenny
So that the Old Road
flies.

North Atlantic Books,
Berkeley, California

Ⅹ·19

Portland

Published by
North Atlantic Books
Berkeley, California

Cover art directed by Stephen Jenkinson
Book design by Happenstance Type-O-Rama
Printed in the United States of America

Come of Age: The Case for Elderhood in a Time of Trouble is sponsored and published by the Society for the Study of Native Arts and Sciences (dba North Atlantic Books), an educational nonprofit based in Berkeley, California, that collaborates with partners to develop cross-cultural perspectives, nurture holistic views of art, science, the humanities, and healing, and seed personal and global transformation by publishing work on the relationship of body, spirit, and nature.

North Atlantic Books' publications are available through most bookstores. For further information, visit our website at www.northatlanticbooks.com or call 800-733-3000.

Library of Congress Cataloging-in-Publication Data

Names: Jenkinson, Stephen, author.
Title: Come of age : the case for elderhood in a time of trouble / Stephen Jenkinson, MTS, MSW.
Description: Berkeley, California : North Atlantic Books, 2018.
Identifiers: LCCN 2017054215 (print) | LCCN 2018014084 (ebook) | ISBN 9781623172107 (e-book) | ISBN 9781623172091 (pbk.)
Subjects: LCSH: Older people. | Aging. | Experience. | Wisdom. | Generations. | Conduct of life.
Classification: LCC HQ1061 (ebook) | LCC HQ1061 .J465 2018 (print) | DDC 305.26—dc23
LC record available at https://lccn.loc.gov/2017054215

2 3 4 5 6 7 8 9 KPC 22 21 20 19 18

Printed on recycled paper

North Atlantic Books is committed to the protection of our environment. We partner with FSC-certified printers using soy-based inks and print on recycled paper whenever possible.

It is impossible for a servant to serve two masters, otherwise he will honour the one and treat the other contemptuously. No one drinks old wine and immediately desires to drink new wine; and they do not put new wine into old wineskins, lest they burst, and they do not put old wine into new wineskin, lest it spoil it.

Gospel of Thomas, Log. 47

TABLE OF CONTENTS

FOREWORD

Cultures older than our own widely believed that words carried a magical, generative power. They were not mere symbolic ephemera, arbitrary signs connected through arbitrary social convention to the real world of things. Words were emanations of land and life, partaking intimately of the beingness of the things, processes, and qualities they signified. To name a thing was to invoke it.

All the more potent, then, was the arrangement of words into story, and the enacting of those stories through ritual. The world was narrated into existence, and upheld through the telling of stories and the performance of rituals. Thus it was that older cultures widely believed—or should I say widely recognized—that the degradation and abandonment of their rituals portended the End of the World.

Who can say, surveying the calamity that befell those cultures when Christian conversion and market economies swept their rituals aside and replaced them with school, money, law, and medicine, that they were wrong?

Today the dominant culture faces the same fate as those it destroyed. Our own rituals and stories seem to be withering, along with the power of word itself. We live in a world of spin and hype, messaging and image, of official lying so routine that it has lost its ability to shock us. Therefore, no longer do the hierarchs of Western society seem able to proclaim, "So shall it be," and thereby speak wonders into existence. The mystical incantations of the Federal Reserve no longer conjure prosperity. The rituals of the medical establishment, despite their hyperbolic elaboration, cannot dispel new-wave diseases like autoimmunity, allergy, Lyme, and cancer. The rites of the injection, the pill, the divinatory test, and the procedure have lost their magic potency.

No longer do we gape in superstitious awe at the power of our high priests, the scientists. No longer do we believe that a Brave New World awaits us, but one or two inventions away. No longer do we believe in the glorious Ascent of Humanity to overlordship of all beings. We are still mired in the habits and institutions born of those beliefs, the whole tower of certainty built on them, but we no longer know what we believe or believe what we know. We are entering a space between stories.

When our stories waver, so does the world built upon them. This book has the potential to unravel reality by severing the threads of some of its main defining stories. Neither I nor Mr. Jenkinson uphold the postmodern conceit that we human beings are the authors of the stories that weave the world. In that regard, postmodernism is not "post" modern at all, but merely extends the centrality of the human being yet another step, arrogating to ourselves meaning, purpose, intention, agency, and all the other qualities of a self. This conceptual robbery of the world sets the stage for its material plunder.

Or could it be the other way around—that the material plunder of the world, the reduction of its stones, soils, plants, animals, and water into commodities, the economic reduction of quality to quantity and values to value, suggested and then demanded its conceptual reduction? Whichever came first, our present predicament is that the story maintains the system and the system maintains the story. They are an inseparable whole, a being unto themselves.

I mean that literally: we are participants in the life of an organic entity that, like all beings, goes through various stages of life. The being we might call "modern civilization" is obviously in a stage of senescence, though whether this precedes its death or its metamorphosis is probably beyond what anyone within it can know. Either way, the question we face is not how to prolong its youth, under the banner, for instance, of "sustainable development" or "green growth." It is not how we might sustain the familiar, but rather what we want to become. Actually, let me retract that statement. The question of what we *want* to become may be premature, because our wanting bears the indelible tint of the delusions of our age. It is more a matter of listening for what we *are* to become. The question "What story shall we create next?" is new wine in an old skin, contaminated with the dying story of man in the driver's seat, master of his own destiny, master of the world, master of the wild, master of the mystery, onward and upward along a triumphal arc of progress. Better questions might be "What story comes next?" "Which new-and-ancient story offers itself with the most beauty?" And "How might we prepare to accept it?"

These questions veer close to the subject of the book you are about to read. Stephen Jenkinson explores (among other things) what our cultural fetish for youth and growth, security and control, have done to aging and the aged; why we have so many old people and so few elders. The attempt to prolong and preserve youth, which amounts to a denial of death, is precisely what thwarts the transition to elderhood. In my understanding, an elder is someone who knows she is going to die, someone who knows failure and limit. By "know" here I mean that the reality of death, failure, and limit has obliterated internal structures of denial and humbled the edifice of meaning. It is proper that the youth act as if he would never die, that he be ignorant of failure and limit. The over-protected youth in the age of "safety first," insulated by classroom walls from genuine failure, is fated to reenact other people's failures, not his own. Protected from the painful and dangerous encounter with limits, he is ripe to adopt the civilizational ideology of limitlessness.

To put elderhood into such a tidy package ("an elder is someone who ...") reveals, perhaps, my own lack of qualification for such an office. That's OK. Speaking from early middle age, the torts and insults that life visits upon my Story of Self and Story of the World have not completed their work. This book, coming from a seasoned man, attempts nothing so crude as a direct definition of elderhood. I must confess to not fully understanding this book in one reading. I encourage the reader to do the same—to not fully understand it, by which I mean: do not be too eager to fit it into existing categories of understanding.

I am not optimistic that the reader will abide this suggestion. As I read quotes to a small group gathered around a table, I witnessed them translating Mr. Jenkinson's words into conventional pieties and containable solutions. "We need to respect our elders; we need to have initiations into elderhood...." Please dispense with your expectations of what this book will say, and do not hope that it will fortify the way you understand elderhood and aging. It is much more likely that if you engage it earnestly, this book will leave your understanding in tatters.

Alternatively, since you are the kind of person who reads this kind of book, you may recognize and welcome this as another step in a long process of disrobing. The vestments of the story we inherited never fit very well anyway, did they? You've clawed away at them your whole life, yet still the rags remain, and still something pinches and chafes. It is the undergarments, so familiar that we mistook them for our own skin. They are the unconscious ground perceptions of the modernized human. If you, like me, yearn to be freed from their confinement, you will likely greet this book with more joy than defensiveness as it helps you strip away what was never comfortable to begin with.

Returning to the idea that an elder is someone who knows the reality of death, failure, and limit, it is clear that what Mr. Jenkinson says about the individual applies equally to our civilization. Can we not see that its fetish for growth is a doomed attempt to prolong its youth? Doomed, I say, because limit awaits in the end (as the locution "in the end" suggests). Ignoring that, we remain frozen in a parody of youth. The collective equivalents of the trophy wife and the sports car, facelifts and hormone replacement therapy, mask the bitter truth of our growing incapacity. Gone is the can-do spirit of the 1950s and 1960s, when hardly anyone doubted that the future would bring space colonies and robot servants, the conquest of all disease, limitless atomic energy, and the extension into the social realm of the successes of material science. We would engineer our social problems out of existence too. Such is the naïveté of youth.

Since then the totalizing ambition of science and technology has hit one limit after another. While vestiges of the old technological utopianism persist in some quarters, few people actually believe the breathless assurances that nanotechnology or genetic medicine or Total Information Awareness will finally open the gates of Heaven. Our lived experience of social decline says otherwise.

As social systems deteriorate and collective ambitions wither, our inherited certainties grow brittle and shatter at the slightest tap of misfortune. What once seemed unquestionable, real, and permanent is revealed as so much illusion. Blinking before the chasm, we might try to summon the illusion anew: Make America Great Again, or achieve the UN Sustainable Development Goals. Or we might turn to the undisguised illusions of fantasy novels, fantasy football, reality television, video games, sports fandom, and the staged brawl on the *Titanic* that we call politics. When the stories that give life meaning and direct us toward our reason-for-being dissolve into a postmodern funk, all that is left is Debord's *Society of the Spectacle*. Yet we have another possibility: to turn back toward the abyss, embrace the unknowing, and thereby come of age.

Having lost faith in our story, we return to the aforementioned questions of what story wants to come next. The story of interbeing, the story of humanity in service to the healing of Gaia, the story of reunion with place, nature, materiality, and life are all worthy candidates, but let us take a pause here. Let us take the same pause I counseled earlier when I warned against trying too quickly to understand this book. Faced with the wreckage of our moribund old stories, we might channel the newly freed energy toward a hasty reconstruction project, recreating the old in some new-and-improved, rebranded version.

To pause here does not mean that we must wander aimlessly forever, prodding among the rubble. Yes, let us not rush too quickly to build a new structure, but know that when the time comes, we will build one. We will build another edifice of knowledge that will serve for a time to order life, to give meaning, to contain a span of years, and it too will someday creak and crumble under the strain of too much.

I have suggested we listen for a new story, but how? To listen for the future starts with listening to the present and the past; that is, to come face to face with the reality of our failures and our limits. It is to let them in, to allow them to dissolve our story and our certainty. It is a process of humiliation and of grief. There are signs that it is beginning. In the United States, for example, the old story of "America, land of the free and home of the brave, bringing peace and democracy to the world" is cracking under the hammer blows of one ignominious revelation after another, from My Lai to Abu Ghraib to police brutality, child abuse, and sexual assault; meanwhile, growing awareness of the genocide and slavery in its origins chisels away at the story's very foundations. So far these revelations have been housed in the ghetto of "unfortunate exception" and "that's all in the past but we're better now." Nonetheless, the certainty is hollowing out from the inside.

The story that is disintegrating in our time is much older and deeper than 1950s technological utopianism or nineteenth-century cultural imperialism. Stephen Jenkinson traces it as far back as the Roman Empire, which with grievous violence supplanted place-based cultural belonging with the universal Roman citizen. Others trace it back even further to earlier empires, which from China to the Levant to the Americas developed social inequality, dislocation of culture from place, slavery, conquest, and environmental ruin. Anyway, moving forward from Rome, Christianity erected upon the scaffold of Roman universalism a further edifice of separation: the abstraction of spirit from matter, leaving the former generic and the latter inconsequential. The former multitude of stories and lifeways, each an organic outgrowth of a unique place on earth, was reduced to the universal brotherhood of man. Then came the Scientific Revolution, which, far from overthrowing Christianity, extended its basic perceptions still further. It completed the transition to world-as-thing and the ascension of humanity beyond it. Viewing matter as nothing but atoms and void, a random melee of mathematical forces operating on standard material building blocks, it confirmed that human destiny was to harness those forces and build with those building blocks. Agreeing with Christianity's abstraction of spirit from matter, it celebrated the imposition of human intelligence and design onto a world that possessed neither. The cardinal virtues of this program were predictability and control, established through the elimination of variables, the conversion of quality to quantity, and the testing of hypotheses.

This is the context for the derangement that this book laments. Certainty, regularity, universality, predictability, and control are well at home in our systems of money and industry, science and technology, and, most saliently for present purposes, medicine and aging. They are the air the modern individual breathes. Today we explore the furthest extremes of separation: the conversion of reality into a data set and the biosphere into dollars. The wild would seem to be nearly abolished.

In this book, Mr. Jenkinson invokes the concept of the *welt*, the liminal zone where the human world engages the wild. He writes, "The welt is sustained by the wild, that which lies out beyond what sustains culture. And the wild is sustained by our willingness not to go there, or live there, or plunder the place, or imagine it as a natural resource."

If we do continue that plunder, the result may not be that we will perish. It is that we will no longer have a culture. Culture, says Stephen Jenkinson, can only persist in relation to limits. Culture is the negotiation of a place in things; what we call our culture today has no place—quite literally, it is placeless, everywhere and therefore nowhere. Having usurped the places of other-than-human beings, it has nothing upon which to brace itself; like a spiderweb with no anchor points, it collapses inward. We see that today in its endless involution, its mounting layers of self-referentiality. Without the external anchor we might call wilderness, it becomes merely about itself. And so we see phenomena like *The Lego Batman Movie,* a film based on a toy that is based on a film that is based on a comic book, that is itself a kind of degenerate myth or, worse, an imitation myth. We see a political culture that has degenerated into cartoonish postures in place of beliefs, raw emotion dressed up in whatever meagre opinions are available, the devolution of civic discourse into infantile good-guy/bad-guy chauvinism. Ignorant of what Bayo Akomolafe calls the Wilds Beyond our Fences, we cannibalize what remains of the culture we inherited. Just as we consume the wild in the process known as development, so we consume the ancient welds of thought and story, imagining ourselves to be their creators rather than their tenants.

The rent is overdue. The payment is the sacrifice of certainty and control that comes in engagement with the wild. That is what renews the weld. That is the breach in the dam that sends the floodwaters over the land, spreading the silt and fertilizing the soil.

Climate alarmists and social collapsists are fond of saying, "Now we are going to *have* to change." But as Stephen Jenkinson observed, in the "death trade," the prospect of annihilation often provokes not change but more strenuous attempts to resist it. What other impetus could there be for change? Among climate activists, human extinction is generally agreed to be the worst-case scenario. I can think of one far more chilling. It is that we succeed in replacing ecosystems services with technological services, ushering in a concrete world with algae pools for oxygen, giant carbon sucking machines, bubble cities, food grown in vats, pharmaceutical happy drugs, and hi-res displays of bygone nature scenes for aesthetic relief. All of this will be accompanied by endlessly rising indicators of wealth and health: more goods and services, more floor area per capita, rising GDP, longer lifespans, and so on. It is a world where everything quantifiable expands at the expense of the qualitative; where the domesticated expands at the expense of the wild, where we lunge toward the appearance of wealth to compensate for an unspeakably desolate poverty.

Can we say that we have not proceeded step by step toward such a future?

To invoke survival fear to force change is to invoke the very same mind-set that causes the crisis to begin with. It suggests we devote ourselves more diligently and cleverly to survival. Maybe we need to give up that campaign and devote ourselves to love rather than safety, beauty rather than growth, and participation rather than control. That is a revolution that would reach to the foundations of our civilization: its science, its economy, its medicine, its ways of birth, death, and everything in between. The book you are about to read is an incitement to that kind of revolution.

To undo the edifice of knowledge whose fraudulence the present crisis reveals, is a much bigger undertaking than to replace one set of facts with another. It is not merely that what we thought we knew, was wrong; we now come to doubt our very ways of knowing, what knowledge is, and what it is for. The subversion in these pages goes that deep.

This book does not offer solutions for civilization's predicament. No "solution" is possible when the cause of the malady is no less than everything. The rush to a solution is, at this point, part of the problem. We fight crime with prisons, terrorism with bombs, weeds with herbicides, depression with drugs, and climate change with biofuels plantations and mega-dams, in each case fighting the symptom while exacerbating the causes. Yes, in a healthy culture, we would respect our elders, but exhorting people to respect old people today glosses over the question of why and how we came not to. Yes, in a healthy culture, men and women would receive initiation at every stage of life, but our own lack of initiations is a symptom too. For an initiation to be more than a weekend workshop adventure, the culture must hold a place for the initiate to land. Elderhood is not a state of being that the separate neoliberal subject can achieve or not achieve; it is a communal function born of social, ancestral, and ecological relationships. The dominant culture does not hold a place for the elder. *Elder* is a word with no coherent referent in our cultural mythology, no traditions of relationship or practice, and no social institutions except its mockery: the "elder care facility."

The question is not whether but when we will finally face the reality of failure and limit. Mr. Jenkinson says that elderhood is not an inevitability, not the mere consequence of aging. Without contradiction, one might also say that it is indeed inevitable; that our culture merely postpones it to the point of irrelevance. It postpones it to the death process. The terminal agitation he speaks of, that frantic encounter in the last hours with the reality of dying in which the enormity of one's loss and one's folly pierces the fog of antidepressants and narcotics, is precisely the rite of passage that will initiate a person into real elderhood. Sadly, for many in our society it is the only such rite of passage available.

I wish for our civilization that it need not wait until the death process to face its limits and losses, failures and follies. Untold riches lay on the other side of that passage. Growth gives way to deepening. Ambition gives way to service. Certainty gives way to wisdom.

Let the agitation begin now.

—Charles Eisenstein

LAUREL LEAVES AND
TORQUES OF GOLD

Books seem borne along by surging convictions about what humans seem capable of and about why a particular corner of the world is in the shape it is in. Like a cross-country skier, a writer leans upon one conviction to get the thing moving, and when that conviction's momentum is spent for the moment, he or she leans on the other. But convictions are where convicts live, holed up for a time against what prevails. So books—or the writing of them, or the way I seem to go about it—strike me as an intrusion into the natural order of things. This is an existential and domestic verity. What to do? Well, many people had to cover for me while I tried to cover open ground, harrowed ground, holy ground. So, to send out letters of credit where credit is due, and to remember some of the willing and some who became accomplices unaware, I begin by invoking the privilege of bragging a little about who I know.

For all those local Fecal Agitants and Agents of Disarray and Sudden Impressarios of the teaching tours I've been honoured with over the years in Australia, New Zealand, Tasmania, Bali, Maui, Iceland, Ireland, Wales, England, Poland, Israel, Austria, Czech Republic, Mexico, the US, and Canada, who laid the currency of their person down on the off chance that I could deliver, who lost friends in the bargain and stayed with me anyhow: bless your boots. Let's do it again.

For the Miscreants and Malingerers in the temples of want and Benefactors who've made a home for their grievous, tempered souls for a while in the Orphan Wisdom School when they could have done any other sensible thing with their money and their give-a-shit and their dream for a better day, and for the Scullery Royalty and for Kaz Amaranth who keeps it cleaned and fed and housed and afoot: here's proof of what you granted me.

For Tim McKee, grace maker over this banquet of rant: you stood there, mister, and wouldn't take the deal, and I don't forget that.

For Natasha Kong, one of the first reckless faith keepers in all matters Orphan Wisdom, stylist of each of my book's look and feel, and giver of grandchildren: mercy to your greying. For Christopher Roy, hand on the tiller of our Orphan Wisdom scow, looking out into the surf, making chips: that story is for you and your kids, good trade for the blades.

For Martin Shaw, and for his kind words of years past: "We'll Both Be Old Men" is yours for the reckoning.

For the band, Gregory Hoskins, for the little walk, for the field, for the demon and the dark, dark wood: companionship for your witness.

For Aaron Berger, who kept the B-roll rolling, and for Susannah Hicks and their New One: blessings, twenty minutes out in front.

For Duncan Passmore and Sian Passmore, and their proper brood, who voted yes way back then: your grace come round.

For Ian Mackenzie, who scored my sorrows for his peers: all the gratitudes.

For the rabbinic Matthew Stillman, who, by all appearances, lives his name, who served me the port and the alchemy: bittersweet to your cooking pot.

For Sean Aiken and Danielle Petersen, weepers in the cathedral grove of who has been, cosigners of this deal to put an end to anarchy, and for their New One: goodness and mercy rolling through your days.

For the Four Corner Posts of the Mead Hall: Dustin Ryckman, who came in from the cold; James Nowak, who credits his mad grandfather and gave me the gale; Daniel Stermac-Stein, who doubled back and doubled down; and Beat Ulrich, who shouldered the beast and got me to say yes. For all those who lent hammer to the peg; for Lolajean Gentles, Chantal Hopkins, and Emily Adam, who've brought their dreams to my doorstep and fed all in the workhouse; for the New Ones born;

and for all of their generation who want to be mistaken about some of the grey heads in their midst: would that the days to come grant you the grey wisdom you wondered about.

For Douglas Varga and Karen Paule, Gary Dillon and Elfi Shaw, Javier Espinal and Panya Clark-Espinal, who stood for matrimony, and for those with no standing: it was crazy to try, wasn't it? All the mercies and the greying heads to become you.

For the old people left in the dust: would that you see yourselves and your sakes here in these pages, that you find yourselves yet in the Conclave of Worthies in the dusty rafters of these very days, raised up for good reason.

For the keepers of the rusty keys, the great rememberers, including those who, for want of regard, hold on tight to what has been entrusted to them: would that your elderhood comes back to you in the young.

For those in the back room and the basement who kept everyone I've mentioned here afloat in the fury: nobody on this end forgets that work.

For Jesse Jenkinson and Gabriel Jenkinson, who know themselves in the Reasons for it all: love and grace, and an agile heart for the storm.

For Nathalie Roy: that some of all of this comes back in the cooling light, and crowds your hearth.

Stephen Jenkinson
January, 2018
Tramore, Canada
Oaxaca, Mexico

OVERTURE: THE ROBBERIES OF AGE

I worked for quite a few years in what many call *end-of-life care* and I call *the death trade*, an honourable enough and entirely accurate name for the enterprise. I was adrift for much of the early going. Having a couple of master's degrees in hand in those days, I was pretty much left to my own devices. I was in my forties, too, and I had just enough life ballast to hold in a storm. And storm, it did. Benign administrative neglect was the order of the day. I don't complain; it suited me. But there were troubles that came with questioning aloud the wisdom of the day. And should you come of age in a grief-illiterate culture, as I did, there isn't much that can equip you to abide at the ebbing away of the lives of strangers, the ardent madness that can ensue. There's no training that can genuinely qualify you for it. You secretly count on the simple idea that there are times crafted by the Lords of Life to bring out the best in everyone involved, crunch times that eclipse the old grievances and family hurts, the old convictions, turning them into pocket-sized regrets and odd notions that can finally be lived with. You figure you could help that along. I haven't given up entirely on this idea, but I know now that dying is, as a rule, not one of those times.

There are exceptions, no doubt, but it seems to me now that crunch times in human affairs tend not to transform very much. Instead, they seem to congeal and to intensify what is already there, sometimes to an almost impenetrable degree of faux clarity and indefensible, intolerant conviction about right and wrong, about love and leaving and limit and ending. Crunch time turns out to be one of those times when "right" and "wrong" are only two of a handful of possible actions and outcomes. You'd think that getting old enough, and old enough to know better, would serve someone in good stead, that good judgement would prevail. It turns out that getting old is one of those ragged, dissembling crunch times, too. If you wait for the wisdom of age to take over, you often wait in vain.

I was adrift in that early going because the practitioners I worked with had gathered around themselves a hue of professional certainty that I couldn't trace back to the outcomes of the work. It was a preemptive certainty, something they brought to the work, not something they really gained from it. It was rarely something they drew from how the work actually went. I was taxed and troubled in those days.

Going into their dying time, dying people were often sure what they feared most. It was physical pain and the symptom/treatment regime that prompted it. The professional arsenal mobilized around that fear. The skill of the physicians in pain and symptom management was such that, routinely, dying people rarely came to the point of the unendurable. Their worst fears never materialized. Yet they were routinely treated with antidepressants and, at the eleventh hour, a degree of sedation that often made them inert. "Patient resting comfortably" was often a euphemism for "slack-jawed and drooling." They were diagnosed with something called *terminal agitation*, a degree of frank existential turmoil that had rarely shown itself in the early stages. By the end, it was unhinging them, even though the end was well-known and practiced and discussed and utterly no surprise. Something worse than pain fears had come to claim them, most of them. There was no treatment for it because there was no diagnostic category for it and because it seemed that no one on the professional end went looking for it. I wrote about this in *Die Wise*. It might have been *the* reason I wrote the book at all.

It turned out that dying people feared most the likelihood that they would disappear, in every sense of the word. That fear drove them to the cliff edge of sanity and lucidity, and beyond. If they were old by the time they were dying, many already had enough practice in being all but invisible. It was, and remains, a reasonable fear to have.

So there were legions of dying people. There were skilled, trained, professional people paid to care for them. There were clear though sedated signs that things were not going well, especially at the end of peoples' lives. And people older in the work and older in life than I were assuring all who listened that everything was in hand, that there was, yes, room for improvement, but that the proper hands were at the wheel. We had our marching orders. We were to deliver on everyone's right to a quieted, reined-in, dignified (read: *managed*) death. We had more practice models to guide us than we knew what to do with. There was little practice wisdom to reconcile death trade workers with what the onslaught of Big Pharma technological innovation was doing to dying people's expectations of us. We were in the death-prolonging business unawares, and that confounded what we expected of ourselves. We were in the customer satisfaction business in a culture that detested dying. And we were professionally and culturally elderless.

There is more palliative care and hospice care and end-of-life care and whatever else it gets called than there has ever been in North America, and I suspect there is more terminal anxiety and thrashing in the midnight hour and sedation than there has ever been. Let that settle in for a moment. Something about the accumulating professional expertise and front-page yammer about dying is not translating into an increasing capacity to die wise and well in the general population. There are practitioners in the new self-appointed parallel universe of conscious or positive end-of-life care, hankering after their place in the mainstream. There are more books on the subject (I've contributed to that), more talk shows about it (I've been on a pile of them myself), and more death literacy (often of the casual kind) than ever, and yet this is not translating into a way of dying that doesn't need palliative care and psychotherapy and past-life regression and antidepressants and sedation and medically assisted death and *Die Wise*. More people are dying than ever before, and more people are dying badly, in my view.

Something has drawn our attention towards expertise and familiarity and comfort and away from mystery, and we're missing something fundamental about what it means to be human and to be coming to the end of our lives in a way that traces our humanity, that leaves the rumour that it is good to be alive, even still, in the air, that makes of us ancestors worth claiming in the times of trouble that are surely coming. And this haunts me still.

⚜

In North America, there is at least one item-for-item parallel to this odd, disturbing, managed mayhem that prevails at the time of dying. Ours is an aging population. There are more old people among us, both numerically and as a ratio of the population, than there have ever been.

By any measure, we are in trouble where aging is concerned. Typically the public discourse on the matter centres upon the burden on the healthcare system and on the welfare system and on the social security system that an aging population brings to bear. We are frankly obliging old people to live ever longer, often at their insistence, and the beginnings of regret and resentment are now sniping across the generational lines, with the younger generations openly questioning what this means for their resources, their pensions, and their lives to come. So, here's a question:

When did a plurality of old people turn into a burden for the culture? Who voted for that?

Maybe it's a question of critical mass. You could say that there are too many old people drawing down from the public purse, too few younger people contributing to it. Certainly that is in the mix. But my question is about the consequence of age, and I am wondering how it has come to pass that the fabled treasure trove of experience that old people have traditionally been in "traditional cultures" has somehow not appeared in this dominant culture of North America. There is the burden, yes, and there is the Boomer bulge, God knows, but there isn't the "national living treasure" aura that should go with it. If you think I am overplaying this "burden" card, please consider that in my time in the death trade the fear of becoming a burden to their families was often the principal cause of dying older people opting for euthanasia. The sheer exponential presence of the aged and the addled has become burdensome. It is no surprise that one answer they've come up with is to disappear.

It used to be that age was held in some esteem, considerable esteem even, as the concentration of life experience. Life experience and its many lessons were once the fundaments of personal and cultural wisdom. It stands to reason then, that with this many old people around, we should be awash in the authentic, time-tested, grey wisdom that should emanate from them. And there should be cultural initiatives that expose the general population to this wisdom. And this should deepen the culture's sanity and capacity for sustainable decision-making. And that should make us all ancestors worth claiming by a future time, now that we've come to our elder-prompted senses and begun to proceed as if unborn future generations deserve to drink the distillate of our wisdom and our sustainable example. At the very least, the distillate of aged wisdom should balance the burden and the books, and old people should have worth as they might once have done, and the culture should break even on the deal. You'd think that this is an inevitable result of an aging populace in a civilized place. We should be smarter, deeper, wiser. Especially wiser.

I don't see it. Maybe you don't either. I see more senior centres, more assisted living facilities, more old folks homes than ever before, but I am unable to read in this concentration of resources any veneration of age. If anything, building a service sector called "senior" seems to have reduced old peoples' visibility or presence in the general urban tangle of North America. They're off now in their own places, places "better able to care for them," places set apart from the homes and workplaces and meeting places of the rest of us.

We have more ways and means of caring for old people fine-tuned for their needs. We have the restorative surgeries, the rehabilitative measures, the leisure sciences. We have the technology. So, why do so few of us seem to want to get old and, once we get there, to *be* old? We are not neutral on the subject. There aren't a lot of shrugs of the "what are you going to do about it?" kind when aging comes up. There's hand wringing and sentiments of concern, and there are diversions of every kind and outright disavowals, and sooner or later there'll be a prescription for taking your life when it suits you. There is not a lot of keenness about this, the "next adventure of life." The exponential math of the thing is plain. If neither you nor I die young or middle-aged, and current trends prevail, and we don't do anything about it all, and now, we're probably headed for institutionalization and invisibility, and rampant addiction to competence, and to its deep intolerance for ebbings and for endings, which will claim our heirs, just as it claimed us.

I don't think this is because younger people or middle-aged people are not attuned to the wisdom of age, nor because it has, for the moment, escaped them or passed them by. It's because they can see aging in North America for the shell game that it is. They can see—hell, anyone who wants to can see—that this concentration of resources in caring for old people isn't the inherent nobility of age getting its due recognition. They can see that it is a coping strategy, and that our way of aging is a trauma, and that fifty years on the culture is still singing that juvenile, jet-fuelled jingle: I hope I die before I get old.

Well, here is what is becoming glaringly obvious: there is nothing inherently ennobling about aging. Nothing. There's no sign that anything lends old people steadiness or wisdom or magic from on high or from down below. If we don't train young people and middle-aged people in elderhood, we will have no elderhood. There is no such training. Without culturally endorsed deep employment of this treasure of experience that could be elderhood, aging is just more of the same with less of the give-a-shit. It's all swoon, the sordid lunge for enduring at any cost. It's an extended-play version of middle age, plus infirmity. And it seems to me that this is what the aged among us have become.

Something has happened to aging. Something has happened to what it does, to what it means, to what it asks of us all. There are more old people than ever before, and it seems that there are fewer elders than ever before, and it seems that there could be a causal connection between those two things. Something in the fabric of life in North America inveighs severely against limit and ambivalence and not firing on all cylinders all the time, and this something is being driven to panic by the daily news, and in the panic you'll find the refusal to age. This something *robs age of elderhood.* No one would seem to benefit from the theft, and it isn't likely that anyone would vote for it, but there is a general willingness to forgo aging, and to live without the elderhood that could have come with it. *Wisdom* is a personal thing now, and nothing more than another opinion in the opinion fest of popular culture, and agedness is at best a prolonged, unextinguished middle age, and the therapists and life coaches are busy.

The young people are watching, wondering whether there is anything lying out there beyond their forties that is worth the trouble. They already seem convinced, many of them, that at best it is a con, that dread is what follows fifty. They are, even now, inheriting a world that their seniors milked for all it was worth, and their seniors are in their timeshares now. The resentment on this matter is almost incalculable. If we do not take up this work of elder-making and begin to make age credible and mandatory, the children not yet born will have the hangover of sweet, toothless platitude and their elders' abdication of duty for their inheritance. In a time of trouble such as our own, those children deserve from us a sign that some are willing to go on as if they are to come.

The day will surely dawn when young people will come to you—as they have begun to come to me—and ask what you did about the troubles, and whether you knew how bad it was, or whether you handed over to them a diminished world with a shrug of compassion fatigue and a vacant wish of good luck, or whether you stood up for them. Until that day, you and I are—we must be—elders in training.

So I set before you a task, a pilgrimage of a kind. Let us see if there are enough among us who can grow sturdy and sorrowed from the labours of a deep and disheveling contemplation of what has become of age in our time. We know what's becoming of the old people in our midst. *It is savagely unbecoming of a civilized people*, and it passes for compassionate care, and it can bear no scrutiny without dissolving into the withering, ghosted sham of compassion that it is.

If I can manage it, there'll be a deep draught of the old wine in this book, the kind of bracing tang that is sweetness tempered by time. Fortified, we might approach the vacated throne of elderhood. It isn't any longer a matter of inviting elders, those of them left, back into the fold. They aren't out there, waiting on our invitation. *They aren't out there.*

Elders are a sentinel species for humanness, and like other forms of life in our corner of the world, they've mysteriously gone missing. Young people are, often involuntarily, looking for them, and they can't find them. How about this: *old people are looking for them too.* The retreat centres attest to it. If you're looking for signs of the end times, that alone might do.

This is not a training manual for elders. It is not a five-step plan for spirit rehabilitation, and it is not in any way pretending to be a frequent flyer reward for any man or woman having made it this far. It is not, for the sake of our corner of a troubled world, a recipe for personal triumph in the Third Act of your life. This is a dirge for the old world. It is a death song for the interminable twilight years of infertility and staring out the window wondering what happened, where everybody went. It is a love song for young people who wonder how and when it all went haywire, who suspect that maybe it has always been this way, who already seem all but certain that it will be the same for them, soon enough.

Mostly, this is a ballad of courtship for the aging and for the old. I am calling them to come back to the shuffle and the sway of our mutual life, to join us in the village square of what is to come, to forego the climate-controlled inner life. I am not telling them that all is forgiven, that things are better now, that we get it, finally, and we need them after all. They aren't forgiven, and for the most part we don't seem to believe we need them. I am just making a place in the banquet hall of this teetering corner of the world for a few of them. I'm not making promises of fidelity or fealty. As it stands, too few of them could really be kept. I'm only making something like a proper place, something like a seat of honour and a proper hearing for the voice of age.

I am making the case for elderhood, not for easy agedness. I'm doing so mostly by wondering what happened. Because something happened. Something happened to ancestors and elders and honour. There's work to be done, and there's an old wisdom to be learned where there used to be the wisdom of old, and you can't fix what you don't understand. That's where we're headed: to grievous wisdom. Let us see if we can bear the sound, the particular sound, of no hand clapping.

This is a plea and a plot for elders in training.

THE FIRST ACT

1

AN EYE UPON THE YOUNG: A FABLE

Y ou probably have ideas of what you might do with yourself in your waning days—good ones, too—but imagine instead that a kind of retirement has been foisted upon you, or soon will be. I know, as you do, that there's no such thing as real retirement anymore. No one can afford it and like most of us, you'll work until you drop. But the commute alone probably would have killed you, so there is a kind of mercy in workplace reorganization or your waning commitment to the regime. So let's say that you've taken up the siren song of retiring to the country and the farm and its many responsibilities. You've cashed out of the urban housing market. You found a little place, something you can afford, with room enough for you to do everything you've not done before and waited until now to do, a good place to take your ease.

The pastoral woodcut visions you had for this portion of your allotment are the first casualty of the farm life. You've probably dreamt of darting dragonflies and dusk and the murmur of the stream coming down the mountainside. There's that. You may have thought that soil was soil and dirt was dirt, but your little patch will teach you otherwise. There's talc and dust for soil, too. There's enough dirt to sustain a scruff of twitch grass and not much more. There's a bit of green on those last few acres along the river, and nowhere else. With the weather changing, there's as often as not no river by mid-summer. There may be animals, too, and the hundred cares that they bring. You're starting to find out why the old guy sold it to you.

And then there's winter, the unvarnished deity of northern farmers. Winter is a rough God. Most people don't dream of winter when they dream of this life. The place is now in a foot of undreamt-of hard pack that's halfway to ice, and you're in an eternal January in the north of the hemisphere.

On the farm, the mauve shadows are everywhere, and there's more twilight than daylight. This could be early morning's first light coming through the hoar frost on the window. That's how similar they are. In your care-worn places, it feels so late. This is an extreme time of year, and like all extremes winter simplifies life into light and dark, yes and no. It doesn't seem like it can be morning so soon. The slurry of worry runs the days into a stream of sameness. General fatigue persuades you that these must be evening chores that are coming on. So you pull on the torn overalls, that unfortunate hat.

You're on a well, and off the grid, you are sustainable as hell, and it's midwinter. Water is hard to come by, and you're a water miser now. You mop the furnace room floor of what you spilled while you were pouring straw and melt water that you were trying not to waste from one frail plastic bucket to another. The plastic buckets are from the sheep yard. They were a donation from the donut shop in town that's a half-hour from your place. Read the labels on the bucket and you'll never eat a donut again. The pails are useless or worse at −35°, with handles that snap off when pressed into light duty, but they were kindly given, and the gift was community minded in a place where community is more and more a seasonal phantom worn thin by the onslaught of cottagers.

The sheep you've dreamt of could come to you in any number of ways. Some farmers can't bear the expense, can't bear the plunge in meat prices, and they give them away. Some quietly bring them to the back forty and shoot them behind the ear, unable to watch them go. You could risk the auction, but not knowing what you're looking at could cost you dearly.

Yours might have come to you from a dissolving marriage, from an ornery, soon-to-be ex-wife of a gentleman farmer. She lets it be known to mutual friends that she'd rather see them dead by the side of the road than with that bastard. But she's settled for them being spirited off the place under cover of dark without her soon to be ex husband knowing, stuffed in the back of a loaned pickup, and driven four hours by accomplices to your place. You have no yard, no fences to speak of, and not much experience with sheep manumitted from a dissolving hobby farm. You note that you'll probably need a pickup of your own soon. The expenses of the simple life are mounting. That's how things start, your spectacular foray. People will say that you're living the dream. Maybe you are.

⌘

You hand fed the pigs all summer and learned their quirks, and they're gone by late fall. There are those two grievous weeks, the butcher table slick with their fat, their bristle caught up in the snow melt and ash, smoke on the meat that's hanging in the shed.

The bees have long since been driven into their hives by the cold, and you've blanketed and tarped them in a way that will never keep them warm it seems, or alive. But it's all you can do. The herbicides make it hard for them to find their way, and the mites are riding them, and two-thirds of the bees will die by spring anyway, sprinkled on the snow in a path to their hives like rose petals in a wedding aisle, no matter what you do.

The chickens are not coming down from the roost tonight to eat; it's too cold even for their fleshless ancient claws. By now the winds have wicked any moisture away, and everything's brittle in the cold. The river ice moans. It sounds like whale song in the night. Sometimes a sapling freezes so hard the contraction makes it explode in the bush.

The sheep have fleece enough to be oblivious to the stiffening cold, rolling their rumination round their mouths. Their blank look has you considering goats sometimes, for the sake of having a little personality around the place. But you're fond of them by now. That thick funk they leave in the frozen air pulls on an old thread in you, and sometimes you get a glimpse of how it might have been in the ancestral days of transhumance. Most of your worry you'll probably reserve for them, defenseless and idiotic as they seem to be, even though they're the warmest ones on the farm tonight, warmer than you.

And then there are the coyotes, who the locals will tell you are an inevitable consequence of the appearance of sheep in the county. In idle talk in town an old farmer will tell you this, a scrawny chip-of-grizzle of a man who tried sheep years ago and learned that coyotes are deeply fond of sheep, fond of the grassy funk of their fleece, fond of their panic, fond of the bolt and reel and sudden ebb of their defense, fond of them to their very bones. Most farmers here and maybe everywhere feel that you raise sheep *for* coyotes, not by intent but by consequence. Up until now, your country's particular coyotes have respected whatever boundaries have kept them from their ancestral sport, though the coyotes may not see it that way. You'll probably mistake the absence of coyotes, for now, as a sign that you're doing everything right. You probably already have. Later tonight, there'll be your dogs by the house, riled by the yelping at midnight coming at them through the black and violet frozen air. You've got some fence down along the river that the drifting hardened snow has already turned into mere annoyance for any determined meat eater in the starving months. You did everything you could think of, alas, but the first hard freeze brought an end to your plans for more fencing.

So you see to the sheep. You skim ice from the buckets if you can, if their water hasn't frozen into a block. Forking over their bedding, you calculate what they don't eat and scatter across the yard instead. You do the quick math on how much it's costing you to bed them. It'll be more than you spend on yourself and your spouse—restaurants, clothing, the works—in a year. And tomorrow, when you come to them at dawn, you'll see they've left ghost thaws in the snow, refusing shelter and bedding and the warmth of sleeping close all the hard night long.

They'll refuse any of it, that is, until those cobalt nights of lambing, when spring becomes a dawn flirt of hoarfrost after a day in shirtsleeves, when, like the dowagers the squat ewes are, they deign to go inside to drop their young. You'll get up every two hours all through the night to fret and watch, the stillest you'll ever be, adrift in the amniotic funk of life coming on again, the farm's future laying wet and dazed in the straw.

Tonight, though, you hope the bale feed in the shed will last until the pasture greens in early June. It never does, though, and you know already that in a couple of weeks you'll be petitioning farmers in other towns for the leavings at the back of their barns. There's a largesse that can bloom between people who don't know each other so much as know each other's troubles. It sometimes appears after you've stacked the bales you purchased and tied them down in your trailer, you and the other farmer in the yard shifting from one frozen foot to the other and talking about the weather, both of you saying things that the both of you already know.

You'll find out every year that you alter your sheep's feed in midwinter at considerable risk to your very peace of mind. *Contrary* barely describes the thing. They'd rather starve in an endless frozen night of bawling than torment their gums with the stranger, coarser stuff. You'll fork it into the troughs, though, and they'll watch you do it, and they won't move, hungry and petulant and set in their sheepness. So you're buying what amounts to more bedding they won't eat, that'll end up as wildly expensive mulch on next year's tomatoes, tomatoes that no one will buy, and unless you send them through the sorrowful contortions of the slaughter house for its blue stamp of authority, you won't be able to sell an ounce of lamb or mutton, or give it away without fretting. And you know you are doing that very thing, even as you are counting out the twenties for the feed man and shuffling your frozen feet.

You come in from feeding them shaking your head, your own weariness so profound that it seems like another kind of weather. If it wasn't for the young man who's mysteriously come to you, looking for something, after he read something you said or heard somebody talk about you, you know your age and your breath wouldn't tolerate many more years of this. But appear he did, and he's stayed, and he'll probably come to love this life as much as you ever will. Most of the farmers in the township are old, single men, their wives quitting them and the futility, and there's the forlorn sight from the highway at dusk in late summer of two old farmers scrambling in the tractor's dusty headlights to get the second-cut hay baled and on the wagon before the rains, their life-long self sufficiency coming to haunt them now, not a young person in sight. You haven't thought much about the future of your place, but the coming of this young man last year has you doing that very thing, and so you're coming to see how lucky you are. Maybe you'll wonder who to pass the place along to, when you're done.

You sit down by the window for the first time since you got up lo those many hours ago. On this night, when the mercury all but disappears, when the limelight stays in the sky, it seems even after the darkness comes, there's comfort in the fire snapping at the stove glass, in the stack of seasoned wood in the shed that mysteriously makes you feel like the regent and the rich man.

There's burden and worry, too. The river has its skiff of ice just thick enough tonight to hold the roamers half mad with hunger in this, the starving month. They've stayed on their side for years, but tonight their yelps are too close to the shore. Your dogs have finally agreed to shelter on the porch, and they've just now begun to trade news and insults and unconvincing taunts with the coyotes. It's enough that you figure one night soon, maybe tonight, the coyotes'll test the ice and their nerve and follow the sheep funk wafting, and visit. The sheep's only defense is the other, slower sheep that gets taken down first. It is unthinkably grim. And you'd only find out in the morning that they'd come.

Yes, the sheep seem built for cold, and you've shorn them enough to know that the hard frost could never find them. Still, there's that sound at the edge of your day's end, in your settled bones and your sighing down into the chair and your reading light, and it's that sound that's calling your comfort to answer for itself. The end of the day is a feeling only. There is no end to the day. There is only the deal you strike with your weariness.

That's what's out there. You catch sight of your reflection in the window glass looking out on the cold indigo night. You look into your eyes.

❧

Well, getting older and contemplating a day off because you've worked enough, when you know young people are courting pious despair and enduring a madness that wafts across the industrial centuries and the creeping suburbs like radon gas: that is something like putting your feet up at day's end in midwinter, with the pigs gone, the bees in colony collapse, the dogs cowering and the coyotes nosing the ice, the sheep in the yard griping on changed hay and no feel for menace it seems, and the sky minus thirty and falling.

There's you there, dogged, imperial, bound to the better things, head askew, half asleep in your chair, wrapped in your earned rest. It won't get any darker or colder this winter. The night seems beautiful and still and auspicious, and it is all of that, scored now with all the signs of the beginning of the endless season's end.

But there's trouble out at the field's edge, all revenant, all but certain, and it may be closer to the house than you or anybody's counting on. There's frailty and there's madness where there used to be reasons to live, and there's faceless conglomeration and early retirement where there used to be old people to turn to in times of trouble. Everything is in change. You've seen a lot of things, and you've learned, and maybe only because of that it isn't clear that you should be sitting by the window, taking the last light, writing things down, your corner of the world tidy or taut as it is.

The old wisdoms have waned, and the grim competition between younger and older for the same certainties has waxed on, and you've crossed over from younger to older without notice. You are the sentinel species of the Anthropocene age. Nobody told you. There's no dab of ochre above your door granting you peace, or a pass. Something like a conscience is alert, and troubled, and muttering. There's no retirement from the siren song of a troubled time. There's a restless compass by which to make your reckless way instead, and young people are in the offing. And there's a question: *who are they to you?*

The Roar and the Storm at Dawn

Probably like you, there've been times I've looked up from something I once thought important or worthy, my little life's work, and I've thought: "What the hell am I doing? Why do this?" In my case, this question has heaved up frequently in the last decade. Now I'm self-employed, so the judgment of the management team is suspect from time to time. I once characterized this whole Orphan Wisdom enter-prise as one in which I am troubled aloud, nothing more. Lately I've taken on intercontinental-scaled lamenting, so the reasons I choose to do or not do this little life's work of mine are magnified somehow by the travel and the travail.

I have an accountant to add and subtract for me and make sense of the governmental harness bestowed upon all enterprises, and he routinely informs me of two realities that now accompany this enterprise of mine:

You are remarkably successful for a one man act.

(I am not a one man act, actually, but that is how it appears) and

Your business isn't worth a cent the moment you die.

By this he means that I am the only product I have, and that without good succession planning, the whole thing comes to a halt when I do. So whatever I'm doing, it doesn't seem that I'm building equity.

I encounter a lot of nay-saying out in the craze, which is what you should expect when you call a bit of the current regime into question. There's the White Light Lost and Found, by which I mean the New Age personal truth opinion fest, feasting as it does on the upside of democracy. This operation is very hard on the idea that something like wisdom can come from experience, from older people, from tradition.

There's the insecurity that is forced upon you as you are scrutinized by security forces in airports and the like. There are the exhortations to be vigilant for suspicious behaviour, which if you obey them make you the most suspicious-looking person in the place. There are the important safety announcements that banish safety at once. There are the in flight microbes and magazines, the questionable food, and the sorry state of affairs that invited you to appear and prompted you to action in the first place. There's this:

> I often recommend to those people who have, in defiance of good judgment and the mandate of equilibrium, entered the Orphan Wisdom School that they obtain for themselves a new, lined journal and dedicate it to recording faithfully and as fully as time and devastation allow well-discerned signs of the End Times. I try to follow my own guidance on this. One recent example might give you a feel for the thing.
>
> I am on yet another plane to somewhere else. The middle-aged man beside me is reading what appears to be a kind of primitive skills/survive-in-the-wilderness book. It has loads of line-drawn illustrations. As the flight wears on and he goes deeper into the book, there are primitive urban skills galore, ones I never imagined. There are elaborate descriptions of How to Escape a Car Jacking, How to Barricade An Inward-Closing Door, How to Respond to a Bomb Threat, How to Elude Ransom Attacks and, this being U.S. airspace, *How to Detect an Inspired Terrorist*. Amazing, useful stuff when the proverbial fecal matter hits the HVAC.
>
> Nowhere, I would guess, is there an account of How to Survive an Encounter with Such a Book, what it would do to your soul or your regard for fellow humans, how it would prompt you to hoard beans and bullets, how it would predispose you to an assumption of predation, of kill or be killed, of the whole thing in a time of disarray amounting to "you and yours" versus "the madness coming over the razor wire."

So, there are reasons enough to leave the road to itself and its citizens to their pleasures and decline the odd invitations to appear that come my way. The invitations are well meant, of course, but almost no one in these climes is hankering after an evening of lament and trouble, of grief and mystery. There's too much of that during business hours. Without "hope" on the marquee there aren't many takers. If I were a preacher, I'd get away with it. I have the inclination, I suppose, and I can work on the clothes, but I don't have the credentials, and I don't have the congregation.

Well, there are my peers. Maybe *they're* why I do what I do. I *am* trying to do something about that recipe for calm and withdrawal that prevails, that's true. I've banged on the bars of the retreat centres and the workshops, yelling for the warden, making a scene. There is a time of life, I suppose, when many try being okay—or try getting to okay—and as a culture, we've been trying that for a while now, isn't that so? How is it working out, this experiment with selective satisfaction and personal growth?

I don't insist that anyone be troubled as I am. It isn't improving, not necessarily. I don't advise getting comfortable with discomfort. That's the same shell game. I don't advise anything, really. I don't have the answers. I have a few questions. That's all. Still, I don't have a lot of takers in my demographic, say 55+. If anything, things don't go appreciably well when my demographic is overly represented at something I do. A few of them ask me in emails to keep going on their behalf, and I probably will, but most of the time I am an ambassador from a failed state. I have no constituency, no position, no marching orders, nothing to return to should I be recalled.

So I am left with the idea that what I'm doing might be for younger people, after all. Our fateful, clanging corner of the world is tumbling towards itself, and it won't slow, not of its own accord. Globalization and the dot-com-funded lunge for the eternal is at play now, and the long black snake of resource extraction is burrowing across the continent. There are those damned personal-use drones, executing for all time the idea that there's somewhere you can go and not be watched. There is the digitalization of every blessed thing. This too is the Anthropocene.

Here's what haunts me: what will hold the young people in good stead? Should things get worse in the wake of our passing from among them—and this *should* seems like an indefensibly neutral way of wondering about it, given everything—to what might younger people turn? To *whom* can they turn?

⌘

If you give the First Act of your life over to the notion that you were born to some purpose or other, and that there are reasons for your birth, and they attend you, then your task seems clear enough: *find out why*. Risk censure and accusations of self-importance and bombast, and find out why you were born. And try living accordingly.

Somewhere along the way, you will enter the Second Act of your life, usually without notice or fanfare or a parade down the main street of your days. It'll only be apparent in hindsight that you've done so. This isn't a time to reap the rewards of the seasons of your life. There are new reasons for living that can come to you only at this point in your life. In sum, they might come down to this one thin thing: with whom are you to live out these reasons for your birth and life? Who shall be the witnesses, the heirs, the beneficiaries of the reasons for your life?

The answer just cannot be the gated community of your peers. It can't be. Your crew has to include people half your age, a third your age, and their young. They are the ones who stand a chance of drinking the wine that might come from the vineyard you planted as you sought your life's purposes. There's that to consider, once you start not being young anymore. Of course, they might never taste wine in their lives, not if you haven't lived and planted the vines as if they'd one day appear. If you persist with the "why's" of your early days well into your Second Act, and if you keep looking for the payday and the amen that you're sure has so far eluded you, younger people might never know the deep red rush of a human life. They'll be your *competition* for that rush, instead. There's that to consider, too, along with whatever plans you've made for retirement.

I'm old enough to have unspectacularly passed from the First Act to the Second, so this question about companions and witnesses is part of the architecture now for me. What should I be doing with whatever is left to me? If I'm capable of anything, how should I lean upon it now? That is not idle contemplation these days, if it ever was. That *is* my days.

⚜

A year or so ago I was invited to appear in a small seaside city in southern Australia. It was mostly a Victorian-era place that had been overdeveloped starting in the eighties. The outskirts were endless suburbs and industrial zones, as you'd expect. It seems to me that one of the signs of a living town is whether you can find a hardware store on the main drag. Citizens of a place need a hardware store from time to time, much more than they need another barista café, and sanity requires that the land prices and taxes not make hardware stores impossible. When the hardware stores are banished to the suburbs, that's a sure sign that things are dying fast, that the crack cocaine of tourism has got almost everybody going. I didn't see a hardware store on the main drag we came in on, and the downtown had the ghosted museum look that so many tourists find charming. The hotel was a block away from the city beach.

The onshore wind was picking up, sign of a probable blow or a storm. That, and the prospect of a 7 a.m. live radio interview and a gig later that night, drove me from the restaurant on the strand to my bed. I counted on six or seven hours' sleep after a long travel day. But sometime before dawn a syncopated roar came down from the dark sky. It was a hellish way to wake up, all panic and bedlam and Krieg lights through the curtains. *Here was the egregious, disconsolate monster of my netherworld come to call*, ominous, oracular, hovering outside my hotel window. It was all shambles and nightmare and screaming machines, and it didn't stop when I started to think. It got louder, the room riven by garish light. Breathless from a broken sleep and from panic, I went to the window. All but blinded for a moment, my eyes like two piss holes in the snow, I saw only light.

When my eyes focused and I came to, I saw that it was a rescue helicopter a hundred feet in the air, sweeping slowly up and down this bit of ocean shoreline, the search light raking the surf. When the helicopter turned the floodlights blasted through the buildings along the shore. It went down the beach again until it was just out of sight. It wasn't clear that it would come back. But somewhere out there it turned again and did come back. I leaned my forehead on the glass, panting in recovery, and watched for signs of life in the black surf. The helicopter did this for maybe an hour or so, and then disappeared as dawn broke. It never landed, never hovered, never dropped a line down nor drew anything from the grinding boil of ocean. I suppose they didn't see anything, not this time, and someone told them that it was enough, and with the beginnings of dawn, they just went back home.

I sat back down on the bed with this vision, the room suddenly quiet again. And then it came to me.

"Yes," they said, *"this is what you do. This is your work, the work that comes to age, showing itself as a waking dream. This is the strange summons that has begun singing your days to you.*

Something has happened in the storm of these last few decades. It's been blowing everything to the shore. Something's overturned out there beyond what most of us remember, and wreckage may be in the sand or in the greasy foam. There may be signs to read. And there is a call that's come in. Some didn't heed the storm clouds and the rising winds. Some are unaccounted for in the surf. Go out in the dark, in the roar, and hover. Stay aloft as long as you can and watch. You can't prevent it. It's already happened. You might lift some from further harm. You might find signs. You might find nothing at all. But sweep the shore until dawn, in case life continues, in case someone wants to know what happened, whatever it was. After that, well, come back with the gathering light. People can see for themselves then."

I suppose the day can dawn upon you when things become myste-riously simple for a while. It won't last long, and you'll be back at the abacus of abstraction and allegation, thinking about things. But for a while, it can all become alarmingly clear, and all the conjecture calms down into *getting it.* Maybe what follows is one of those times.

Imagine that you have endured long enough that the habits of your one true childhood have, for the most part, taken their junior position in the scheme of things. Imagine that you are not old yet, not by the lengthening standards of the day, but from where you stand, you can see "old" coming on. Imagine, too, that you are not caught up with the new spate of instruction manuals proposing to guide you through this new phase, that you haven't given yourself over to the care of the reassurance brigade and their ministrations or to that soothing sound of having the best part of the thing ahead of you, of sixty being the new forty, or whatever those integers are. You've observed by now how the advertising for anything but sexual performance enhancement devices, arthritic reversers and endless retirement in the sun has utterly passed you by. You are still of the numeric majority, yes, but the vibe of the times isn't yours anymore.

The temptation—and it's a strong one—is to go with the music you remember, the recreational drug you remember or barely remember, the friends you've grown accustomed to and the classics you haven't read yet, and wish younger folks a good day. You're haunted with becoming a burden to your grown children, and though they don't want to hear you say it, you're more than a little relieved that now that they have begun legalizing marijuana they'll get around to legalizing medically-assisted death in your district, hopefully in time to help. And LSD's becoming popular again for people in their waning days, so there's that to con-sider. It's a consumer's proper denouement, serving your unswerving demand to be on top, to be self-directed, even then. Still, with all of that ganging up on your conscience, a part of you thinks about what kind of a world you're about to pass on. You move on from the morose things that you can't change, but this business of young people tangles you. With luck, it won't go away, and this version of the serenity prayer will begin losing purchase.

⚜

It is at just such a time, should the Gods prevail, that someone one-half or one-third your age might come around. Maybe an errand or a delivery brings them to your door, or some meeting brings you to them. You fall into casual banter, glad that the chasm of years has closed enough to permit casual banter. Then the page turns, or the pall slips, and without seeking your permission or your forgiveness first, and without much in the way of preliminaries, that younger person asks you a question:

When you were my age, did you know what was happening?

Questions that come from the Lords of Life, questions such as these, aren't answered by a yes or a no. Certainly not this one. This one has to be answered as if many a thing were at stake. This is the sound of younger people turning to you in times of trouble.

But most of the troubles these days aren't personal. "*Is this it?*" they're asking. Can you hear it? Can you hear the unleavened mixture, half dread and half plea on behalf of scant sanity? This person isn't asking about how cool you were back in the day, how hip or aware or awakened you were. This person is asking about *whether anything means anything at all*, just for starters. This person is asking whether the madness of these days has always been there, or whether it came on on your watch. Best be alert.

So the answer that you give, among the most authentic and faithful answers, won't cover for your inattentive days or those years-long bouts of legitimate self-absorption. The answer won't satisfy, may not ever be able to satisfy. It won't answer for the grudge and the grievance and the greying of their technicolour world. Your answer could come to sound something like this:

Well, in those days, given everything, anybody who wanted to know what was happening could have known. It was there to know. But not everybody wanted to know. So not everybody did. That's the way it went. For all I know, it's still going that way.

It seems that there's only one other question left, after a faithful answer like that. This person might look you in the eye right about then, and ask

So, what did you do?

This book is written as if that day is coming. I've used the ground ash of my disappointment for ink, my brittle memory for parchment. It's written for the sake of that day, for the sake of that young person asking, and for the sake of that older person being asked. We'll have to go deep into the gale for this one, deep into the sedated satisfaction of a consumer culture utterly bereft of its ability to rise in indignation at what is killing that corner of the world it feeds upon.

This isn't something that requires inspiration to undertake. Expecting to be inspired by what troubles the world before coming to its defense isn't defensible, not among grownups. That's part of what got us to where we are. Inspiration is octane, but it isn't give-a-shit, and it isn't "getting it." This is work, and work is that thing that you find yourself least inclined to do. The time is done—it's more than done—for leaving the work of conscience and of grief-endorsed action to the kids.

Get your heavy-weather gear on, that Gore-Tex you bought for a rainy day. *This* is the rainy day. It's an hour before dawn. Let's go.

2

MODERN ENGLISH

T|his entire enterprise of ours comes down to wondering together, without recourse to certainty or comfort, whether there is any longer such a thing as elderhood among us, to imagining the great change in our cultural fortune that seems to have taken the elders from us, to imagining what might yet be done before even the memory of a time when things were not as they are now goes feral, baying into the bush at the first sound of trouble. And it will be conducted in my cranky, Canadian version of the English language. This isn't remarkable, unless you consider two things.

1. It is likely that something in the modern English language tracks and bears historical forces so considerable and relentless that English itself has become the disease vector of modernism, worldwide.

2. It is as likely that modernism has born witness to and has helped prompt the eclipse of the function of elderhood in our midst.

Using English to wonder what modernism did to elders is hair-of-the-dog wisdom.

It is no secret that the West surrendered or abandoned something ancestral and indigenous, something fundamental to its mythic and poetic well-being, when it agreed to be an icon or a mascot for all things civilized, cultural, and Godly. Its old soul was left in the weeds. It is no secret that the various sojourns into empire making, slavery, resource exploitation, coercive religious conversion, urbanization, demythologization and rationalism, global market conjuring, World Bank manipulation, and a few other notable things have come back to haunt the West. These have burdened what is left of its middle classes with coping with refugees and with a ghosted half memory and world-class resentful guilt where there once was a conscience that might have leavened privilege with duty. The poorer classes are left with a chronic, alienated grudge that rears up at election time to enthrone a former greatness that never was. The governing elites are opting for statelessness, their only serious allegiance saved for shareholders and boards of directors, and each other.

What might surprise you is the possibility that the modern English language is now the lingua franca of postmodernization and globalization, precisely *because it is the ghost language of empire.* It is the default language of the stateless, and it is the default language of that postcolonial blur called multiculturalism. Modern English is also a child of empire. It has been informed and deformed and reformed by serial invasions from Rome, Frisia, Norway, and Normandy, by the harrowing of the disenfranchised, landless workforce—namely the Industrial Revolution—and by the unseen hand of the marketplace, free-for-all Capitalism.

For all of those syntactical precursors, it was the converting religion of the eastern Mediterranean, Roman Christianity, that claimed, corroded and becalmed the Old English of Anglia, giving us the Middle English of Chaucer and Shakespeare and Marlowe. What binds them together to become the Modern English language and world and mind is Plato. The early Christian church had Plato, not Christ, as its philosophical authority. It was the Platonic Ideal, the untempered apartheid of spirit/body, eternal/corruptible, true/incarnate that powered the engine of conversion.

The more original and spiritual a thing is, the more being it has and the higher is its dignity. The highest possesses the 'beautiful' in itself, the 'true' in itself, the 'good' in itself … God is the highest being. Constant and consonant, this 'being' was the functioning deity of Christendom, and still is.

—Thorlieff Bowman,
Hebrew Thought Compared with Greek

By virtue of its mania for the foundational verb *to be* and its many errant descendants, modern English's syntax is obliged to an essentialist view, and not a relational view, of everything. By this I mean that I can ask you how *you* are doing, you and only you, and omit all and sundry responsible for your well-being from the inquiry. I can isolate *existence* from anything that might sustain or describe it. I can distinguish the inner from the outer, the body from the soul, the ephemeral from the eternal, the Truth from everything else, human being from human doing. The language and its syntax encourages me to do these very things.

The Industrial Revolution hammered a wedge between the generations. Driven from the agrarian life by closure of the commons, a landless, urban working class was the invention and pride of systemic capitalism. Its social engineers sent children who were not strapped to the milliner's bench alongside their parents to school. The old, unable to keep up with the shift-work severance of family life, were left to decay in the fetid alley. And all of this was carried by the casualties seeking after freedom and improvement, and it was planted with their every footfall in every land they thought they discovered. This new culture of industry, as much as anything else, stripped the modern marketplace and the main street of elders, turning them into inefficient old people. This continues to happen before our very eyes now, in every generation. Stropped into trim by the Industrial Revolution, in many ways a product of the Industrial Revolution's penchant for urbanization and its disparaging of dialect in the name of easy productivity, modern English was made to order for standardization and for internationalism. Evidence-bound, utilitarian, binary-oppositional, cause-and-effect addicted, litigious, and virtual, midwife to the internet's metalanguage, modern English is more peoples' second language in the world today than it is their first. Modern English gives us a way of imagining and describing a world that begins with us and our generation, with what we care about, with our habits. The essentialism of the language is what gives us a way of divorcing experience from essence, past from present. It is the fortress of the stone-faced solitary I, and its existential playground is "being." Relational linguistic syntax is the de-facto relational reality of intact village life. Modern English has no such syntax, not on the street or on the screen. Village-mindedness was a casualty of modernism, and in the same way the standing of elderhood was an early and enduring casualty of Modern English.

And yes, I am proposing to approach this caravan of misfortune that has impoverished the West so spiritually and rewarded it so materially, that has made Western people so recognizable when we travel elsewhere, the very misfortune that has trivialized wisdom and marginalized the aged among us, by employing the same language so instrumental in mobilizing that poverty and that trivialization. One reason: it's the only language I have. Another reason: language is powerful business. Language is a spell caster, and it is a spell breaker. The same skills are used for both. It's a risky business, but I mean throughout this book to break the spells Modern English has cast on the modern mind by using Modern English—and the memory of from whence it came—as the spell breaker. I have good practitioners who have preceded me.

Setting out to write a book is something akin to setting out to discover a continent when the evidence and the general mood tell you that every continent worth finding and exploiting has already been found. That's how it strikes me, anyhow. I've done it a couple of times. The project slides often from the "doable" to the "must-doable" for its seductive inclination to coalesce into the revised standard version of anything I ever thought or meant about the subject at hand. And now I'm at it again, maybe one more time, before I revert to speaking for the duration. Wrangling the contending propositions and allegations is hard work—hard enough—and then comes the line edit. This is where the publishing house that professed to be enamored of your voice might set about aligning it with a voiceless style manual. Regional spellings and dialects are often sacrificed on the altar of the easy read and the global market.

I wrote about money and the soul's desires years ago, a wiry and contentious little book that deserved more concerted attention than I lent it at the time. The publisher claimed general satisfaction, and later went bankrupt just before the book appeared in the world. But I didn't know that then, and I was awash in the full blush of "first book-itis." A couple of days after submitting it, I got a phone call from the administrative assistant to the managing editor. We ran through some tedium, and as an afterthought she mentioned that the publishing house had an editorial policy, compliance with which ensured a civilized product. She said that wherever the word *God* appeared in the text in the plural, it was automatically granted a lowercase g. Editorial policy, she called it.

A spell by another name, I'd call it. I suggested to her that it was much more theology than it was policy. She shrugged a phone shrug and reiterated the caveat nature of the thing.

"Anyway,"

she said,

"you can change it however you'd like, so long as it conforms to the editorial policy."

By this time I was a little chagrined. I could feel my heels looking for solid ground to dig into, and they found it.

"I tell you what,"

I said.

"I have an editorial policy myself. It goes like this: when this book comes out—if it comes out—it will have God in it. At the least it will have the word in it. We'll be consistent about it too. Everywhere the word appears, be it singular or plural, it will always have either the capital G or the lower case g. To be flexible, I'll leave the choice to you folks. Let me know your preference."

They chose the upper case G. And I've come to this book the same way, with the same willingness for all the Gods to have their day and their say, if I can manage it, including the God who's fairly sure he's the only One. Early indications are that the present publisher might be willing to go along with me on this one.

Anyone reading this who has a graduate degree in theology knows how marketable that learning is. Should you find yourself with a theology degree and no recognizable denominational affiliation to speak of, as I did, you will learn the very limits of translating the details of your education into the yammer of the marketplace, as I did.

And so I was for a time a teacher of English as a second language in a kind of fly-by-night language school for teenagers whose families were rich enough or well-placed enough to spirit their kids out of Guatemala and El Salvador when those places were lethal, when there was no middle ground, no apolitical zone between the army and the guerillas. I was tangentially qualified for the job. The tone of the place was grim. Hormonally claimed and with that arcing, plaintive expressivity that Latin America is known for, these kids wanted to get news from home much more than they wanted to get English grammar from me. I, with no serious background in English grammar as a teacher or as a student, had to get by with whatever creativity with the language had survived my formal education to engage the students. Often we read the newspaper for the news from home.

One day I discovered that the syllabus dictated that prepositions were next up in the course of study, and that night I had to look up *preposition* in the dictionary to get the hang of the thing. Preposition Day dawned, the young exiles sprawled across their desks utterly free of curiosity about English grammar, and I launched into a story free of any rules or exceptions or learning to account for prepositions. In other words, I made up a story to explain why the prepositions are what they are and do what they do. It went something like this:

> You've noticed that there are a lot of English words that you recognize, because they are very similar to words in Spanish. The reason is a simple one. The Romans conquered the English homelands, forced their ways and their language upon the people, just as they did upon your ancestors, and that common Latin conquest is in the root words that you recognize. You may not have noticed which kinds of words are the recognizable ones, though. They are mostly nouns and verbs, with the attending adjective and verb forms. What they aren't, for the most part, are prepositions. Unlike the names for things and for actions, prepositions do things. They answer questions, for the most part: When? From where? Which? How? Their function in a sentence is to establish relations of cause, influence, consequence, purpose. That means that prepositions are there to provide the syntax of the sentence, which is where the meaning appears.

> You could say that the house of a paragraph or story or a language is made of bricks—the nouns and verbs, adjectives and adverbs. But the mortar, the minor layer that lends the whole thing durability and purpose, that is the preposition at work. Prepositions are the magicians of meaning, and they carry what you mean to say when you speak or write. So they are meaning's midwife.

> And, for the most part, they aren't derived from Latin or Greek. How did it come to pass that most of the old English names for actions and for things succumbed to the Roman conquest, but most of the lowly, monosyllabic prepositions did not? I suspect it was the English people's way of resisting, their guerilla warfare.

When you are a conquered people, the visitation of the conquest upon your daily life is incremental, cumulative, generally unspectacular. In order to contend with the conqueror, you have to learn the basics—their names for things, for places, for doings—and this gives you the chance to, in some fashion, fit into the new order, and perhaps after a few years or a decade, or a generation or two, to benefit from it. But the English seem to have kept their words for making meaning of the foreigner's strange language, their prepositions. You could say that after the Roman conquest, they spoke differently, but that in some fashion they kept their tongue.

Upon this rickety branch of the English tongue, with its rogue prepositions and its vagrant, poetic, skaldic soul, I propose to drape my dread, my contrition, my pleas on behalf of elderhood among us. There are etymologies to consider, prepositional subversions to administer, poetry to revel in. I hope you'll find that employing a language to subvert its madnesses and emerging with a syntax of sanity in a troubled time is worth the considerable trouble and attention to detail and disciplined sorrow that it will take. It seems to me that much is now hanging in the balance. There are young people, hosts of them, watching the self-absorbed bulge of boomers passing from this mortal coil bedraggled and betrayed by the old promises of limitless potential and self-actualization and personal growth, and retirement savings plans. They see the retreat centres full of retreating, the gated communities full of retiring, just at the time when everything points from bad to worse, from anger to apathy, from vexation to the vast, vast extinction of What For? A good many of these young witnesses seem full of disdain. They rightfully are, but secretly they seem to be wishing they are wrong about the old people in their midst. Some part of their grievance wants to be wrong. With no faith that can stand the tests of the market place, still some of them seem not quite capable of going it alone, or of wanting to go it alone, another youth cult, the Sixties again.

They don't have generations anymore. That's already gone. They have decades instead. The breathless ramping up of change, of excess and extirpation, of chronic must-havery and limitless gadgetry, drives many of them to polygamy and peyote and the business casual, gold star, private priority lane of anything. "Is there anybody out there?" they're asking. "Is there anybody to ask?" How has it come to pass that in the era of more old people per square kilometer than the world has ever seen here in the dominant culture of North America they have so few elders? Has it ever been like this? Where's the wisdom? Has it always been like this?

I'm circling around God, and around the ancient tower
And I've been circling for a thousand years
And I still don't know if I'm a falcon, or a storm,
Or a great song.

Rainer Maria Rilke, "I Live My Life"

This is Robert Bly's translation of the great Rilke poem, and the poem is probably truer now than when he sent it out among us. Here in the last part of the poem is something like a clear and dead reckoning of how it might be for young people to be looking out onto their almost elder-free world. When I first heard the poem, it sounded like mystification. But it sounds more like a lament to me these days than at any other time since I committed it to memory thirty years ago.

In Middle English there is the uncommon word *staniel*. This is the name of a small raptor bird, of the same order as a falcon. The name comes from the Old English *stangiella*, literally "stone yeller," a likely reference to the call and the habitat of the bird. There is a frequent migration in the pronunciation of English from the harder sounding "g" to soft-palate friendly "y," and you can hear it here. It is from the bird's name, *giella*, that we get our verb *to yell*.

And we have the word *to regale*, clearly a relative. It has a celebratory or banquet or showy raconteur context for us now, and properly so, because it has the older meaning of "to yell or to proclaim with vigour." So, too, the antique English word *galan*, which means "to sing, cry out, cast spells, sing charms."

And there's more to this lineage. *Gale* has the meaning, of course, of a very strong storm, and the word brings together all of these meanings: breath, force, chant, conjure, proclaim. Remember Lear in the storm on the heath. The Old Norse equivalent, *galinn*, has the feel of being "bewitched by magical singing."

I don't know if Rilke knew of these evocations, but it doesn't seem to matter. They coalesce in his poem anyhow. What does matter to me in these strange times of ours is that we have a poem a hundred years on that seems to have foretold what was soon to beset young people, how it would come to pass that the deep uncertainty about who and where they were in life meant that, all but abandoned by those charged with caring for their souls, their lives would become some tangle of predation and tempest and possession and lament and proclaiming. Circling around an ancient tower, they are looking for signs, all but abandoned by age.

Rate of Change

In my years working in palliative care the doctors often dreaded the question they knew was coming: How much longer do I/does my beloved have? They dreaded it because they knew the answer would always be approximate. They dreaded it because no matter how delicately they put the answer, it would always daunt and make dread wherever it landed. More often than not, the answer would tend towards offering quality over quantity. "Nobody really knows," was the equivocation that seemed to serve.

But privately, in the team meetings, we almost certainly could know how much longer that person had to live, and our clinical decisions often relied upon it. We weren't always certain of the day, though that did happen, but almost routinely we were certain to within a few days, or to the week. There was a kind of back-pocket technique of divination that routinely proved itself. Its particular genius was not to track the days or weeks or months, but to track what changes were occurring in those days or weeks or months, and especially to track *the change in those changes*. We referred to this as *the rate of change* and used it to anticipate the time of death and to achieve some ability to help families draw close to their dying kin in a timely way. The idea is a simple one. There are changes, and then there is the rate at which these changes occur. That rate of change, if it was observed to have accelerated to weekly change, for example, allowed us to generally predict that the patient was in area of weeks of life left, and not months. When the rate of change was daily, they had days left, and so on unto hours and moments and the end.

It turns out that the agile and timely use of this pocket divination tool is a transferable skill. If you apply this measure of the rate of change to culture, what do you find? We are, as any student of the age will tell you, in an era of accelerating change. The rate of change bearing down upon us itself is changing. It is going faster. And there is no sign that it will do otherwise, nor that we are likely to turn voluntarily to restraint or hesitation. But in which direction is it going? To what end?

The English language is changing. Better still, it is being changed. New editions of dictionaries are breathlessly enshrining words that didn't exist five years ago. "Bucket List" was a movie once. Now it is a moral order bossing old people around, marching orders for the acquisitive and the experience junky. Etymologies are abandoned. Learning is traded in for adaptation. The language is being changed to suit change, to serve momentum. Irony, cleverness, quippery are the Gods of the market place and the kitchen table. The Rough Gods of our recent excesses are haunting the Clever Gods of coping with what we cannot or will not change.

> Should you be halfway through the flu, say, and should you have a penchant for utter, impotent futility, occasionally interrupted by gauzy bits of hope suspended in the ooze, be sure to spend a convalescent afternoon sorting through a friend's social justice documentary film collection. You'll probably emerge fairly sure

in which direction the whole wreck is speeding. Here's a good rate of change marker for you: the atomic bomb was dropped less than a century after the invention of the repeating rifle. That film collection itself is a fair sign of the End Times. It will probably visit that very rate of change upon your imagination. You may end up making an oath to yourself or your spousal equivalent never to do that kind of thing—watching an animated version of the caravan of eco-misery heading into the gloom, or a phalanx of wizened talking heads pledging you to hope or to hellish resolve—to yourself or each other again, come what may, hell or high water.

The rate of change in what we surround ourselves with or involve ourselves in is probably a fair iteration of that broader calculation of culture change. I know a man, about forty years old and working in IT, who knows for a fact that regardless of his expertise, he is being lapped by people half his age. He knows this because the sheer rate of change in the gadgetry beggars his experience. It is already obsolete. He is all but obsolete. That's a fairly good indicator of where this rage for innovation is heading. It discredits any experience wedded to time or place or circumstance. Take another step or two on that escalator, and you begin discrediting memory and its handmaiden, habit, as being impediments to adaptation to change. You can already tell what some of the implications are for how we think of aging and of the aged, when we think of them at all.

Well, you know the yammer as well as I do: of course (in principle) change is good. The more that's left behind, the more room there is for improvement. The quicker things are left behind, the sooner something better can come in. Change is like bad publicity: you might not like it sometimes, but at least it's happening.

Okay, then think of what seems to be a fairly clear and rising incidence of neurodegenerative diseases, the ones that affect *memory*. That is happening among old people. It is beginning to appear more and more possible that if you live long enough—and we have the technology, and we are living plenty long enough—you'll eventually while away your mindless hours not knowing you're you. This is a maze the likes of which may have prompted Kafka to his extremes. We are engineering longer lives and the proliferating frailties that come with them, and we are legislating medically assisted death as a solution to that engineering. That scene is not even in the future. That change has already happened, though most are just beginning to sort through the existential snakes and ladders of their ebbing days. We have what seem to be increasing incidences of a disease that obliterates memory at the same time that this increasing rate of change is making memory obsolete.

Attention Deficit Disorder is the order of the day among younger people now. It is a fact of life in the educational system. The inability—or the unwillingness, or both—to focus for the sake of scholastic and social and personal success haunts the classroom. I don't know the science of these things that prevail upon the young and the old among us, but the lived realities of it all are enough for the civilian to carry around at one time. We don't seem to know it now, but the day will come when these afflictions of the young and the old will be the second-hand smoke of the age, the vulnerable ones suffering from the majority exercising their rights and having their way. It is already showing itself as an existential, soul-level response to the accelerating rate of change that binds and propels us. The young are deeply under-persuaded that, as obsolescence trashes the cultural and environmental landscape, paying attention pays. It isn't easy to defend the idea that attention span is the social or moral obligation of the citizenry any more. The cost for doing so prohibits it. The cost is trying to pay attention to what's going, going, gone, pretending it's good for you to attend to the ghosted emotional and social landscape of an era in thrall to change. The old are muttering cantos of obsolescence, they themselves the trash on the landscape of their burdened adult children.

The young and the old are the canaries in the Anthropocene coal mine, our sentinel species. The accelerating rate is benefitting them least, harrowing them most. There is existential whiplash in the book-end generations. That's what the rate of change seems to be doing as you sit and read this. Young people are unable to defend any instinct they might still possess to pay close and abiding attention to the relentless, autonomic windmills that haunt their ontological horizon. Older people's memories have become museum displays of quaint gadgetry during the course of their own lifetimes.

And what of the people in the middle? Seemingly oblivious to what this means for them, seduced for their approval at election time and fed upon thereafter, many of them are working without end to put away enough to be cared for adequately when the rate of change comes for them.

Yes, change is changing alright. It isn't nearly as good as it is relentless. It compromises the ability to be alert and to remember, but it also brings disrepute to the instinct to do either, the necessity of doing either.

Take a breath, look out the window and assure yourself—because there's more—that the world's still out there, and it's still worth serving, somehow. Then, if you would, consider this: Is there such a thing as new old people? Yes, of course, aging might be new to them, if they notice it, if they have a sustained curiosity about or even a willingness to consider what their aging means. But does that make *them* new? Don't older people strike the rest of us as the least new people around, the least changing, now that they're old? The least changeable, now that they're old? Aren't the aged in our midst something more akin to apostates—lacunae, even—in the Gospel of Change, the ones change eventually caught up with and left behind some considerable time ago? Do they not appear to be the least likely to learn, to change? Does the rate of change not predispose the rest of us to see them in just this way?

At first hearing this might sound harsh or inconsiderate or judgmental. Well, who do you suppose that iPad you use, with all of its consequences for social etiquette, job readiness and the like, was designed for? Bifocaled, vaguely arthritic older folks, to make calling their adult children in times of trouble easier? You know it wasn't. It was designed for people who can adapt so fast to the next version of anything that they never land. The change-begotten life of the urban person now is akin to that of an in-transit flight attendant. But many urban people change planes in midair to take advantage of the next new possibility coming at them at the speed of sound. The entire enterprise has the fathomless and breathless clarity of an in-flight magazine. All of this is for the competence addicted, the novelty besotted, those at the height of their powers, gliding through the towers of power, business casual. Doubt not the deep intolerance shown to anyone slowed to a shuffle by contemplation or doubt or a willingness to consider. Or by memory. You can see around you the trance-inducing power of momentum, of novelty for its own sake, of changeable change.

Years ago Robert Bly wrote that it takes courage to be idle when practicing the writing life. Not indolent; still. It is truer now, I think, than it was when he wrote it, and not just for writers. For all the attention he gave to his time, for all of the verses of redemption he committed to memory, Mr. Bly is wrestling his neurodegenerative demons now, from what I hear. And that IT man not yet forty years old? He knows—not fears; knows—that no matter how much re-upping he does in tech tune-up, he's too old for the job. What kind of old age awaits him and his peers? Are they already ashudder at the prospect of a stage of life that is (or used to be) still twenty-five or more years away? Or *is* it that far away? Has the rate of change that seized modernity when almost nobody was looking already begun lapping itself? When do you get old now?

People on this continent are living longer than they have ever done, so far as we know. Does that mean that more and more of us are younger longer? Or does this mean that we are getting older sooner, that we'll be old longer than ever before? Where does this "more time" place us in the arc of life? And when does this "more time" that is here for us to enjoy actually happen, now that we are hurtling along the changing rate of change? Is it sprinkled throughout the life span, extending all the stages of life by some mysterious increment? Or is it all saved up for the ignominious denouement, age having become not much more than an over-extended time for fingering the rosary of loss?

And where do we calculate and bear in mind the consequences of our ever-lingering lives for this living world? Do we even do so? What of the natural order is served by Western humans living ever longer, drawing down ever more by living our intransigent and unsustainable ways of life that grant this very protracted life span? Do you see wisdom rising from the ash heap of limits that change is making of age? Do you see anything sustainable coming from it all, for humans *or* for the world some of us still claim to love? I can tell you this: I haven't read many books on this subject of aging (I read a few and I couldn't bear it, eventually), but each of the ones I did read came to aging as something to be dreaded for the canticle of derision that it often is, or as something no more unnerving or undoing than a bad attitude, or as an arbitrary, scant proposal and a thin veil of hoping and doping and coping with the grizzled certainty that yes, aging isn't good for you. Yet the tech higher-ups are designing a near-future for the rest of us that includes—that requires—*more age* to go along with our more time. Do you remember any item from your consuming life that took on greater value in the cultural or spiritual or consumer economy as soon as there was more of it?

> Years ago a pair of young men interviewed me for their podcast. One of them asked me a brilliant question. Clearly haunted by limitlessness, he let me know that, while it might be too late for me, Big Pharma is working on a serum that will within a generation prevent people from dying.
>
> "If I take the serum, and I don't die, what will I be missing?" he asked.
>
> Hoping then, and hoping still, that I could be equal to that well-wrought question and to the one who asked it, and to all of his age kin, I answered him this way:
>
> "I'd say that the question is probably more like this: If you take the serum and you don't die, what will the rest of us miss?"

The smart money, the dot-com money, is on eternity, cancer-free life, and Mars. You know it is. And that programme is being driven and funded by people in their thirties and forties, trying to engineer a better deal than aging while there's still time. You know that's where modernity is headed, if it has its way. It banishes elderhood. It leaves behind what can't keep up. It sneers at limit.

Well, take another minute for yourself now. Look out the window again. I'll admit it. The sheer rampage of the last few pages seems like a visitation of that very rate of change you contend with pretty much every day. If so, it is a rendering of the state of affairs that is faithful to the state of affairs. Until faith in change is cooled, until innovation is subject to the real scrutiny and governance that can only come from credible experience and considerable time-in from those who have lived without and then through the changes that are howling for unanimous approval, until practice wisdom draws abreast of the rampage of technological innovation and bridles it, you and I and all that we hold dear in this world will be subject to all manner of change in the rate of change, without notice. That is what is turning experienced people into aged people and old people into speed bumps on the superhighway to Betterland.

And what of the elders in our midst in this time of breathless change? Those of them tenaciously and incredibly left are limit without limit, boundless boundary, the proper, melancholy metabolizing of potential and heroism and the never foreclosed-upon future, the very incarnation of time passing and passed. And that's one reason why there are so few of them just now. They get in the way, and they don't get it.

Yes, there are more old people, in number and in ratio of the general population, than ever before in the West, and there are fewer elders than ever before, and the record will show, sooner or later, that these are not coincidental bits of information in a relentless information age.

These are the cause and effect of dread. We have fewer elders than ever before because we are living longer. That's the thread I am pulling. That's the poorly kept secret of the age. Something about the suspension of limit and ending compromises the function of elderhood, even the appearance of elderhood, because there is something about limit and ending that conjures elderhood from age.

Cultures are cultured not because they have more books, or more leisure time, or more well-being, but because they have glimpsed the deep unwelcome consequences the concentration of too many people visit upon the place they claim to love as their home. The spirit algorithm of the thing is part tragedy, part love story. Societies are brought to the tempered achievement of "culture" by seeing and learning the end of what they hold dear, and then by entering into a self-governance of restraint and obedience to limit. Endings are the midwives of their ability to love their home places, their Gods, their ancestral matrimony and patrimony. Being willing to live with less, to be less—not all—of what you can be, that is how cultures serve their world. Without the tutelage of limits and endings, you have no elders to practice and incarnate the wisdom of "enough," no culture recognizable to cultured peoples, no record of noble restraint that would make of you an ancestor worth claiming, no defeat of the nobility-making kind. Rilke's wish for us was that we not prevail, that we be undone by ever more nobler things, that our culturedness be wrought by that undoing. The rate of change has swept that kind of wisdom to the curb.

It may be humane to extend our lifespan because that's what people want, and because we can. That is holy writ in the death trade. But I do wonder how human it is. Perhaps the time will come when *humane* will be understood as a kind of human-centered calculus we make to mete out compassion. *Human* will be recognized finally as the world-centered compassion that we are on the receiving end of. So it seems to me. Perhaps we'll find a way of living where our humanness is no longer our possession, but a life-affirming, world-enhancing way of living our souls are entrusted with instead. This is not that time, it wouldn't seem. The poet W. H. Auden wondered whether we are a people now who would rather be defeated by the consequences of what we shouldn't have done than persuaded ahead of time that we shouldn't do it. The dominant culture of North America has grown mysteriously fond of defeat. We seem to prefer defeat over limit. That's what we rely upon as the regulator of innovation. It absolves us of restraint. Defeated, we don't have to choose to stop, or even slow down, or obey the knowable limits of our knowledge. Persuasion—voluntary limits—is for chumps now.

Here's something else to consider at just such a moment as this. It's not a balm, not a cure. It's a pause in the parade of getting ahead and going on.

You the very old, I have come to the edge of your country …

William Stafford, "Waiting in Line"

With this flourish William Stafford's begins his very fine poem.

I remember Robert Bly telling the story of talking with his friend William Stafford about Stafford's practice of writing a poem every day before rising from bed. The exchange, as I recall, went something like this:

"Every day?" Bly asked, and Stafford told him, "Yes. Every day."

"They couldn't all have been good," Bly said, "and there must have been the delicate pressures of the morning."

"True," Stafford said, "All true."

Bly asked him, as one pro to another, "Well, how did you keep writing, knowing it wasn't a good poem?"

"Oh," said Stafford, "On those mornings, which weren't infrequent, I lowered my standards, finished the poem, got out of bed."

Probably a bit more alert to the passing of time when he wrote "Waiting in Line," Mr. Stafford acknowledges in the poem that by the time he did so even he

can achieve your beautiful bleak perspective
on the loud, the inattentive boors
jostling past you toward their doom.

Does this sound bitter? Does it sound like he wishes he were twenty again so that he could get in on the jostling? I don't think it does. It strikes me as born of the courage Mr. Bly prescribed, the courage of pausing without doubting. It describes what this accelerating rate of change that sweeps everything in our corner of the world to the curb looks like in the increment of an ordinary moment, slowed down just enough to register. And it describes the unbidden thrill that comes in, the gratitude that rises when you see that you've now lived long enough to risk being utterly, temporarily alive:

…like you
I have stopped at a corner and suddenly
Staggered with the grace of it all.

Frailty enlisted for the sake of thanksgiving, frailty as the Angel of Slow, both visitation and advocate of grace: that can be the consequence of being reined in by age. Giving uncommon voice to the reined in and the staggered and the ebbing away, the poet tries on his shoes:

You others, we the very old have a country.
A passport costs everything there is.

And I suspect that's what many of us will find, should we lapse in our momentum and give diminishment its due. We will find that the coming of age is a costly affair. It costs, among other things, what you thought coming of age would be like, or what it would ask of you. It asks that you end your endless wager upon more, upon the next thing, your restless drawing down upon tomorrow. It asks that you occupy utterly the wane of want that has come to call, that you vote for the slowness of gait and mind that has come anyhow whether you sought it or not. It asks that sometimes you look younger people in the eye and you become not the something more, but the something else, the discrete truant from the Academy of More that they sorrowingly, secretly seek.

3

LEARNING OLD

I am lucky enough to have a school, and doubly fortunate that people come to it from many places, and the fortune trebles when they return every six months or so for another round of contemplative mayhem. The motivation of the scholars to expose themselves to categorical dishevelment and ambivalence I don't pretend to understand, though I have enormous gratitude to them for doing it, and their fiscal and existential decision-making in attending can be questioned. But they are my contemplative kin, and our companionship in the heavy weather of wondering how our corner of the world has come to be as it is is a feast in a famine. When we are labouring up another counterintuitive, habit-violating semantic or phenomenological incline, dragging the ten ton stone of what passes for sanity in the West up the hill of habit and into the light of courteous inquiry where it belongs, I often offer this cool comfort: *the language will not fail you.* Think about how you think, I tell them, and talk about how you talk, and patient attention to the means by which you think and talk—the language—will serve you and the world you are desperate to care for. The language will not let you down.

Freud called his new medicine the talking cure. It has been around for a century or more in one form or another, and the return on this particular investment isn't looking good. Maybe a bit of our time could be given over to curing the talk, just for a change of emphasis. Having recourse to the standard dictionaries is a start, but there is a static, stifled inertia and a poverty in them. That may be an inevitability, given the modern impatience with learning and the insistence on mystery cashing out. Many of them are tombstones of inquiry, places where perfectly healthy and agile words go to die their semantic deaths. What is missing in most of them is the passage of time, the mark that time leaves on language, on the subtle service it grants its practitioners, the changes in nuance and import that signal sea change in the culture. Those are things that could help whoever wants to know how we turned into us. In the case of the English tongue, there are many fathers, and the dappled phonetic and semantic gene pool is there to be learned and revelled in.

That the meaning of words changes over time is not a spectacular claim. Most people would grant the likelihood that words haven't always meant what they mean today. But what might escape our attention is the timing of those changes, and the semantic direction in which those changes tended to go. Think of a kelp bed. The uppermost leaves, those closest to the water's surface are all aligned in a certain direction, and they tell you something about the current of the water in which they grow. Our language is our kelp forest, and its semantic shifts murmur about the spiritual and ontological tides that have prevailed. These changes in meaning show us something of the massive, subtle currents at work that have crafted this strange and troubled time, that have troubled and compromised the work and the very presence of elders among us.

Etymological dictionaries give us one way to track these changes in the English language. They do this mainly because they allow the passage of time back into the understanding of meaning. Etymological dictionaries are the tolerant and enduring elders of the semantic trade. They remember pretty well, and with that memory they testify to inconvenient histories and times that aren't the authorized version of everything that we learned in school. They bear inefficient mysteries,

mysteries that won't give in. They betray the allegations that stand in for tradition.

Our word *old*, these semantic treasure troves tell us, derives from a pan–Northern European word root, recognizable to this day in the Nordic and Germanic languages: *alt*. It is cognate with the Latin "to nourish," "to grow," and also "to cause to grow." This link to Latin is as you might expect, because it is a sign of two historical events whose consequences are far from spent: the conquest of Germania, Gaul, Iberia, and Britannia by the Roman Empire, and the subsequent conversion of these peoples and places, and their northern neighbours and adversaries, to Christianity over the following seven or so centuries. With conquest came the dominion of Latin over the indigenous languages. Latin became the language of learning and civility and governance. With the conversions, Latin became the language of devotion. These two events and their howling brood of consequences will be fundamental to the Second Act of this meditation upon elderhood.

This is a tricky and not very wise translation, though, using our current understanding of *growth*, including the notion of "rising above" (as in *altitude*), to suffice for what *al(t)* may have meant. I would like to imagine that the early custodians of what became the English tongue did not share our preference for installing their deities way up out of reach, hovering as those ominous drones do now. They seem instead to have been willing or able to find holiness in the weft and whorl of the little corner of the world granted them, and to have settled for a kind of animism that did not make their Gods or themselves strangers to the world. And they may have not had the aversion to limit and frailty and endings that very much hovers at the edge of what we mean by *growth*. In fact, northern mythologies seem to have had a healthy estimation of what their Gods couldn't do, couldn't manage, couldn't vanquish. There is not much sign that they traded in the degradation and slander of the natural world and of the body that prevailed among some of their contemporaries who were influenced by eastern Mediterranean Gnosticism, aspects of Greek philosophy, and some Eastern religions during the same period. So the spatial and moral hierarchy we might bring to "above and below" and to "old and young" may not have been there in the early going.

The change of the meaning of the word *growth* to something like "unerringly good for you and for the world" signals, among other things, a steep and intolerant shift in the place granted to limit, frailty, age, and elderhood by which our time is now recognizable. In our regime, growth is something between a mania and a moral obligation. In its spatial iteration it certainly evokes the sense of "increase," of "more where there once was less." Growth accumulates. It takes up room. It occupies. It swells. The way the word is used now, *growth* is inherently good, in much the same way that *natural* is good.

When the business reporters gravely report that the rate of growth has slowed this quarter, though you are no economist, you can take from their voices that this isn't good. The rate of growth itself has to grow, because the alternative, the opposite, is … What? Contraction? No, not really. In economic terms, contraction is just this side of the apocalypse. Functionally, ideologically, the opposite of a growing rate of growth isn't a growing rate of contraction. It is a slowing rate of growth. They aren't the same thing. But if you are in a time and place utterly strung out on momentum and change, they sure seem like the same thing. In such a place, *the mandate to grow itself grows*. It brooks no doubt, no challenge. Some working in and out of the geopolitical economic world have begun now to question or warn us away from undertaking growth for its own sake, which is proper and long overdue, but I suspect the lion's share of people in North America continue to endorse growth, especially the financial and the personal kind, for its own sake.

Look to the self-help industry, the retreat industry, the personal-growth industry in North America. There you will find that growth has become a moral order unto itself. Personal growth is secular salvation for the nonaligned, for that demographic swell that elbows its way to the front of every line, and the personal-growth industry strikes me, for the most part, as an elder-free zone. Younger and older, all of them seeking betterment. The sense of personal inadequacy that drives the thing seems to have become the great social leveller, the great generational equalizer. The democracy of growth is the antidote to hierarchy in a culture that no longer believes in wisdom and ancestry.

Personal growth: the atomization of benefit, the obligation to leave the baggage behind, to shed and shuck what binds you and precedes you, and to strive. It is the great leveler of merit. "Oh, I'm always learning," people say. "If you stop learning, you start dying." I see. Bad news for dying people, that is, especially those who thought they could learn how to die. But it's one or the other, proliferate or perish, for the growth addicted. It's something like that morose menace we ascribe to sharks, who must drive water through their gills by forever going forward, or die for want of momentum. Personal growth is the psychologization and interiorization of the world. Ectopic victory over the vagaries, monotheism without God. The age of the Anthropocene.

⚜

Consider the tumour. I am no anatomist or oncologist, but it strikes me that the tumour might be best understood as growth. Not "a growth," which is a common way of referring to it, but *growth itself*, both the essence and the incarnation of growth. Now, unchecked or untreated, the tumour is likely to proceed, consuming as it goes about its mandate of growing. To what end does it grow? you could wonder. When has it grown enough, so it can finally just be a tumour and stop growing towards being one? The only answer I can think of that is consistent with the tumour's way of going about its business is this: there is, ideally, no *end* to the tumour's growth, in either sense of the word *end*. This means that there is no termination foreseeable or permissible. It could also mean that there is no purpose that either legitimizes or employs the growth. A tumour is a relentless incarnation of growth for the sake of growth. A tumour is growth untethered to, ungoverned by, the consequences of growth. The end result? A tumour loses by winning. It kills what it draws its nourishment from. It grows itself to death.

Growth untethered to its consequences strikes me as something like artificial intelligence. It is ingenuity unburdened by conscience, utterly unaccountable, sociopathic. Naturally, the smart money in a growth-addicted culture is on disembodied, homeless "intelligence."

Growth for its own sake seems to be the mantra of the self-improvement industry in North America. It has enjoyed unimaginable growth from the 1970s through to the present time and has done so during precisely the same time that genetic manipulation of the food supply and remorseless fracking-style extraction have been engaged in, Brave New World style. Years from now, these may come to be recognized as developments, or growths, that were joined at the hip.

⤛❈⤜

Alt is probably the older form of our word *old*. When it is used as a prefix today, it means something like "high," and it carries the subtler association of "fully done," something like "having become complete." The much older and more widely geographically distributed Indo-European form of the word is *al*. Like the ancestors of most of our words, *al* was a verb, signifying something that was performed or done, the semantic predecessor I would say of all nouns. In this case, we can translate it in its two functions. It means "coming to fullness," and it also means "causing to become full," making it an alchemical conjurer. In other words, the meaning of *al* in English's ancestral era carries an understanding that whatever and whoever the word is used to describe is both an incarnation of the idea of "fully realized" and an agent of full realization. It is, for all of its two letters, a potent idea. The presence of something or someone who is deeply achieved has the consequence of prompting or fomenting deep achievement, both by example and by inducement.

Given all that, it is a deep running thing to consider that in Old English, the semantic predecessor to Shakespeare and to you and me, there was the word *eald*. It carried all the meanings I have described here, and its superlative form, its congealed and incarnate form, was *ealder.* Elder: not the one who grows without end, come what may, but the one who causes depth and fullness by being deep and full, the one who prompts and is prompted by the ebbing, by the failure and the end of growth. Considered in this way, a life lived chafing at limits is a life that thwarts the advent of *old,* and of its crowning achievement, *elder.*

So we might consider translating *al(t)* not as ascending or swelling or taking up more of the inner or outer horizon, or taking more, but as something like "deepened by diminishment," which is a radical restatement of what is usually meant by *full.* It may be in the manner of *old* that it enables by agreeing to be less able, by surrendering wide-ranging competence with increasing grace, and by ceding agility and mastery of its time and place to others, by refusing the accolade of *timeless.* Old may serve most by relinquishing the centre stage of life—the principal seduction of middle age—and in so doing, it may prompt capacity and depth in the younger generations. The elder serves best by toasting the coming of the next new day while he or she stands there at five minutes to his or her personal midnight.

Wine is a good example. The passage of time doesn't increase the amount of wine you have. It confers upon some of the wine you manage to make the status of age. Wine does not increase in volume but deepens in richness as time passes. It can bestow a sense of well-being, but it has to be spilled to do its work among us. In its aged form *old,* the adjective and the noun both describe the function of "nourishing," "sustaining." It seems that the sustenance flows in one direction, from the aged to the aging. It passes, yes, but its passing is bequeathed to the young and to their present. *Old* gives those beginning to age a place to appear by slipping away at some mysterious appointed hour. *Old* serves notice to the young that their time of service is at hand, and that transience and frailty and the failure to persist come what may *is* the passport to the Pantheon of the Worthies that the Ministry of Time grants. And the young in turn sustain the old, by being willing to be sustained by them.

From this brief, contentious contemplation of *al,* the story of *old* and of *elder* seems to have appeared. The words themselves haven't failed us. They seem to tell the story well. To be old is to be willing—sometimes more so, sometimes less—to be drawn down from the heights. An elder, the deep etymology suggests, offers up in some metabolized form the strange elixir that can be drawn from the breaking down of cool remoteness and tyrannous competence. The old competence of youth and middle age is tapped and tempered and brought true by all the leavings, the thinning of the ranks that the passing of time performs. This is a kind of private understanding that cannot be easily shared with those still aroused by the imperious dominion and the anthem called "my life," those still confusing "the human lifespan" with "life."

The presence of the elder is of great consequence. The presence of the elder forsaken by growth can prompt this deepening, this skill of being slight, in the witnesses. Rather than "old growth," you might say "old, grown." *Elderhood is the antidote to personal growth* and the fret of personal inadequacy that drags it along. It trades salvation for sorrow and sanity and a late-coming chance to get it right. This is what Leonard Cohen, the Patron Saint of the Orphan Wisdom School, Unawares, could have meant when he sang:

> *And I lift my glass to the awful truth*
> *That you can't reveal to the ears of youth,*
> *Except to say it isn't worth a dime.*
> *And the whole damn place goes crazy twice*
> *And it's once for the devil and it's once for Christ*
> *But the boss don't like these dizzy heights*
> *And we're busted in the blinding lights of closing time.*
>
> —Leonard Cohen, "Closing Time"

L. C.

Leonard Cohen dies. Three words. My daughter sent them to me one afternoon last fall, knowing how close I'd felt to his example, his faithful witness, in case I hadn't heard. Within an hour, the media deluge was on. His wane was out there, had been out there for some time. The last record, *You Want It Darker*, put it out there: *I'm ready, my Lord.* So they had their stories ready to run, of course, their on-demand obituaries. They just plugged in the day, plugged in the way. The reviewers made room in the registry of luminaries for the Loss of the Great Man, and the bouquets, and other relevant things. They fell over the transom and over each other, getting the word out, harrowing his field for the gravel of signs, finally acknowledging the unfurled flags of infirmity that flew for years over what he cared to say.

Well, "It's all a joke." He said that a few times. Don't leave that out. In one of his last interviews he said he was ready, told the Lords of Death as much. But the wave of his time's refusal of endings broke over him when he said it. And he recanted. Playing the old card, he declared his vow to live forever instead. Shrugging the shrug of the servant of the clear and the cool, he looked the other way. I've no inside track on the man and those waning days, but I'd guess it probable that he may not quite have been willing to stomach how accustomed so many were to him, how much required reading he'd become. Now he's become required quoting.

Why not finger the rosary of good fortune back *then*, when gratitude could have taken its place alongside finitude, when he was still with us? That's how we could be with people whose heartache or exhortation we hold dear. We could miss those people while they're still there to be missed, still there to hear it. Here's what could have happened: before he died, those who would miss him could have missed him *with* him. Maybe they were. I hope they were. I don't mean family and close friends. I mean the beautiful parade of listeners that came to his work later in his life. Then, they could have taken in that slurry of grace that was his dying, their love for the hard-to-think thought of his goneness back where it belonged, the grief and the grace of it, and they could have risen to the task of taking him under. As it is, we get another nostalgia-sanctioned "forever" instead, washing over us, the one called "He's gone," to add to the collection of inevitables that we've gathered up to gird us, some of us, so that days like this don't happen. Or if they do, they don't end. Read it for yourself in the internet obituaries: he'll live forever now, they say.

I myself had nothing written down for that knowable day. I was prepared to call it off, though, give up the work and the struggle when I heard. The departure of a Worthy makes me question the worth of what's left, for a while. I don't say I was ready. I wasn't ready, had no desire to be ready. I am a veteran of the death trade, but I can say in earnest that he was so valiantly old, it seemed from here, that there was no longer any *reason* for him to die, strange as that might sound.

I know. I know all the mutterings about the gift he was, and going on, all of that. But I have no obligation to surface, to shuffle across the fields as if people are watching, as if going on is the next thing to do. As if it makes sense to go on without a dark, achieved light like that. There are reasons for all that "going on" business, but there's no rhyme. The light's still on around here. But the rhythm's gone out. That's how it seems. Stay in the warm room of his achievement and his heartache long enough, you think the world is warm.

Well, here's the part that could've been known, all of you who are secretly bereft by his death: there's always been the leaving. And the getting left.

He settled into the leaves and the dust of uncertainty so slowly you could've watched it happen if you had the discipline. Not the will, not the stomach. The discipline. *Discipline*: that which you bind yourself to in the name of the love you have for the one you propose to learn from. It takes a kind of discipline to see down what you admire, what you've found, what's held you in good stead. That's what it took to see his farewell unscrolling.

There was the grace. That's something he could do. Looking down into the boil, looking off in the direction the loved ones go—he could do that, too, I believe. The songs might not seem much to go by in this regard, but now they're going to have to do. He sent signals of bewilderment, but he counted the grains of sand granted him, and he did it aloud. He dropped the coins of age into the cup, a couple at a time. He didn't leave that out. He seems to have let them fall in the manner of one who reads, knowing that turning the pages obliges all that's been read to vanish. It seems to me he did it slowly. A coin falling into an empty cup is something loud when it's the first one. But when they begin to add up, you hear not the sound of the fallen but of the falling. He gave himself over to be counted among the falling, all diminished and deep like burgundy, like that voice.

Let others—and there are, plenty—tell you artfully how there's nothing to say when a Worthy hits the dark road heading out of town. No sense disturbing their day. But he said those nothings, and he catalogued the leavings, and he didn't do it once. He was aged for so long. I wonder if he got used to it. He was old longer than he was young, that's the way it seems. He slowed it and he showed it.

> *I've always liked it slow. I never liked it fast.*
> *You want this thing to go. I want this thing to last.*
>
> —Leonard Cohen, "Slow"

You don't get to see your youth coming on, it doesn't seem. It's not in the eye. It's not on the screen. It's not in the ear. It's busy. It's electric, it's busy being seen. You're never young, of course. You're young in hindsight, but never at the time. With courage, though, you're old when you are. That's your address. That's where your mail comes. That's where they can find you, your days mystified by overhearing the song of their end, you testifying by waking up again and lurching up again, until you don't, and by making your way as if all of this is in the wings, in the cards, nothing to wait for anymore. Old time.

A few months ago I was walking in Montreal. There was a kind of wall mural festival going on, and the artistry was widespread, and it was a sunny morning. I caught a glimpse of something green and grey to my right. I backed up to look down an alley that ran north. It afforded me a view of a building maybe half a kilometer away. It was ten stories high, or more. Across the entire windowless side of the building a mural of L. C., the Orphan Wisdom School's Jewish Patron Saint, Unawares, ten stories of his fedora and his age, wry and attentive and uneclipsed. He was getting The Treatment, the uplift into the Pantheon of Worthies. I loved him all over again. Bless Montreal.

✤

Closing time: a good way of testifying to the willingness of age to forgo all the other possibilities. Not defeat. Stepping down instead, the subtle segue that doesn't need an enemy. The agreement to be bound to time, to be gathered up in a way that seeks sustenance. *That* might be the thumbprint of elderhood. Think again of the actual meaning of the alleged compliment where things and people are called *timeless*. It isn't "enduring," or "tested and found true," or anything of the kind. It means "life has passed by without any sign that it has." It means "the whole thing is an allegation, nothing more." It means "there's no way to know." It means something like "oblivion." Any ability you might cultivate through your life to have a willingness to be known by what time has made of you might come from the slow, dawning realization that in the days of seeking sustenance, you were on the take, on the receiving end of that sustenance and of that ability to be sustained. Now, with the coming of age, you are awake to it, and you aren't taking much more than some tea as evening comes on, something stronger if it's winter. Your example is the wine younger people are fortified by.

✤

Here's another etymological journey for you. It strikes me as recognizably so, and it should be so if it isn't. We have this word *awake*. It now means "to come from sleep." In philosophical and religious circles, it means something like "to emerge from error or confusion." The lineage between the two is to be found in the word's close association to the Old English *waeccan*, "to watch," from which comes our word *vigil*. That's what the dictionaries will tell you.

Here's some more. *Wake* is a noun you'll recognize as meaning "something that ripples out behind you," as in "making your way through water." But a wake is also that event that is prompted by endings of all kinds, and by death. Put them together and you see that *wake* means something like "the array of consequence that fans out from what happens or what is done, intentional and otherwise, whether in water or in life."

Then there is the *a-* out in front. This is a mercurial prefix in Modern English. The negating sense of *a-* comes into the language from Greek and Latin and applies only to words of that origin. Given that our word *wake* is Old English and not Latin in origin, the general meaning of *not* does not apply here. This leaves us with its Old English prepositional meaning: "in," or "on," or "of." Taken altogether, you could say that *a-* in this word has the effect of intensifying, by locating. It congeals, in place and time.

When we reassemble the word *awake* as *of the wake* or *by the wake*, we have something close to "to be gathered up into the tangle of consequence," "to be afforded a place in the outrageous fortune that is human life." In other words, as *sleep* is the time of childhood and ecstasy and ectopia, so *to be awake* is to become a citizen of your time and place, to come of age. I myself love this little treasure. Wakefulness, far from being a recipe for disdainful remoteness from the hurly burly, means instead to be taken in by the Big Deal, by the Whole Thing, to be included and to know that you are, to be a faithful witness to the wilderness and the town and the places where they meet, to be harrowed by life and winnowed by the winds of change, to be burdened and privileged by living long enough to know that you are well and truly alive, and to pay the Lords of Life for the remarkable grace of the thing by living down into the depths, and by testifying on occasion. To be an elder, in other words. That's the condition of elderhood: to be gathered into wakefulness.

Consider, then, the frank aberration of the natural order of life perpetrated by boisterous Boomers who've begun to insist upon being at their own wakes. *Your wake is prompted by your death.* That's what it is. If you're there, it's just another party. They call it life affirming. Maybe. But it seems life subverting. It follows that fault line of this age, the great levelling satisfier of the marketplace, the creed of the times: *it works for me.* We need a new word to describe the event—*dewake*, maybe, the final undoing of *awake.*

This old-person realization resituates you. No longer at the centre of it all, nor at the forefront, no longer drawing down and taking. Maybe you're unwilling now to be above it all either, no longer meaning or willing to prevail. You're the master practitioner of sorrow and longing and belonging instead, the incarnation of endings, fraying, failing at eternity. So it's come to this: by doing the work of deepening by diminishment, you are lending younger people endurance in times of trouble.

This function is a temporal one, meaning that it is a consequence of obeying the passing of time. One's elders are one's past, but not the kind of past that means "gone," or "behind you." You look towards your past, and there they are, *before you.* They are what—if fortune smiles and you do your work—might become of you. Your elders are not passing away from you. Time bears them as it bears you. Same tempo. You are not standing still on the shore of life watching the river of time bear them away. You are in the river, too.

How about this: *your elders are no closer to their death than you are to yours.* Your death and theirs are at the end of the shuffle of your days and their days. Oh, you may have more upright days than older people, if you were to start counting the days from now. But why call today the magic beginning of *anything*, no matter how important you feel today, no matter what that fridge magnet in your kitchen says? We miss the beginnings of almost everything, truth be known. We catch up to them after they've already begun, if fortune and mercy mingle and the Gods prevail. Most everything in life begins somewhere in our hindsight. That's when the elders learned their elderhood: in your hindsight. You know the saying: "the older I get, the smarter some of the older people become."

Chances are that your elders were callow youths before you were born. The distance until your death and theirs is not measured in days until then. It's measured in life. It's always been there, your death and theirs, the daemon at the end of your lives. It is the constant companion, the uninvited houseguest who, with discipline and a good example before you, prompts the radical etiquette and the zany hospitality you may yet extend to endings of all kinds. Both you and your old people have the same thing left: the rest of your lives.

The elders can be as alive as you can be until they die. If you manage to evade the haunting promises of eternal life in the decades to come, and if the institution of elderhood is somehow restored, you'll see. Their way of sustaining you by how they lay down the raging glories of youth, before you even *know* of them or those glories—that is the *now* that your life happens in. If they are elders, they've done that laying down—and a lot more besides—some time ago. Their way of proceeding out beyond their middle age, that is what constitutes your *present*, the time that you were born into. That is how the present arises. It is the sustained, the ongoing iteration, of sustenance. The generative power or consequence of the past is what we call *now*. That is how elders prompt deepening in their juniors. They are the imperative of the present, the Would That It Be of now.

All of this, without exaggeration or fancy, is to be found in the contemplation of the subtleties of a two-letter word that comes from the ancients of the English tongue. With patience and the discipline of learning, this tuition is there to behold. Practice this patience with *al* and *old*, and somewhere in there the elder appears. And then consider the consequence, the wake that fans out from old peoples' refusal to age overtly and clearly, in public, and how that robs younger people of their deepened lives, their present.

4

CABIN

*You start off in
the light and you
end up in
wisdom,
if the Gods are
prevailing.
Otherwise, light.*

"**O**rdinarily" is not a great way to begin a sentence, but ordinarily I would finally stop looking for something I'm sure is somewhere but can't find. Stymied I am by the Gods of Reorganization who visit my stuff from time to time without warning or clear mandate or a by-my-leave. It isn't extraordinary for me to find things gone. (This section of this book is no exception. I've written it once, transcribed and, I thought, improved it on the computer. I opened it up two days later to find that entry gone.) I don't know whether it is better to have grown used to finding things gone by now, which I haven't done, or to refuse to grow used to it in the name of not losing things, which I have tried to do. Either way, the stuff goes. And either way, a strategy is in order to contend with whatever anhedonia attends to the losing of lost stuff.

I've been rooting through things looking for a writing book on elderhood I'm sure I began some years ago. I'm haunted. I swear I can see the word *Elderhood* on the front cover, or on the front page, the book properly begun and tracking whatever I'd come up with on the subject up to that point. But it is nowhere to be found. I am beginning to wonder if this is what is in the cards for the duration, me certain only about what is gone, no breadcrumb trail through the undergrowth of my memory to follow. This is where you entertain thoughts of what a very early stage—or, gads, a not-so-very-early stage—of a neurodegenerative lifestyle might be like, you with a small card pinned to your lapel that, instead of your name, says, "Do you know where … is?" and has room enough for you to write down what you've lost, the particulars of which you will eventually not remember either. Self-diagnosis is a holdover from my days in the death trade, an occupational hazard that no longer requires the occupation to persist.

> I often walked the long death road with people who lived their entire conscious lives, so far as they recalled them, as atheists, or agnostics, or generic naysayers regarding What Happens When You Die? and other Big Questions. Whether or not this gave them comfort they seemed not sure about, but it gave them a kind of functional certainty, a kind of night sky crowded by stars but free of constellations by which they made their certain way through their now waning days. They were, it turned out, the lion's share of the dying people I met in that large urban centre, and they were troubled in a way they never saw coming. Now that they were fairly sure they were dying, should they want to have been right their whole lives about the inevitabilities of Oblivion or Meaninglessness or Storylessness, now that these were no longer concepts, now that it wouldn't come down to what they knew, but what they figured, or what they hoped for?

Or should they wish to have been wrong their whole lives, on the off chance that everything is Otherwise?

Imagine hoping that you've been right all along about what is soon to take you from among us and banish you from the scene, you amounting to a persistent allegation, for the sake of consistency, if not for anything else, the moral high ground now more like a stall in suburban strip mall of opinion. Imagine hoping that you've been wrong all along, all those moments of life you gave over to dismissiveness or faux clarity that you know now were not nearly as deeply considered as they might have been when the What ifs? came to call. And those moments are now up near the front of the line in the caravan of your regrets. And all of this imprecision and self-doubt has entered into your mind at five minutes to midnight, just in case there *is* Something Else. It isn't easy in life's tender and taxing times to tell the difference between conviction and casualty. Nor, does it seem, is it supposed to be. That's what enough time-in can give you a feel for—consequence.

If losing things has become chronic, you are probably dangling from the antlers of a dilemma particular to an advanced life. Do you want all this losing to be a kind of character flaw that more learning or more stuff doesn't seem to change, but oh well? Or do you want it to be a cognitive synapse kind of thing that says nothing about your person but promises a lot about your future? A sign pointing forward, or a sign pointing back?

Anyway, when I couldn't find my writing book, I was in tribulation, just enough tribulation to feel irresponsible and wayward about this latest misplacement. Then I thought, "Now, what might an elder do at a time such as this?" And I do recommend this question to anyone routinely visited by the goneness of their stuff. You might think that this very plight of routinely losing things is very much like an old person mingling in the growing crowd of his or her afflictions, just a part of the deal. Or you might think instead that the skillfulness of elderhood is to be found not in avoiding loss but in knowing how to lose, learning to pay the price with more grace as you go.

I am not clear whether this gets me any further down the road on the theme of elderhood that I have come to so often over the last decade or so. I have returned to it for so long now that occasionally I am credited with the title or the job description by others. That does make me wonder sometimes whether the preoccupations and habits of mind I have cultivated over the years are a sign of elderhood, or a consequence of elderhood, or an impediment to elderhood. Do elders wonder in this fashion? I wonder.

What the wonder did do was to get me out of leafing through everything one more time, *just in case*, which was welcome. It did persuade me, too, that some little leaf of the rest of my life was blowing by while I was bent over the pile of my writing books trying to find that fledgling book on elderhood, which itself seemed a fable of some kind. And it did persuade me that there were limits to the tiresome sense of responsibility to unfound and unfindable things that I have. So I've given up trying to find the thing. I remain underpersuaded that I'll be forgiven for giving up on the book, and I'll have to contend with that. I've learned over the years that giving up looking for something helps with finding it, though I don't know why. It just seems that it helps with the feeling-tone of the quest and somehow takes the heat down a bit. Maybe it's my version of the serenity prayer. Almost certainly my wife has *organized* it in some fashion, and she will find it, now that I've given up being able to, and I'll forge a temporary détente with the moral order I carry around. Marriage can be like that, sometimes. It is among other things the transactions of lost and found. Elderhood can be like that, too, I imagine.

I don't have the answer, really, to what an elder might do about losing things, but I know what I decided to do, having run out of schemes for peace of mind. Time went by, and then a few days ago I went down to the writing cabin to write this stuff down again. It was the first time that I'd done that. I'd written before, in various places, but I'd never gone to the cabin to do it. I formally gave up what I'd written down so far on the subject, watched it carried away by the River of Going, Going, Gone, and chose another book that had no writing at all in it, an expensive one I'd been saving for something important, and I peeled off the clear wrap, deciding that this was as important as things were likely to get, and wrote a brief account of my defeat, as a beginning. That's what I did. That's what this is, the one you are reading now.

It was not until all those little defeats of memory and organization gathered round like chicks to a hen that something came to me, sitting there in the writing cabin for the first time. It *is* a strange arrangement. Something finally comes to you when enough other things finally don't. You could say that there is something in losing that can bring flexibility to the grasp. Whatever the machinery of the thing, an unbidden memory came calling, came reeling then, a day or two ago, just around the time when the panic of the search was morphing into something like infinite resignation to the ways of the universe of errancy and stuff, when the teaching of impermanence was messing with my plans.

❧

A year or two ago, a few of us commenced unplanned work on a little structure on the bank of the River of Abundance and Time that marks one boundary of my farm. It started out its life as an outdoor kitchen, but the idea didn't take. I spent more money, used the bones of the thing as a kind of exoskeleton, imagined myself sitting there by the river, scribbling away. With my father-in-law's help, we finished it up into a little one-room writing cabin, pine clad, tin roofed. I called it a "cabin" at the time because it wasn't formerly housing chickens, for example, or fodder, or dried cans of paint, or the recycling, so it was never a shack. If it had been a shack, that would have meant that I could have launched myself again into the redemption business and crafted a moral silk purse from the ruination of time leaning so heavily upon wood outdoors, as it does. But there was no shack to redeem. In fact, since moving here, I've caused to be built a few lean-tos and coops and so on, all of which are inconsiderate of the building codes in the area, all of which are fated by disorder and not design to become shacks fit for redemption into cabins for someone else years from now, should that person see the world that way. "Writing cabin" I called it because I was encouraging myself.

It was built, and it sat there, unmoved into, for a season or longer—quite a while. Turning some pine walls and plastic windows and tin roof into a "writing cabin" requires writing in that space somewhere in the equation. That isn't optional, I don't think. It is an honourific title at best, and it's downhill from there towards ignominy in your mind if you look on your architectural folly from the house and admire it and so on, this cabin of yours, and leave it to shed rain and snow and to freeze and swelter for a year or more, and you don't go down to write in the thing. That's what happened, though.

A few items went in, books and pens, the formalities. But I didn't go into it, barely at all, for the longest time. I looked at it sometimes, felt a pang of Protestant propriety about the money spent, the addled plans, the sheer single-purpose folly and pomp of the thing. Well, the snow did settle on the roof. Spring came, the snow was gone, and still the cabin sat empty, a little caldera for my grand plan for taking time off from the road, for self employment as a writing person. I am not a writer. That much is clear. I am someone who has written some things down, occasionally, just in case it happened enough times that something book-like came around. An animist, I had a pang, too. This little house was not being called into life very well, while I sat and looked at it unoccupied, unaddressed. Reasons for the elderhood book came and went; reasons for it not being written came and stayed.

Now, in order to write, somewhere in there must linger the conviction that the "whys" of writing have been met and to a certain degree subdued, that there is merit to the enterprise, and that some skill has found its feet and its saunter. The entire escapade would perish in a heap of scorn and self-loathing—or it would in my case—if the writing cabin preceded the writing, or if they were born together in a season of imagined plenty. Even if all the preliminaries are gathered in a row, and all the requisites met, and even if the cabin is paid for and no debt of the usual kind lingers over it, there is the matter of going there at some point, more often than not, and, in my antique case, putting pen to paper. All the preparations in the world would insult even the simplest part of you should you not court the Menial Gods of Scribble and Screed by bending your head and assuming the position and writing something down. Well, I felt by this time that I had a few thoughts on the subject that might produce book-length trouble, and I had written book-length things before and knew I had the discipline to do it, but whatever I had wasn't enough to get me down the hill to that cabin.

And then I did go down there, and the memory came, a quiet, ruthless memory that had lain unremembered for sixty years. I wrote in *Die Wise* about my tangle with spinal meningitis when I was four years old, but I didn't say anything much about the time afterwards, except the detail that somehow, lamentably, I'd grown used to having nearly died in the name of carrying on, that it'd become something like the wallpaper in the hallway of my younger days, something I'd passed through on the way to *now*, something that had stayed put, back there. Call it trauma and call it coping, call it getting on with your days. However you slice it, it still doesn't strike me as advisable to get used to having nearly died. It should change you somehow. It should call down the Saints and the Worthies to attend to your procuring your daily bread. But it doesn't, not necessarily. Then and now, it is relentlessly easy to grow accustomed to what nearly undid you, all the while upping the ante on undoing.

Well, like everything, there's more. There were weeks of convalescence back then, me bound to the bedroom and the bed, looking out the window on the sunny days passing by without me, alone in there, obliged to get better. There were strange contraptions of convalescence, though I can only recall the table a neighbour made and spray painted robin's egg blue that spanned the bed to hold whatever I ate and couldn't eat. Catching just a glimpse of that memory of looking out that window at four, my life going by, when I was sixty-two, looking out the window on the little cabin I wouldn't move into, it all came crashing in. I realized then that I've resolutely resisted resting, lying down in the daytime, studying indoors in spring (which made exam time at university a genuine torment), taking any naps while there was light (which made teaching in Iceland at the summer solstice a year or two ago seem insurmountable) for pretty much my whole life. *My whole life.* I look like I do now partly because of the speckled and inconstant kindness of heredity, partly because of the road that has claimed me and obliged me to travel on, but probably because I've sworn off resting. Resting is too much like illness at four years old, I guess, too much like being kept away from life.

Imagine, swearing off resting. But I realized in that moment that this is exactly what I've done, for decades. It seemed all life affirming, all positive and eager and capable, every time I thought I chose it, like so many manias do. People credit me with having energy and staying power to burn. I've been on international teaching tours whose pace might kill someone half my age, and it must look like the Gods are with me, the Gods of the Harangue, at least. They may be, but I don't think now that it was any of those things. I think it was a forlorn madness for the light.

And so I couldn't come out to this writing cabin that enforced the same one-room solitude that my body seemed to remember very clearly and sit down. Yes, some part of me voted for building the thing and, yes, you could say that part of me knew something of all this and crafted this proscenium arch under which I could self-discover, though I wouldn't say that. It sounds too victorious. The truth is that the person who is writing this didn't know it at all. The truth is that I didn't want to recuperate, not again. So I didn't move in. It seems that for those few rolling seasons, I could endure the folly and the recrimination of money poorly spent, and I could endure the taunt of imagining a new book, even of declaring that I'd do it and signing the publisher's contract. But I couldn't approach the old altar of solitude and infirmity. I couldn't walk down the hill, go into that stillness, sit down to table, be troubled aloud, testify, be the faithful witness.

It seems to me that something about growing older, and then being old, understands these foibles and fables, and might even have something like fondness for the fact that they are still prevailing, still being told. But it doesn't tolerate them much. It doesn't look the other way. The older part of us has learned too much it seems, and it cannot betray what it was entrusted with for safekeeping, and so it serves the time it has lived long enough to see by remembering, by gathering back together that which was once whole and well wrought and has since, because of strange days and sorrow, been rent asunder and let scatter and been called "gone."

Perhaps this is something that can appear when the invitation to age appears, just the odd, unsought memory of a sorrow indistinct, of a frantic bird in you that won't settle in the bone, a strange disquieting unwillingness to lie down while there's still light. More than likely, that's how it will be in the end. Lying down while the sun still shines, when the earned fatigue is with you, seems like good practice for the endings entrusted to you. I've talked about it enough over the last two decades, but doing so never got me close enough to that little restless memory to remember it. It took losing what I'd come up with about elderhood. That seems now to have been the exchange. It strikes me as a fair deal.

I don't know what this memory will change. I'm no more amenable to rest than I was, which won't help with whatever infirmities are gathering in the wings. I'll be grappling with this for the duration, I imagine. But I'm glad to remember that boy pining for health enough to leave his room. This reunion has taken a long time to come around. Maybe we'll meet out on the deck on the lee side of the writing cabin while the early evening light goes magic, all amber and violet, now that the biting bugs have settled for the season and the leaves are russet on the ground. That's what I'm up to these days, seeing if I can make peace with a young lad, no longer dying and not clearly alive, looking out onto the living world through his window and wondering on his place, by writing something about elders, and how they get that way, and why there are so few of them now, and why there are so many old people instead.

Firewood

I'm sitting in that cabin now and writing something about elderhood that seems patient enough to have waited me out, and it is early winter. As it happens from time to time, life can grant you dispensation from this mandate of memory and for testifying you set for yourself, and all their prompts. Life provides copious reasons for forestalling. The ramshackling memory comes in, the furniture is overturned, the property values plummet for a while, but before you know it, the well-known human skill for adjusting sets in. It sends other claims upon your attention and your give-a-shit.

There is the matter of your income to attend to, the life in your house up the hill from the cabin. There are the people who look to you. There is the machinery of notoriety to be reasoned with, all true enough and ongoing without end. Where I live, there is the particularly strong dispensation that comes in the form of a real, substantial and persuasive winter.

Winter here is another character in your play, not part of a moveable set you can strike when the mood shifts. When you live off the power grid, this means you have a semi-yearly programme of making heat, typically by firewood. Procuring firewood has the synergy of life affirmation and simplicity all about it. At least it does for the first few winters. You are, as a banker informed me after I moved to the farm, "living the dream, baby." After that "dream" part comes and goes, the finding, hauling, stacking, drying, moving and restacking, fetching, splitting again, and stoking occupies the place in you that the Stations of the Night do for monastic people. The endeavour is part dedication, part discipline, part necessity, part grind that seemed like a good and noble idea at the time.

It is well-known in off-the-grid circles that softwood gums up the works and weeps creosote as it burns, gathers in the flue and stack and is ripe for making a fire somewhere up in the venting. Softwood has a good look to it, compliant and affable and plentiful and fast drying. It is a good starter if it is dry but trouble otherwise. Hardwood, now, *that's* the grail. Split and stacked for drying two or three years before, it is harder to find, not as plentiful, more expensive, and worth the sometimes considerable trouble that comes from keeping it at hand.

As you'll be able to tell later in these pages, I have a bent for things monastic, proverbial, and devotional. My programme for self-abnegation in the late days of autumn has been to trim mature softwood from around the place of its dead limbs, cut them to length, and stack them for winter. I know in my heart that the heat from them is meager, and on an early morning of –20°, that has consequence. I sit by the stove, ablaze with cheap, plentiful softwood, whose nominal heat leaps up the chimney more than it tempers the stove top, and I feel the frost on my shoulders, on the top of my head, on my fingers, and it steals body heat like a cynic steals good cheer. It forbids focus on anything else, and it is the peripheral thief-companion of my winter writing, crackling and nattering like a spooked chipmunk in the firebox.

And yet I persist with the softwood. Why? Because the whole enterprise is a *taking* enterprise, that's why. That's what I tell myself. The building, the land it sits on, the river view it affords, the tin roof, the indulgence of writing: how can I atone? I can atone with making do, with softwood in the firebox. It's a moral code for puritans and lunatics and fundamentalists, and for me. Though no one has told me so, I'd say this proves I have Scots—or Calvinists, for sure, as close as I can probably get to ancestral *penitentes*—in the family line. I do know, even as I continue with it, that this is a shell game of sorts, one that I cannot win.

But this morning, I think I may have lost less severely than usual. Here is what struck me while I was choosing among the softwood possibilities: my firewood is my words. Simple. They are what I have to warm the place. The consequences of being too careful with the good stuff are unavoidable. I mistake cool for heat, inactivity for contemplation, colossal close-fistedness for care. My intention with the whole charade is kindling and little else. I try to do less harm, less taking, and don't go with the good stuff until some kind of mythical crunch time comes when the enterprise deserves the good wood, the good words. I *could* save some of the good stuff for later, for the proverbial better day or rainy day, or the next writing project. I could. I've done so before. Or I could spend them wantonly, putting all of the good ones I can think of in the firebox *this* day, at *this* writing table, in *this* writing, forsaking all others to come, reckless, irresponsible, failing at parsimony, ignoring the allegation of a future, of another book, or another day sitting at the window.

"You see," I said to myself this morning, "you've already built the cabin. There is nothing to reduce or save. You have already given some of the second part of your life to scribbling at times. It isn't a collapse—*unless* you cheapen out, go for the discount, modify your dent on the general predicament, under-function. *Then* it's a collapse. But it seems that writing, like heating a writing cabin you don't go into often, like trying on the brittle garland of elderhood, must be, should be, can't not be the spending of what's been granted you, as utterly as you can bear. It's parting with what you instinctively want to hoard for a more worthy time, a more needy time. But *this* is the worthy time, and God knows it is the more needy time. It's also the *only* time. It is the time for spending the good stuff for the sake of the good stuff, because it's good."

So, you probably know what I did. This morning I dipped into the hardwood. Not too much, but I did. It warmed the place, I have to admit, right into the corners, quicker, truer somehow than the other mornings. And when the joints of my fingers softened, I wrote this account of things down, dipping into the hoard, not waiting for a better day for it all. The softwood belongs, mind you. It's good for the ants and scuttlings. I'll leave it where it falls. Me, I'll burn the hardwood now.

❧

You can see how it can be with getting older than you were. There are these auspicious stories that gather your memories about them, and there is the dusty business of making a place for your reasons for being born to appear, and between these sentries the mystery of your ordinary life passes. And so I never found the writing book, in case you've been wondering, and I had to start again. And I've done so. This is what you are reading. It seems to me now that the book I precociously began vacated the place that the old memory of being a shut-in came to occupy. It's mysterious. I set about writing something about elderhood, the preliminaries disappeared without a trace, and an unbidden memory from childhood upped the ante on the whole thing, finally giving me a place to sit, warmed by parting with the precious and the propitious, auguries all. Welcome to them. Welcome to you.

5

I'M JUST DOWN THE ROAD

ome of you have a website. People in the know tell me that it is *the* slam-dunk business decision to make, that insolvency awaits anyone not so represented in the aether. This may be madness, or it may be true. Some people seem to have websites devoted to the business of being themselves, and it seems that business of that kind is booming. I have mixed feelings about having a website. I knuck-led under to the idea, but peace is elusive. It is like having an agent who is there for you, yes. But this agent does need encouragement and a wardrobe upgrade from time to time, so there's maintenance. There's rent to pay and a fee for the privilege of calling yourself what you call yourself, year after year, even if it's the name your mother gave you at birth. Ask your agent via the metrics game if he's earning his keep, and the answer is almost always yes.

But it is a seductive business. If you are front and centre in the website, there's the illusion that you are *there*, available and affable, like a late-night convenience store when somebody's got the munchies and there's nothing in the fridge. There's the illusion that you yourself are legible and discernible and a clear running stream, another product somebody can add to their cart. And if your face appears somewhere on the website, people seem to feel that they know something about you.

And it can get strange, too. With the dubious discretion that got me into the internet game in the first place, I'd say that having a website amounts to having a shit magnet attached to your house. It can, and often does, draw down the errant fecal matter of the universe, and some of that matter mysteriously has your name on it.

There are urgent people out there, and a good number of them mean well, no doubt, but this veil of anonymity in the arrangement has the God function that seems to make anything possible. Literary standards are an early casualty. It seems to suspend good judgement on one side of the contact or the other for the duration of the encounter, too, and from time to time facelessness calls the shots.

> This example can cover the lot. One woman dreamt that God had come to her with a message for me. (I don't claim to know the transmission preferences of the Great Beyond, but it's already an oblique tangent—from God to this lady's dream to my website to me?) I was to film my dying days, with several high-definition cameras, from different points of view, and send the live feed out into the aethernet. When things like that come in, my wife pushes away from the square-eyed Cyclopes, calls me over to her desk, and informs me that the entire operation will be shutting down, the teaching tours canceled, the writing projects suspended until further notice, and the interviews turned down, that the pigs and sheep and pastures here to for will receive our full attention, that I will be settling into a proper job, and that the marketplace will go along free of my suggestions. That is the kind of business meeting those messages prompt.

So the people managing these things thought twice before forwarding me a message that began: "Hi. I'm just down the road. I'm thinking about coming over. Would that be okay?" This sounded a bit creepy to those who read it. Unless "just down the road" was a euphemism for "in the same area code," it was a bit too forward. It turned out it wasn't a euphemism.

Now, just like your life, life here can be busy. Farming doesn't stop, it doesn't really even slow down, and it goes on as long as there's light, often longer. When you're a farmer, you take the vows, and you're a lifer. You're self-employed, yes, but you have a lunatic abbot for a boss. And if the muse has your address, she's a serious contender for most of your waking hours. That's how it is. So there isn't a lot of wiggle room for impromptu droppings in, for contemplating the eternal verities, if there are any left, with strangers. So we demurred. Over the next few days the messages continued to come, just as persistent as the first, but with a change in tone. They expressed a deepening courtesy and appeared to recognize that we didn't have a drop-in aspect to things, that what was being asked for wasn't a casual encounter. Finally enough courtesy was forthcoming that I thought the place could manage the seeker, and I offered him the one hour in the one day that seemed less given over to the mandates than usual.

When he appeared, he was much younger than I expected, in his mid-twenties at most, probably younger. His head was shaved close, he dressed in well-used clothing, and he was understandably a bit nervous. He had a kind of honed, barely contained instinct for calculation about him, a knack for figuring what might be had and what it might cost. He was on what was probably his version of high alert. Though it was his idea all along, once he got here, he was spooked. After the preliminaries, I asked what brought him here. He said he wanted to see what sustainable farming looked like, in action. It turned out that he was hundreds of kilometers away from his home, which was in fact in another country— a long way to come for a farm tour. So there was probably more to his story.

But he talked farming, said he farmed where he lived, and soon enough, the allotted hour was almost up. He could have gone on. It was clear he wanted to, as if he hadn't yet come to his business. So it fell to me to reinstate our time limit, as the sheep needed tending just then. Before he left, he asked to buy everything that I'd written or recorded. His arms full, he thanked me and walked down the hill towards his car, and I stood there with the dogs and watched him go, wondering if he'd found what he came for. About halfway down the lane he stopped. Before he could think about it more, he came back up again and stood in front of me as if we hadn't met. He took a long breath, put the goods down, looked out across the river, and said this:

> I didn't know what to do with myself a while ago. I'm Jewish. I took up the Israeli government on their offer to bring kids in from the diaspora and set them up with a Jewish life. It went pretty well. I got caught up in the national feeling. It was the first time I ever felt part of something big and grand and full of purpose. I started off on a kibbutz. I don't know how or why—not even now—but after a while I joined the army, like everyone I met had done. I'm not the army kind of guy, but it was in the air. And my timing was very good, or very bad, depends how you want to look at it. There was another uprising on the West Bank, and before I knew it I was there, with the uniform and the gun and the troop carrier to get us into and get us out of the trouble. They sent us out for the first time to patrol. Before I knew it, there were rocks and bottles smashing into the windscreen, and everyone was yelling to scramble out, and we did, and the guy in charge was maybe twenty-three. And there was a crowd at the end of the street that came out of nowhere, throwing things at us. A lot of them were children, and older women. It all happened so fast. I had my finger on the trigger. Something went off beside me, and before I knew it I fired. I don't know if I hit anybody. I don't think so, but I don't know. And they went nuts then, and the guy in charge yelled to get back inside the truck, and in another minute we were driving like hell to safety. Then everything was quiet. Nobody said a word. And suddenly I couldn't do it anymore, and the bottom of the whole thing fell away. I guess I had something like a nervous breakdown a bit later. They let me out of the army. I came back to the States. I don't know what I'm doing. I'm working on some guy's farm, but I don't know what I'm supposed to be doing.

He stopped his story. Everything was quiet again. Then he looked at me in the eyes for the first time since he arrived, and he said:

> You know why I came here? I just wanted to find out if you were for real.

Let's say you have a teenager or two at home. Let's say that might happen someday, and it'll be sooner than you bargained for. Just like it was for you and your parents years ago, there'll be those moments of genuine confrontation, some principle or other transgressed, some boundary that needs defending or enforcing, some propriety cast adrift. You'll ask for a talk, which the teenager knows is code for you doing most if not all of the talking. So the chances are that, if you still have some respect floating back and forth between you, the teenager will submit to the talk, might even participate to some degree.

This is where you get another chance to decide whether it is worth fording the generational Rubicon, or whether there's another way. Chances are good that if things get heated, and you feel unlistened to or disrespected a bit, you'll start focusing the whole discussion down to the teenager, to his or her manner or speech or tone of voice, and the whole thing will wheel around and become an inquiry into how the teenager figured this or that was an okay thing to say or do, and how the teenager came to be as he or she is.

And that's the fatal error. For the purposes of that discussion, you're probably not going any further, no matter how much longer the thing goes on. Shutdown has already occurred. Somewhere in there, from frustration or from a sense of futility, or from some other place, you slipped into the old, familiar role of trying to figure the kid out, and you did it out loud, to the kid. You made the kid the object of your scrutiny, and you mistook that for an act of genuine concern. And, probably, the seating arrangement said it all. You moved around until you were opposite the teenager, and the teenager couldn't see anything but you and your inquisition.

There is an alternative, though it won't likely seem like one at the time. It's a simple shift. Move your seat, that's all. Not alongside him or her, all chummy suddenly. But move your seat so that you are, in some fashion, looking off in the direction that the teenager is looking while trying to avoid your inquisitorial scowl. Instead of trying to see the teenager, as tempting or mandatory as it might seem at that moment, see if you can see what that young person sees, instead. I don't mean see what the young person sees when he or she looks at you. I mean, try to see what the teenager sees when he or she looks out onto this world you have brought them to. And you'll find it a remarkably challenging thing to do. You'll find that there's a reason that you were trying to see them instead. It's easier to do that than it is to see what they see. It's safer, too.

There is change in this world, of course. Seasonal change, stage-of-life change, fashion change, and the rest. And, of course, political change, or the changing illusion of change, and technological change that washes up on the doorstep almost every day. And then there is the *rate* at which these things are changing, which accelerates all the while, which explains why all the climate change logarithms overheat and burst into flame. They cannot account for the cumulative consequences of the changing. The simple truth is that the world of your youth bears so little resemblance to the world of a teenager today that it must be all but abandoned as a reasonable basis for understanding life as it stands now. In your youth, you could not be killed easily or at all by sex or the sun or the imported food supply or the domestic food supply, by the genetically altered grain or animal, by the insulation in the house, by the phone. But they can. They can be killed in their youth by things you probably don't know exist. This doesn't make you obsolete, not neces-sarily, but it does make you unsteady and in deep need of reimagining what is at stake with young people. It doesn't make them geniuses, not at all, but it makes them overrun by a world that is allegedly there for them, and it makes them dependent in spite of themselves on some even rudimentary guidance, some anachronistic something that could be wisdom, that could only come from the likes of you, someone twice or more their age. That's the deal now.

It doesn't happen every week, but kids do get in touch with me, they do come to the School and to teaching events, and without encourage-ment from me then or now sometimes come up the farm lane like that young man did, their hands curled into fists. You could think that they are curled in anger. Often they are, though it has been swallowed for so long that it takes a while for it to break the surface as anger. You'd think, with the energy bound up in keeping those fists as tightly closed as they do, that they're afraid to lose what they've brought. In a strange way they are afraid. I say *strange*, because they are holding those fists out towards me, not in threat but in plea. Holding on for dear life, they ask me in one indirect way or another to pry them open, to take from them what they've been carrying.

In one hand these kids have an impotent rage, a rage that has had the energy leached out of it by futility and pointlessness and the chronic collapse of faith, all heat and no light. In the other is an aimless, wandering, principled anxiety, dressed up as brittle conscience, all light and no heat. And *these* are their prized possessions. And that's why their hands are curled around them. Some of the time, maybe much of the time, that's what they have. It's all that they have. Their formal education, their political education, their media education, by these they have been persuaded that awareness and prescience in a troubled time means burden and troubled sleep and rancor in the marketplace of ideas. It means merit so compromised as to be an allegation. It means there is no tradition of their own worth claiming. It means seeking out a cooler, intact, café-au-lait spirit tradition that they can be nursed by. It means trading in a sense of well-being for a sense of compromise and a label of *privilege*, just to feel something like legitimacy, just to survive a casual conversation about how things are. It means fashioning a hair shirt out of conscience. It means enthroning misanthropy, just the time christened the Anthropocene dawns. Good luck with that.

I have mothers contact me from time to time. Their requests come down to this: "Please take my teenage son." She sent him off to university in the fall, and he's come back at Thanksgiving unrecognizable—sullen, inward-turned, wounded, dragging a phantom limb of well-being. He's in a liberal arts programme, and in more classes than not, he's learned that he's the face of privilege, he's the one with the class problem, he's what's been wrong for a long time, he's at the top of the food chain, he has to stand in for the whole, wretched thing. "What do you want me to do with him?" I ask her. "Just help him to be a man. Help him to be a person," she says. "Find someone from

where you live," I say, which is the right thing to do, to seek sustenance from the place that seems to have compromised him so deeply.
And she says, "There isn't anybody." So she'd rather send her son to
somebody who's no more than pixels on a screen than to anyone she
knows. Such is the devilry in some places.

Yes, such is the shaky moral high ground of young people being
alerted to the troubles of their time, that *these* are their prized possessions. And though this seems to surprise them as much as it does me,
they are pleading with me to pry open their hands, either hand, and
take these prizes from them, or at least one of them. That's one of the
more urgent reasons they come. They don't make the trek to show
me what they've accomplished so far. They haven't come to be seen,
not really. They've come so far to have their misanthropy vandalized.
They don't think they are wrong about what we've done to the world.
They've mistrusted and hated people my age for years. They're about
to inherit a world whose deep compromise they had no voice in per-
petrating or in solving. They don't think they're wrong about who
can't be relied upon. But, somewhere in there, they *want* to be wrong.
That amounts to something like a plan: *find an older person you could
be wrong about, and be wrong about them to them.* If that's as close to
wisdom as you can get for a while, that'll do.

Yes, the young man who bought the books wanted his story heard,
and yes, there's some merit in that. He'd seen I'd been in the death trade,
though. He'd read that sometimes I had something to say about trauma
and heartbreak, about grief. Maybe that's what drew him, some Google
search for grief. But all of that didn't matter that day. What mattered
was this: could he afford to be wrong about me? Could he risk deciding that somewhere someone learned something worth learning, knew
something about life worth knowing in a troubled time? That someone
of the age of clear culpability might be something more than culpable?
I think that's what he meant by "for real."

Listen: if you are that person that someone one-third your age comes
up the hill to lay eyes on, you already have life's later-day prize laid at
your feet. If you're wondering whether the young man finally decided I

was for real, I with respect say that you are asking the wrong question. You might be looking for reward for an uncertain life and you might be looking to a young person to give it to you. You're asking the wrong person for the wrong thing. That's like going to the hardware store for bread. Young people don't have that reward to give you, don't have that absolution to bestow, and they have other things on their minds than to reassure you that your life has been worth living.

I don't know what he decided. He didn't tell me, not then and not later. But he came up the hill, you see. And he did it twice, which must have taken some doing, with the time ticking away as it was. He sought me out. He made the move. He extended his fists, and somehow he said, "Maybe." *Maybe* today is a synonym for "I don't know," but its ancestral tone is closer to prayer. It whispers: "May it be so even yet...." Something like that prayer is what he brought to me. My job was to have lived a whole life as if that moment might happen.

⤷✦⤶

A few years ago I was asked to talk about elderhood in a yoga studio in the Vancouver area. You can tell by looking at me that it isn't likely that I do a lot of yoga, or by listening that I don't know a lot about it. I sit, but not for very long. That's all I really know about the thing. I walked into the studio at show time, and I thought to myself, "Hot damn, I'm becoming quite a commodity." There looked to be easily three hundred people in a place I'd never been to, maybe more. Things were looking up. I might have a career in the trade after all. And it took me a few seconds to realize what I was looking at. This being a yoga studio, there was a floor-to-ceiling mirror the length of one wall. There were actually about seventy-two people in the place, and I was seeing multiples of them. So I was taken down a few notches.

I assumed my position at the front of this meager assembly. The organizer and I had arranged to do a question/answer kind of session. I didn't know what he would ask me about. So after the introduction, this man in his late twenties turned to me and, without irony or wit, began the evening this way:

All my friends are depressed. Can you tell me why?

Bullshit, and playing for time, is easily recognizable in a moment like that one. I did what I could.

I suspect there's a correlation—a devilish correlation—between the demonstrable fact that there's an extraordinary incidence of despair in the culture, and among young people in particular, and the AWOL status of elderhood in the culture. That is what I talked about.

The aging demographic was well represented in the audience that night. There was mournfulness at the front of the room, unmistakable mournfulness. It wasn't rancor, and it wasn't grievance, and it wasn't accusation. It was grief. It wasn't a rhetorical question. He was asking because he didn't know, because his friends didn't know. Because maybe *somebody* knew.

Had there been elders in the room that night, they might have been recognizable in how they carried themselves and what they did in the face of this mournful declaration. One of them might have picked up a chair and brought it to the front of the room, and put it on the other side of that young man, and sat down beside him and said something loud enough that at least the first few rows could hear, something like this:

Listen son, I don't know why people your age are depressed. I didn't even know that was true. I sure don't know why it's true. And I'm not sure I have anything for you that would help. But tonight you aren't going to be depressed alone. You're going to be depressed with me sitting beside you. And you're going to have to deal with that, as I will try to do. Let's see how it goes.

That is what could have happened. But nothing of the sort happened. Something more thinning, more threadbare happened instead. One of the older people took umbrage, serious umbrage, objected vehemently to the tone of the proceedings, and defended himself as follows:

I'm a good grandfather. I Skype my granddaughter every week.

But no one had said anything about grandparenthood that night. Why did he? No one called into question how good a grandfather he was—no one but him, it seemed. To this older man, they were the same thing.

We seem now to have traded in the function of elderhood and its very iffy status for the biological mandate and the vague affirmation called grandparenthood, as if they are the same thing. In an elder-bereft time, it may be as close as many older people can get to elderhood.

6

THIS IS AN IMPORTANT SAFETY ANNOUNCEMENT

Learning and Knowing

Some years ago my wife and I were looking out the proverbial window, contemplating the rest of our lives, what they might be taken up in. She suggested out of nowhere, so it seemed to me, that we start a school of some kind. I could imagine nothing that I would teach, and no one coming to learn that nothing, but she could, and she did, and the Orphan Wisdom School came from it. Likelihood wasn't required, it turned out. The feasibility study came down to whether it sounded right. After a while, it sounded right. I'm glad we called it a school, glad because it does imply the distinct possibility—bordering on obligation—of learning.

Strangely, this learning aspect of the School has caused problems. In the North American imagination, a certain indignation rises up at the possibility of learning something, strange as that may sound. We didn't suspect it at the time, but this allegation of learning was its own calamity. Attendance at a school devoted to learning *is* a calamity of sorts, because the school proceeds with the clear inference that the scholar has not learned all or perhaps not even "nearly all" of what needs learning, or that there are gaps, or that there is work to be done. Such a school trades on perspiration, not inspiration. That's what I've seen in most sessions. People do bring their experiences and their personal truths and other such things to the School, and there is the expectation that a valuable and useful learning enterprise will corroborate the most precious or the most mandatory of what they bring to it, of what they've grown accustomed to, of what they know. I don't argue the point. I assume it. So it falls to me routinely to read aloud the bans, the mercy clause of any such school, the love letter to the psyche. I announce that *they are under no obligation to know anything as a precondition for learning something.*

You'd think the scholars would feel something like relief after being told that they are off the meat hook of relative omniscience, but there rarely is relief in the short term. There is suspicion instead that, excused from the clear verities of personal experience and conviction and utter fidelity to most of their prior knowledge, they are now disarmed, and chicanery and villainy and theft of valuables will probably ensue, perpetrated by the person with the microphone at the front of the room. So convictions abound where you'd bargain for wonder, and it turns out that one of the first things to be learned in the School is the difference between learning and knowing.

You know as I do that in this era, learning things *seems* to be encouraged and *seems* to be rewarded. Of course it does. The school arrangement, though, just calling it a school, reminds most people of grim childhood slights and shames, and much of this is reconstituted when they come, even though attendance at the Orphan Wisdom School is—more or less—their idea. It reminds them of the real reward system of the schooling they were subject to: get the right answer as quickly as possible, then go on to solve the next problem. No, the subtler story is that learning is tolerated as a preliminary stage in the royal road towards knowing things. Learning is the lamentable but mandatory crimp in the pipeline of certainty and self-assuredness. Learning is something to be gone through. With enough learning comes the coalescence, the alchemy, of knowing: that's what many of us learned about learning. There's "taking in" and "take aways," "processing" and "digesting," and there's personal style. Give some attention to the language you use for learning, and you might be surprised how much taking and consuming appears. That's what many of us know about learning.

Well, knowing might be a lot more like a self storage unit on the edge of town than like the sanctum sanctorum of prestige or personhood. Think of those things, how they have proliferated like mushrooms in a dank forest floor out on the cheap, lapsed farmland at the edge of the action. Think of what's in them: all the stuff you'll need, sooner or later. So you're renting a small, one-room house for all the stuff that won't fit into the house you're living in, stuff that you'll need eventually. That's how important it is. You've arranged for it to have its own house *and* paid for it. *You* don't even get your own house. You have to share it with the stuff you live with. But your other stuff doesn't have to share its house with anybody, because it has the hallowed status of being on-call.

You're currently living without the stored stuff. Mysteriously, that increases its value, because it really lives in the realm of *probably*, as in *you'll probably need this stuff*. But only if you get rid of it. As long as you have it, you probably won't need it, which is why it has its own house out on the edge of town. Remarkable insurance, when you think about it. You are living without it, proof positive that you don't need it. But life has taught you by now that if you give it up to the waves, you'll regret it soon enough, because then the day will surely come that you'll need it. And so you hold onto it. And, minus a yard sale or you coming to your senses or the odd thing going to one of the kids when they get their first basement apartment, you'll add to it as you go.

Knowing as a goal of life, as a moral imperative that settles in on adolescence and coalesces into adulthood, strikes me as working similarly to the storage-unit scenario. Knowing goes its way acquisitively. That is what PhD also means: piled, higher and deeper. Things that you know don't *replace* things you once knew. You don't unknow things, not really. They are added to the pile. Replacement is for beliefs: "I used to believe that. Now I believe this. As soon as I believed some new things, well, there went what I used to believe." But you don't really say to yourself or to anyone whose opinion you trust or require, "Well, I used to know this. But then I knew some new things, and I didn't know that old thing anymore." Knowing seems to hover out there like a dirigible in the endless sky, untethered to necessity, unburdened by limit of any kind, growth for its own pristine sake.

And so knowing has a kind of secret overhead, a burden that comes with the territory. It takes up a lot of inner real estate during the course of your days, and that real estate needs maintenance. Knowing is like the rate of economic growth you hear from the six o'clock news—it is bad news if it slows down. It's a perpetual motion machine, and it needs new stuff. It needs to be added to, like that mother wad from which alternative people make their sourdough bread.

And elders know the most. And, miracle of miracles, the best of them are out there defying the atrophy of age and still adding to their cart. Any learning that is to be done, if it's useful and earning its keep, adds to what you know, turns into knowledge. That's what you probably "learned" in school. Knowledge amounts to that uncertainty that you've decided you can afford. You probably didn't learn that in school.

But learning really doesn't acquire, gathering as it goes. It is possessed by puzzlement and by wonder, and wonder courts uncertainty as its maid of honour. And *the first casualty of uncertainty and wonder* as mythopoetic or spiritual practice *is knowing*. What comes under serious scrutiny when learning stirs are those aisles and aisles of time-tested conviction from which you supply your needs for the day. Learning is hard, yes it is, but not because the older you get, the more the synapses dry up, the more likely you are to be a creature of cerebral and contemplative habit. That happens, but it is not in the circuitry of learning to be habit forming or habit ridden. Because of that, learning is in many ways counterintuitive, particularly in a time that rewards information literacy and has five hundred channels for achieving it. So, learning is remarkably difficult, certainly when compared with knowing, because learning is so expensive. From a learned point of view, knowledge looks more like the limits of uncertainty that can be born, like the kind of imprecision you secretly accede to. Learning is hard on knowing, like kids are hard on the furniture, like life is hard on the body, and it costs you considerably to learn, and there are casualties along the way, and there are things that you part with. And the parting with isn't voluntary much of the time. It's too costly. By that measure, *elders have learned the most, and probably know the least.*

So imagine now a culture that is making a sacrifice at a propitious time of year, perhaps harvest time, and that they are doing so as a way to keep up their end of the human/divine circuitry of sustenance. They are parting with some of their harvest, perhaps the best of it, the first born of it, partly for thanksgiving and partly as a way of supplicating and pleading with their gods for the coming or the continuance of life. Historically among herding and cultivating peoples, this practice has included the slaughter of animals. So the blood is flowing at sacrifice time, and plant and animal life is being ended by the priestly class so that human life might continue. And you know that there is in making sacrifice a memory of a time back in the mists when the priests slaughtered people, probably so that the world might continue.

And in the midst of all of this partition comes an old woman in tatters, with the waft of poverty all about her. And she burrows down into her tatters and dredges up some modicum to add to the pile on the altar, perhaps a penny or two. She puts her two cents into the fray, then makes her way out of the theatre of sacrifice and restitution of the primordial deal.

After a moment of silence the place explodes in calumny and recrimination: she could have changed or washed, she could have done better, she should know what is at stake in times of sacrifice, that volume counts, that future harvests hang in the balance, that food enough for the children is in the balance. And she should have found some way, as everyone up in arms did, to part with more.

And someone comes to his or her senses in that moment and offers up this bit of, well, sacrifice: "Everyone gave considerably in the name of the future, in the name of more, and there might be merit to doing so. We'll see. And it must be so that everyone did so from the full pocket, from the cache of what he or she had to part with. And there is merit to it. But that old woman a moment ago, she came without much, and she parted with a bit of it, and it came from her poverties. It came from her empty pocket. Since we are keeping track: who then gave more?"

And that is what I mean by claiming that learning is so hard because it is so expensive. Learning is forever reducing, diminishing, winnowing, because it is animated by wonder, and wonder is the courageous capacity to test and prod the very ground under one's feet in the name of determining how it all might have come to be as it is, and whether it will continue to bear you. And this is the very ground of divination. It is acute attention to the details of the present. Learning has a hard time accumulating certainty, since wonder is given over so often to contemplating and testing the certainties that have been settled upon. Learning is a willing engagement with impoverishment, with the threadbaredness of what has claimed the attention of the family, the workplace, the sanctuary, the elect, the culture. Learning, you could say, is the more or less unbidden encounter with unwelcome things about what you know.

Learning is unnerving. It puts the edge back on almost everything that has lost it in the name of being user friendly and ego affirming and safe to be around. It knows certainty to be an unrepentant and possibly temporary lapse in judgment. Learning is like divorce. An arbitrary sandstorm of rancorous, debilitating loss has come, and it has ground away most of what you unwittingly agreed to be, along with almost everything that was never really there, and when the grounds cool, only a few things are left standing, one of which is the reason for your birth, another of which is some kind of burnished, barely enduring "you" that can now draw some sustenance from the ash and dust and take something like its proper place in the proceedings. This "you" is now the junior partner in the enterprise. Remember these days frequently enough and you'll always be the junior partner in your life. An old person might say that he or she has forgotten more than you've known. An elder might say that he or she has lost more certainty than you've had.

No, that is not hyperbole. Learning is that demanding, and its calamity visits in direct proportion to the body of knowledge that holds sway. Certainty, you could say, is the rent that knowledge pays for all the inner real estate it takes up. Learning, and the wonder that animates it, brings that rent down to something livable. The programmes of certainty are an assault on mystery, bringing mystery to heal, training it to pee in the box in the corner. Learning is something like a counterintuitive willingness to be mystified, to be on the receiving end of a world that, in its dignified manner, does not give itself away, or succumb, or dissolve into its constituent parts. Learning is the case you make for mystery, and ambivalence is the courtesy learning extends to what it would romance.

> Turn again to the great treasure, that story that is the family tree of words, the etymology of what has come to us as English. We have this word *ambivalence*, and we know what it means to us now: something like "indecision," or in a stronger form "paralysis," that comes from being pulled in incompatible directions. Never understood as any kind of strength or competence or ability, we are warned away from ambivalence at an early age and experience some real anxiety whenever it comes to call. Ambivalence is something of a moral failing in a time of certainty addiction and heroism.
>
> That is a recent meaning. Its constituent parts track the change and give us something of the existential lineage of the word. We have the prefix *ambi-*, which in one sense meant "both," or

"pertaining to both." But its older meaning is closer to "around." So you can see that the prefix doesn't calculate or count. It is a relational word, and it signals something spatial, and it registers something like "plurality," like "the consequence that rises up from diversity, something that rises when you move around the possible and the impossible things."

And then we have *valence*—a word used most often now in physics, but whose Latin origin means "strength," and which gives us the word *valour*. This signals something like "the proclivity or capacity by which something or someone can be recognized." If you employ the poetics at the soul of the language granted to you at birth and that have probably slowly eroded during your formal education and encourage these two words back towards each other in semantic reunion, a little revolt in the fiefdom of your certainty gets underway.

Ambivalence is "the capacity to entertain a diversity of possibilities or tendencies at the same time, without recourse to the premature and often unnecessary decision to vanquish plurality for the sake of certainty." In other words, the etymology tells us that ambivalence has, for the balance of its semantic life, been a skill born of being a child of a diverse world, not an affliction born of weakness of character or a lack of self-awareness.

The change in meaning of this word tracks a change in the dominant culture of the West as it appears in its English-speaking form, a change in what it values and what it slanders and suspects and is discomfited by. You could entertain the idea that whenever there is an increased premium placed on information and technique and certainty and singularity of purpose and precision and the like in the culture, it probably signals a growing ill-at-easedness with plurality, diversity, and the particular wisdoms of place, and an increasing uncertainty about personal or cultural identity. Real cultures affirm other real cultures, as initiated humans do initiated humans. They aren't unnerved or diminished by them. For a culture deeply at home in the world, ambivalence is a skill that learns as it goes and mitigates against accretion. For a culture adrift, habitually exercising dominion wherever it goes, ambivalence is an affliction best treated with certainty, the more the better. The change in the meaning of the word probably signals a kind of homelessness of the soul in a world not of its choosing, a vagrancy that began to haunt the places where English was spoken somewhere around the time when it was obliged to take upon itself a scheme of belief that traded a home in this world for salvation in the next. That is, when being something like a stranger in a strange land, and the mythic alienation it brought, became something like a point of pride. And yes, that *is* a lot riding on the shift in meaning of one word.

Learning is savagely, unjustifiably expensive. It ravages your prior life. It opens the box where everything once called *dangerous* or *useless* was placed long ago, and it mixes them up, switches the labels, makes it harder than ever to tell the difference and be sure. Learning is ruthlessly proceeding without recourse to your readiness to learn or to proceed otherwise, without preventing consequence or considering it first. Not learning, alas, is more expensive yet.

Asking "How do I start to learn?" takes mystery too much by the neck, bringing it to heel, where it disappears altogether or morphs into something housebroken and destined to do your bidding, a condition more commonly known as strategy or solution or "knowing." But you could ask this instead: "How does *learning* start?" Getting yourself out of the equation will help, and placing the emphasis on learning instead of on feeling better about imprecision will help too. Learning rarely seems to start with an intent to learn. It can start with an almost aimless willingness to stop what you were doing. That's all.

What you were doing was living in the house—the citadel—of what you knew to be so. This seems to be what prevails in the early going. For decades, you are haunting the Tower of Should, which because you return to it every day after work, you are certain is home. How do you begin to learn about that? Are you already a little impatient about this book not quite being the how-to book on geezerdom you counted on? How do you learn about your old habits of getting safe and secure instruction on the "shoulds" of life, of turning everything into a servant of certainty? The beginning is to not come back home for a while. Just go out of the house, the holding cell of certainty and conviction, and consider that a legitimate place to be.

"But the threshold is what kept me alive and safe." You could believe that. Both of us have probably believed that for years. *"But behind me is every true and noble thing. It's madness, it's irresponsible, to leave it."* You could believe that too. Behind you is certainty, where you'll find every familiar thing. The handle of the door is an angel you wrestle. Exhausted by the work and driven near to madness because there's still a handle and a door after all that, you let go of it and lurch through. Whether in that moment you believe this, or believe anything, you lurch through, and it is done. That's crisis for you: going outside. That's the old meaning of *ecstasy*. Not "thrill," not "joy." It meant "going out from what prevails."

Then, no matter how you feel about all this, no matter whether your conviction or your discontent survive the threshold being crossed, you are outside the home that has served you so well by not changing much, or by not consulting you first, or by submitting you to a regime of despair you grew to know as The Way It Is. The door swings on its hinge behind you. You could go back. You could always go back, and you probably will from time to time. Yes, there is a guard there, of sorts. He or she is the guard of habit and shame, that kind of guard Kafka wrote about, the kind who looms without acting, forbids without enforcing, interferes without intruding, like many teachers on the self-improve-ment circuit do now.

You are already outside, though. You're already on the wander. (Our verb *to err* has only meant "to be mistaken" lately. Its older meaning is "to wander," to step outside the furrow, that's all. The shift in meaning brims with the addiction to certainty and to habit.) And you could go back. And they're both true. Even if you don't take another step—and often you won't—you are there now, and the house is, for once, behind you, not inside you. It's a place, suddenly and finally, and not a feeling. Now big things can happen.

Sometimes a man stands up during supper
and walks out the door, and keeps on walking,
because of a church that stands somewhere in the East.
And his children say blessings upon him
as if he were dead.

—Rainer Maria Rilke, "Sometimes a Man Stands Up"

Desperate sounding and not very grand—that's what the beginning of learning often looks like. And that's from the *inside*. From the outside, those who care about you craft their concern according to how far away from the person they know you to be you have moved. But look at that sudden shift in the last line of the stanza. The man's children are stirred to blessing (*blessing*: two parts affirmation, one part invocation of divine protection from the madness that has claimed you) by this sudden, unexplained, fairly reckless abandonment of the order of the table. Though it is hard on traditional family values, it isn't a bad outcome.

Receiving the blessing of your children as you pass through the door of learning that may part you from them for a while or for keeps is far from guaranteed, that's true. But passing through the door of learning is your end of the deal, and it may stand as one of those things your children most deserve from you, whether they see it that way or whether they don't. It may yet come to pass that your departure from the dishes and demands for a while stands as a high-water mark of inconvenient courage for your adult children. They may yet see it as something a learning human is bound to, and they may forgive you for it. Forgiven or not, you are out on the saunter now.

> *Saunter* is from *san*, as in *sanity* or *sanctuary*, the fundament of health, and from *ter*, *earth*. A *saunter* is a procession across holy ground.

The language will not fail you.

Two Apologies, and a Bicycle

Learning is a bit like being young. You don't usually get to know that you are learning when you are. Hindsight tells you you were learning. You'd think that when you are learning the veil parts, the walls come down, the waters recede, and the new reassurance comes in to retire the old, and that the old goes willingly. But that is routinely not the case. When learning is occurring, it is too much like things going haywire to be persuasive or consoling, and it tends to raise your hackles and your inner border patrol. It is mainly with hindsight and the sheer going-on-ness of your days that your learning comes swimming up towards you like a salmon from deep water, and that it seems now that, yes, you *did* begin to learn back in that calamitous time. Learning, you can see, is almost counterintuitive in a culture addicted to novelty, information, and competence. The reason? Because it is so relentlessly hard on the status quo, and because the status quo and its high priest, knowledge, are so notoriously habit forming and habit ridden, learning is often indistinguishable from losing, from grieving, from paralysis and confusion and going down.

Because of this, I have been properly obliged to issue the Two Apologies to all incoming scholars of the Orphan Wisdom School and to revisit them routinely for a few years. The quiet persistence of the School over the last eight or so years has granted me the privilege of standing before thousands of people from many countries and troubling them with unauthorized histories and grim, unsuspected collateral damage. That they return is a questionable wonder, but that I owe them that sort of fidelity is not. On the whole they seem to agree, though they do so mostly in hindsight. Somewhere in the first session, when the certainties that brought them to the school initially can't keep them there, when the cost/benefit analysis reveals that this enterprise is by any measure too dear, when it isn't fun anymore, when the return on investment has dipped below the poverty line, it is time for me to fess up.

I apologize first for the irreducible consequences of wondering aloud about officialdom in its personal and political and spiritual guises, the consequences of uncertainty that will visit their domestic and contemplative lives in the months and years to come, none of which will be reassuring or seem redeemable, all of which will tease out a meager tightrope of homespun by which they might traverse the short span from indignation to shame to befuddlement to defeat as the bizarre sham histories of the West and their personal counterparts lumber into view. You'd agree probably that to do that to someone who is probably just trying to do the right thing can hardly be justified. I agree to that. Hence the first apology. Coming to the School is likely to be hard on your close relations, hard on the automatic life, and so it is hard to defend. In fact, it can't be defended. I am told that divorces and resignations ensue. Mea culpa. I can warn you away from the School and its calamitous tuition, but that you might take as just being part of its charm. It'll start sounding like an inside joke that you're now in on. Mea culpa. More calamity's to come.

The second apology comes down to this: if, after my best efforts, the scholars find that on balance all of this is no big deal, that the first apology is all bombast and bile, signifying nothing, that they can return to a life unchanged or unblemished by these considerations, shaken a bit perhaps, but in no enduring way stirred, curious but fine, that they can simply pick from the School's offerings as it suits them and wedge the pickings into an undisturbed life and leave the rest where it lies, on the killing floor of opinion, then I have failed them utterly and wasted their time. There's been no learning. It's all come down to affirmation or slander. It could happen that way, and sometimes it has, and when it does a deep apology from me is proper. Mea ultima culpa.

So this is probably an odd beginning to a learning project, though it has earned its keep as an honourable practice. It is faithful to the spirit of learning, as I understand it. For all that, though, it is a preamble to a story I have to tell, sooner or later. Once the apologies are in place and the passing of time has tested their authority, it seems that the scholars are more able to consider the Two Betrayals. In school, as in life, sometimes timing is everything. Timing might be the scrawl of the Gods, writing your life down for you to read.

I imagine that some time in your life you have taught a young child how to ride a two-wheeled bicycle. You'll recall the posture of the thing, you bent over, one hand on the handle and the other on the back of the seat, steadying. And the rider barely on the seat, all askew and akimbo and destined to wreckage without your ministrations, barely touching the pedals, the child knowing none of this, you knowing all of it. But you move the whole operation forwards anyhow, with pronouncements—demonstrably false pronouncements—that the child is doing a good job, though no rumour of the wonder of balance has presented itself to him or her yet. And you know in your heart that the child has no idea at all about the enterprise. Encouragement disassociated from merit is the order of the day in many of our dealings with children now, afraid as so many of us seem to be of crushing for all time the fragile crust of ego (theirs? ours?), unwilling to risk their disapproval. That's what happens when you enthrone the inner child. They're the vice-regent of a world free of its depths, and you are their court jester, a yes-man angling for uncritical positive regard. Unalloyed free-floating praise unattached to any accomplishment: this seems a precondition for accomplishment in a time like ours, so addled as it is by symbolic ventures and symbolic, Pyrrhic victories and platitudes and allegory.

None of this would have reached the stage of tin-can encouragement had the child not wrung from your soul a blood oath, a vow so incontrovertible and inviolable that it seems to come from the time when desert saints came down from their caves and visited the town squares and stilled the gaggle of opinion and conviction just by standing there. The child either extracted the oath or you, helpful to the end, offered it unsought. The oath? *Of course I won't let go.* Having made that vow, you are now in hell.

You agreed to the oath in order to get the child on the swaying seat. But the necessity of your hand remaining on the seat is only fleetingly dictated by the mechanics of learning balance, usually. The lion's share of its meaning is emotional and symbolic and, yes, moral. If you swear to not let go, you corroborate the child's vision of mayhem and crash landings, and you corroborate their view that you have the power to spare them, and that you should spare them, and that you will. By swearing, you are colluding with their utter refusal to fall or to fail. Which is to say that you are colluding with their refusal to learn how to ride a bike as they pretend to ride it, as you pretend they are.

Clearly, most people learn the happy medium of balance by straying into the weeds of imbalance, on bicycles and in life. Balance is mute. *Imbalance* tells you where balance is. *Falling is the teacher. Failure is the tutor. It doesn't make things better; it makes them so.*

Well, that sounds right. That doesn't sound like Aesop. That sounds like life. On the other hand, though, there is the iffy business of letting go. Of course you do your best to calculate the moment of doing so—if you do so—for maximum gain and minimum tears, lots of ego affirmation and no gravel in the knee. How does the child find out that you have let go of the seat? Almost uniformly in the early going, it is because they keel over. So the hell of the thing is that "the right thing" is not that obvious. There are two betrayals available to you once you have made your oath, and you will perpetrate one of them.

The child believes you when you promise not to let go. They get on. You go along for a while, and sooner or later you know that if you break your oath they might get to learn to ride a bike without you back there underwriting the whole affair forever. And that is the first Betrayal. Having given into a child's version of security to get them onto the seat, you, for the sake of their learning and the subtle life lessons you hope are in the mix, betray that childish understanding of security and promise and unerring adult fidelity. And you let go. You *must* let go. When you do, you will sooner or later have to endure their calumny and ignominy, their rage and shame and hurt, and you do so, frankly, for their sake, though the fidelity is utterly lost on them. This takes some discernment and some courage on your part, some willingness to go ahead without any understanding coming to them as to why they fell, as to why you let go, as to why life can be so strange sometimes, and how love can be so confusing.

Otherwise, you keep your promise. You go along, maybe for hours, telling the child that he or she is riding a bike when you know he or she is not, as if enough misrepresentation of the state of things will change the state of things. The falling never happens, at least not on your watch, or is so controlled that reentry is genteel and confidence is never tested. You keep your promise, you don't have to endure that look of pure violation. Maybe the whole thing can unfold without the falling down. Yes, maybe. But the chances are just as good that you keep the promise you made, and the second betrayal is at hand. You betray them by keeping your promise, and that child goes off into their teens and twenties and beyond, you still holding the seat, collusion in that fidelity, the child pretending to ride, you pretending to respect.

And those unfallen children become consumer groups and special interest groups, don't they? And troubles come as troubles do, and the understanding of promises kept no matter what—an understanding that is proper to childhood— deepens in their middle years into a kind of faith, a faith that "the rules apply," that "you get what you deserve," that "if you stay between the lines you win," that "God loves your country," that "there are good guys," that "good guys win," that "*you're* the good guys."

And lo, those children will grow old, some of them, and the world around them and its troubles will remain unaddressed and untempered by that faith. And that faith will sooner or later look more like paradise unfound and unsought, more like a dereliction of duty. And young people one third their age will come to them then, with that bewildered sorrow that has so much principle and so much anger in it, and they will be looking for one human example of grace under pressure, of a conscience tethered to the troubles of the times. And what they will get is this cant of faith, that Fate or Goodness or Life or The White Light or The Big Guy is steadying the swaying seat.

But the seat isn't steady, and things are getting worse, and the aged among us look blindsided by their changing bodies and by the implacable rate of change in the world around them, and they look betrayed by the unkept promise the world seemed to have made to them when they were young and upright in the seat, that it would all work out. And aging is the siren song of humiliation and trivialization. And "random" is the best adjective. And there are no reasons. And dying is an insult.

And so it strikes me that this is what life practice of the deepest kind must be, a kind of love that betrays what would betray it. And it strikes me that this is what elders do, or that this is what they are. They will betray whatever would betray life. In a time of unconquered naïveté, in the domain of the inner child, that makes elders a dangerous proposition indeed.

I've had the privilege of travelling in the world and talking as I go and making a living doing so. The enterprise has brought me to venues of every kind, it seems. There've been church basements and sanctuaries and decommissioned churches, bars and auto body shops and dance halls and Rhine River barges. There've been proper concert halls, television studios and old cat houses and back rooms. And then there's the retreat centre, or the adult learning centre, or the personal development emporium. There's the workshop clearing house, and there's continuing education. These places tend to appear wherever there are congregations of people who in days gone by forsook the cash economy, forsook the standard visible means of support, forsook the clock and The Man and made a go of it in the boondocks, out of the glare and out of the way. They tend to favour temperate climates, benign local customs, low property taxes, and the like. Such places can have more power animal veterinarians, shamanic life coaches, crystal repairmen, and colonic irrigation specialists per square foot than the local Deities normally permit. They can outnumber the locals sometimes, which begs this question: once they have tuned up the locals, who might they be practicing their mojo upon, to stay in fettle and fighting trim?

Allow me for a moment to be troubled about workshops and retreat centres. The very name *workshop* brings out the worst in me and doesn't seem to help a lot of other people either. It carries a division of labour, and it reinforces the inertness of an audience. We know who is supposed to be doing the work in a workshop—the person at the front of the room. Say all you want about the inner work of the attendee. If in the first hour the leader offloads the work to the audience in the form of breaking off into little workgroups, or by sending people off into the woods by themselves to write a poem or on some other personal quest, there'll soon be some kind of uprising among those who properly expect to be on the receiving end of the leader's knowledge and wisdom in the form of hearing about it. And this leaves the attendees to do what the dominant culture trains them to do: shop. Like old people on fixed incomes at the discount racks, workshop attendees can sort through what they hear from the person at the front of the room, picking up some things and holding them up to the light, putting them down again, trying a few on, finding them too, well, not worth it, taking fewer bargains home, fitting them into the old wardrobe.

And then there are retreats. The entire conceit of the thing seems to be to withdraw from the field of contention, laying your burden down, letting others drag the stone up the hill for a while. There is much to be said for retreating when the going gets tough. I can't say it, though. That I'll have to leave to others. I'm told that some people retreat routinely, every year. And what is the direction implied in the word? "Away from," or so I've seen. We've had retreating on the front burner in the self-improvement kitchen for perhaps half a century. How's it working so far? How is all that self-improvement improving things? What's for dinner? In times of deep disarray, such as we have now, is there merit in retreating? Now that nerve and give-a-shit is in ebb, does an elder leave the heavy lifting to the young, those with all that untried dexterity of limb, and wish them luck, and lock the door to the gated community behind them, and take the week or the season off? It's understandable. It's elderly, in the current sense of the word, and it seems unbecoming.

Anyway, I was invited years ago to teach at one of these centres, and they asked me to do something about elderhood. I already knew by that time from prior experience that, of all the things I present, it is this theme of elderhood that mysteriously prompts the most intense hurt and outrage and objection. This is noticeably more prevalent among the older people who come. I suspect that it has to do with the fact that so many attendees come assuming that what I do is present the Three Phases, the Five Stages, the Seven Sages, or the Twelve Steps of being an elder.

There is nothing in what I have written or have been recorded as saying that would encourage anyone to believe that I have the technical drawings for the elderhood generator, or any strategy for how to get there from here that I could franchise out to the highest bidder, but that doesn't staunch the expectation, the demand for step-by-step instruction, and it doesn't moderate the intense resentment when the how to's don't appear. Over the years it has become clear that beneath the demand to be given the keys to the elderhood kingdom, many of these folks expect recognition of their innate elderhood, expect that these sessions should be anointings of a kind. So these things tend to be volatile, and the back rows can be seething with not-very-well-contained indignation and more. I've noticed no similar expectation or demand or resentment among younger people who come and, mystery of mysteries, younger people continue to come.

I had to take a ferry ride to get to the centre. I sat across from two young people I knew who were heading to the session. The woman's father had just unexpectedly died, and she was pregnant and awash in grief. She was fatherless for the first time in her life. And her child would only hear of a rumoured grandfather. And she sat there in the ferry seat, awash in the Great Mystery of the thing, her man solicitous and hovering. Just as the ferry eased out of the berth the intercom crackled with a prerecorded message that was misshapen but timely. It began this way: "This is an important safety announcement from the transit authority." And though no one asked me to do so, I finished the announcement before the recording could, loud enough only so that the two people across from me could hear it. I leaned over and I whispered:

"There isn't any. *That's* the important safety announcement. There's no safety."

It turned out that the message and its timing was oracular and about to come in for heavy trial.

I got to the retreat centre a day early and had the afternoon, I thought, to uncoil from the travel and the wear and tear of life on the road. I took a seat in the sunshine on the porch, and it wasn't a minute before the doors opened and a woman erupted with,

Well, *there* you are!

In the normal human back and forth this observation doesn't allow for much response. I *was* there, to our mutual surprise. I nodded, and she went on to say how excited she was that today, after she'd gone to pay her bill for the modern dance session she attended, she'd seen my name in the list of upcoming teachers and spontaneously signed up for the session on elderhood. Now this was complimentary, and I thanked her for her excitement and for letting me know, but I had some misgivings, too. She was of the demographic that tends to be troubled by this consideration of mine, so the odds were that the excitement wouldn't last, mainly because in the early going the sorrow of the thing often prevails. It could, but in truth it didn't seem likely that it would. The first evening came, and the woman sat in the front row and seemed to enjoy herself.

The next morning at breakfast two other participants, probably in their mid-sixties, approached me with the information that they were withdrawing from the session. Now there were financial consequences for me for them to do so, given that I got paid on a per-attendee basis, but deeper down I was dismayed. Whenever that happens I wonder at once what I did, in what way I contravened things. I don't defend the response. It is just there, me wondering what I did wrong, the pangs and the sense all around that I might have done otherwise, or should have. But I nodded and thanked them for letting me know without simply disappearing. After an awkward pause one of the them asked if I wanted to know why.

"Okay,"

I said. She said,

> "Well, we're here on a holiday, and what you're doing just doesn't fit into our plans. We're here to enjoy ourselves."

They were the people I had most in mind when I came. They and the lives I imagined for them were some of the reasons I did so. I know that bound them to the enterprise not at all, but still, it was dismaying to hear older people trade in the chance to be in on a contemplation about elderhood with a good number of younger people, and to be something like a living example to them of grace under the considerable pressure of persevering in an age-phobic age, for the distractions from the enterprise their busy lives obliged them to. It was dismaying, and it was a sign.

As the session went along, the heavy weather of considering the unlikeliness of elderhood in a time hankering after growth and personal development and the rest began to take its toll. There was disappointment, and there was offence, and there was grudge. The excited woman wasn't in the front row anymore, and she didn't seem very excited either. By the last morning, she was back against the far wall and glaring. At the lunch time break, the woman who managed the centre asked for a few private moments in her office. In a grim voice she told me that someone had withdrawn after the morning session, that this someone had threatened legal action against me and against the centre and had already contacted her lawyer. She had announced that I was deeply disagreeable, that she had a friend who would take notes on what I said to bolster the legal case, and so on.

> "Well what did she say I did, or said?"

The manager said that for the balance of the meeting she actually wasn't sure what the accusation was. She finally asked, and the woman said,

> "I just don't feel safe."

So, that was it. I remembered at that moment something I'd read in one of James Hillman's books. He wrote that he'd lived long enough to see a time in which there was no difference any longer between feeling abused and being abused, that they'd fused and become the same thing. I told the manager how disappointing the whole thing was, and in particular how disappointing it was for the woman not to have said something of the kind to me directly.

"What would you have said to her?"

she asked. I said,

"I would have told her that she was right."

Well, she didn't feel safe. We know that much. But is that a description of how things just tend to go for her, or for someone her age, or for everyone, eventually? Does it describe the habits of feeling that she or many her age bring to bear upon their days, rendering them down to integers of threat, real or imagined? Does it describe what the slings and arrows and extremes of life or the extremes of Jenkinson talking about elderhood and its considerable demands and unlikelihoods for a few days does to people?

Is it so that we legitimately require feeling safe as a prerequisite for wondering about some of life's big deals? Has it ever been so? Is any encounter with the oracular, the knowable unknown, ensured as to its probable outcome? Are the consequences properly contained beforehand? Is that where this safety lives? Are safety and mystery found in the same area code? And what is lost, untested and untried, when the belief in feeling safe has to be there before we learn anything about what we believe? Before we learn anything about safety?

My point here is this: the need to feel safe, if it is a need and not a self-serving demand, is understandable. It is worthy of consideration and of compassion. But it is the first casualty of those moments ripe with indecision and ambivalence that are the handmaidens of wonder, the midwives of learning. You have no way to know everything will be okay once you get to the other side of learning. And it is deeply unbecoming of people steeped in years to hold out for feelings of safety before risking it all for the sake of a better day, and it is compound dereliction of duty to do so in the presence of people one-third their age.

Here is my proposal: the life of an elder is not an exercise in risk management or damage control. That is the life of an actuary. It is because of that duty not taken up that the woman at the retreat centre (and retreating was what she seemed to be doing) indeed didn't feel safe, in both senses of the phrase. She surely and understandably didn't experience safety as we wondered about elderhood, and she surely wasn't safe to be around for anyone weighing out the merits of getting old.

There is a moment in the James Hillman/Michael Venture exchange called *We've Had a Hundred Years of Psychotherapy and the World's Getting Worse* where one tells the other about the end of marriage, leaving an ex-wife, the inexhaustible result of neediness, and the ardent fugitive running down the street whom he once called "safe." "Love," one of them says, "is a very strange place to go to for safety." Elders are another strange place to go to for safety. If *safety* means "anything goes," if it means there are no consequences for your self exploration or for taking a few years off from the strange days or the heartache of being awake, then *elders endorse danger by their unwillingness to collude with you.* They are faithful to a fault to life, that's all. Sometimes it looks as though they're your friend when they're faithful that way. Sometimes it doesn't. The difference comes down to whether you want to hear from them or you want to hear yourself come out of their mouths. You're not safe, and they see to that, and that's it.

THE SECOND ACT

7

THE ORPHAN WISDOM FORENSIC
AUDIT METHOD

I n my early farming days in eastern Ontario I was often in the position of needing to borrow things. It was not usually a tool or a piece of machinery. Borrowing these things in the country is understandable, maybe even necessary at times, but rarely wise. It isn't that people aren't willing to lend them. They are, often. But it does set a precedent and an impression in conservative people that sits and solidifies and turns into their take on you.

Having to borrow things doesn't mean that you have figured out how to do what needs doing. It means that you couldn't figure out how to do the task without the tool or machine you are borrowing. So it means that you are relying on the ingenuity, the good will, or the stock in trade of a neighbour. But what are neighbours for? I know, I know. Neighbourliness is there in the mix, to be sure. But turning to neighbourliness to get you out of a jamb you really shouldn't be in in the first place has a flaw in it somewhere that doesn't dissolve when the tool is returned. It's still there. Self-reliance is such a mandatory presence in farm life, whatever's left of it, and it conserves, and it doesn't doubt itself. It is another religion, a moral order of the same kind that enables the bank to punish you for having to borrow by calling the punishment "interest." It is a moral order that comes from the gross vulnerability of the settler days; you were in some kind of trouble and there was a neighbour every five kilometers of car-less, snow swept country road in the killing month, February, and you couldn't count on help. It is a moral order that should have changed with the changes and the times. Most of us don't live that life anymore, but so many of us still honour the outworn code of utter self-reliance.

I've tended to borrow experience, instead. Yes, people did feel lauded, in a way, and held in good regard when I asked about their take on a given dilemma with the sheep or the corn or the soil, but I could tell that the proper arrangement was to make every conceivable mistake first, several times over, figure it out, and then tell the story of my chronic mistake in idle conversation that was allegedly about anything but what I was asking about. I found out that if I did that, generally the hoard of plenty was opened and I might get the benefit of the ages. You can imagine how taxing and inefficient learning this way can be, and how hard it is on the machinery of farming and living, but this is one way by which local people can calibrate your willingness to live their kind of life here in their kind of place. It is a way by which you can be known that doesn't rely entirely on how you manage someone else's impression of you. You learn this bit of rural etiquette and you learn something of the willingness to be known. It's a kind of education whose manner and style and skillfulness stays with you long after what you learned has become just another thing that you always knew.

And so it happened that I was on the native reserve close to my farm. I was there to pick up some lumber that someone had for me. I couldn't figure out from the directions I had where to find the house, and so I pulled into the gas station to ask. A few old timers were shooting the breeze with the attendant, and the place went quiet when I walked in. I told them the name of the man I was looking for.

"Oh, yeah,"

one of them said. A whiff of cautiousness was in the air. I mentioned picking up the wood.

"Uh huh,"

he said. And nobody moved or said anything else.

"Any idea how I could find the house?"

I asked.

"Uh huh,"

one of them said.

Then everybody waited, to see if I knew how to wait for what I asked for, probably. Somehow or other I passed the subtle test, I suppose, because then one of the men got up and walked out the door and stood there looking down the road. I realized I was supposed to follow. I went out, stood beside him, and he pointed down the road with his chin.

"You see that there?"

he said.

No idea what he was meaning, I said,

"Where abouts?"

"There"

he said again, gesturing with his chin.

"Yeah,"

I said, realizing that I was going to have to figure this out once I was in the car again.

"Well, that's where you turn. There, where the old schoolhouse used to be. Just turn there and you'll find the place."

They were confounding directions at the time, but eventually they became wise to me. Of course, in one sense, they were directions any local person would have understood and therefore not required. Directions, like maps, are for people who are uncertain of where they are, even though they are standing right beside people who are certain of where they are. (Consider then what the mapping of every square inch of the earth itself means about how foreign so many of us are to this world, even to our little corner of it. Consider the reflexive habit of Google mapping every time somebody goes somewhere. Consider that the drone that oversees your peregrinations now hovers where once "the Spirit of God was moving over the face of the waters" (Gen. 1:2), and consider that they both seem to have ended up with the same job.)

The assuredness that comes from knowing where you are isn't really contagious. It is a learned thing. But in another way, telling me to turn where something used to be was a way that old Indian man had of being at home, and his being at home relied more on being able to read the signs of time passing than on being able to read the road signs. And it seemed to mean that anyone at home is place literate. And that might be one good understanding of *indigenous—place literate*, the ability to read the presences that constitute a place. And that includes all the presences of what once was there, what once was so.

As it happened, the old schoolhouse was the place where the provincial government enforced the assimilationist course of study, and those old men in the gas station were the last generation with a memory of being taught how not to be native people while being taught math and history and so on. The fact that it was torn down by a generation not schooled in it meant something, too, something subtler than victory, more mixed than victory. But the school house remained a fixture in the landscape of the old timers' lives, where it was, what it did, why it was, and it was as enduring and resonant a place, at least, as the gas station and the cultural centre and the elder's lodge offering bingo on Friday nights.

Being a white man on the reserve looking for lumber that day didn't entirely exclude me from all of this. We didn't have the same history, but it wasn't a given that we couldn't stand in the same place and see something of the same thing. That's what his directions meant, I think. They meant this:

> If you go down the way I'm showing you, there will be signs. Not road signs. Signs that make up a place. You don't need to know all the things that happened there. What you could do is see the presence—the particular presence—that absence has. You could see it in the kind of ground cover that would grow on recently disturbed ground. You could see it in the kind of trees there, whether they were the sentinel species that signaled the beginnings of forest regeneration. You could see it in the mature trees, whether they grew away from something that is no longer there. You could see it in the subtle furrow that came in off the road, something that might be a signal of a path grown over made by thousands of small footfalls decades ago. And from all of this, you could grow some proneness to the human life that came and went this way. You could.

And this is what I mean by the Orphan Wisdom Forensic Audit Method. You can learn how to read the signs of what made the signs. It isn't "the real story" I'm talking about. It's the rest of the story, the unidentical twin of the story you know and may have grown accustomed to. It's the unclaimed bastard sibling of the authorized version of anything.

⁓❦⁓

In a time whose changes, and whose rate of change eclipse much of what went before, the ability to see what was once so might seem a waste of time, or misplaced attention, or folly, or an old person's melancholia blooming again. Certainly it doesn't seem to be embraced as any kind of skillfulness, unless it is devoted to the skill of avoiding the doom of repetition. And it might seem that to call it a forensic method is to deepen the ghetto funk of the enterprise. Allow me to propose that the study of words serves the speaker as it serves the speech, and that the particular troubles of our time might ask now that we cure the talk, that we rescue our way of speaking to each other from the chicanery and missed apprehensions of the political arena and the marketplace. Etymological pondering can help with the cure.

Etymology, that is, and not the dictionary. Dictionaries, as I said earlier in this book, could properly be regarded as the place where perfectly healthy words go to die, suspended in a formaldehyde of fixed, enduring, unrepentant "meanings." Consult a typical dictionary with an active imagination and watch your curiosity swoon and heel over, vanquished, not sated. Etymological dictionaries are stories, first and foremost, of how a given word swam the seven seas of subtle change to come to us as it has. In an etymological dictionary words have their raiment, the crazy quilt of their many lineages, their quiet endurances. You read an etymological dictionary, and with work you find semantic riches forbidden, ignored, or abandoned by the current regime. Yes, and you find drastic shifts in tolerance, often not for the better. You find a pall in the modern period, a drift of change towards contracted poetics and an assault on subtlety and imprecision and mystery. You also find mystery, and the sure hint that sustains your suspicion that it hasn't always been this way. In an etymological dictionary, the old stories are still stories, still old, still there. Dictionaries of the abbreviating kind are what happens when literacy is forced upon language.

> We and whatever oral leanings we have left were once served by the telephone. People tell me that this is all being lapped by the monstrous infliction, that all-in-one communication and command post that fits paper thin into your breast pocket. The voice, for all its fidelity to what you actually mean to say, is not enough anymore. I leave a phone message. Nobody calls back. No one, they tell me, listens to voice mail anymore. It's not quick enough, not immediate enough. Imagine: the human voice leaving a message in real time is not *immediate* enough. So texting is the thing. *Texting:* the latest triumph of the written word over the spoken word. Here we go again.

Etymology, though, is language slipping the snare of suspended animation and nosing its way back into the underbrush of time. Etymology is the Old Gods of noble speech murmuring their names, us overhearing, our One God of fact and information caught for a moment unawares, all the evidence hinting that he isn't the only one.

Imagine that language is not the precursor to literacy, that verbal peoples were not and are still not hankering after the obvious improvements to their speech, their thinking and perceiving, their very lives, that literacy is alleged to lend. To describe some peoples' stage of development as "pre-literate" is to collude with the literate prejudice that literacy is a deep expression of the yearning all languages have towards improvement, fixity, standardization, sophistication, and the page. It is akin to referring to some peoples as being pre-Christian, pre-Muslim, pre-industrial, pre-virtual. It is a steep learning curve indeed to encourage literate people to credit the possibility that literacy-free peoples once had a degree of attention to the world and to each other that has suffered everywhere literacy has proliferated. I do encourage the consideration.

Translation is at best an allegation, and it often heads off in the direction of misrepresentation promptly, unrepentantly, thoroughly. Languages are not "names for things." They are entire semantic consolations and constellations and worlds. They are place- and time-specific, and in that sense at least, they are indigenous. They are attestations of a human encounter with the dwarfs and the deities, the drumlins and the dead, the dim and the dread, the very weal and waft and warp and weft of this bright, blue, turning world. The specifics of these things have no obligation to generalization. Languages belong to places. That is their fidelity and their service, that they are willing to be faithful to what bore them. When another language slips beneath the waves of standardization or globalization, that is more than another library burning to the ground. It is Ground, burning to the ground.

One aspect of this fidelity to place is the sounds of a given language. It doesn't strain the nobilities of speech to imagine that its origins are mimetic. If so, it may be that language stirs in humans when the sounds of the living world are overheard. Imagine that all the sounds of the world are the world murmuring to itself, giving its voice, saying its many true names. Imagine that humans get to overhear this murmuring when they obey the living world. Imagine that our obeisance is our speech.

One example, partly imagined and partly remembered, might help with crediting that possibility. As a guest of longstanding in the homeland of the Algonquin people, it struck me as a rudiment of respect that I try to learn a bit of their language. My aim was not to be able to converse, as fine an accomplishment as that would have been. It was simply to be able to have a few of their words for places, the details of place, the ways of walking through those places, count-ing on the possibility that having them might loosen the Angliciza-tion of landscape, inner and outer, that I have inherited, enough to hear and see my corner of the world a bit differently. As I did so I found that the tendency to translate back into English confounded this simple devotion. The Anishnaabe-English dictionaries tended to do the same thing.

The Anishnaabe language has a word, the spelling of which, as is proper for any language contending with literacy, is a bit arbi-trary: *wawashkesh*. When I learned this word it meant "deer." Certainly the word doesn't imitate any vocalization a deer makes, so far as I know. There is another way to approach this with a bit more sub-tlety and elegance. You could say that humans *vocalize*, while the world *sounds* as it goes its worldly way, and *wawashkesh* is one of the world's sounds.

Now it just so happens that in the corner of the province I live in, the field grass grows about knee high by early August, if the rains are kind, and no higher. The sand beneath it and the cool-ing evenings would have it so. Even with the rainfall the ends become brown and friable by that time, a sign that summer is making its autumnal way. And as it happens, the fawns born in midwinter, those that survive, have grown by mid-August so that their stomachs are brushing those brown ends as they make their way through a meadow. Deer are all stealth when moving, especially in the open, alert in a way that would induce coronary arrest or free-floating anxiety in many humans I know and that would tend, perhaps, to make them suspect the worst.

Given all of this, if you are downwind of them on a calm day as they make their hesitant way, and you are stock still at the right time, and if your jaw is hinged open enough to extend your hearing to the cavity of your mouth and cranium, and if your creation story and your psychology has not placed you squarely at the centre of life and so you've managed something like an existential humility known as humanness in other times and places, you might hear a kind of swishing sound as their bellies course the grass tips, a whisper of late summer song in grass. If so, you, too, might have come up with a word that imitates a yearling deer coming through yearling grass at summer's fine, burgeoned, opportune blessing time, and it might have sounded like what it was: *wawashkesh*. I don't know this to be the origin of the word, but it may be in there somewhere.

This is to say that language, in its origins and among its able practitioners, is a charm of place. It is the murmur of an animist soul, the only kind of soul there is in this world, that humans get to overhear. That is how we become enchanted.

⚜

Now to this forensic method. *Forensic* pertains to things legal, often criminal, as we use it today. But once it referred to a place—the forum—and to the meeting place of ways of inquiry particular to the forum. From this you could imagine that in its older iteration, *forensic* described the particular means of ascertaining the reliability of a certain claim or idea that relied upon attestation in a public forum. It described some shared take or impression or encounter with the light of day, and it described an understanding of the subtle verities brought to bear upon what was being considered, and not private rumination on the "truth" of the thing.

And there is our word *attestation*, or *testimony*, and the root verb, to *test*. Currently this means something like "to bear witness to." But for a much longer period it meant "to assay," "to try," from the Latin for "clay pot," a crucible for precious metallurgy. The word derives from a process for drawing essence from dross, what is wanted and valued from what bears it. It is an aspect of alchemy. And alchemy was, for centuries, a dabbling in the dark arts, the distillation of matter. So this business of attesting and assaying, and the linguistic murmuring that carries it, probably goes back into the mists. It probably tracks the earliest storied encounters with the Iron Age, all of its transmutations, all of its murky traffic in the molten domain of the Gods. The notion is at least that old.

With this handful of words we have in linguistic form an existential transition of immense consequence. *Test, attest, try*: these are a kind of Braille, a means by which we might partly imagine, partly remember a time in some early stage of the Indo-European language root, where the crude beginnings of open pit mining, smelting, and forging—of taking rock from solid to liquid to solid again, of bending the mantle of the earth to the purposes of humans—changed in a rudimentary and irreversible way how people of that time understood, lived with, and venerated the ground of their being. The semantic hint we have of this change—though *rupture* might be a better word for it—is in the mingling of *test* and *true*.

With this lineage in mind, it isn't hard to see how the verb forms of these words would be employed in the project of determining *truth* (which I'll look at closely in Chapter 13). The idea of *truth* once stood for "what is assembled, or braided, or woven, or gathered together in a purposeful way." You can get the feel of these associations by considering the words *test* and *text*. Both are the root of *textile*. In their early forms, they designated "a thing crafted by weaving," from the Greek *techne*, the skill of craft, assembly, design. *Techne* in turn is related to *tetra*, the number four. It remembers the four-cornered shape of any woven thing, from which we get our adjective *four square*, as in "full" or "fully manifest." Perhaps it remembers the help of companions, human or otherwise, holding the four corners of the cloth or the world, necessary for crafting a worthy thing.

But it seems that the cumulative, probably older meaning of *truth* might mean something closer to "the way of attestation, a consequence of assembling those whose name and standing in the community lend credence to what they attest to." In that understanding, *truth* is true because it is attested to, assayed. It is an assembled thing and a consequence of humans assembling. Truth is learned by contextual observation, and patience, and it is learned from the recurrence of the true thing.

In this tangle of *test* and *try* and *technique* and *forum* and *four* you can finger the probable limit of abstraction and disembodied speech and the likely lineage that merges observation and contemplation and incarnating speech. I mean that this gaggle of associations has a direction and a momentum, and in that is a recollection of the dappled wonder of human ingenuity, the wonder that rises in the maker and the witness when a made thing sees the light of day.

Consider the simplest loom, the back-strap loom, for example. It maintains the weave by ensuring a dynamic tension that enables the threads—thread, which is wonder enough coming from conjured fleece or cotton—to be articulated into a pattern. The loom mediates (literally, *halves*). It insists upon separation, and it does so by re-creating the hands that might once have held the edges and corners in a cooperative quadrant form. The fringe, and the knotted bundle of warp threads at the corners of blankets (Navajo blankets are a good example) all remember the helping hands, their willingness to attest to the weaving.

And so, no surprise, we have the words *texture* and *textile*, showing us how *text* and *true* and the others remember their origins in shared conjuring work. And then there is the mystery of the warp threads. In many forms of weaving they make up the visible design, gathered around the no-longer-visible weft threads, the hidden fundament of the seen. The unseen bearing up the seen, not in hierarchy but in mutual regard—it is a sophisticated cosmology. The little miracle of the woven thing is to be found in its incarnate memory of the means of its assembly. The woven cloth, you could properly say, is *testimony*.

So all of this heads off in a certain direction that can't be commanded, like your dog does when he noses an old imperative in the bush and heads off into the undergrowth, deaf to any authority you once enjoyed over him, he is now beyond your command. We have before us a confluence of *forum* or *assembly*, and *truth* and *hearing*. The crucible assembled, the edges or corners remembered by the weave, the capacity to hold a consequence of the memory of being held at the corners or edges, the capacity to hold a consequence of the tenacity of memory, and the willingness to hold memory, to testify to the presence of the absence of things: all of this is a fair recipe for humanness. You can see that this caravan of consequence enthrones human memory as the workshop of the Gods, the place where oblivion is doctored by the skilled willingness to recall, when doing so gathers grief to memory's side by calling out, by regaling, by speech. Human memory is one place where the Gods advocate for life, all of it, in all its raging glory and ramshackling power, where the alleged apartheid of past/present/future is rendered down to its proper fluid ambivalence.

Soothsay It

So what I call the Orphan Wisdom Forensic Audit Method is something like soothsaying, I suppose. It is a means of reading the portents, some of which are present and others of which are signals and augury. It is the antidote I offer to the oracular degeneration of the age. You could think of it as you would whitewater canoeing. My nominal experience in that adventure has taught me that, while the whitewater is certainly real enough and deserving of all the attention you can manage, particularly if you are in it, whitewater is, for all of that, a sign. Reading the whitewater is really reading what made the water white: current, plus the rocks that lie beneath the foam and the roar.

This is a divinatory skill, and while surely it is not reserved for older people, it is just as surely something that should properly coalesce in older people in marked valence. As things stand, the proliferation of aged people among us has current, and it has something submarine.

There are more old people, in ratio and in real numbers, than ever before. Many of them seem reasonably content to leave our corner of the world and its considerable troubles to younger, more trouble-inclined people to manage. Aging is slandered, and it is slander. It is all but impossible to fashion a compliment from the word. All wither and collapse and indignity now, it is no wonder that so many older people seek out the comforts of personal growth and retirement and each other's waning company and painting pictures of flowers in the spare room. As I mentioned earlier, every time I bring these matters up in a forum dedicated to learning in a troubled time, I get the fiercest objections and attack from older people, from those who stand as most likely to be ennobled by it. They come to be seen, to register on the radar of merit, to be accorded their allotment of automatic high regard. When it doesn't go that way, there's more trouble still.

How to read the troubled waters? Perhaps—no, probably—none of this comes from age. It more likely comes from what has happened to age in our time. No person-making rites of passage to speak of exist in the dominant culture of North America. There are ghost versions of such a thing, frank shams, desiccated husks of vacated tradition, globalized greeting-card affirmations. If that is what prevails at birth, at puberty, at matrimony, why would that anemic poverty not gather in a pantomime of reverie as age gathers? The assumption that we are automatically human at the moment of our birth, automatically adult at the moment of our majority, automatically engaged in matrimony at the moment of our marriage: how can this not lead to supposing that elderhood is automatic at the moment of our irreversible infirmity?

> *Automaton*: the dictionary tells you that it comes from two Greek words, *self* and *moving*. I suspect that the second word has another inflection, a more primordial one. The *mat* root might signal here what it signals in most other places it appears: *mother*. I suspect the word describes an abomination that in our time has taken on the guise of a skill: to be *self-mothered*, or as is often said now, *self-made*.

Anything in human affairs that has gained the reputation of being inevitable has shed the possibility that it was once a skill, a worthy and iffy endeavor that required patience and discipline and learning and failure, in equal measure. And so getting old and being old have become the inevitabilities that accrue when you are not middle-aged any longer and are not dead yet. Period. The odometric fascination of the current regime confers upon the age years ending in zero some symbolic import. Reaching sixty or seventy and being forcibly retired is a withered, ersatz rite of passage for old people. It achieves nothing. Instead, it merely records the clicking past of time. The only attribute that seems to be acknowledged or rewarded is endurance, or persistence. Among us, being old is something that happened to you because something else didn't happen to you. Aging is rarely talked about as a truly achieved thing. Much more often it is talked about as an endured thing.

Something in the whitewater of our way of aging needs tending to. If becoming an elder was a consequence of aging, we'd be awash in elders right about now. But it isn't so. It might be worth considering some kind of unsuspected relationship between the proliferation of old people and the ebbing of elders that is causal, not merely coincidental. I suspect it has something to do with the limit-defying lengths available to us to thwart the passage of time and the marks it properly makes upon us as it goes along, to thwart the proper limits that settle in for the duration, to thwart for evermore the idea that there is such a thing as "your time to die." I suspect the stone under the froth of our resentment of age is the suspension of any obligation to life, the eclipse of most life-born limits, the prolongation of life according to our preferences. Under the torrent of time are the boulders of mastery and autonomy, swamping the procession of wisdom from one generation to the next. I suspect that something about the arbitrary power of life, the limits without end that belong there, and the death time that is our proper inheritance together weave the capacity for elderhood out of the fraying threads of aging. Without those limits and endings, we are bereft of the elderhood that is woven by them.

Playing the Mercy Card

Should you agree to live a long time: as odd as that might sound, the signs are that it will come to that, likely within your lifetime if you are under thirty. You are master of your allotment, now that dominion and control of your life has reverted to the proper hands, subject only to the "shoulds" that suit and serve, accountable mainly to what you've grown accustomed to. There is medically assisted demise, of course, extending our repertoire of self mastery, but subtler things are at play. Now that we've been saved from what was routine demise a generation ago, and have a life prompted and prolonged into a kind of duration unsought and unfamiliar, we are living out the dream of a deepened, self-determined time for all who want it. The great unnerving unknown is looming up out of our technology and mandate of mastery: this "more time," this increased life span, when does it happen? When does it appear? Is it sprinkled through our lives, fairy dust on our dreamy youth, sawdust on the workshop floor of our middle years, ash on our diminution? Yes, our lives are being extended. Do we get more youth because of that? Do we get more middle years? Is it tacked onto what would, in the old days, have been the end?

It's early yet in the life extension business, maybe too early to tell for sure, but it seems to me from my years in the death trade that this question, "When does this more time come to me?" isn't answered by the high priests of medicine or technology or Big Pharma. It's answered by how you feel about getting older, and how you have lived out those feelings in the days when you weren't old. What I saw persuades me that if you abhor limit and ending and what seems like the ordinary arbitrary injustices of a life in unravel, the chances are very good that the time you cadge from what they offer you will be tacked on the end, *adding* to those limits and ends and ebbings away you found so unpersuasive, so optional, in your days of physical and emotional mastery. It has very much the cadence and the cant of the Kafka deal, the Catch-22: defeated in victory, undone by getting what you bargained for.

What does it cost to age in a graceless age? What is the tariff of flagging? What is the tax on limitless limit and postural decline? You learned your body when you were young, and you did so incrementally. As you grew and learned the rigours of energy, you probably pitched forward from one cresting wave of agility to the next, as if it had never been otherwise. And that centripetal sway of "the next thing," of learning the coming-onness of things, carried. And that is the thing that is going to bow or bend or break if you live long enough.

So, there's the canto of despair awaiting its aging voice. Aging around here is you on the receiving end of caprice. Like the unwitting ex-spouse whose marriage took the assent of two and its ragged dissolution only took the disavowal of one, the aging person in our corner of the world is a tail on the end of life's kite. Aging doesn't require your agreement, your acknowledgement, even your awareness. It just seems to happen. The settling in of your aged self comes as hard weather does—in blows and bursts, eating the horizon of possibility and potential by which your course was once set, all aboil and sudden and finding you wanting another moment to prepare, to demand recourse or consultation, your rightful due. Arbitrary, and random, like all hard weather is, that's aging for you.

Then might come mercy. That might be the hard ground of the thing, you playing the mercy card. You never needed it in times of plenty, when you exerted dominion over your days. You hardly practiced pleading for it when you were drawing from your full pocket and from what you could afford to part with, and it was so easy in your times of plenty to confuse mercy with getting your way or being ignored by tragedy.

But now you're older. You've grown into the fullness of your years, yes, but you've done so in a place and time that is all but elder-free. An etiquette of diminished expectation and decorum settles around you, but nothing instructs you now, nothing vindicates you having lasted this long. The whisper campaign says that the kindness of life grows thin with age, that the frailties of the time are a sign that you are being left behind by life, that the Gods have other business now.

Imagine that you'll come into your fifties or sixties with little or no experience before you of the grace under pressure that elderhood makes of aging, you yourself by then all but aged. It might be that you're an amateur at mercy, both its exercise and its petition. It might be that you wouldn't know mercy if it wrecked your threshold or crowded your hearth. All those years of learning the body and becoming a self and growing that fine addiction to comfort and competence are done. The endings are coming into view. It's not a failure of the will or the imagination. It's the unbidden realization that you are deeply into the second half of your life, that you've seen far more of life than you're going to see, that the end of everything you hold dear is what will come from you holding it so dear. If any wisdom survives the heavy weather of age coming on, it kicks in just about now, and you ask for mercy.

There are habits of the heart, and they are often broken in crude ways. Mercy being what mercy is, infirmity will break these for you. In the sway of all that loosening of the old ties, it may not have come to you yet that you lasting this long, with all of its allegations of loss, *is* the mercy that you seek. It isn't all goodness and light, mercy, but it is a faithful sign that you growing down into your age is there, pending, hovering, possible. And, for the sake of the young people around you, mandatory. Your aging, you see, is not coming *to* you. You are not its recipient, its victim after all. It's not inflicted upon you, any more than the quiet, enduring presence of the reasons for your birth and your life were inflicted upon you. Neither its master nor its teacher, you are age's practitioner now. Your aging is coming to those who attend to your latter years. It's coming to the younger people around you. It is one of the examples that they will bring to their aging time. *Your aging—its meaning and purpose—is happening to them*, you see, not to you. You practice aging, or you endure it, or you refuse it, and that turns into younger peoples' lives.

So, mercy *has* come. It has burst the hinge on the treasure house of your mastery and self-determination, splintered the lintel of the mansion of the hopes and expectations of life that were born when you were seven. Ravening from neglect like a dragon come in on the mist-bands, it has come to warm itself by the hearth of your certainty and your confidence in life set ablaze. Only now that it is in the house do you ask for

it. You learn this mercy by coming to know that the unsought fundament of your days is the ending of your days. Your days are granted even
now and not withdrawn. They are allotted not according to the calculus
of merit, but by some other augury that seems to bear you in mind not
very much, but which may be a sign of how life reinstates itself there at
the edge of your limits and your understanding.

You are being eldered by life itself, you see. That is how the elaboration of endings comes to you, as mercy, tutoring you in the syntax of
mercy, crafting the sound of the thing. Endings see to it that the canto
of mercy resounds in the world by drawing their breath across the holes
that open in your schemes and convictions, playing the polyphony of
age, retiring the relentless cadence of mastery and all the aphorisms
you've held to until now. And if all of this is happening not in the purgatorial privacy of your own misery and mind but in the presence of
witnesses and in the light of day, in the forum where it belongs, where
its meaning is born, then mercy is coming in, and younger people are
being schooled in what is possible now.

When we say "the love of life" we seem always to mean the love we
might have for life. It's good if we have such a love, but it doesn't seem
to occur to us that life may well have a love, too, that *this aging entrusted
to us*, and all its fracas and foretelling and fortune, *might be the love
that life has*, coming into the world this time by riding us. If you're old
enough to recognize something of all this, it's likely that life is loving
aloud, in the form of your age, as things have turned out.

You might grant, no matter how well the enterprise has gone for
you, that there is a cost to love. Weighty, restoring, fulsome, and as
dire and dear a brush with the Divine as is likely, it is all of that, and
it is costly too. I mean here not the inconstancies, the weather of love.
I mean the scripture of conviction and desire you bring to the thing.
What love costs you is love, surely. Every allegation, every vapoured
notion of justice about love that you bring to the undertaking is taken
at the door, replaced by nothing much at all. What you've known love
to be, whatever nobility barely tested in the jangling marketplace of
cohabitation you attributed to your best self, all of that is the casualty,

the cost of proposing to make a go of love in this world, in this body, at this time.

And o my love, be not afraid
We are so lightly here.
It is in love that we are made
In love we disappear.

Leonard Cohen, "Boogie Street"

Well, amen. It can, of course, be devastating, and usually is, to know that your understanding of love will not survive your practice of love, and that nothing will take its place on the broken foundation stones. There be mercy. And so it is with the tuition of elderhood. An elder is the devastation of conviction. He or she is the one whose certainty is over, whose plans are in ruin. The presence of an elder has that consequence for his or her allies and adversaries and neighbours. That is the cost of having an elder in your midst.

A tool, it seems to me, is an extension of the primate hand. A machine, though, is not an exponential tool, not a tool at all. A machine extends the human will. As creatures limit-borne, elders are not the machined extension of mastery over life's vagaries. Elderhood is the extension of life's hand, weaving and fashioning humans by the calculus of calamity. The elder's ragged example is a revelator of the untried, the mandatory testing and truing of the unbroken. And for this they are rarely thanked, such is the rancor this devastation and this revealing prompts. But they should be thanked. If you can find one or two, praise them for that noble service, no matter your age, that you might brace and gird yourself with their example, that there might be a few more elders in the time to come.

8

THE RIVER OF ABUNDANCE AND TIME

Current

It is likely that you have spent some time in the water. As a wader or swimmer, young or uninstructed or both, there probably grew in you a subtle skill of rippling and eddying, of being born again by current, of feeling how it prevailed and prevailed upon you, and in that current you remembered something of the skill of being born and being carried, reminded again of the purl and sway of your beginnings. That memory is a skill vital to the human tasks, and it's there in the water. In our souls we are amphibious.

Along the way you may have come to watercraft, and so to the canoe. In its birch incarnation the canoe is a mingled genius of indigenous lifeways. If you held it in its proper regard, you would see that the canoe extends the reach of your skill of being borne along. When in the water, the canoe's skin extends your tactile sensoria, and its bones extend your skeleton's reach into the world. When in a birch bark canoe, you remember the amniotic nights of your making, the amphibious days of your coming among us. That isn't too much to say. I've been in them. I've made them. It's a true story.

The birch bark canoe is a seismograph for subtle motion. It reads any nuance of wend or wave or wake in the water and amplifies it and makes it known to you. You can hear it and feel it in your jaw bone. The canoe is a shell to the ear of the shoreline, too, and it reads the echo of all the ways you are making through water, all of your faithful arriving. Faithless and true, the canoe is a pitiless amanuensis of the eddy and excess and the jaunty paddling style of what it carries—you, in this case. Lean to the left by a hair and your course will feel the effect. That is how reliable a witness the birch bark canoe is. In my corner of the world, the paddler is advised to part his or her hair dead centre, down the middle, ere the course of the canoe will go awry from the imbalance. The canoe doesn't inflict stability upon the world, nor does the canoe require it. The canoe is built to rollick and to roll; each paddle stroke is a clutch of shudders, even in still water. But still water is not the measure of a canoe. Torrent: that's when the canoe and its denizens learn themselves and Braille their limits.

Now, a torrent is not made by water. An abundance of water and a descent in elevation helps, but you'd have something like a canal then. No, the roil of a torrent is made by whatever lies beneath it. White water and a birch bark canoe—this is a combination made for gamblers. If you've gambled and won before, you know that the key to the whole affair is a steady hand and some luck, surely, but more so, it is the capacity to attend to all that prevails, to endure ambivalence, and to read the signs, the subtle and the broad, the welcome and the fraught. The white horses of the boil are rearing, and the terrain below is making them rear. The water is testifying to the sunken rocks, turning away from them, raging over them.

The shift in the meaning of words, the pitch of this change, its momentum, the era the change occurred, the conditions attending the change, the reversals and subversions can all be read, in the same way water can be read. Some changes, the traumatic ones in particular, have such charge and devastation that the memory of any time before them is an early and often permanent casualty. One sign of trauma, personal and cultural, one way for the instinct for striving to be blunted, is to forgo the memory of trauma at all, and to collude with the vacant, morose canticle that intones "It hasn't ever really been otherwise. It has always been this way." The great merit of memory, personal or cultural, lies in the ability to recall the "otherwise."

Should you live beside a river, and should that river be moving still and not throttled, damned, bifurcated, or driven underground in the name of public security, and should that river still serve all things riverine and not carry the refuse and detritus of the sedentary, you may be gifted and entrusted each day with a living, adamant vision of time, making its timely way. And your time among us here in this world might be marked and born by that distillate calm of the tempered and the trued, a tone entrusted to you by the river's faithful seasonal sway and swath. And from all of that, you may have the markings and the signs of being a national living treasure, nothing less, bringing the rest of us the news the river of time has brought you.

Steady, loyal, and a salve for the fixed and the fast, the river in spring remembers those mauve and silent and enduring frozen nights of winter. It breaks the oath to keep to the steady shore that it never really made, and floods its banks and maroons the forgetful and the rich man's country house, cursed and attended to again. The tempo of the river shows when it quickens, when it eddies and ebbs. The pulse of place, artery and artifact and an old God, the river bears and burdens, bestows and bedevils, faithful that way and a guide to the perplexed and to anyone willing to be quieted and rendered down by the passing and the steady roll of days.

So, in this world time is probably river borne, or riverine. Or a river is time murmuring its song, willing, it seems, to be overheard. And there are a few salient mysteries to drape the notion across. You could decide the river of time has a clear beginning, and you could say so, but you won't find it. You won't even find *your* beginning. You'll find headwaters, but these are places where the beginning has already begun. Headwaters are gatherings. They are the proper stilling of the clamour for the one true origin, that monophony we've grown so accustomed to humming.

It comes in waves, the river of time does. Give it any attention at all, and you'll see the river of time pulse, constantly inconstant, in obedience to some lunar sway, in thrall to some solar flare. It seems to slow, then to speed, then to disappear altogether, and then to reassert itself as the very medium of memory. Though there's not much in it that you can plan, still the river of time is the fundament of every scheme you make, including all those plans for your life and its web of purpose.

And the river of time has a current, a discernible testifying that bears it along. Step out into any river and go knee deep in its steady urge. Do so blind or blindfolded and you'll still know from whence the surge comes, and whither it goes. You can feel it murmur on by you, rippling along your legs, you mysteriously going along with it for the moment, but at a different pace, different enough to feel the river.

Turn then in the direction of that place to which the river is bound, and think again upon this river of time you are a witness to, and ask yourself these questions: What *time* am I facing now? *When* am I looking to? What time does the river of time flow *to*?

Most all of us who have been graced with a public education in North America know the answer before the question is struck. We were taught the proper understanding. There was no time class to attend or be truant from, because *every* class was time class. You could not avoid the tuition. It is in the fundament of our grammar—*tense*—and so it is the fundament of our imaginal life, too. Our early time lessons are where we gained our understanding of the verities by which our metabolic life is governed. It gave us the warp and weft of our mortality, and our suspicions and our dreads about what is to become of us in the great by and by. Whatever we imagine, whatever sway we grant to our imaginings, they are bound at the hip to this certainty without end that the current of time goes to the future, to the not yet. Say it to yourself and it'll come to you like a bee to a flower: the river of time bears you and all that you love from the given to the ungiven, from the known to the unknown, from the has been to the hasn't been, from the past through the present and to the future. Likely, every plan wrought and wrecked by your higher self was cast according to this conceit about the current of time, every scheme for fortune and contentment, for defeat and dominion. Cast your bread upon the waters, and to the future it is bound.

"You have your whole life ahead of you." Everyone reading this knows what it means and what it does to you to be told that. It means that the future is out in front of you, that you face the future when you put the past behind you. It also means that you're young. What it does is craft a moral order that enthrones fantasy, deifies hope, and binds you to *what you haven't done yet*, that allegation foisted upon you as a young student.

Well, this statement must be true for everyone if it is true for anyone, regardless of age. Older people would seem to have their whole lives ahead of them too, no? But it doesn't actually feel that way, does it? It's what you've been told, that the past is behind you and the future is ahead. Probably it's what you've said, many times. But it's not quite how it feels, once you begin to consider.

The phrase is routinely used to get young people to line up at the productivity trough, and it is virtually never used on older people. Why, do you suppose? Because our general view of aging comes from our understanding of the passage of time. Because aging and time put everything behind you, in the file folder marked "Done," that's why.

Now, the observable ripple of the thing is that everyone's life is the same length. By this I mean that every life has its allotment, the duration of which is confirmed at its end. Measured not in days but in fullness, each life is a completed life. A fifty-year-old's life is no more full than an eight-year-old's—particularly from where the eight-year-old stands. It is the rumour of potential that prompts that strange conceit that the eight-year-old hasn't enjoyed the kind of fullness that can only come from an as-yet unlived life. No one's life is more ended, in other words, than another. They are all ended.

But this amounts to pointless nonsense in a culture that covets growth and hope and plans and possibilities and duration and What Could Be. Here's why: it's that old river of time that we are persuaded every day bears the past away as it bears us towards our entitlement. It is our understanding of the current of time that steals from the old and burdens the young. And the young are burdened with this allegation we call potential. *Potential*: the word comes from the Latin for "power." Yet it is our conviction about the direction of time's current that subverts potential, attributing it exclusively to the future tense. It's a strange phrase, when you let yourself be bothered by it a little: *you have*—present tense—*everything that hasn't happened yet*—future tense. How can you possibly have any of it? *Potential*: all those things you've not yet done, those people you've not yet been, everything you could be, all of it, at least in principle, known to the shamanic guides and the life coaches and the parents, and unknown to you. *Potential*: the carrot and the stick of striving. Leaning out into the allegations and the maybes of modern life, you face promise. The past is well abandoned to itself, all of it conviction and constraint, spent and—if you've got a good attitude—no more. That's what we know about time. That's what prompts the next trip to the mall.

For all of that, we seem more and more modern and a little homeless and confused by freedom. We're born adrift and not aloft into a future and away from all that has come before, each day compounding the giddy and the greying isolation, the past as gone as anything that's ever been. In my years in the death trade, I saw the forlorn, death's-door algebra of the thing. The dead we claim to love even still are consigned to the past tense, to the over and done, to the gone. *Lost*: that is what so many say when they mean *dead*. And there is consequence to saying *lost* over and over. Nobody I remember from those days chose to lose their loved ones and their dead, but that's what they said, and they did so every day. They did so every time they said, "I lost him," "I lost her." And they had conspirators: "I'm sorry for your loss." They had paid professionals waiting in the wings who colluded with the hope-benumbed project of "getting on with your life," as if your life was what waited for you, as if you were owed a future that you were now free to draw down, as if you had an obligation to lean out over the precipice of "over" and towards the future, as if there was still this allegation called "your life" out there, ahead of you and pending, as if there ever was.

You might think that how we are with our dead is a deep and enduring consequence of our agility and our aplomb and our devotion where
love is concerned. All of that is surely in the mix, at least when the
better memories outweigh the bad, when we *want* to remember. Love,
yes. And all the tangled garden of habit and persistence and the having
grown used to the measured passage and the footfall of the day taking
its leave in evening—that is there, too.

Friends, imagine that it is not the mishap or the disease that ends
it all, not the funeral business that takes your loved one under. The
funeral director could not have come up with something like "passing
away" on his or her own. With due respect, it's too vast, too utter, too
final for a celebrant or an event planner. No, the palliative physician,
the undertaker of the dismal trade, and the grief containment brigade,
they all take their marching orders and their cue from the grammarian.
It is our English grammar, with its three parsimonious and intolerant
tenses. It is this past/present/future parade. It is the intractable draw of
the given and the gone. These are the architects of how we live and how
we die and how we come to love and to leaving.

"I lost him" is not a synonym for "he died," not in any way. But if
your grammar deeply discourages imprecision of tense, and if your river
of time heads to the future with purpose and hasty rhythm, and if the
very measure of your sanity comes down to being willing to swear off
all other possibilities and instead be consistently moored in the present,
then being lost when you die isn't an expression, and it isn't a possibility, either. It is fate. And it is as inevitable as the goneness of this very
morning, and of all the others before it.

> I fell off the beams when I was taking apart my crumbling barn
> roof a few years ago. Eighteen feet later I lay in the mouldering
> straw and listened to the cries of alarm that went up from the
> helpers all around me. As my friends scrambled down from the
> ladders yelling for help, I tried to move my fingers and toes.
> Miraculously, I could. By the time they reached me, I was kneel-
> ing. I could speak a little, but there was a lot of blood. I'd scored

my scalp at the hairline on the way down, and a hospital visit was required.

In the triage room a nurse had what seemed like hordes of questions. But as I focused on them, I came to see that she was asking me the same few things in different ways: Where are you right now? What day is it today? How did you hurt yourself? She was of course checking for a concussion or worse head trauma. But she was doing so by testing my allegiance to the English grammar that tolerates but one tense at a time, and my willingness to forsake all others for monogamous enthrallment to the present, and to do so consistently, and to agree, in other words, that yesterday is gone and tomorrow is not yet, that the present is bereft of the former and bewildered, beguiled, and besieged by the latter.

A Line

Every childhood classroom in which I was educated had, above the chalkboard and below the Queen of England's faded photograph, a timeline. Its beginning was usually in a corner, and it progressed left to right in the manner of Western literacy to the next corner, turned right down the next wall, and so on around the room. Its content arbitrarily determined by whatever the syllabus obliged us to learn, there were a few illustrations, a few faces, and plenty of dates. It was presented to us as a faithful rendering of the sentinel events that became us and our wondrous, modern life. It was studded with conflict and strife and, above all, winners, prevailers, anointed by history, the proper progenitors of the students gathered to learn it, we ourselves the pinnacle of merit and victory and time's own design.

It was heady stuff for an eight-year-old. And it was, unmistakably, a line. A straight line. No one in the room could have misunderstood that time moved with all the confidence of a caesar from the distant past through the recent present to.... Well, no one ever asked, that I recall. Things might have become interesting indeed if the teacher put any particular day of the current school year at the end of the line, or any particular person we knew who was still alive, or any person in the room.

But that never happened, and year after school year the frolic of dates and wars and the rest went inevitably on, cutting across any ability any of us might still have had to see anything otherwise, leaving us to dead reckon our way through our subsequent lives, that timeline the very fringe and frontier, the intransigent limit of our imaginations. It was orderly, though. And there was progress, the inevitability of progress, from the simple to the complex, from the single to the diverse, from the literal to the abstract—and, for some, from the sublime to the ridiculous. That line went right on, until, literally, we ran out of history, which is what the present is in a culture where the past is mostly gone. The present is where you run out of history.

This linear timeline that we were taught was relentless. It reeked of survivalism. It had the shrill refrain of triumph about it, and it was as intolerant as any staunch conservative or eco-warrior can be. There was no limit to the timeline, no real variance to it. It left behind the weakened, the defeated, the spent, and the old, the detritus and debris of time grinding away what has been, forever reborn and renewing. Its cadence was regular. In its Gregorian and Julian forms, the timeline had a mysterious claim of origin to a particular year and day, and birth, flinging everything that came before into the outer realms of pre-, before, so that everything prior flooded headlong in purpose towards that moment, and every subsequent thing emanated from it.

The very idea that you could start time by designating a year or a moment or a person as the first year or moment—or person?—was garish and breathtaking and, with a bit of reflection, made no sense at all. All of those people who lived before time began? What were they? *When* were they? Still, the whole thing never came into disrepute, not that I recall.

When you learn that time is a line moving ever forward, what does *repetition* mean? It means regression. Repetition is lack of discipline in a timeline culture, the collapse of learning into recurrence, the tomb of tradition. It means dwelling upon the past or, if left unchecked and untreated, dwelling in the past. It means trauma. Too much recurrence, the swarming of the present by the past—that is the definition of neurosis. We were learning the past so we could progress, so we could matriculate and graduate and, in the immortal, rancorous cant of the timeline, get on with our lives, that pageant of progress that lay out there, ahead of us.

And memory? What is it, and *why* is it, in the principality of linear time? To remember is to take what is need for the journey from the past and, plunder complete, deke its limits. You hear it in every canned commemorative speech: learning from the past, living now, looking to the future. Of course, none of this was said in school, not that I recall. It was taught by correction, not by instruction, and years down the road (there's the linear image again) it is still hard to recognize, and harder still to realize the thorough legion of consequence fanning out unintended from this unconsidered conviction that time bears us away from all that precedes us, towards what awaits us. If time is a line, the future is a snowflake—unique and precious and stand-alone as is each one of us, never having been before, its novelty a throne and a God. If time is a line, the past is as gone as gone can be, and the oldest among us are mostly gone. That's what it does to them. That's what it will do to you.

A Circle

So there was lots to remember and to be tested on up there on the wall, but there wasn't much to wonder about. You'd think that when the idea of circular time came around—or, more in keeping, came around again, then again—because you or someone close by had come across some Buddhism for Westerners, or the *I Ching*, or Beat poetry in the black and white City Lights series, there'd be celebration. I myself remember a giddy sense of being in the know and in on something esoteric and becoming. It seemed a more sophisticated vision, the eternal return. It was the friendlier-seeming circle of life, if you were a fan, the circle game if you were not. It seemed wise, authorized by the ages. It seemed time-tested and lent a tinge of world weariness to any twenty-year-old looking for a little gravitas to anchor his day. No alpha, no omega, a user-friendly, inclusive curve to the thing that calmed the striving. It neither rose nor fell, began nor ended. It was reassuring, in a dusty and saffron-tinged sort of way. The shape seemed to rein in the excessive progressiveness of linear time and bring some much-needed humility back into the story.

Here's why, perhaps: there's nothing much that's new. Like a snake swallowing its tail, circular time is more than current. It is recurrent. Circular time has bequeathed to us that somber sounding syllogism that stymies inquiry and might be as close as many citizens of these times can draw to Delphi: everything that goes around comes around. If linear time's time signature is a progress relentless and intolerant of limitations, then circular time's time signature is a fate inexorable, the karmic wheel of fortune grinding aspiration and vanity into cosmic pocket lint.

Where linear time has the potential, circular time has the inevitable. Circular time delivers every made thing to its beginning and its recurrence, again and over again. Its adherents claim for circular time a sophisticated humble arc that turns striving back towards itself, that blunts bombast and triumphalism. It does so with more than a little futility, though, and a refrain of "ashes to ashes." The circle of life, typically a vision of wholeness, seems as much a vision of ultimate sameness, where all is vanity.

Circular seating is the choreography of choice in retreat centres and workshop settings, probably to contend with this new age's (though how "new" could the New Age be if it's really "the circle of life"?) misgivings about hierarchies and power and the like. I found out what kind of claim the shape makes upon retreaters and workshoppers when I began to teach in such places for a while and asked for the seating arrangement to be changed to something more random-looking. Many people were disturbed. They liked the equi-distance of the circular seating, the allegation that they could see everything and everyone at a glance, the antidote to that power-at-the-front-of-the-room association from school days, and the level-ing that provided a stage for their personal truth to have its own airing and presentation and merit.

⁓⧓⁓

What does *recurrence* mean when your vision of time is circular? It means that you finally are getting it. It means that the illusions are going clear, as are you, and that repetition is the fingerprint of God, as enduring a sign of fidelity as we are provided in this world awash with apparent change and the hoax of progress. And it probably means that whatever parenting you received is largely what you will draw upon in your later years, as did your parents as they parented you, and they theirs, and so on back into the parental mists, and onward into them. This would be something akin to fate. It is not repetition so much as "same stuff, different day." The variance comes in how you will be with what routinely comes towards you.

You could say that the idea of linear time is akin to a young person's untested conviction that everything is possible, and that the idea of cir-cular time is an older person's life expectation reduced to this: most of what is possible isn't likely. Circles of time are lines of time that through attrition and consequence and futility grew tired and could no longer maintain the demands of infinity. It is no wonder then that Western cultures, and the dominant culture of North America in particular, as the new kids in the culture-making game, remain the breeding ground for the giddy excess of linear time and its allegations of progress. Their weariness with time hasn't quite appeared. It is no wonder—literally, no wonder—that the Children of the Time Line are drawn into the trance of progress. Places with more time-in retain the idea of circular time for the fundament of their spiritual and religious practice.

A Spiral

It wouldn't be much of a story or much of a contemplation if there were only two choices in this matter. There is at least one other possibility. It employs a bit of imagery from each of the previous ideas, but it seems to me to subvert them both. Perhaps time comes and goes in eras of such abundant and gradual ellipse that it is more like Yeats's widening gyre, its shape a spiral. You could imagine it this way, as a line still vigorous, now tempered by its spare way and its solitary habit, grown not so sure of itself, not so willing to leave everything behind, looking over its shoulder for a sign of life. You could imagine a circle lifting up from itself, rising and remembering its penchant for returns and for the old ground, but opening to what is stirred by the whorls. Granted, it is a visual image and so probably not the last word on the shape of time. But the spiral has an expansive quality to it, and so it has the capacity to gather as it goes. Of the three, it is the only one possessed of a real third dimension. Your own life experience might whisper to you that this spiral has a depth that widens, deepens with the days. So this spiral shape I imagine for time going its way is consistent with the quantum continuum that binds time to space as two aspects of the same event, just as physics imagines them to be.

The spiral of time goes on by doubling back, you could say. So it leaves nothing behind by proceeding, and it curls back over what precedes it, fingering the prayer beads of when and where it has been, the very time signature of time's memory. It eddies, it curls, it slows and reverses. It drifts, it lingers, it hurtles, it abides. It is mercurial and will not be herded or brought to order, but it will bear your efforts to do just that. As it wafts it restores. It has the bearing and the tuft and the nap of memory all about it.

I have been maintaining all along that the way in which you imagine or picture things carries a whole wake of unintended consequences too, to go along with what you mean. In the case of imagining the shape of time itself, each shape conjures all manner of existential and primordial chimera, and determines the claims we make for fidelity to ancestry, regard for tradition or wisdom, or for elderhood. Surprising as it may sound, of the three, spiraling time seems to be the only one in which time actually appears. In the line and circle time is two dimensional, collapsed and shorn of its depth. In the spiral, time has volume, and that aspect of depth is where the going on of time registers and appears, and where we and our memory appear.

Spiraling time is the one shape that seems to credit experience, to grant a seat at the table in the feast hall of life for what is learned and for its reappearance in the present as a tutor and abiding titular spirit. You could say that spiraling time is the horse that wisdom rides into the human endeavor. If you are labouring away, crafting your normal life, enduring the spectacle on occasion, and glad of the steady road, you could be thrown, and perhaps you have been, by the sudden appearance in the proceedings of that which you'd dealt with, resolved, put away, sorted, and foreclosed upon years before.

A handy example might be your various challenges with one of your parents or the other. Of course your childhood was wrought by him or her, and you were your parents' best ideas of what a human should look like and how one should be crafted and behave, so there's that. And you come yourself into your twenties, shuddering somewhat with that experimentation and glad to be in the land now of self determination, and you may have found to your dismay that your own romance is crafted to some degree from the shattered and abandoned examples of the romance that begot you that you forsook. You work on your "stuff," as it is sometimes called, enough at least to consider parenthood for yourself. Five years into your parenting you find yourself saying and doing things you distinctly recall forbidding yourself from doing years before. Perhaps under some marital duress, you submit yourself to the particular, exquisite minuet of counseling. You aren't an hour into the thing but here comes the childhood business again, your "mother stuff," your "father problem." And so on it goes, into your fifties and sixties, the parental spectre shading the proceedings.

Spiraling time credits these recurrences as your right and proper inheritance, partly personal and largely ancestral, something in the manner of the build of your face. But it does more than credit them. It credits the time that bears them to you, and the times between. Its counsel might sound something like this:

> Yes, it's distressing when what you thought was done appears again in the fingerprints you leave upon others and upon the world by your striving and dreaming. You thought you were done with the old foibles and their claim upon you, or you thought you were done with any chance to better yourself. Do not surrender to the old taunt that this is the same old thing, though, and that you're nobody worth being all over again, and that this is just the way it goes. You are no longer seven years old, nor twenty-seven, and that old learned futility is the first casualty of being obliged to come to these old sutures and binds with the new grace entrusted to you by the time afforded you since.

> You are hereby granted another chance to befriend your days and what they've made of you, by bringing to bear what you've seen and learned and lost and left since the last time these things claimed your recalcitrant attention. Consider this grace: the first time these things swam towards you, or the fifth, none of them were your one and only chance to get it right. They were not. This is not fate, nor is it doom. This is mercy, carried to you by these days of yours, days not lost but coming round again. You are flirting with wisdom now, as wisdom is flirting with you.

That strikes me as the blessing bestowed upon us by spiraling time. It *credits the passing of time as the medium of wisdom.* It is not inevitably a wisdom bringer, but possibly, or more than possibly, the spiraling of time brings the restitution of experience. It brings the currency of wisdom in the looping current of time. The possibility that the past is not gone from us nor binding us to repeat it, the real possibility that experience plus time can bring a wisdom tried by endurance, a wisdom eclipsing prejudice; this is the understanding of time that underwrites elderhood.

Hierarchy. The word has a bad PR firm working for it. Symptom bearer for a woebegone and elderless age, *hierarchy* is the straw dog for every misanthrope, every convicted anarchist, every defender of the ninety-nine and foe of the one. Get rid of hierarchy, and you're halfway to heaven.

Until you learn the history of the word, that is. Once you reconsider its constituent parts, the grudge match might be over. The dictionary tells you that the word refers to graded ranks of ecclesia, and by extension, of any organization. The Greek prefix *hier* means "of things sacred." It does not automatically mean "above" or "raised up," nor does it seem to carry any inference of superiority that comes down to us from any ectopic, creation-slandering religion. It imagines *sacred* as one condition of this earthly life of ours.

And then the root word, *arche*. You probably know it best from that resonant pronouncement regarding how everything commenced: "In the *beginning* was the word...." But you would also recognize it in *archaic, architecture, archer, archetype, arc,* and a score of other words. Here it begins to lose its later associations with "ruler," with "overlord." The thrust of the thing is closer to *fundament,* or *foundation.* It carries an understanding not of single cause or origin, but of "enduring upholders," or "nutritive predecessors," and so in its pre-monotheistic incarnation, it is plural in its nuance and sustaining in its function.

Reassembled, *hierarchy* gives us something like this: "Those who locate holiness in this world by underlying the world, by coming before." With this understanding and function you can see that the elder is the hierarch of his or her time, that the spiral of time is the medium and the engine of the wisdom hierarchies which are your proper inheritance.

Go back down into that river of time now, and wonder, if you would, about the same questions we began with. Where does the river of time bring everything and everyone to? What is its way? The answer seems properly to be that the river of time goes to the past. When you obey its current, you are facing the past, which is out there ahead of you. The past is where everything that has been has gone to, none of it ever gone. That is where the river of time will bear you to, *is* bearing you to. You and I are headed towards all that has gone before us. That is what is before you, and yes, that is what is to become of you. In this one sentence you can see the spiral of time making its eliptical way. What is to become of you is already before you, neither repetition nor fate, only promise.

In that way elders are your future, a future that is here, a future that gets old, that ages before your eyes, if you are patient and inclined that way. They have their personal memories, yes, but as elders *they are memory incarnate*, one way life has of testifying to the presence the past has.

Consider Alden Nowlan's poem:

As long as you read this poem
I will be writing it.
I am writing it here and now,
before your eyes,
although you can't see me.
Perhaps you'll dismiss this
as a verbal trick,
the joke is you're wrong;
the real trick
is your pretending
this is something
fixed and solid,
external to us both.
I tell you better:

I will keep on
writing this poem for you
even after I'm dead.

—Alden Nowlan, "An Exchange of Gifts"

The gift he is talking about is the enduring presence of the past, the spiral of time moving over all the things of this world, the abundance of time becoming this present that we meet in. He made a promise in the poem that today, thirty years after his death, he is keeping. "I'm writing it here and now," he says. "What I once promised to do *is* this moment between us." He is eldering us now, in other words.

It is in the mystery of elderhood to duck out from under the straight assignment, the steady thing, the unerring time parade that seems to carry everything worth knowing and worth being away. One example: elders won't last, not the way you wish they would. *But their ending lasts.* It lasts a long time. It is there as long as you're willing to remember it, and wish it were otherwise, and awaken to the realization that you forgot all about them and their endings, and your own, again. That's how long they last. They'll get back to you, after they're gone, and they do it by your unwillingness on occasion to go it alone, and by your grief-endorsed willingness to turn to them, even after they're dead. Especially after they're dead.

9

THE FOURTH TEMPTATION

I doubt many of us who grew up in North America in the 1950s knew it was "the 50s." The sheen that the 50s acquired with hindsight—the cool, the beat, the bop—wasn't so obvious at the time. The ash of the Second War was already ploughed under, the walking wounded were turned into a work force and a consumer group, and the fields on the edge of town were being turned into more town.

And then there was television, the cathode calm of watching, the great grey-green glowing leveler of town and country, young and old. The television business was in its infancy in Canada at the time, and most of the trends and technology then followed the American example. As it happened, the consumer delights available on the television didn't actually exist for us on the shelf or the street. Some did, but for the most part, what we saw on the television came at us from Neverland. All manner of running shoes vaulted thrilled kids over every obstacle, and there were chocolate bars that delivered a delirium of well-being and power with every bite.

And there was the Southern Baptist preacher. Unimagined, unheard of, and unknown in our part of the country, he was an apparition looming out of the two-tone tube, deeply exotic and unrestrained, all aswelter and aglow and utterly out of control or reach. Out of reach, that is, until a fateful fall New England afternoon, one of my first few days of attendance at the Ivy League divinity school that took me in more as a consequence of the demands of a foreign student quota than of any stellar scholastic achievement of mine.

There are times in a life when good judgment does not prevail. It isn't because we are more foolish than usual just then. It's because we are in such a time of life, and the weather of that time is foolishness. *Weather* might be a good way of saying it. There are times of life when the weather is so persuasive that for years afterwards you remain quite sure that it was your mastery and capacity for self-direction that was prevailing. There are those times you recall for a while with rickety certainty, and you anoint them, and say, "I won." Often those are times, recalled later with a bit of hindsight and chagrin, that you were at the steering wheel indeed, singular and factotum of all you surveyed, careening off into the weeds.

If you are prone to the Gods, if you grant them some kind of bit part, at least, in the scheme of it all, there can be times when you hope that you are doing their bidding, that you've been successful in getting out of the way of your purpose or your fate. Those times, too, you'll probably recall later as times when your will and the will of the Gods synced up nicely and seamlessly, as times when you couldn't tell them apart. They can be magical memories.

But when the caveats of age begin their whisper campaign and your recall is more willing to attune to the crazed allegations of your younger days, those times tend to loom up more accurately as times when the Gods were mute, as they sometimes are, and *you* provided the voice-over of purpose, direction, and the meant-to-be-ness of it all. These are wince-worthy episodes. In the story that follows, maybe the Gods were calling the shots. Maybe they were in the wings. Maybe I was filling in for them. I'm not sure.

Summoned, like all of us were who'd entered the white-collar programme, the Master of Divinity, I appeared at the appointed hour to articulate my vocation and the means by which it was to be realized. The Southern Baptist preacher who awaited me was a vision. There's no other word for what I saw seated there. I took the empty chair. He, with the demeanor of a minor regent that reward and the passage of time had neglected, looked out the window—and, in fact, never did deign to look at me directly over the full course of the audience. He just looked out the window. He had the dew of exertion all about him, though the morning was comfortably cool, and he had the performer's way with a handkerchief. His array: an impossible-to-find-for-yourself robin's egg blue suit, a polyester blend with a few episodes of sheen at the elbow that spoke of being well-worn, lapels like wings, as befitted his station in life and a particular style of the times. The white shirt, also a blend, so white it was turning in the direction of blue, adhered to his generous midriff, not entirely accommodating him in seated repose. A glimpse of the hirsute between the buttons completed things. There was the tie, a slash of complimentary grey and crimson, the enveloping throne of lacquered, alma mater black and gold, the expanse of desk, the pen in his hand, and the remoteness of the sage.

The pen he held as if it was a scepter. It was a Waterman, a high-end writing machine, its girth that of a modest cucumber, its hallmark there on the cap and legible from a fair distance. During our meeting, the Southern Baptist preacher unscrewed the top of the pen very slowly, and screwed the top back down again continually, his only activity apart from asking me, as it turned out, four questions by which my very life's path was to be determined. It was a daunting business for a young foreigner.

Screwing and unscrewing, and surveying the collegiate domain through the window beyond, he began. With the requisite drawl that still had a Celtic lilt about it, the adjudicator of my future said to me,

Now, son. We have before us the obligation of ascertaining the whys and the wherefores of your vocation. I have one or two questions, none of them difficult. As to who sent you: what is the name of your sponsoring congregation?

I don't believe it showed on my face, but inside I froze. I recognized that this was the narrow gate by which I would come to my chosen place in life. I was sure then of wanting to be a clergyman of some kind. But it became very obvious in that moment that to pursue such work one had to be sponsored or spoken for by established ecclesia, preferably of one's home place, and it was obvious, too, that I was entirely ignorant of the requirement.

But I was light on my feet at that age, nimble of thought when necessary, so that moment of brief panic was brought to an end by something I thought sounded the right combination of contrition and self-assurance. I said,

"Well, I haven't worked that out yet."

The preacher called up collegial reassurance in his tone, the sound that only comes when a senior member of a given fraternal order gathers in a younger would-be member but holds him at a bit of a distance. He said to me,

"Oh, that's alright. For now, just give me the name of your *denominational affiliation*."

These last two words he wrung out until he seemed not to be asking about whatever allegiance had claimed my spiritual striving but instead intoning the name of a recently discovered volcanic island in the South Seas, using something beyond the normal eleven syllables to do so. I was two brief questions into discernment of my life's chosen track, and I could see the lights going out, and I could feel the sediment under my vision liquefying and running to lower ground. I hoped he wouldn't notice, though the sheer scope of the man and his position already guaranteed that he was probably already out ahead of me on this. With whatever shards of certainty that were still available to me I answered,

"Well, I haven't work that out yet either."

Now, among those running amok in the hortatory trades, Southern Baptist preachers had until recent years something approaching a monopoly on drama, and on drama's proper midwife, timing, and this man had both, in spades. A third question was looming, and something like fate seemed en route. With another couple of turns of the Waterman lid to mark the eternity that passed as this inadvertent confession of mine lost all lift and fell upon his desk, and with a tone that mixed practiced affability with a whiff of the purgatorial, and landing heavily on the third word, he said,

"Son, where do you go to church?"

All was lost by then, of course, and I knew it, and he probably knew it, too. I was the prey run to the back of the pen, finding no escape. I turned, so to speak, and faced the end of my life's plan. I said,

"I don't go to church."

He hadn't quite done the broken math of the moment, I don't think. It was either that, or he couldn't fathom the self-deception or artless naïveté I'd managed to nurse until that moment. The third word bearing the brunt of his wonder, he said,

"Well where *did* you go to church then?"

No recourse left to me, my career as a nonaligned cleric in shards before it began, I told him what he knew, what until that moment I hadn't imagined would have constituted a serious obstacle to ordination, what sounded now more like negligence of the criminal kind than it did oversight or bad planning. I said,

"I didn't go to church."

At our end now, divination of my employment and spiritual future complete, sounding very much like the Wizard of Oz dismissing the four vagrants and the dog, he said,

"Let me see if I understand the situation. You propose to go into the ministry of something or other, you hadn't *never* been to church?"

And I said,

"Yes, that's right."

Well, he sat there, as the chicanery of the thing became apparent. And then he said, as only people entrusted with the gentle drawl can say it (in transliteration),

"Well. I nevuh."

And I agreed with him. I said,

"I never neither."

And, with that, it was finished. In the coming days I was firmly counseled, without recourse, to reconsider my life's path and see it rerouted to one that would spare some parish in the future and me my inexperience, to one more scholarly and academic, one that required no attendance at any recognizable house of devotion, and so I submitted instead to the Master of Theological Studies regime. I don't remember feeling a failure, but certainly I had no idea anymore what was to become of me, now that my entrance into the feast hall of the hortatory arts was barred.

Which is why I was dumbfounded when a year into that programme I was approached by the PhD student in charge of such things with the invitation to preach—yes, *preach*—in the weekly church service in the school chapel, a service attended by many of the students and august faculty. The embers of my imagined career disturbed back into a temporary warmth, I agreed to do it. Bear in mind that I'd never been to church, that I'd never seen anyone preach in person. Still hadn't.

What I had done, though, in the meantime, was enter into an undeclared apprenticeship with a magisterial storyteller, a wordsmith and master practitioner of the skaldic arts, a raconteur of the most sublime kind, a black street griot and easy American equivalent of an Indian holy man, powerful, dangerous, serious, doing his God's work, forgoing permission from the tower or the bunker. Brother Blue was his street name, his running name, known to immediate family as Dr. Hugh Morgan Hill. He was the kind of man I didn't know was alive, and it was an apprenticeship I didn't know existed.

I didn't know any of this in the beginning, when I played harmonica behind him in a Unitarian church service while he fairly sang some Delta blues version of The Good Samaritan (*This is what preaching is? Where have I been?*), but he and his wife Ruth gathered me into their travelling-road-show lives, and I was glad for it. There was magic there, potent and old-feeling. I grew to love this old man, though I didn't really know how. By some magic I didn't command, this meeting between a homeless white kid from the often frozen north and a wily grandson of African slaves who had been fashioned years before into a full-time servant of some Other World began to fashion in me a capacity for gratitude and the whiff of life purpose.

He made it clear over and over that his life came *to* him. Whenever I asked him how he was doing, his answer always was:

"I am the luckiest man in the world. I found what I was born to do."

I now see that he was telling me over and over,

There *is* such a thing as why you were born. But you don't invent it. It was there first. You obey it. It is bigger than you, luckily, and your job is to get out of its way by finding a few ways during the course of your days to say, "Yes."

We often performed his version of King Lear, which he called "Blues for Old." I was too young to know it, but in his late-sixties by then, he was singing the song of a life that had already come to him.

So he was the surge of life under me. He was weather and wind and current, all in an hour. He was no teacher, and so the finest of masters. No instructor either, he was a practitioner instead, and he never pointed to some other time or place or possibility more worthy of being learned than the one we found ourselves in. He proceeded instead as a man of enormous wealth, entrusted with something precious and necessary for his time, properly upright, guaranteed to detonate the vigilantes and homeland security wonks as he went along, en elder in every sinewed joint and phrase, foregoing acceptance and steady pay, calling down the mighty.

I appeared with him, supporting his performances with the best music playing I could manage at the time. I probably added as much arrhythmia and clamour as anything else, but he carried himself up there as if he had a well-oiled backup band, and he'd introduce me that way, overstating things as he was want to do. Ruth and Blue invited me to accompany them on a short tour of the Midwest. I was under-rehearsed and overwhelmed, and I said yes. Pay was discussed. I knew they lived on not very much. But more so, I knew that I was a child of fortune at that moment, and my recompense was my tuition. I learned that from him, too. Determined to take no pay, I approached the Divinity School for a loan. I described the outlandish idea to the Dean of Students, who responded:

"So, you want us to lend you money so you can miss class?"

And he did so, and he still has my deep regard for overcoming administrative good sense and contributing so deeply to my soul's education. I got a job from the limited range of temporary employment available to me as a legal alien, custodian in a shopping mall, responsible for maintaining the limited hygiene of a public place, where I learned the Elysian mysteries of women's bathrooms, among other things, and had whatever remained of a childhood curiosity about those places sated for all time. And I paid that money back.

I remember the tour as a great success. I discovered that Blue was a more masterful practitioner of radical and ribald living in the downtime *between* performances, as hard as that was to imagine. Many times I had to beg him to stop storytelling, his humour so relentless that I feared for my entrails from belly laughing without inhaling. And many times I saw his love of being alive spill out over the levee of "the show," and his enormous generosity and grace in the face of the awe and animosity his storytelling prompted in others. Doing what he was born to do, he set a high and restless standard for anyone wanting that for himself or herself. His example so implacable, his capacity to love this living world so thorough, he was by turns a visitation of the Old Gods and a bracing tutor of the soul. And so he was often hard to be with, as unrepentant elders can be.

We arrived back in the city at the train station downtown late of a rainy, chilling fall evening, draped in road fatigue and lugging baggage. I had Ruth and Blue wait inside with the luggage while I found a taxi out in the street. I was gone for maybe three minutes, but it was time enough for the transit authority police to begin rousting them as late night, down-on-their-luck loiterers. There was a strong charge of racial tension in the city in those days, and the authority that night was young, untempered, and white. I came down the stairs and saw this going on, and I was adrift in the sudden sea change from road victories against all the odds to my soul's parents being harassed by authorized bigotry.

I was all rage looking for a handle. Blue looked over the shoulder of the looming cop and saw me coming and, such was his mastery and resolve and road-tested elderhood, he caught my eye for just a second, and, as best as I can translate it today, his look said this:

Listen, son. I know what this is to you. I know you'll pour your rage on these guys, to make this right. Well, everything's not going to be right, no matter what you do, and you're about to make everything a whole lot worse than it is. And you won't bear the brunt of what you're about to do. We will. Don't you think my life has given me plenty of chances to learn how this goes, and how I can live with what I know, and how to keep going anyhow? You think it all comes down to this? Just come over here quiet and respectful, and get the bags. Learn something now about the world.

So my preaching invitation came not too long after that evening, and I probably said yes to Blue's incandescent, incendiary example when I agreed to do it. But the truth was that I had no idea what to say in that hallowed chapel to that august company. The weeks went by, during which my utter lack of church time had its way, and nothing came to me. The afternoon before the appointed day came and went, and still nothing. The sun set, and with it, any sense that I'd done right by agreeing to what would probably be an undignified fiasco.

Sometime before midnight it came, and it came entire and sudden. The appointed chapel hour came, and I preached (I suppose you could call it) for the fifteen or twenty minutes allotted me. I called it "The Fourth Temptation." I can't remember anything beyond polite acknowledgement afterwards. Many years later, I was invited to the Jung Institute in Zurich to speak about my reservations about the psychological mandate of individuation. I called the session "Individuation or Initiation?" In that session, I told the story that came to me that midnight hour years before. I can't remember anything beyond a psychological scrutiny from the Jungians in attendance, and the vague suggestion that Jung himself had said much the same thing maybe seventy-five years before. All of this isn't much encouragement to tell it once more, but by now I've found the strange convolutions of the age I'm born to to be reason enough.

Preaching and Prophecy

No news to anyone reading this, preaching has a poor reputation, much of it—maybe all of it, or almost all—richly deserved. The spiritual arrogance that often animates it is a mockery of what it claims to serve, and it is not to be borne, and that arrogance is in gaudy, tawdry array in the clamour of fundamentalisms of all stripes. Lurid, baleful, visiting upon hapless auditors what it pretends to warn them away from, spiritual arrogance is a shell game. Each person I know could enjoy a rich and full life, in all its wild raiment, without resorting to the utter, relentless certainty that spiritual arrogance exudes, without resorting to the unsuspected servitude of the spirit and the self hatred it begets. There is a scene in *Griefwalker*, a documentary film about my work in the death trade, where a fairly satisfied preacher is using a woman's funeral to thunder on about everyone being a failure in life and just not good enough, about God saving everyone from themselves, and from death and hell, and there's an old man in the pews, and you see his bowed head submitted to this poison from someone half his age. It still rankles, all these years later.

But in its older incarnation the verb *to preach* means something closer to "to cry out" (hence its synonyms *to proclaim*, and *to clamour*, both having the old root *to low*), and to do so publically. So the thrust of the word is not contemplative really, nor coy, nor quiet and withdrawn, and it says nothing of the merit of what is cried out in public, only that this must be the forum, the occasion. Can crying out and being troubled aloud in a troubled time be done without the grotesqueries of condemnation and obscene self-assurance, as if the proclaimer has the ear and is the tongue of the Almighties? Rare as it seems to be, I can imagine it so.

The world has been blessed from time to time by the bloom of wisdom traditions that know their limits and respect their ends, that have no swagger and will not succumb to the spells of universality or eternality, will not promulgate them unawares, and will not missionize others. They have an aspect to them that tends to the prophetic, instead. There is an elegance to the architecture of prophecy that dispels spiritual arrogance and the messianic impulse that often swells from it. It comes also to the unlikely, to the unpromising. When it comes, it can prompt a kind of radical etiquette, something like this:

> "I am not able to care for this thing that, in mysterious error, has come to me."

It sounds like self-effacement, and it is. But more is at work here than humility. A deep, unbidden understanding is rising, where everything is alive, including this strange imperative that seems powerful and frail at the same time. It implicates and compels and still needs translating into the vernacular of the prevailing maelstrom, and it needs and deserves its proper nourishment and shelter. These are ways the summoned one often knows next to nothing about.

So, prophetic traditions have this almost comical aspect (comical, that is, if you are not the one so summoned) whereby the response is more reflex than reflection:

> "Me? It can't be me. Nothing like this has come to my door before. Others are more worthy, are more able to carry this around. There are others who know what to do. I know a few of them myself. I could give you their numbers."

Which is all absolutely accurate. There *are* others more seasoned and proven. There always will be. Alas, the normal design and criteria for merit is often the first casualty of the prophetic call. This is usually written out of the official version handed down over the centuries whenever a religion heaves itself up around the advent of prophecy, making the religion itself look preordained and inevitable. But prophecy seems to be neither meritocracy nor democracy. It is, among other things, an anointing of unlikeliness. It affirms the demonstrable facts of the unlikely.

And it goes further down this unpromising road. Prophecy prompts serious doubt and challenge about the wisdom and judgment of from-whom/whence-it-comes.

"You are mistaken, this time."

This is the last line of defense of the summoned. And the response of the Great Beyond seems only to reinstate the summons, without elaboration:

"Do you know the suddenness and the implacable presence of this moment to have something of the Other World in it? Hear it now."

And the one so summoned can see the holy logic of the thing begin to foreclose on his or her old understanding of the deep etiquette the call deserves. And the defeat of merit is close at hand. So the radical etiquette of the prophetic tradition can prompt a kind of humility that moderates and lays low and ennobles at the same time. Translated, the summons could sound something like this:

We have come to you now, as you are coming to see. So this is what has become of you and your allotment of days. Your worthiness and your abilities on this matter have already been established. It isn't required of you that you feel able or ready, only that you proceed dumbfounded and prone to this, and that you are seized by an imperative that you are yet to translate, that must be translated.

That is all for now.

In a place and time that honours and practices prophecy, the prophetic role isn't something sane or well-adjusted people would seek for themselves or their children. It isn't a way of getting ahead. You could say that unworthiness rarely begets prophecy, but prophecy tends to beget unworthiness. It is not much to hang a religion on—which might be part of the architecture

There was one who recently left us to our devices, with winter coming on. I remind you of a few scraps of evidence he offered up in lieu of credentials during his time among us:

The flood it is gathering
Soon it will move
Across every valley
Against every roof.
The body will drown
And the soul will break loose.
I write this all down
But I don't have the proof.

—Leonard Cohen, "The Roof"

There'll be a breakdown of the ancient Western code.
Your private life will suddenly explode
There'll be phantoms, there'll be fires on the road
And the white man dancing...

You don't know me from the wind, you never will, you never did
I'm the little Jew who wrote the Bible
I've seen the nations rise and fall, heard their stories, heard them all
But love's the only engine of survival...

Your servant here he has been told to say it clear, to say it cold,
It's over, it ain't going any further
And now the wheel of heaven's stopped
You feel the devil's riding crop
Get ready for the future, it is murder.

Things are gonna slide, slide in all directions.
Won't be nothing, nothing you can measure anymore.
The blizzard, the blizzard of the world has crossed the threshold
And it's overturned the order of the soul.
When they said, "Repent, repent"
I wonder what they meant.

—Leonard Cohen, "The Future"

Now you can say that I've grown bitter
But of this you can be sure:
The rich have got their channels
In the bedrooms of the poor
And there's a mighty judgment coming,
But I may be wrong.

—Leonard Cohen, "Tower of Song"

And this last one, with a bit of cheek, he places in the mouth of the one who summons him:

I love to speak with Leonard, he's a sportsman and a shepherd
He's a lazy bastard living in a suit.
But he does just what I tell him, even though it isn't welcome
He just doesn't have the freedom to refuse.

—Leonard Cohen, "Going Home"

All of this is to say that the prophetic tradition begets a kind of elaboration of the soul. It begets a relentless, implacable etiquette that renders down preaching and its proneness to spiritual arrogance until they serve the place and the time to which the summons has come, often taking the form of speaking the troubled thing aloud, for others, while full of misgiving and a vague sense of being the pretender, and having no sense of authority. Eagerness to take up the prophetic work typically is a sign that prophecy and its authors have left town for now and are nowhere to be found. This is true for elders, too. No elder hopes they are one, but in private they know the claim that has settled upon them.

Wilderness

The Spirit immediately drove him out into the wilderness.
And he was in the wilderness forty days, tempted by Satan;
and he was with wild beasts; and the angels ministered to him.

—Mark 1:12f

We have before us the story of a boy. His age isn't clear, but the architecture of the story in its other versions (to follow) eventually whispers that there is something here of the onset of puberty that is one of the great prompts of human life, or can be. So this one is perhaps fourteen years old or so. The story is written in Koine Greek, the vernacular language of literacy over much of the eastern Mediterranean in the centuries on either side of the advent of the common era. But it was not written by or about or probably for Greeks. This tells us something of the convolutions of the time. The language of learning and literature is a foreigner's language at this time, and these people turned to the foreigner's language to record and circulate this story of theirs. And it grows more wrinkles. The story is a version of a bit of oral tradition of a liminal Jewish sect. The story has several iterations and probably circulated as such before it was set down in Greek in a backwater province at the eastern edge of the Roman Empire, an empire at its zenith just then. So there are degrees of cultural upheaval and existential dislocation hovering around the story.

The version we have here is one of three that are known. The other two are more elaborate and literary and argumentative. This one is the oldest, written probably within a generation after its subject's death, and it has the sound and tenor of a story more often told than read. It begins abruptly and without preamble. Ευθυσ, it tells us: *Immediately, suddenly.* Without warning is how it happens. *"Immediately,"* it says, *"the spirit εκβαλλει."* This word means something like "drove him out," or "banished him." From this detail a good story hearer hears two things: the man/boy is on the receiving end of the story's momentum, he's prone to it, and he's not there voluntarily or because he sees any merit to the arrangement. He is driven out, banished. In centuries to follow, this aspect of the story would be glossed over or abandoned outright as unworthy of the man this boy became, or the symbol the man became, and with that the bones of the story would be torn from it, and it would be preached as a set piece, a bit of formal decorum that ratifies the fix that was in from the outset.

But none of that tone is in the old story. The vocabulary used says it clearly, in a way that the spell of inevitability can be broken. It says that the boy would have chosen otherwise, just as you would have done. It is an aggressive word, to be "driven out" or "banished," and it seems to whisper without quite saying so that something had to be overcome or undone or defeated for the story to proceed. I think this "something" was the boy's deep running domesticated habit of staying home, of staying inside everything that the word *family* can conjure: safety, sanity, belonging, lineage, legitimacy, purpose, and future, to name a few. The end of this first sentence tells you plainly that *he was driven to the ερημον, to the barrens, the blighted heath, to "a place made desolate."* Our word *desolate* means "completely lonely," "a place left alone."

You are becoming an adept story hearer now, so you've heard clearly that this word *desolate* doesn't describe an inner state, an emotional condition, a psychological predisposition. It describes a place, one that is the origin of the emotional condition we too often take it for, a place made in aloneness that in turn makes us lonely. And that's where the man/boy is driven to, and that's why he's driven there. He'd never go there of his own accord, and he must go. He is driven to bewilderment, to have the wild visited upon him. That is not preamble; that is *amble*. Bewilderment *is* the story here, the bewilderment it describes and the bewilderment it incarnates or begets in or entrusts to the hearer. We're on the road heading out of town now. And all of this is in the first sentence.

Next: *the man/boy was bewildered for forty days*, certainly a number that has the mark of exponential increase about it, a fabled kind of number, numinous. *Forty* serves notice that the desolate land of bewilderment cannot be reached in a weekend. It's farther away from home than that. The land of bewilderment visits the proverbial upon the one driven there, and it is the home of deities or denizens not housebroken, not domesticated to the shrine or the temple.

And now they come. The story tells us that the man/boy was πειραζομενοσ. This word is generally translated as *tempted*, and if you know this story, you probably know it by that name: *The Temptation*. Having taken on a tone of the salacious now, and suggesting something of a duplicitous and evil nature in the one tempting, it seems to me no longer a worthy translation of an elegant and authentic telling of this kind of encounter. The story and the wilderness and the man/boy in it are all better served by this phrase: *He was tried*.

It is in the place where the human and the wild meet that the human is on trial, or where humanness is tried. Not "accused," not "innocent or guilty." Instead, "human or not." The wild is where the human is wrung and wrought, or prized. *Prize,* from the Old Latin "to take hold, to seize, to grasp."

That is not the *purpose* of the wild. The wild is not an extension of human purpose, something that can so often be lost on Green advocates and land developers. But the trying of humanity is the visitation of the wild upon humans exposed to it. Better to imagine that the wild is a place and condition free of humanity, where humanity—the conditions for being made human, or not—is conjured and annealed and tempered by something that is not human, nor proto-human, nor crypto-human, nor metaphorical, nor symbolic. This is a very important detail so often lost on people gathered in sedate domestication or virtual reality. *The wild is not an aspect of our imagination.* It is there, out beyond the edge of our imagination. It is not a petting zoo for the human soul. It is that which we cannot imagine. It is a strange place to be driven to for the sake of one's humanity, but wilderness is where the story is headed. And *humanity* is why.

A bit more about the wilderness. Human culture seems to me now to be an achievement forged by a glimpse of finality, of limit and end, a glimpse conjured by the willingness to see and to be bound by the consequences such a gathering of people has for the place that sustains them. Cultured peoples have seen what drawing down from their home place in the name of belonging there can do. They live within the limits their belonging reveals, or they agree to cease continuing in that way, in that place.

There is a tripartite covenant of deep sustenance that culture participates in. Human culture is sustained by what lies out there just beyond its end, a place you could call the *welt*. *Welt*, "the place where two things meet," is related etymologically to the verb *to weld*, describing "the joining of two things." It is also related to *field*, "the place where civilization meets the wild." The welt is the place from whence a culture's material sustenance and spiritual well-being are drawn, from pasture, farm field, park, fallow place, and all the riverine equivalents.

And the welt is, in turn, sustained by the wild, that which lies out beyond what sustains culture.

And the wild is sustained by our willingness not to go there, or live there, or plunder the place, or imagine it as a natural resource. We *could* do so, and we do, but the reciprocity of the covenant bids us not to, and continuing to do so finally will compromise our capacity to be cultured humans more than it will compromise the wild, as we may even now be seeing.

So the terms of the covenant are clear. The willingness of the human to be sustained by what lies at the edge of humanity, and to not grow beyond it, is what sustains the wild that the human never inhabits. The wild comes to us in the form of the welt, the place from which we draw food, and comes no further, and human culture is born there, in that configuration. Human culture, the covenant decrees, and all its rules and norms, suffers to the point of prolapse by direct exposure to the wild. Thoreau was probably, though inadvertently, right: wilderness is the salvation of civilization, but *only when the civilized are bound by the obligation to not outgrow what sustains them*. So, no eternal life. No making cancer history. No misnomers like "life support." No climbing every mountain because it's there. No following the dot-com millions to Mars when everything starts going south in earnest. The wild stays wild, the welt keeps us apart, and human culture is spawned by that separateness. Humanity—our crafted capacity to be human—is forged in a temporary, blistering, habit-breaking, rule-withering, meaning-free encounter with the wild. And that, no matter what else you've heard from the pulpit, is the thrust of the story we have before us.

All of this contention and torment over the human's relationship to the wild hovers behind the story, written as it was by and for townsfolk in a place that had seen plenty of deforestation and agriculture-induced drought, and this contention and torment comes clearly down to us in the words *driven* and *wilderness* and *tried*. It isn't new.

Tempter

The earliest and simplest version of the story we have, the one attributed to Mark, says that the Spirit did the driving out, and Satan did the trying. It is a compact, open-and-shut rendering that has something of spiritual apartheid about it. In the name of having the wind of imagination open the story a bit for us, I turn to another version, Matthew's, written probably a generation later, where the trying is more fully described.

And the tempter came and said to him, "If you are the Son of God, command these stones to become loaves of bread." But he answered, "It is written, 'Man shall not live by bread alone, but by every word that proceeds from the mouth of God.'"

Then the devil took him to the holy city, and set him on the pinnacle of the temple, and said to him, "If you are the Son of God, throw yourself down, for it is written, 'He will give his angels charge of you', and 'On their hands they will bear you up, lest you strike your foot against a stone.'" Jesus said to him, "Again it is written, 'You shall not tempt the Lord your God.'"

Again the devil took him to a very high mountain, and showed him all the kingdoms of the world and the glory of them; and he said to him, "All these I will give you, if you will fall down and worship me." Then Jesus said to him, "Begone, Satan! for it is written, 'You shall worship the Lord your God and only him shall you serve.'"

Then the devil left him, and behold, angels came and ministered to him.

—Matthew 4:3f

173

The "tempter" makes three offerings to the man/boy, each of them faithfully attesting to the physical and existential suffering that exposure to the wilderness visits on humans. There are formulaic offerings and formulaic responses. They are formulas because by the time this story was written down, it was being used as evidence to bolster claims of the boy's divine identity and lineage and purpose. In this context of contention, the tempting became a set piece, a bit of preordination theatre for the boy's innate and inevitably occurring capacity to contend with otherworldly adversity and prevail. The tempter became a symbol whose purpose in the story was to confirm the victorious, auspicious beginnings of the glorious march to Jerusalem, to Christhood, to the end of history and culture. And, I would say, to the end of humanity.

But the beauty of the story is that its real bones keep sticking up through the gauze of symbol and metaphor and doxology and set piece victory. Told faithfully, the hovering presence of the wild unnerves the metaphors. Allow me to try.

The man/boy is in many days of hunger. The fast has been forced upon him. He is asked to consider conjuring bread from the stones around him. It isn't a symbolic nourishment. And it isn't just bread. Bread is "the staff of life" for cultivating peoples, and the very emblem of civilization and of sedentary human life, historically a huge step beyond hunting and gathering. The offer is much more subversive than it appears. The trier would have the boy turn something of the wilderness into something of the civilized, extending the pall of a kind of progress untethered to its consequence. For the sake of ending human hunger and suffering, he's prompted to extend the edge of human culture into new places, to make the unpromising make good, to press those places into servitude as raw material, to *develop* them. This is the very hallmark of expansionist agricultural peoples. This was how Rome occupied Europe and the Middle East. The entire undertaking is what has become of the "New World." The Monsantos of our time take their corporate mandate from this trial. The "stones into bread" episode is an extraordinary, prescient, and hauntingly modern trying of human being. It recognizes that desperate, emboldened people can visit deep and enduring consequence, unintended and unawares, upon the world they rely upon, the one entrusted to them.

This intrusion into the covenant of sustenance (the subject of Chapter 10) begins the end of human culture. Now, you might recognize something modern, something of the compromise of spiritual ecology, something in the order of a mania for development and for problem solving that the West is well-known for in this moment. Perhaps you have heard stories of subdivisions being thrown up at the bleak edges of town or out in fallow fields, and of how bears will pass through the place and run amok, and of the mayhem and "wildlife management" that ensues. Well, the humans, with no memory of the place nor of whom it once was home to, think it is a subdivision where they, by virtue of being mortgaged, now belong. The bears remember their paths, even though the paths and most other markers of terrain are gone, and the wild is there in their memory. The wild has memory and belonging, and the human amnesiac has habit and possession. The human solution tends towards sedation, or relocation, or euthanasia for the wild—*and* for the human, as these things go. The memory that the subdivision has not always been subdivided, that it has not always been as it is now, and the conscience that goes with it, is euthanized by these solutions.

The formulaic trying carries more than the promise of food. It carries the promise of home, too, and family, and all that human community seems to come from, and it offers it up. It says, *"If you are the son of God, command these stone to become loaves of bread."* It means:

> *Make this place into your home. Be sustained by trading on your lineage. Eat your ancestry. Flex the unbroken chain of the human and the potent that is your rightful inheritance. Consume what gives you life, so that your life might continue. So that nothing of you ends, or is constrained. Belong. Lay claim. Exert dominion. Make everything in your own image.*

It is a modern trying of human being and human civility. The man/boy is invited to extend the pall of civilization, nothing less.

His answer startles. He thwarts the first part of this trial by giving in to the second. He loses by winning, as humans are wont to do in the mirrored hall of parable. True, the stones remain stones. But the Pentateuchal quote used here says it plainly:

"I'll consume my father's will and direction and example instead. Here in the wilderness, where lineage just has no purpose or purchase, I'll invoke it anyhow, and remain as I am, sustained and defended and certain and free of bewilderment."

This second trying ups the ante. The man/boy is drawn up to a high place and invited to jump. The trial:

"Your life, and maybe your humanity, is in peril. If you have a father, get him to father you now."

The Adversary is not dull. He has noted the man/boy's citation of his people's holy book, so he cites it himself. It is a scriptural throw down, verse for verse. And then, for a moment, the axis of the trial swings round, and the unthinkable is roused. It is the father who might be tried by this travail, as much as the son, tried in the form and the figure of his fatherhood. The son speaks up to save his father for fatherhood.

"Take me down from this height, he says, so my father might be spared time in this wilderness, spared what it might do."

It is frankly a strange thread, to allow the possibility that God might be subject to temptation. But that is what it says. There's a bit more to say about it, which might better appear at the end of this retelling.

Because three is the other resonant integer, the potent calculus, there's a third trial. The Adversary comes to the finer points of the prizing of human being. The Adversary tries him thus:

"Here are the principalities and powers of the world, here's where the power to do real good is, and here is the deal: turn from your old allegiances, and turn to the one who has tried you, and the dominion you

may seek will be yours. You want everything to work out, right? You want all the wrongs to be made right? Here's your chance. Here's how."

It means:

*"Have you grown accustomed to this contention now? Fond of it, even, now that you seem to know how it goes? Master of the one liner and the bon mot, all the authorities at your beckon call: shall we dance? Shall we betray all the particulars, the snags and corners and God-given wrinkles of this world in order to save it? Shall we subvert the ways of the world, pretending we are preserving the world when we do? Shall we have dominion, and answer every deviant or broken thing, and unbreak what we know to be broken in this world, and then keep dominion in hand, just in case? Shall we war on mystery? Shall we **know?**"*

The subtlety is stark. The Adversary knows an awful lot about many things, and he or she seems to know human beings quite well. The offers make a dead reckoning of the thread and thrust of human striving, in particular the deep uncertainty people have about how their humanity comes to be, and what it requires, and how it is to be maintained, and whether it is universal or inevitable, like weather, or whether it is an achievement far from guaranteed, or whether sanity and sanctity can ever prevail. The Adversary knows, too, that it costs human being mightily to come to the details of its time, to the confounding, implicating sway of the banal tragedies it can traffic in unawares. The Adversary knows of the sob upon awakening that is the lot of the lucid one tethered to what is illumined.

Well, the man/boy chooses the father God, as you may have heard. He has a perfect score of canonical refutations. He's young, but he's on it. With the Adversary apparently now in full retreat, and with the laurel garland hung on his brow, the man/boy is ministered to by angels and goes confidently into his life with a resolve beyond his years, so the story seems to go.

On that example you could hang the beginnings of a religion. It is a winning story of victory for those assured of their place at the head of the spiritual lineup, and it is certainly preaching-amenable. It's a story of spiritual victory, spiritual heroism, of the particularly adolescent kind. But it isn't the whole story.

That kind of shrug at the end just does not strike me as worthy of the sustained brilliance of the story that is there from the first "Suddenly." The brilliance of this story prevails here, too, in a kind of quiet cliffhanging there at the last victorious shudder, so quiet that the brilliance goes without notice. This is it: the ending doesn't happen. The story stops, but it doesn't end. Real stories are that way, to be sure. They don't swagger across the finish line, moral in hand, slathered with life lessons free for the taking. They aren't metaphors in story's cheap threads. They happen with the telling. They are incarnations of what they advocate. They make things happen. Real stories wonder if you the hearer are still there, whether you'd like to pick up the thread and ravel it into your days, whether it counts at all that you've heard it, whether you *did* hear it.

There's a crack, an opening there at the end. You remember that the young lad was driven into the heart of darkness by something called the Spirit. That's how he got there. It was not at all his idea to be there. And you remember that he met the Tempter, so savvy on matters of the human soul. That's who kept him there.

And then he's back in town. No mention of how he got there, or why, or whether it was his idea. Instead, there is this momentum of restitution, as if he would inevitably return to from whence he came, as if the whole point was to get back into the race with new credentials, as if nothing really changed out there in the wilderness beyond the Great Affirmation, the imprimatur secured, the seal affixed. The Good Guys: 1. The Bad Guys: 0. Just the next thing. Inevitable. And not a great story.

Adversary

Allow me to tell this story again, briefly. There is a boy, and there is a wilderness, and there is someone or something out there that seems to be unsurprised by his appearance, and so there is mystery. There is hunger and creed and the draw of home. There are trials of a kind, though it is not clear what is being tried, and there are solutions, though it is not clear what is being solved. Then there is an audience hearing the story, and a story being cried aloud. And there is consequence to the speaking and the hearing, such is the power of the incantation.

A young boy is sure, as young people can be, that his father knows it all. He is equally sure that he sits at the very centre of his father's life and times and purposes. The paternal arc of heaven is above and the filial life is below. His job is to swell to the full occupancy of his position. If you've had an adolescent in your house, or have been an adolescent, you know something of this, if the memory of it can be borne. His life goes its young way, and that doesn't change, and there seems no reason for it to change. And it won't, not without some big overturning of this order. If his father orchestrates some rite of passage to turn the son's attention to the wider world, this only confirms to him his father's omnipotence, and the son's place at its centre, and all remains as it was.

A father can know this much, if he is willing: he can know that his son is out there, at the limit of what he, the father, can understand and do in the world. Wherever the son sits, there is the full exhaustion of what the father can conjure and contend with or manage or ordain. Every son, you might say, is the limit of his father's omnipotence. (I write this as father and son both, and leave it to women to craft some similar symmetry for their ways together, if there is one.) So, for his son to ever know something of the wide world and his necessary but minor place in it, the father will need help. He needs someone or something that will work beyond the pale of paternity, an outlier unbound to the etiquette of the hearth.

Those references we use to speak of the divine in the world—those references left, anyway—so often use parental terms that it could have you thinking that this is the most inevitable and most enduring relation humans have had with their Gods. When the Gods are your parents, that's quite a lineage, a lot to live up to, yes, and a lot to ride on. Or be ridden by. The truth is that using parental terms to refer to the Gods is far from universal.

The parent/child relationship is not the most benign nor the most predictable construct of modern life. It is often neither the parent's nor the child's idea of a good time, never mind their idea of heaven. What happens when God is your parent? A punition/petulance cycle ensues, that's what. There are other things in there, but that is the emotional tone of the devotional bone house. Obedience is the spine of love. You can see this with abundant clarity in the creedal overlay of the story that gave the Adversary his various names. Each of them grants him the temptation function. In each iteration of the "temptation," the scriptural citation makes it clear that it is fidelity to the father, filial piety, and singular devotion that is being tested. But who tests such things? In the vernacular familiar to us all: Whose problem is this fidelity?

Clearly, the whole enterprise is not the son's idea. It isn't his problem. And the tempter isn't behind the scenes, pulling the levers of power and influence. Who drives the son into the wilderness? Our version of the story says the Ρνευμα, the Spirit, did so. If this is a test of faith, if it is the temptation story that most bible-based traditions hold it out to be, then you end up with one of two doctrinal threads. The Father is entirely confident in the fidelity of his one true son, and the jaunt in the wilderness is a kind of school-play level proving-out of that fidelity for the conversion project that follows and continues. Or, the Father is deeply uncertain of his one true son's fidelity, and he sets up this drama to adjudicate. Either way, if you take this as a story about Temptation, you end up with the Father in charge, dialing everything in. Then the whole thing is driven by the father's problem, the father's uncertainty, the father's need for a demonstration of obeisance, the father's need for a son. It is a monotheist's natural order, his or her moral order.

Enter the wilderness. The wilderness is there just beyond what the father can do or be for his son. The wilderness is everything the father and the family and the village and their ancestors are not. It isn't Home. It isn't Belonging. The story makes it plain that the father is nowhere to be found in the wilderness, and he plays no part in what happens there. Or better to say that the father's part is to absent himself, and this he does. It is strange that a monotheistic religion claims this story as a fable of divine omnipotence, demonic tempting, and human prevailing against considerable odds, since in the story the father is absent and silent, the demon is empathic, and the human is programmed for certainty.

The wilderness is not bound to the well-being of the son or anyone else in the story. It cares not a whit for peoples' cares or souls. The wilderness is obliged to all that is not human. And the wilderness is the very limit of human being. It is not hostile to humans. It is indifferent to them, an indifference that usually plays out as more hostile than any predator might be. And why is that? Because to an unvanquished childhood, the wild's indifference has no whiff of this "human as the centre of it all" to it, and for that, it is more punitive, more in the manner of a disapproving parent who has withdrawn attention in the name of discipline. *"How can you not care enough about my precious self to steal it from me?"* That's the callow muttering under all that "the wild red in tooth and claw" business that swept through Victorian prose. To the wild, you might say, an undisturbed, chronic childhood extending well beyond adolescence is the clown of creation.

Enter the Adversary, creature of the wild it seems, whose job it is to not father, under any circumstances, not to extend the domain of the home or the human by an inch or a moment. The story as we have it now saddles the Adversary with traditional names for evildoing and the like, but none of them authentically render the function he or she performs. The Adversary nurses the boy in ways neither the boy nor the hearers would recognize as succor. The Adversary serves the boy and Life best at this telluric moment, at the cusp of human fertility by *knowing human being well*, as you read him or her clearly seeming to do, and by burning away the childhood, the centre-of-the-universe certainty of this time of life. Maybe, in so doing, a life-tethered servant of the world who deeply obeys its limits—a human being—might appear. The Adversary superintends—no, inflicts—the means by which that might happen, and the Adversary is bound by the radical etiquette of the wild. You might say that the Adversary is the wild's way of being itself when people stumble into its midst, or are purposely driven there.

There is parabolic mystery afoot here. It is important to say this, and say it again: the wild doesn't play by the rules as we know them. But the wild *is* governed by a kind of ruthless etiquette. It does not preserve itself by subverting its wild soul. Who among us has not been on some camping trip or the like and seen the inexorable creep of civilization coming on, the intrusion of distant neon in what was once a dark night? How many times have you heard older people remember a time, not so long gone, when every developed part of your life was in their childhood a field of Queen Anne's lace and deer spoor? How many of you have harboured a wish that something of the wild would rise up and smite Big Pharma, or Big Agra, or the Military Industrial Complex, or your local bad-guy equivalents, Armageddon-movie style, just enough to reinstate the boundary line and lend us a little hope, and then forgive the rest of us enough to allow a little conscious ecotourism to help with the maintenance costs? The wild seems terribly vulnerable in our time. Were it to respond in kind to the indignities and rapacious practices we oblige it to endure, the wild would practice our kind of "desolation by payback," our kind of retributory justice. It would be the very undoing of the wild's other-than-human ways of being itself. So this defenselessness sustains the wild's soul, you could say. It is heartbreaking. And if the wild expires at our hands in decades to come, species by species, place by place, it does so as the wild does, not in soullessness, not in punition, but in wild silence.

So there is a reversing alchemy to this thing. The principal means by which the Adversary upholds the soul of the wild is by crafting humanity from very unpromising maybes, and by doing so in ways that are wildly faithful. He or she does so in this story by giving the boy every chance to get back to town unscathed, unshaken, and infantile. He or she hands the boy's childhood back to him, three times, *in this fashion trying to take it from him.* Of course, if the boy does so defend himself against the wild's power, by invoking lineage, home, and the rest, and if the boy takes the Adversary up on his or her offer of a reconfirmed, innate, inevitable illusion of humanness, the Adversary has failed.

The Adversary's job is to give the boy—and his village—the slender opportunity to have his world-serving humanity be born, but this has to be done with an authenticity equal to the task, and *authentic* means burdened and bolstered by every chance for failure and retreat and death and clever slander and nothing much happening. So the Adversary risks every possibility of failure for the chance of human being. The Adversary tries the boy, as you read, and does something for him that the father could never do. In partnership with the father's absence, the Adversary courts the indifference of the wilderness in these matters. The Adversary shows it the greatest respect and carries himself or herself in concert with its ways, all the while with a weather eye on the nascent tendril of humanity that might yet be born in these harsh conditions. The Adversary reinstates the Natural Order of Things through the entirety of this story, in the name of a human being being made. He or she does not subvert it.

Why? Because it is in being in close, deliberate, guided, and momentary contact with the humanless, unsettled, mysterious, naturally occurring jangle of the wild that human being is forged. It isn't in town. It isn't in the nest of the family, or in the web of relations in the community. That's where human being is acted upon and employed. That is not where it is made.

Town

And now to the missing piece of the story. The boy is there, affirmed by angels, fixed and tried and prized, so it would seem, enthroned on the field of his victories. So far, a disaster, though it wouldn't seem so to almost anyone reading it these days. Another spiritual warrior has been victorious, another inner child served, another unvanquished childhood about to be loosed upon the world, that's all. Filial piety resorted to and restored, another One True Religion ordained by the Father in the offing, the sanctity of the family polished and granted a place of pride on the mantle. And he has prevailed against temptation. He's made the team. He's won the gold. So, why go back to town? Whose idea was that? How did he get there?

It is just at this moment, when the attention wavers and the ordinance of tradition slackens, that redemption's crazy wisdom might appear. Life will never again be as clear, as winning, as sorted as it is at this magic moment. Life in town will be the trying of everything he saw and won in the wilderness. No one will get it. No one will be moved by what moved him. What will any of it mean to those lives lived amidst the cups and the dishes, in the madding crowd? The home he left is lost to him now, though he doesn't know that quite yet.

What you have here is a story with a parabolic curve, and it overturns every domesticated, sensible instinct, the very order of the soul, and it does so by employing the indigenous wisdom of the world. The wisdom comes down to this: *if you win in the wilderness, you lose at home.* That is what is hanging in the balance by the end of the story. Remember that brief consideration of prophecy, the damage done to anyone's understanding of merit and morality when the summons comes. You can see it here again. If this boy comes home believing he's prevailed against the armed and arrayed Forces of Darkness—which is how the story is typically used in the hortatory trade—then the rest of the story, the Big Story, the rest of the synoptic tradition as we have it now, is nothing but a victory march, an empty affirmation of what was guaranteed all along. It's an allegory at best, little better than advertising sloganeering, and a lousy story. Well, that is precisely where he is at the end of the story. He is on his field of victory, and his world is no better off for it. Making the wilderness his new home—*that's* what sanity seems to dictate. That is the Fourth Temptation: to stay in the wilderness, where it all makes sense, where you are so perfectly understanding and understood, to be on the right side of history, firm in your victory and God on your side, the denizens of the wilderness your new family, another Desert Father. It sounds like every Paradise Found story the mythically bereft West has come up with these last thousand years.

I say that this young man did not go back into town willingly. I suppose that it was the Adversary who, in his or her final act in the name of making human being, drove him just as ruthlessly back into town. Town is crazy, yes, but town is where the myriad skills of human being are employed and endorsed and recognized and needed. The wild doesn't need human beings out there in their all-weather gear, seeking sanity. It needs human beings to be human in town, on our side of the weld and what we know and what sustains us. It doesn't need *us*. It needs our *humanity*, planted in our corner of the world. That corner is what I meant earlier by culture. *Culture* is the place where achieved human beings live out the world-loving limits they have agreed to live by, knowing the wilderness shimmers out at the edge of humanity, fingering the welt.

And that's what prophecy does. It fingers the welt left by the brief and blistering contact with what isn't human. Again, in parable, if you lose in the wilderness—if the little black tent or red tent of your spiritual quest is brought to ruin by the proper desolation of the place, driving you back to the place that needs this learning about failure that you don't yet treasure—you win at home. Because you may end up there. You may yet become a storyteller, a master practitioner of failure. You will not be failure's ruler. Live in the sorrowed bustle of town long enough and you'll begin to see what the Adversary did for you and for your world. That Adversary was in your corner the whole time. You are now on the road to becoming—if all goes crazily according to Hoyle—an elder.

So this is a story of the conjuring of human culture and the iteration of its limits, in the form of an initiation story about a young man. What is at stake in the story is not rubber-stamped obedience to a remote God. What is at stake is the wildness of the wilderness and the humanity of the human. The whole thing happens suddenly, without warning, meaning that the young man doesn't see it coming, such is the pervasiveness of his childhood. The father is out there at the very edge of the story, coming no closer to the proceedings, knowing, I suppose, that to approach would be to subvert the spirit and means of the doings. The mother is nowhere to be found. The Adversary is the initiating elder, his or her love for the world *and* for the wild finding its deep expression in his work on behalf of one more human being perhaps seeing—and being seen by—the light of day. And the wilderness is the wilderness, just as it appears in the story, mother to all these proceedings.

Adversity's Right-Hand Man

We have legions of people now, across the dominant culture of North America and beyond, who themselves were never as young people claimed in any way this story describes. Some of them are, with noble intentions and with a probable retroactive longing for some person-making, childhood-ending ritual that never took place, borrowing or cadging from every existing culture still undertaking such work that they are drawn to or authorized by and taking younger people into woods or deserts to engineer some rite of passage. For the most part, so I have heard, they then deliver them back to a town and family utterly uninformed by whatever might have come to them out there, by this Fourth Temptation story. In so doing, they oblige the young people to endure all the slings and arrows of returning to a time and place that has no interest in the ordeal, no way of recognizing or employing what came to those young people or what they saw, no need of them. The temptation is immensely strong for those young people to set aside the event as trivial or poorly imagined, or illusory or stupid. Equally seductive, they could be driven to lionizing or fetishizing the event as conferring upon them the inalienable status of the Primitively Skilled, the Awakened, the Alt-Elect.

That might be a part of the story you didn't see coming. You are young, you are court-mandated, or new age–claimed, or self-directed. You go the requisite, desperate distance of a deeply unfamiliar shenanigan, keen and sorrowed and bargaining one more time to be on the inside of something right, or real, and you're heaved up onto the reef of Nothing Much Changed. What's the point? *The fifth temptation might be this*:

> Without a throng of elders to welcome the younger people into a home place changed utterly by their strange ordeal, without those elders being in on it from the beginning, the wilderness is trivialized, a sound stage where the inevitably victorious drama of the gifted, permanent child can be celebrated yet again.

"C'mon. You've gotta start somewhere." I hear that objection. Yes, you do have to start somewhere. But this doesn't strike me as a promising start. It strikes me as the great grief-bypass operation it probably turns into, despite everyone's best intentions. Instant ceremonies airlifted from exotic peoples and places, rituals that don't come from your home place, a home place that frankly remains a stranger to you and you to it with every ersatz ritual mosaic you craft, these are solutions to a dilemma so few seem willing to learn. In fact, they seem like solutions dictated by an unknown low-grade something that could be sadness and could be anger. They seem like wars started by bored generals, fires set by bored firemen. And they seem likely to keep this elder-free poverty—*our abandonment of what preceded us*—from us. A deep, learned, sustained, unalloyed, undiluted draught of our cultural poverty, learning how it got like this: that is what seems called for. That's where we are. If you're looking for your Old Timers, they're probably already there, on their own, wondering if you'll ever find them worthy of your dream for a better day, wondering if you going again and again to someone else's traditions might be the surest sign of how deeply they let you down as they lived, how irrelevant they've become. Imagine the dire thing this is for the old.

Given half a chance, these young people dangling from the thread of instant transformation could well go feral, their domesticity slipping, imagining themselves wild and free and dangerous. Dangerous: that much is true. That is the old adage—there's nothing more dangerous than young people who are needy unawares, who are not gathered towards what needs them. All of this has come to pass in a time and place where elderhood is in eclipse, where wisdom is relegated to opinion, where age is endured and not radically learned from and employed, where seniority trumps sagacity. That is no coincidence.

So, there is an alternative. Tell *this* story. It's a genius story, and in some fashion I don't pretend to command, it sees all of this modern confusion about doing the right thing coming. It foretells it, going so far as to make that confusion part of the story, the part that occurs with the telling. It is prophetic. Consider telling the story in something like the fashion you have just read it. You may be put off by the book the story came from, or by the traditions that have marshaled the book in defense of their ways, and that is understandable. You may be put off by this book, too. But I have tried to show that, perhaps, the people who preserved the story didn't know the subversive power of what they preserved. And there it is anyhow. No preaching, no creed, no being born again is necessary for the story to appear again. For whatever reason, in whatever rankling form, they preserved it, and I am grateful they did so. There's magic in it.

If you do think of telling the story, please work over it, breath over its coals, and learn its reversing, ramshackling power. And then please consider this: when the story is told in a society very short on memory and sure of itself, competence addicted, youth addled, and hope ensnared and drunk on bites of information, the story *is* the Adversary, and whoever tells it well is Adversity's right-hand man. An elder, in other words, soothsaying.

Then tell it to the kids.

10

THE FIRST ANCESTOR

I have come to set father against son, and daughter against mother.

—Jesus of Nazareth

reeze through a few world mythology compendia and you will come to the realization that many cultures seem to have foundation or creation stories that include one you could call "the first ancestor," or the primogenitor of the tribe. This first ancestor sets the cultural values and practices, and is often credited with entrusting the tribe with the best of its mutual and material life. In this way, the first ancestor is the fashioner of the tribe's soul and the ways by which it recognizes itself. That first ancestor is regarded, spoken to, and esteemed accordingly.

The first ancestor is often referred to in the academic literature as a *totem*. In fact, the word *totem* comes from a particular corner of the world, the eastern seaboard and Great Lakes basin of North America, where I live, from a particular language group often called by outsiders the Algonkian. The word seems better transliterated as *dodem*, and its more elaborate meaning is something akin to this: "that one who kept the first ancestor alive." In a monotheistic imagination, this would probably amount to *God*. But that is not the meaning of *dodem* as I understand it, not at all. The spirit of it is one of interitance, not as I understand it, not at all. The spirit of it is one of interitance, not commandment and obedience. It relies upon a cosmology of mutual reliance and sustenance, a place that itself is alive. *Dodem* doesn't rely upon a cosmology of debt and trespass and redemption, or an inanimate place that is the staging area for life. When people speak of their dodem in ceremonial times in the area I live in, they often use it in conjunction with their "Indian names." They are introducing themselves in a way that does not trade on family line but on kinship, by which they are making themselves known to the conjurers of their spirit, their Old Ones. Their animal dodem is the medium of that kinship. Think of the totem pole. Occasionally there is a human figure on it, often in a junior position or relation. That human stands for the human ancestors of the clan, as I understand it. But the rest of the pole is made up of animals or mythic beings, and they are the ones who sustained the human ancestors. They are the deep running ancestors of place. They are what make that clan and its ways of life indigenous.

Mutual sustenance is the archetypal relationship of life. So it is possible to say in contemporary English without any confusion of sequence or cause/effect that whatever sustained your first ancestor *is* your ancestor. You could call that One your original first ancestor. And for the traditional people where I live, all of those *dodemug* (plural of *dodem*) are animals. They aren't mascots, or pocket-sized symbols for characterolological inspiration. *Mascots* are what happened to the natural order when this understanding of ancestry devolved into human-centred DNA inheritance, when animals became exemplars of human traits. There are a wide variety of totem animals, and not all are of the hefty and awe inspiring power animal variety. Some are mammals, some are birds.

So here is a little mystery worthy of contemplation. How is it that some human cultures understand their culture and their humanity to have come in a fundamental way from animals, not from an upright Adam or Eve, not from anyone or anything we might call human? Do they just have a kind of mythic imagination that steps adroitly over the obvious question of how human genetics include animals? Not that I know of, no. It doesn't take selective ancestral memory to come up with this understanding. It takes *inclusive* ancestral memory. The Western imagination might now need a kind of mythic primal moment where the wild inseminates the human to make sense of this idea, but we might be in the minority there.

One of the principal acts of creation or conjuring for these cultures is nourishing or feeding or sustaining. These are acts of love, and they are architects of village mindedness. They are generative, generous, holy. So this sequence of sustenance is the web of environmental, emotional, spiritual, and cultural health and life, and *that web is the warp and weft of kinship*. A totem animal is that one who gave life to the first human ancestor, perhaps by giving himself or herself as food, and in that way, acted as ancestors do, by living in the presence of and according to the generations not yet come. (Our word *accord*, meaning "agreement" or "harmony," comes from the Greek *kardia*, meaning "heart.")

So, if the first ancestor is the one who kept your ancestor alive, then your lineage was maintained, yes, and *your lineage was maintenance*. In every way it can be meant, this cadence of sustenance is the lineage binding present generations to those not yet born and to ancestors and to the Old Ones, the first ones. How does that work, though? How can acts of feeding and the deep etiquette that attends them *be* lineage, *be* kinship? Not "represent" or "symbolize" kinship: how can etiquette *be* ancestry and kinship?

I read a brief caption under a picture of a Lacandon shaman in evident distress. He had asked the anthropologist present for aspirin for a headache. The anthropologist asked in turn why he didn't resort to his "traditional" ways to cure the headache. The shaman responded that the aspirin helped the Gods to do their work. So, *that's* how it works. Lineage in this understanding uses DNA and the other mechanics of inheritance known now to Western science (and uses other things as well) as the means by which this covenant of maintenance appears, informs the present, and continues recognizably through subsequent generations. DNA, you could say, is one way the First Ancestor sings to his or her grandchildren, granting them their days, and those songs *are* the lives the generations of grandchildren get to live. And the grandchildren's memories of their ancestors are those songs being sung. That is a powerful thought to think: you have memories of things you've no lived experience of. Those memories aren't yours. Those memories *are* your ancestors, murmuring their songs of life, songs that you get to overhear.

The habits of mind Western education entrusts to its citizens are in sharp relief when we question and wonder. Many of us have a mania for the monolith and the sequence and for "the one and only beginning." So this is a dilemma, isn't it, this business of the first ancestor not being human? You might say, "Alright, I can imagine this maintenance function being the way ancestry is passed down. But then who maintained the ancestor of the first ancestor, the dodem? It had to start *somewhere*. There had to be one single beginning. That's what the word *beginning* means." Well, that's one of the things that it means. Everything changes—everything does—when you put an "s" at the end of *beginning*.

Let's say that the dodem, the first ancestor, is a deer. Then who kept the deer alive? This question mutates in answering it, you see. Do you mean what food kept the deer alive, or do you mean what *underwrote* the health of the deer? Allow this idea of sustenance to touch your idea of what *alive* means, and what *beginning* means. The deer is an herbivore. So if you are thinking of sustenance as food source, you might say, "Young twigs, or tender shoots of anything. That sustains the deer." So, do you see? By the mandate of sustenance, the first ancestor of the first ancestor deer, the dodem deer, would not be the first deer, but the first born of shrubbery. Then, you ask the same question of the shrubbery, and by that time you enter into a kind of creeping regression inquiry that resembles the barbershop mirror that reflects the back of your head to infinity. But if you think of ancestry as something underwriting health, the unsettling of this "certainty of firsts" can happen. Could it be that the deer's *health* (a more generous understanding of sustenance or feeding) isn't found in food?

Health is a different consideration. Health is one's negotiation with the limits of health, not the vanquishing of those limits. Think of the current, almost uncontested view of health that animates, for example, our healthcare systems in North America. Health here has become the absence, or failing that, the heavy, tech-reliant containment of what compromises health, illness. Health for us is largely the default condition of an illness-free circumstance. So we don't really have a healthcare system. We have a disease management system in not very convincing disguise, and it is thrown into high gear not by the appearance of health but by the appearance of disease. That is why we spend about eighty cents of every healthcare dollar in North America in the last six months or so of a person's life. It is a war on infirmity, not a health crusade. If health is derived from the absence of what challenges or compromises it, there is no health to care for. Life is full of these challenges and compromises. Health, then, is what you manage to wrangle as you keep life at bay. You may not believe that at first, but consider how it may have insinuated its way into your dreams for sanity and for a better day, into your fears about your waning years, into your homeopathic regimes.

In this dodem understanding, the deer's life is food reliant, of course. But the deer's health proceeds in constant back and forth congress with genetic frailty, injury or weakness, age and illness. Enter the wolf. The wolf is the tooth of life for the deer, bringing the compromise of health to bear upon individual deer through predation, yes, and leaving the strong and the able to procreate. In feeding herself and her young, the wolf culls the weak, the lame, and the genetically disadvantaged from the deer's gene pool. The wolf is the guarantor of deer health in this understanding. The wolf is an ancestor of the deer, and if the deer were to congregate in ceremony, their aged ones might in making themselves known to their Old Ones murmur *meingen dodem*, wolf totem. By this reasoning, one very compelling to me, Big Pharma is becoming our ancestor, is it not?

So, you could say that by this understanding and way of living the elder is a visitation of the Old Ones, one's ancestors. By giving over his or her waning days to the young and the surrounding generations, the elder takes on the sustaining function of *old*, the totemic function. And then, in generations to come, the achieved elders are gathered up in kinship with the Old Ones and with those *dodemug* who granted them life, and they are counted among the Worthies and the Saints, conferring dignity and worth upon their heirs from the rafters. This is what elders in our midst are: *lineages of maintenance.* Sustenance is the currency of ancestry, and adversity is that currency's guarantor, and elders are the grace note of that currency.

Covenant

I agreed to an interview for a worthy literary journal, a kind of literary/ current events magazine in the US, some years ago. It's always a delicate dance, seeing if you can find those bits of your life, what you've been granted to see, that might be useful to people you'll never meet somewhere inside the questions you are asked. But months went by, and then a year or two, and the interview never appeared. I gave up on the thing entirely, largely because I was no longer sure that it faithfully carried what I'd begun to concern myself with by then. I was no longer entirely and uniquely The Death Guy, for example, I hadn't been for several years, and the unlikely appearance of the interview years after I'd done it might give it the look of a nostalgia piece. So I let it go. Perhaps it was this very subject—death—that may have been the sticking point for some on the editorial board of the magazine. But however it cleared the hurdle though, the interviewer wrote a couple of years later that it was on again, and the piece ran.

The interview generally tracked my take on the death phobia of our culture and other related things. Somewhere in there I was asked about what spiritual practices I might engage in to help with the work or its collateral damage. *Spiritual* is generally not a word I use to describe anything I do, or anything else, for that matter. I have no secretly spiritual reason for this. I only mistrust the ideological heredity of the word. I said as much. But, I told the interviewer, I do have the privilege of farming, which obliges me to a web of duties and measures that might come close to what he meant. We have sheep on the farm, I said. They are generally standoffish during the year. They tolerate our appearance in the yard while we are bale feeding them in winter, and are happy, it seems, to be rid of us come pasture time in late spring until well into the fall. But when lambing comes in early spring, we check on them every two hours through the still-freezing nights. We are close as they drop their young, in those first uncertain hours of scenting and bonding and nursing.

They are magic nights, the darkness and our work clothes a waft of amniotic funk, the other ewes keeping a safe, calming distance, all quiet and numinous. It is a privilege of the deepening kind. At those times, that jittery unwillingness to have us around seems in abeyance. I may be wrong on this, but it seems clear enough that the sheep agree to have us there. They give over their flight instincts for the moment to our safekeeping. That, I think, is their end of the covenant we have entered into. They bear their young on our doorstep, and they tolerate our presence in this vulnerable time, and they take the food we give them.

Our end of the covenant is to learn and contribute to their health, after the fashion of the *dodem*. This we do by carefully observing the thousand little things that are their days and doings (what I call "watching the farm channel"), by managing the pastures and mending the fences, and so on, and by slaughtering a good number of them, including all of the lame and the weak and those disfavoured by genetics, and most of the young males, in the fall. In other words, we do what the wolf does. Or what the wolf would have done, had we not interfered with fences and dogs and the regime of domestication and the like.

Here you find the innocence-rending sum of domestication. We have banished the Adversary, the predator, from the lives of the sheep. The dodem is banished. This means we have deeply compromised the health of the sheep. So, if we are not to violate the spirit of mutual sustenance, the αρχη (arche) of human life in the world, the covenant that binds us to the flock, we must take up the work—the soul work—of what we have banished. We do so knowing as they are born in late March what we will do in late November, by not hardening ourselves to the work or shrugging, by proceeding instead in mournful respect of what binds us, privileged and sorrowed in turn, obedient, alive.

In case you are wondering, yes, I know there are many wrong ways to farm, and yes, there is conscious and mindless cruelty at work in the industrialized aspect of the enterprise. And yes, there was condemning mail on this covenantal detail of the interview that came into the magazine, most of it of the vegan vitriol variety, crediting me with elevating murder to a spiritual practice, and the like. In anticipation of something similar, I ask only that you consider this understanding of sustenance and ancestry again before resorting to feelings of a moral order being transgressed by a matanza. And consider, too, that the indignation might be coming from the same place that marginalizes ancestry in the name of self sufficiency and self determination, and from a covert refusal to be bound to a natural order it claims to understand and champion and defend and continues to benefit from.

So, without this or some similar mythic understanding of health and ancestry and time and the gift of life, modern people continue to labour under the lash of a simpler cause/effect paradigm that delivers so many to the irreducible, mythically impoverishing conviction that all the universal ancestries date from one primordial time, the time of first principles and origins, where The One begat The Two. God begat Mitochondrial Eve (God knows how), who begat everything that begat me. And nothing begat God. And so (to go out on a monotheistic limb) God is my first ancestor, the parentless parent of my parents. Everyone who comes from people converted to a religion of the book, no matter their lineage or home place, comes from people who were obliged to trace their people via recourse to someone else's story, to the biblical bottleneck of a cultureless garden. By that story, Genesis, an eastern Mediterranean, sedentary, agriculturalist, monotheistic, abstracted, inanimistic religion's idea of a good time, is everyone's home. The West is in an ancestral trance, and the primacy of the nuclear family is a sign. Self-sufficiency is a sign. The withering of the elder function is a sign.

The Ache of Anarchy

We have slipped into the particular precinct of intolerance known to history as monotheism, and in the West we did that some considerable time ago. I know that this way of saying it probably causes offence in some quarters, and I don't know how to avoid that. Perhaps some wonder might be a balm. Consider what the consequences have been for the hapless generations in the West alone who have grown in life and ebbed from life awash in the understanding that their God is their father, or their mother. Consider the standard parent child dynamic. Among many things it can be contentious, rife with projection, inflected towards protection. Then there's the child, made in the image of the parent, who assumes the voice of the parent in a parentless place, Lord-of-the-Flies style, in the playground. All God's children, none apparently any older, more able, or wiser than others, are angling for approval, or resentful and sullen when the approval seems not to appear, some claiming to be more favoured and chosen even still, some claiming to be the boss's son or daughter.

If we are all children of the one true God, we are siblings of a kind, are we not? Consider the jangle of jealousy and the vying for parental attention that can inform sibling life, particularly when family life is principally parent-child life. Think of what the enormous physical, cultural, and linguistic differences among us have come to mean when we are obliged to that One Story, that one ancestral monolith that comes to us thanks to the linear understanding of time, that one parent God. They've come to signify closeness to or distance from the Source, the Truth, the Way. If we are all come from the same parent, what then do all our differences mean? Or, what have they come to mean? And with that has come this killing conviction: according to many, there are those who are God's people, and then, according to many, there are many who are not. Groups of people are pining for God's blessing upon their nation state, insisting that their socioeconomic order is what God had in mind for the world. And they are not very secretly haunted by a sense that somewhere along the way they got it wrong. Hence the pining. Hence heaven. Hence redemption. The "family of man" is mostly a jangle of monotheisms, each of which claims to be heir to the throne of the first born. Yikes.

If your God is a Father God, or a Mother God, he or she is first and foremost a parent God. Parents give you your life directly. It comes to you directly through them. You come into life through them. There are no intermediaries, no surrogates, no dodemug. That's the inheritance/debt model, the family dynamics model, of the West. It isn't a sustenance model. It is a burden model, a sin/expiation model. Everywhere the idea of debt has come up in the West (and elsewhere), the idea of trespass—the idea that this is not as it should be and that debt is a sign of transgression, and that the debt must be undertaken and paid, probably with tangible and emotional and spiritual interest—tends to come with it.

You owe your life to the willingness of your parent to accede to you, to make you, to grant you your life. And then, as your life proceeds, you begin to acquire something like a massive indebtedness to your parent for the care and feeding that has generally kept you from mayhem and starvation. Your life is, among many other things, a retroactive project of earning the perinatal allocation of parental attention and burden you enjoyed. Your parent stands at the centre of your making and of your life. The contemporary ideal of this arrangement is that parents reciprocate, and follow suit, and enthrone their child in the centre of their lives, *each one the completion of the other*. Yikes again.

This scheme presents massive dilemmas. What is the gravitational pull of the parent upon the child? It is rooted in need, vulnerability, subsequent debt. An obligatory obligation, you could say, one that you have no vote on, no choice in. So there is inevitably a bedrock possibility of resentment because of that pull. There are, of course, other tones to the relationship, but none of them replace or subvert the indebtedness, or the involuntary nature of it. And there are interpretations of these matters that enthrone indebtedness as the primordial condition for humans, a sure sign that we are finally getting it right, humbled and admonished in turn. Ancestry is for them the delivery system of primordial indebtedness.

But there are one or two hiccups in the arrangement, and they throw the binary reciprocity of the geometry off kilter. First, there is the matter of being the child of an omnipotent God. What might your parent God need from you? Not require; *need*. Leave aside the dogmatic convolutions that might keep theologians up at night or render them senseless at dusk, and you are left with the ordinary clarity that an omnipotent parent figure needs nothing from you. Absolutely nothing. *Your* needs are considerable, though, and the only mechanism available to you for reciprocity comes in the form of something like requirement, or commandment. You have things you must do to maintain your status as the child of an omnipotent God.

And then there is the question of grandparents. It is easy to see how cultures with an omnipotent parent God at their head understand their families to be symbols or reenactments of the God/human relationship. But then who or what is the parent of God? To whom does the parent God give anything like respect? To whom does the parent God give the reins? To whom does the parent God surrender the seat of honour? Where do human grandparents fit into this parent/child primordial order? What purpose or function does the centrality of the parent God leave to them? What do you have for your grandparents in a parent/child centered world, if anything, and what have they entrusted to you?

That last part is easy. If you live in a psychologizing age, and you do, parents are the fate of their children. Grandparents are peripheral unless they, by the default of tragedy or mayhem, become pressed into service as stand-in parents. If they do, they aren't much more than an echo of parenting past. Often they loom as a loopy example of parenting, which the parents themselves are responding to or reacting against. So the only relationship your grandparent can have with you is *through* your parent, by your parent's leave. You can see how all of this begins the programmatic marginalization of old people as "spent parents," "benign parents," "sugar parents," the Disneyfied version of discipline. I know there are rafts of exceptions, and I'm glad of it, and you yourself might be the beneficiary of that exception. But this is the modern Anthropocene West I'm talking about, and this poverty is there, too. It's there in spades. You know how old people are marginalized in the dominant culture of North America. They are marginalized in the religious traditions and in the family, and that's where the culture gets its poverties from in this regard.

The grandparent, by virtue of the parent's presence, will have an indirect, softer, oblique presence in the grandchild's life. They are the parenting-light presence. I can assure you that the custody/access assessment aspect of the family law process where I live has in times of family dissolution traditionally granted grandparents an ice-flow status in the lives of their grandchildren, and grandparents are brought to the fore only by a fundamental corruption of the parent/child "bond." Occasionally they have to sue for access to their grandchildren in acrimonious custody settlements, perhaps in the same way and with the same sense of utter anarchy prevailing that indigenous grandparents of residential school children petitioned for their grandchildren's return.

※

Think of a clock face, that old fashioned circular thing with the numbers all round it. Imagine that your life begins at a 12:00:01. That's when you lurch into motion. Remember, though, that many other lives were already in motion before your own. We could say that family life is reset to that time with your appearance on the scene. With that in your mind's eye, where on the clock face of your family life are your parents found? These days, parents are having children at an older age than in past generations. (Bear in mind the consequences for potential grandparents and their grandchildren of this trend: they are often so old by then—if they are still alive—that they are wheeled out at the occasional birthday for the sake of inclusivity, and their grandchildren remember them, if at all, as the wispy periphery of their early lives. Very likely, they'll always be on the "spent end" of old to their grandchildren. Very likely people coming into their parenting time later and later in their lives will soon have the look and the lurch once typical of grandparents. Yikes abounding. Not much to look forward to for anyone.) So it is likely that your parents are at about 5:30, even 6:00, when you are born. In other words, when you appear, they might already be halfway through their lives, or close to it. Where then, are your grandparents, if you are lucky enough to have living grandparents in your young life? They might be at 10:00, or 11:00, or farther along still.

Then look at the distribution of the generations across this clock face of family time, and ask yourself this: who is closer to whom? And you can see clearly that the relationship with the closest proximity, and probably with the subsequently deeper affinity, is the grandparent/grandchild relation. They stand closer together, one close to the way into life, the other close to the way out. The parental generation is about as far away from either of them as it is possible to be. And as the time goes by, that space between does not lessen or close. That affinity is a constant of intergenerational life, the older ones spiraling out over the nascent life of the younger, remembering as they go, each prompting the grace and merit of the other.

The parent life is a life of custodial maintenance, the grandparental life one of spirit cultivation by example, the child the beneficiary of both. That is a fair take on the natural order of family life. As people age, they assume their new place on this spiral, graduating from custodial parenthood into the deepened grace, watching that time of their lives pass from view as their children grow, cued to this by the blandishments of time and the generations passing. They bring the abbreviated, eclipsed functions of parenthood to help inform their grandparent and their elder functions, spirit guardians now, if they are spared, of the nascent generations.

Now this is enormously good news—or, more likely, no news at all—for cultures that practice elder-making and hold age in high esteem, all of that deepened humanity there abiding, coursing through young children's lives. Imagine, though, the consequences for this affinity of grandparent and grandchild when people come to their aging undignified, belligerent, reluctant, slighted, uninitiated into the mysteries of deepening life, surrogate babysitters. It makes the marginalization of and controlled access to the grandparents make sad sorrowful sense, in a way. The natural order of things seems contravened when parents occupy the spiritual and affectional centre of their children's lives.

What then of the Godparent? I've been asked more than once to be the Godparent of someone's newborn. It is meant as an honour, and I take it as such. But think for a moment what the word *honourary* has come to mean these days, and the honour begins to fade pretty quickly. It means "symbolic, euphemistic, a hollow tube taken for a moment for a pillar." It means "not really," doesn't it? And it has fallen to me to clarify what the parents are asking of me: that I appear at the appointed hour to augment and affirm their parenting? That I give them a much-needed break from the ordinary grind of parenting? That I lend whatever gravitas I can manage to some particular proceeding or other that maintains their place at the solid centre of their child's life? The God-parent pressed into service like that is not even a surrogate parent, but more like an honourary parent, a truly domesticated, house-broken version of a parent. A yes man, a yes woman. Does that sound too grim? Then ask yourself, as I have asked of the parents who have asked this of me: When does the Godparent God parent? If and when the "legitimate blood parent" is removed from the scene by temporary agreement or more permanent catastrophe, that's when. And what has become of the God function? It's just more parenting. It's no surprise in a culture that fashions itself around the God-as-parent paradigm that the God function and the parent function are indistinguishable, and the God-parent function is indecipherable, and the elder function is fugitive. It may have been for the sake of the grandparent and the Godparent and the elder that Jesus claimed to have come among his people to set father against son, and daughter against mother.

Imagine, then, the exponential poverty falling down from the rupture of that kinship of awe humans might have had with those who preceded them. Imagine the savage, snarling, stranger-in-a-strange-land aloneness in the world that seeps out into our days when that old grandeur turns to indictment and trial and conviction. In fact, you have no need to imagine. Only look. We are awash and adrift in the trial of isolation from the Old Story, in the primacy of the family and the One Family. And we are so adrift because of the grim eclipse of the abiding, relentless presence of elders in our midst by the parent God. It isn't going too far to say this: One God religions are single-parent families of millions.

So here's what might be the *crux interpretum* of our time: when your culture practices no initiation, no person making, no purposeful and forceful ending of childhood or parenthood or middle age, where is elder hood supposed to come from? Without the undercurrent of elderhood in the culture, then no matter how old you are, you'll always have your parents—and their approval or disapproval of you and what you hold dear (that is, whatever it is you hold dear apart from them)—at the centre of the life that has you at its centre. You and your appearance *made* them parents. Individuation and rebellion are the inevitable projects. They propose to end childhood, but extend it instead. Individuation and rebellion subvert initiation and turn it into another parenting/anti-parenting exercise.

But if there *is* an initiation into personhood, then who stands at the centre of your life? Nobody. And your identity? No one. Who do you replace your self-focus with? No one. Certainly not your parents, nor what you owe them, nor what they did for you, and not the rest. And if you have initiation, what becomes of your parents? They are not the arbiters, the architects of your inner life. (They are, though, more than qualified to be in on the inner life of other peoples' children.) That is someone else's job.

So, is ancestry just the sum total of all that parenting, all of that who-begat-who of the generations? Are we debt-burdened heirs of a chequered, alleged ancestry, even now foisting that debt—principal and interest—upon the youngest, an ersatz identity masquerading as a culture? And is history all the iterations of parenting that we as humans have come up with? If it is, then we have, all of us, been eternally and universally and exclusively and inevitably human, and whatever has maintained our humanity is out there to do so, and there is no crossover of kinship, and we are essentially self sustaining, with all the world seconded to that project. All of the world has us in mind, and we are *meant* by life: the clown of creation. If that isn't precisely the creation story of the West, it is at least the melody by which it has been sung across the generations.

I would ask you for a moment to consider the possibility that sustenance—maintenance of the reciprocal, covenantal kind, with its spiritual charge and spiral valence, its architectural presence there among the fundaments of life, being perhaps the murmur of life itself—*is not the domain of parenthood, not exclusively, not at all.* It is the domain of ancestry, just as the totemic understanding knows it to be. The first ancestor of your first ancestor is an animal or a plant or the sum nourishment of a given place and time, yes, but *the sum of all that*, perhaps, is what God is. Not the first ancestor, not the first parent, but the alchemical conjuring of purpose and awe and the cadence of days from the choreographed matrix of the death-into-life-unto-death, that ground of "why" into which we are born and into which we die. Our end of this choreography, as earth-conjured human beings, is to be willing to proceed as if this were true. It is this way of going on, sometimes heartbroken by it all, sometimes in rancor, sometimes not being able to, that makes of us ancestors worthy of the name. That ragged willingness, staggering out across the generations, is the rumour of worthiness that stymies and stuns and stirs the coming generations. Elders, then, are the means by which ancestry-as-sustenance slips the bind of parenthood. Elders are the way by which the human-scaled mystery of person-making, of spirit-making, comes on.

Think again of the wonder that is weaving for a moment. There are the warp threads. Typically they are the threads that you can see, whose choreography gives you the pattern and the harmonies of the cloth. And there is the weft, those threads beneath the warp, holding it apart and together enough that it is proper weaving and not piles of thread on the floor. *Weaving*: the seen draped across the shoulders and outstretched arms of the unseen. The miraculous "no visible means of support." Seeing that, you can see the function of the elder in a living community. *The elder is the amanuensis of the unseen, its onomatopoeia.* The eclipse of early family allegiance, the concentrated frailties, the utter extinction of potential, and the wisdom that can ensue from that—in this we have elderhood, and elderhood when it is honoured in the midst of a living culture and employed in its ceremonial, political, and economic life is that culture taking dictation from the unseen, from the Great Beyond. Elders do not take their guidance from their Ancestors and their Gods nearly as much as they in their tempered, archaic, implacable ways *are* the mutterings of the Old Ones that the rest of us, with respect and a learned ear, get to overhear. Not the weavers, no—they are the weaving.

⌘

Arche. This isn't a word that stands alone in modern English. It is, however, the root of a half-page of words in the standard dictionaries, and it deserves a second look from us now. As an adjective, it means "clever, sly, roguish." As a prefix, it means something like "chief, principle." It also has the shade of "first, original," which is something closer to its Greek beginnings. Already you can sense the dance in the word.

Now consider something simpler: the *arch.* In the foot, in the doorway of an old building, it is the curved shape that "binds by mutual pressure and can sustain a load." This dynamic, incarnated meaning gives us something like the primordial sense of the word. The arch was an extraordinary thing once. It was a mythic structure in that it was a *nothing that bore up everything* that rested or depended upon it. Peasants who had never seen one coming from the countryside to a newly built church to pray couldn't be persuaded to pass underneath it. They couldn't tell the diabolical from the divine when they saw it, and for good reason, because the arch marries the two.

The Roman arch was something of a squat, Mediterranean affair. It had a wide stance and a modest soar. The Gothic arch, its northern European grandchild, was a faithful sign of the devotional life of its time. It raced skyward, towards the remote one true God, and it did so by contracting its stance, by narrowing its contact with ground it relied upon. It would have swayed with the first strong breeze or collapsed under its own weight had it not the extraordinary ancillary structures (the flying buttress, for one) way up in the air to replace the wide stance it had forsaken for the sake of leaving this mortal coil.

The arch begins and ends not with the keystone in the middle up in the air, but in the foundation stones upon which all of the building—the arch and all above it—truly rests. And there are two foundations, at least two, to every arch. The word doesn't mean "beginning," except to a one-origin believer. It means "beginnings."

Arche is "that which *understands and bears up*." If the ancestral presence, the unseen but attested-to sustaining presence, is the ground of our personal and cultural being—and it is—then the agent of that sustenance is the foundation stones resting upon it, those upon which our personal and cultural lives stand. Those foundation stones are elders, and that under standing and bearing up is what they do for us. Real human life is inconceivable without them. Life without them is anarchy.

11

JUNG'S DICTUM

I am certainly no authority on Jungian psychology or philosophy, and though I did teach once for a couple of days at the sanctum sanctorum of all things Jungian in Geneva, I am distinctly underqualified to make any representation or summary of any of the old man's ideas or of what has been done with them since. With that in mind, I'd like to wonder now about something I've heard ascribed to him several times, and see if it might nudge this ten-ton travail of an absconded elderhood up the hill of history.

Though he contributed enormously to how we consider the individual psyche and its way of doing business, they say that Carl Jung offered up the idea that there was also something legitimate in understanding human cultural life and continuity in collective, even generational, terms. From his work I imagine that each generation of a culture answers to a particular description, assumes a certain slant on things, and generally is recognizable as in league with, but not a pure product of, the generations and ages that have gone before. And so it may be that each generation has a kind of inheritance from the generations that precede it that is more functional or purposeful than it is material. There *is* a purpose for each generation: that is the inheritance from generations past. The purpose of each generation? That is crafted by the times and the terrain each generation is granted.

And so it may be that each generation has a project of the spirit, work entrusted to it by the time and place in which it lives. This work the generations take up on behalf of this blue and brilliant world, and the particulars of this work are granted by the very heft and hue and haunt of the corner of the world that generation has for its home. So all of this spirit work is specific and local. Perhaps it is true that it is in the nature of *spirit* that it is *only* specific and local, that there *are* spirits, that they are all spirits of place, and of time. You might go further and imagine that the specifics of place in this world were not domains or possessions of these spirits, these Gods, in days of yore, before modernity had its way with them. They *were* these Gods. *They still are.* If that is so, then this spirit work is every generation's murmuring and mingling with the Gods of its home place.

The word *indigenous* is currently enjoying heavy rotation in the conscience communities in North America. It is used by the dominant culture to designate certain groups of people who are credited with an honourable, ecologically responsible past, yes, but in common talk today it is more often used to designate the character or nature of individuals, a kind of indwelling and irreducible dignity of the spirit. And the dominant culture's moral history—its inconstant conscience—has, for the moment, divided the human world into two camps, indigenous, and non-indigenous, and the moral distinctions are clear.

But a little etymological pause over this word works wonders. The first part of the word functions prepositionally, and it answers the question "Where?" It says "in," or "inside." The second part of the word describes what happens inside: "to be made," "to be crafted, or conjured, or born." So if you are describing someone as being indigenous, you are observing one salient feature. This person was born and made in a specific place, the consequences of which are considerable. It is not a word that describes a particular person's personality or character. It describes the particulars of their origin place. And it knows personality or character to be attributes or consequences of what you might call deep-running topography. The word imagines an identity that is not personal at all, that is not even human-centered. It imagines an identity that is place-centered. The particulars of place: they are the God-parents of human identity, indigenously speaking

When the warp and weft of the generations is woven, you can see that each generation's task is one of *discernment*, the ability to be on the receiving end of the harm and the hurry of the times; and *translation*, the ability to craft a project of redemption particular to what harrows and hurts in that generation's time. So courage and cyphering are involved, and nothing in it is easy or casual. It is something akin to inheriting a family farm. In times of bounty, the work is proper distribution of the bounty to the workers and to the land, so that some of this may continue, and the work is one of governance. In times of clandestine GMO infestation, sentinel species collapse, and climate change, courage and discernment might ask that the farm go fallow, that some fields be given over to forest regeneration, that the farm might cease to be a farm in its former tradition-sustained way, and you hope that this might be something that your farming ancestors might have done if they had to contend with the same things, and you hope that they might recognize their own love of that land in the stand you take. The work then is one of radical redemption. You can see that this understanding of projects of the spirit does not guarantee that everything will work out in the end. There is no "end." "Things working out" means only that you are not truant from the travails of your time.

Now, imagine some rupture in the continuum of urgency and indigenous savvy, that this inheritance of understanding is disturbed and goes instead from allegation to rumour to superstition and personal opinion. Imagine that "spirit work" becomes an enterprise for the psyche to entertain, and imagine that whatever purpose is served is entirely in the manner of self assurance, self esteem. Imagine that feelings of worthiness and safety have become the goals of spirit work, that spirit is personal, that the particulars of place are there for personal experience, and all the sordid rest. Imagine then that the sense of obligation to place and to the human generations to come is set aside in the pursuit of personal style, or survival. And imagine that all of this means that the spirit project of that given generation is undone, unspoken. What becomes of it then?

If the spirit work I'm talking about is truly an iteration of the time and place of the spirit, *if time and place are spirits*, then that work no more disappears than the time and place disappear. Consequence accrues to the truancy, the rupture. Whole wakes of consequence fan out across the countryside. The following generation inherits now the undone, unconsidered spirit work of its predecessor. The fingerprint of *its* time and place is the smudged fingerprint of those who came before, the needs of its time and place now gone to eclipse, burdened—no, ghosted—by the past, by that old confusion or abandonment or refusal.

And then do the exponential existential calculus of what such a misery of truancy looks like many spent and ghosted generations down the pestilential road. Consider what becomes of the world and its spirits and its citizens when it is all a tangle of the undone, the unimagined, the unwept for, when each generation's spirit work is to endure the consequences of its predecessors gone feral. This isn't ancestral inheritance anymore, or tradition. This is white noise. It's modernism. It's globalization.

12

THE ROCK AND THE
HARD, HARD PLACE

There is in North America a glut of old people: indelicately put, but accurate. Certainly many people in their twenties will agree with the description and the tone. This is likely the case in Europe, too. The presence of old people generally is a good indicator of stable and successful provisioning of the basic needs of life. Across the range of human history the proliferation of old people has meant that the material needs of the culture have been provided beyond a subsistence level, consistently, over a long period of time. It has meant the temporary ease of the survival instinct. Like the very young, the aged tend to be vulnerable to food shortages, diminishment in standards of living, civil strife, and forced migration and the like, and their increased numbers typically signal bounty and stability. Imagine then that in most of those times and places the presence of old people would be the most tangible expression and incarnation of real richness and bounty. They would be the deepest running achievement of their culture, the treasure and the treasury, the blessed and the blessing.

In our case, they mostly signal dominion over the material world and its limits, and the benefits of sophisticated medical intervention and its prolongation of life. The proliferation of old people has not meant the proliferation of elders, not across the dominant culture of North America. The probable reason seems to be this: the presence of elders in a culture turns out not to derive from an aging population. We'd be awash in wisdom here if it did. We are awash in information, and an often inarticulate kind of mass blunt force trauma we call "experience," instead. While it might be true that most, if not all, elders are old people, it seems just as true that not all old people are elders. If it is so that elders are made by and for the snap and the snarl and the deep and deepening travail of the times they are born to, then they are not an inevitable consequence of simply not dying any sooner, of just staying around.

Clearly the prolongation of life that we have wrested from the Lords of Life has not conjured anything like a proportionally grand number of elders among us. It may yet be determined that the extension of the life span by means that include our notorious resort to high-end medical technology to thwart the summons called "your time to die" goes hand in hand with the diminished number of elders in an aging population. It may be that when the late-middle-aged people among us refuse the invitation to join the time parade, it bars the rest of us from the soothing and solid company of time's ambassadors. We are lords of all we survey, and we can do almost anything we want, and we've traded elderhood for belligerent, prolonged, competence-addicted middle age and, when that finally fails, an agedness aggrieved. What a mystery.

There is nothing particularly new about this bereavement, it doesn't seem. If it falls to elders to ease the excesses of younger people by instruction or by example for the sake of the time to come, then the history of the West gives ample reason to imagine that something happened, or some combination of things happened, something perhaps unrecorded or unremembered as calamity enough, and it relegated the moderating voice of elderhood to insignificance. It doesn't seem likely to me that people looked around one day somewhere and decided that they would make a new world or a new world order by going it alone and leaving their elders out on the proverbial ice flow. It strikes me as more likely that, probably quietly or subtly, something happened to the institution of elderhood at various places that eventually produced "the West," and the result was that the institution itself was marginalized, or diminished, or shamed into insignificance. It may be that one of the signs of deep trauma in culture is the inability or the unwillingness to believe in what came before you. In this chapter I imagine what happened.

I remember being taught Greek and Roman myths in school, and I remember being taught why. Greece and Rome were the seats and the sources of all things cultured and worthy. The obligation of an educated white kid in the dominant culture in North America was clear. We were to trace the best of ourselves and our cultural life to the eastern Mediterranean. This is wondrous in its peculiar, tormented way. Something in civilization trumps the particulars of the great peregrinations and the passing of time and all the diasporas that human history, even just the recorded part. You may have no DNA sequence that binds you to Greece or to Rome, and yet the siren song of civility calls you to the paps, to the fountain, to the mythic source of myth and culture, where you will find your deep running self. If this sounds overstated to you, consider perusing the courses of study of universities throughout Europe beginning in the early medieval period, and see whether or not they were teaching the particular histories of those places. As a rule, they were not. With the plundered patrimony of their Holy Land in hand, courtesy of the various and sundry Crusades, they were teaching about the histories and philosophies and sciences of Rome and Athens, places that most of the teachers had never been to, places that had been in disarray for many centuries by then, places whose time had come and gone.

Come the Romans

Study the etymology of many English words, and you get to Rome. Study the laws that bind you and compel you, you get to Rome. The ways and means of real cuisine? The origin of the recipe book as we know it? Rome. Architecture? Rome again. Learned or not, Rome is in your sight and in your eye. The neoclassical period in eighteenth century European culture, a cover story for the anguished spiritual dead end of the time, was nostalgic for and drunk on the old glories of a proper Roman empire, and the sagging nations of the continent fanned out across the world to make empires of their own. Many European philosophers of the nineteenth century, grappling with the relentless rate of change that swept them along, went to the history of Rome for solace and for a map detailing the way to a civility they felt to be slipping from them. For something that passed from the centre stage of Western life so many centuries ago, vast though it was at the time, Rome has a remarkable presence and persistence in the Western imagination. It is in many ways the birthplace of the modern era. Some say that Rome is the spiritual parent of Europe. I'd say that Rome haunts the European psyche, banging on the walls in the dark.

The Romans conjured many Romes from one, such was their particular imperial genius. They were masters of the mechanics of war for centuries, their routine and their discipline overturning the vainglory and heroism of the locals. Here is something mysterious, a kind of sensitivity you may not credit to any imperial enterprise: in war, they attended to the vagaries of local culture, custom, language, and locale. The memoirs of their generals are replete with examples of their attempts to learn the particulars of their adversaries. All their wars were local, not provincial, not global. Once victorious—and for centuries their victory was all but ensured—they ignored the particulars of place almost entirely, and built and settled in the manner of Rome, and planted Rome everywhere they went.

The Romans shipped their defeated enemies—not their leadership, whom they usually killed, but the surviving rank and file soldiers—to the known ends of the empire and beyond. There, in exchange for their lives, they became Romans, to fight for Rome, and to beget Rome again. This was conversion of a kind, and in the manner of conversion the choice was at once compelling and illusory. The resettled, retired Roman soldiers were pensioned off in whatever new land they had wrested for Rome, they took local women for wives, and they made a generation of children who were from both the Roman and the indigenous point of view not quite fish nor fowl. "Roman" was the default identity available to them and to their children.

In the manner of conversion, the grandchildren grew so accommodated to tribal defeat and the passing away of tribal memory that they probably articulated it as a new possibility, as deliverance from tribal darkness, as freedom. In the first generation it was trauma and Armageddon, in the second coping and surviving. In the third the same thing was a new God. You had tens of thousands of conscripts who were fringe dwellers, who never saw their homelands or heard their languages again in their lives, Romans by edict who had never seen Rome, enforcers and victims at once of the Pax Romana, begetting generations of progeny who were secretly bereft of ancestral continuity. No surprise, these generations often became the local ruling gentry. This is foundational to the Europe you and I learned about in school, and goes a long way to explaining why we were obliged to look to "the classical world" as the true home of our honourable and civil selves.

This remarkable capacity to overwhelm local culture and to imagine one's victorious self and soul as the guardian and repository of all things cultured, and to imagine the locals as in some fashion awaiting this particular enlightenment, and to fantasize that all of it was conjured by the act of conquest and by the will of the Gods—this is a hallmark of empire. The Roman Empire was not a clearing house for hyphenated identity or ancestral diversity. Certainly not a tolerant polyglot, not a precursor of any league of nations, the Empire consumed what it conquered and disfigured those people and places in its image. The Romans were road builders, field clearers, ground breakers, planters, and harvesters. There are roads in England and France today, for example, unnaturally straight for up to several kilometers and severing any restraint the local terrain might have bound them to, and they are all Roman, all paved now and still in use.

And the Romans were fabricators of paganry. They *appeared* to convert the surviving indigenous peoples to Romandom, but the genius of their governance was that they more decisively *converted the land*. It was the Roman way to make the countryside feed the town. That's what it was there for. Unbroken terrain to the Roman was just that: a place that had yet to be developed, that was yet to happen, potential incarnate, pre-civilized. Mind you, they didn't have a high regard for people who worked the land either. Our word *villain* meant "the scoundrel in thrall to the villa for his life," and the word carries the sneer to this day. Agriculture on the Roman scale was the prosecution of war by other means, and when the soldiers were pensioned, they were converted to farmers. *They* were the real conquerors. They conquered the land in a way the itinerant army could not.

Roman agriculture was a war on local Gods, on a way of life that knew God in the terrain and the weather and the whorl of springs and the oak and yew groves. In the hands of land developers, the ploughshare is a sword, and the Romans broke ground with that blade, and as they did so, they put to flight any way of life that venerated the land as the land, as the stuff and body of the Gods. It should be no surprise, given that the United Nations is fundamentally a Western invention and so to some degree institutionally beholden to Roman precedent, that the façade of the UN building in New York carries the biblical injunction to "beat swords into ploughshares." This is precisely the Roman programme for pacification of the locals and conversion of them to the global economy of the time, the Roman Peace. Neither the conquered people nor the conquered grounds could distinguish the sword from the ploughshare. Still, history has shown that the conversion of the land prompts the conversion of the people.

The Romans, by that means, made pagans out of indigenous people. The moral syntax of the Roman word *pagan* means having the quality of village life and village mindedness. It means living at a distance from the seat of power and the arbiters of orthodox belief and observance, and living at the shadowy edge of a ploughed field. It designated undomesticated, unbroken bush dwellers, those for whom the light of culture of the eastern Mediterranean kind had not yet dawned. It is a powerful distinction to make, with powerful, enforceable criteria. The Romans didn't invent *pagan*, but they did make pagans out of the country people they conquered. Though the word at this time meant something like "those on land unbroken," the change in meaning to the modern European sense of *pagan* as "enemy of the true religion" tracks the arc from agricultural practice to systematic ethnic cleansing. Through a programme of shame and systematic desecration, they marginalized traditionalists, drove wedges of privilege between families, rewarded collaborators, confounded and demeaned the local languages, compromised indigenous lifeways. They made another kind of war on the indigenous aptitude for living alongside ancestors. Though certainly not the history many of us were taught to emulate or admire, it is there, stones in the sediment of the Europe that founded America.

As the Romans went their civil, ruinous way, they made a point of learning from the newly conquered something of the traditional histories, alliances, and enmities of the area. They learned these enmities not to conclude them but to collude with them and deepen them, to further them, prey upon them, employ them, turning the conquered against the not-yet conquered, holding themselves out as the new, powerful ally who would right ancestral wrongs, securing and obliging and forcing the newly conquered to raise the foreign conqueror to the status of a mysteriously benevolent foreign God. Sleeping with the enemy began in earnest. This is a lesson and example relied upon heavily by Hernando Cortes as he made his ruinous way across Mexico early in the sixteenth century, and it made Cortes a dark legend in the old and new worlds.

Well okay, all very interesting, you might think, but this was an awfully long time ago to be of much consequence now, and this is an obscure way of wondering about what became of elderhood here in North America. Surely that shame and desecration and culture trauma and loss of sacred sites and ancestral ways was local, and far from pandemic, and surely it has long since been eclipsed by the benefits of development and progress and general tolerance. Here is a story, strange and true, something I witnessed, that makes me think that, at least in the England that many of my ancestors called home and then fled, that trauma is still there in the wings.

> While on a teaching tour of England some years ago I had a rare off day that enabled me to visit Bath. The city is built on the site of thermal springs, and there is a long history of human habitation. As beautiful a sight as it is, the story of the place is that

much more remarkable, because the springs themselves were lost track of for hundreds of years. The loss itself is probably a telling sign of dispiritedness and inanimism and ruin. Mineral-rich water coming up from the ground from some unknown source, hot enough to soothe and redeem but not to injure, appearing without connection to any merit humans may have achieved: abundant evidence of the regard of the Creators for the creation and for humanity. How then do we account for literally and utterly losing sight and sense of them for centuries? It is truly an example of the moving and shifting sands of time.

If I remember correctly, a gentleman in the Edwardian period was having some trouble with a wet basement of his townhouse, and the workers he hired to fix the problem dug down until they hit warm water and what turned out to be thick sheets of hammered lead. This was perhaps fifteen or more feet below street level, and you can see the excavation today, plunging down to restored Roman ruins. You stand there gawking as I did, and you realize that the ways of wind and water and human culture and agriculture move the world's skin relentlessly and move tons of ground extraordinary distances. Think on this for a bit and you realize that the terrain you inhabit as likely as not bears no resemblance to what that place was even a few hundred years ago. You could go to sleep at home, and going back—or forward—in time, awake in a panic of foreignness, though you lie in exactly the same spot.

Down I went into the restoration. The exhibits made clear the likely succession of occupiers of the site, noting that it was always regarded by them as numinous or sacred. When their turn came, the Romans developed and built up the place into a series of public baths and spas. Imagine to what depths of disorientation the defeated local people must have been driven to see a sign of their Gods—or perhaps their Gods themselves—disfigured by modernization and development, by desecration. The Romans hedged their bets, though, just in case the place had not been entirely rid of the indigenous deities. In the restoration archaeologists found caches of offerings and Latin prayers, many of them legible still, pleading for bounty for themselves and punishments and plights of the most acute and elaborate kind to be visited upon their foes and neighbours.

Attaching myself to a small group enjoying a guided tour, I was getting the official version of the place's history, the standard state-sanctioned history where no one ever really did anyone else any harm worth recognizing, where situation ethics and what now gets called cultural relativism often absolves the aggressor. This is typically the kind of narrative that traffics in the idea that time heals, that current understandings of justice or mercy or humanity have no place in interpretation of the historical record, and that anyway, the past is gone, and that this display is for edification and for entertainment. It is certainly not for grievance, or for reviving ancestral rites and wrongs.

The guide lingered for a few moments over what remained of the lifeways and signs of what she called the pre-Roman inhabitants of the place. As you'd expect, she referred to them as "they." Moving on to the Roman period, the tone and the pace of the presentation picked up noticeably. This was partly because there was more Roman stuff to describe and talk about, but that didn't really explain the presenter's not very subtle pride at the accomplishments in evidence around her. As she talked about the demonstrable merits of development and creature comforts wrung from the place by the Romans, she referred to them several times, surprisingly to me, as "we." By this she claimed them as kin.

This strikes me as remarkable for a couple of reasons. First, it is a safe bet that the Angles and Jutes and Picts and whoever else might constitute the indigenous peoples of that part of the world would never have understood themselves as pre-literate, pre-agricultural, pre-Roman, or pre-anything else. This phrase is a pernicious recasting of a history that never was. These peoples did not volunteer for a fleeting appearance in *the* historical record of the advent of Western culture. They were not people who awaited the extreme unction of civility courtesy of these visitors, the Romans. In other words, they are not who they are because the Romans did what they did to them and their homes and their Gods. The Romans did not grant them their place in history. There is a second noteworthy thing. Assuming the genetic admixing that ensues with every conquest, and assuming that the tour guide was native in some fashion to the place that employed her, there is a very good chance that these "pre-Roman" inhabitants are present in her DNA, perhaps even in something like a measure equal to the "Roman" contribution. As such, they would qualify as her ancestors, at least as legitimately and demonstrably as those of the mongrel monolith that issued from Rome and the Roman occupation.

As was I, this tour guide was probably subjected to a state-sanctioned education that included introduction to "classical civilization," the waxing and waning of Greece and Rome. It is not a subtle education. She was likely obliged to learn these places and peoples as the apogee of culture. It is no secret that the West traces its imagined and actual civility to Greece and to Rome, and state-sanctioned education has its ways of mingling cultural and personal self esteem with genetic and spiritual lineage going back to The Source. Anyone coming from a class-conscious social environment would be prone to this kind of ancestral cherry picking. When conquest is involved—and the history of the West is largely conquest-driven—this entire process of the crafting of culture means that there is welcome lineage, and there is disposable lineage. There are official ancestors, sanctioned by self-esteem and selective reading of the historical record, and there are outliers, miscreants and pre-ancestors and pagans, banished by education and conversion and by the language of "us" and "them."

The rank and file Roman soldier and settler, conscripted at sword point, working off that mysterious debt incurred by being defeated and then gathered into the fraternity of the conqueror, bore no resemblance in language, custom, or appearance to his military superiors, most of whom would probably have been native Romans. Imagine then the confounding picture presented to defeated peoples by the Romans: an array of superior armament, tactic, and discipline, seeming to be destined and ordained for victory, a polyglot assembly, a supracultural single people who answer in a slurry of accents to one identity, a macabre combination of discipline and diabolical obedience to an invisible civilization, a military and mythic monolith of ruined indigenosities assembled from the wide conquered world. In a generation, two at the most, the Romans, who were organized by homelessness and culture loss into a monolithic military colossus, combined to make another facsimile of the one true city and people and way: Rome. They did so across southern France and Germany, across Spain, across southern England. The marvel here is the deadly efficiency of the eclipse of language, custom, religion, and culture, both on the perpetrator's side and the victim's side. On both sides of the conquest there was homelessness, incarnate and contagious and pandemic. The end of local culture as the beginning of civilization: by this the Romans would have been their adversaries' end times and apocalypse incarnate. And so they were. And so they remain.

Come the Christians

What follows could be taken for a slander of someone's—anyone's—Christianity, and courtesy requires that I speak to that. It is fashionable now in certain places to demean Christianity, and religions in general. Etymology again. The root of the word *religion* is the same as that for *obligation* and *ligature* and *ligament*. It means "to bring into temporary alignment disparate things." There is no moral order or outrage required to do so. (The miraculous structure of the human knee is a good example.) In the case of *religion* it means "to reiterate the alignment," and assumes some dissolution of a prior or primordial alignment. The list of excesses perpetrated for the sake of religion is egregious and heartbreaking and long, and can understandably prompt many to reactionary or ersatz religions of their own, and has. Of course, there are Christians who have lived and died for the sake of a genuine, just and better world, who still do, and their religion enabled them to do just that. What follows wonders over the ways in which a religion relying on the Jesus example became a Christ-reliant systematic religion, and transplanted itself across Europe, the surge and the slights and the sorrows of it. I welcome Christian apologists and practitioners to the fray.

Almost wherever in Europe or the mid-east Rome withered, two things followed: the anarchy of interregnum, and Christianity. Despite being targeted at times for persecution by Roman authorities in the early days of its missionizing project, Christianity became much more a beneficiary than a victim of the Roman way. In many places, within a couple of centuries of its appearance, it became the religion of the realm. Rome is the geopolitical forbear of Christendom in the West. The Vatican's presence and endurance as a sovereign country inside Rome's city walls is no coincidence. The Christian religion in all its early wrinkles fed upon the example and the detritus left behind by fleeing Romans. The Roman example was to set people against people (often people who shared ancestry), and simplify the particulars of culture, language, and kinship until there are but two kinds of people, Romans and non-Romans, Romans and barbarians. This they achieved by the magic stick of instant inclusion and citizenship. By this remarkable sleight of hand they killed the adversity by converting the adversary. That was civilization's messianic way. That was the missionary's way, too. It still is.

Rome began dying away from the outside in, from the empire's outer reaches at the edge of Europe and back towards southern Italy. In the case of England, or example, this was early in the fourth century of the common era. In France, Spain and Germany, it was somewhat later. Its demise prompted what is usually called the Dark Ages in Europe, which refers to the waning practice in Rome's absence of keeping track and recording. It prompted the anxious devising of civil codes and legal codes across urban Europe to cope with the administrative and legal vacuum created by Rome's withdrawal of administrative funds and higher ups. It prompted the calcification of Latin as the language of learning and prayer where almost no one could speak Latin. There was no revival of indigenous wisdom or ritual practices or pride, no restoration, no return, no council of truth and reconciliation. The revenant, the shards of civility, went feral in some fashion, and into this jangle of endings and deep uncertainty strode Christian missionaries, opportunists blessed by Rome and assured that God had cleared the decks and made this place and time for them and their good news. This is the period of church and monastery building. This is the period of the amassing of land holdings by the church, fetishizing "The Book" in places where virtually no one could read. This is the time often referred to as the one in which Christendom preserved civilization. Briefly, here's how that preservation began.

It doesn't seem that the man known to history as the apostle Paul, who was once Saul the persecutor of Jesus believers in Israel, met the man-God he worked for. He wrote that he was claimed by summons and not by familiarity, and so there is no sign that he got his understandings from the one he ascribed them to. But Paul does come into the historical record in the first generation after the crucifixion, in what later came to be called the first century Anno Domini, and most certainly he had contact with those disciples who remained in or around Jerusalem. The early Jesus believers were struggling to find their place among the fractious doings of a normative Judaism that was under the dominion of the Roman Empire. There was sedition, subversion, collaboration with the Romans, and struggles to achieve a shared understanding of Judaism as Jews bided their time and tried to manage the end-of-time advocates among them (John the Baptist would be one kind of example), some of whom believed that armed insurrection was a religious duty. No doubt there were echoes of similar cultural strife going on at the same time in the west of Europe, for many of the same reasons.

Paul's mission to the "Gentiles" was the deal he struck with the Jerusalem-based Jesus-believing Semitic cult that was heir to the remnant order of the original disciples. The entire enterprise was Jewish in the early going, as was Paul, self-consciously so. Had it remained so it is not clear you or I would ever have heard of any of it. The contentiousness that arose early on was whether it should remain Jewish. Those who thought so anchored what became the "eastern" and subsequently Eastern Orthodox aspect of Christianity. Paul's offer to them was to separate entirely from the Semitic root of the Jesus example. This he did by moving west, yes, but his principal achievement was in the imagination, and in what he seems to have learned from the Roman example.

Paul was in the business of winning souls for Christ and for God. His particular genius was to take aspects of Jewish and Hellenic philosophies and craft what amounts to a conversion-friendly understanding of the soul. Paul conceived of the soul as a culture-free, language-free indwelling sameness among people everywhere, something that belonged to God. And he crafted a metaphoric understanding of the culture-bound example of the historical Jesus: though Jesus himself was Jewish, his example and his message overturned Judaism, and any religion or philosophy of the period, and introduced a new world order. Paul employed a few Jewish concepts, and a few concepts from Hellenic philosophy, but he subverted them fundamentally. Primary among them was the ritualized marker used to designate and achieve kinship among men, circumcision, which he made into "circumcision of the soul," the cutting away of the worldly allegiance to culture, tradition, language. This, Paul preached, was a precondition for citizenship in the culture-free, God-ordained kingdom that Christ initiated. Paul proposed to free the flesh-bound, culture-entombed soul. Jesus's death and assent as the Christ was the effective end of culture as the root of identity, such was Paul's preaching, and the soul was the supranational constant of human life, the only place God was to be found in the world.

This was the principal expression of the love that was the heart of the new Jesus-believing faith, as Paul understood it. Christ loved the undifferentiated, post-cultural soul in every person, and *only that soul*. Any tradition anywhere and any traditionalist that predated or resisted this good news was left out in the dark, unredeemed, retroactively in disgrace. In Paul's preaching, Christ's love eclipsed and cancelled culture. Inclusion in the Kingdom of God required the disavowal of identity or membership in the culture into which one was born. In one imaginative sweep, Paul crafted an understanding of love that set those loved by Christ at odds with who loved them and who had preceded them and granted them their mythic, imaginative and poetic lives, and their lives' meaning, and their place in the scheme of things. Devastatingly, the Christian love Paul imagined required and achieved the end of culture, and equated the end of culture with the entry of God and God's affection for humans into the world.

Christ's love was anarchy, in every sense of the term, the voiding and the devastation of the web of belonging that bound people to the world, to each other, and to their ancestors, the fundamental *arche* of their lives. No village hierarchy rooted in tradition or merit; no enduring, time-proven ceremonial mingling with the dead; no esteemed tradition that granted the old meanings to peoples' lives; no veneration of elders. All of it gone in the name of love. The old kinship was replaced by the fellowship of all believers. The old village-mindedness was replaced by the Kingdom of God, freeing anyone from the useless allegiance to what had come before. Let the dead bury the dead, let the ancestors care for each other, now that the new believers won't be caring for them. There, on the other side of this chasm and chaos that the Christian message opened in the town square and in the village soul of every place it went, was the Kingdom of God. The Kingdom of God became the monolithic suburb that believers, now ancestor-free, were invited to take up residence in. And Paul was its Charon. The Land of the Dead was a ghost town, because the ancestors of pre-conversion times were hell-bound.

Eight or so centuries later, the programme of Christian missionizing of the European tribes bore all the signs.

And it is right that every priest eagerly teach Christianity and crush all heathenism; and forbid the worship of springs, and necromancy, and divination and incantations, and the worship of trees and stones, and the devilish trick

people perform in which a child is dragged across the earth, and the super-
stitions practiced with various auguries on New Year's night and at pagan
shrines and elder-trees, and a great many other errors which men practice
much more than they should.

Wulfstan, "Canons of Edgar" in Liuzza

The resemblance of the mechanics of the Roman Peace to the spiritual architecture of the Kingdom of God attributed to the risen Christ
is no coincidence. That realization can shock, or it can confirm, or both,
depending on grievance or grace. You could say that the Roman Empire
founded the West, but Pauline Christianity made the West. If one of the
acts of empire is the bringing of disparate parts into order, then order
the vagrant and indigenous and pagan ways of Europe the Christian
Empire surely did. The incarnations of this ordering were many, but
the mechanics were clean and clear and few. From the gospel stories of
and about Jesus, Western Christendom cadged and cajoled a narrative
arc whose prospect and purpose was to end the diversity of humanity
by ignoring, trivializing, or demonizing human culture, its specifics,
its deep running stories, its histories, it's allegiance to ancestors and to
Gods of place, its indigenosities.

For the Roman and for the Christian empire builder the end of
diversity and culture is the beginning of peace. The eclipse of everything granting meaning to this life is the beginning of a life meant by
God(s). The abandonment of one's ancestors to their fallen state, who
are denied salvation by the cruel hoax of timing, who were born and
died too soon, is the beginning of one's fellowship with the Elect. The
meaning of one's life is not in the hands of one's heirs. It is determined
by one's successful entry into a timeless time and placeless place that
leaves heirs behind. Rome was utopia, the imposition of a generic
civility upon the world. Christendom was ectopia, the deliverance of
the Elect from the world.

At approximately the same time as these movements began to gain shape and momentum, Vesuvius erupted and the city of Pompeii was entombed in a tsunami of searing ash and poison air and molten rock. It was an apocalyptic vision for its victims and its survivors, an end of the world by any measure. It happened so fast that the city was caught in freeze frame fashion in the daily grind of being itself and fixed there. Centuries went by, empires and barbarians came and went, magma settled into soil. Then, sometime in the last century, people started to dig, and they found that the lava had overtaken scores of people in flight or in the futility of hiding and had entombed them there, and the heat was such that the bodies left behind a faithful mold of themselves and nothing else in the cooling rock, a mold so faithful that the stitches on their clothes, the tethers on their shoes, the money in their purses, all of it could be read, lucid and articulate. They had become the negative space, the placeholder, the screensaver to what overcame them, the only sign that anything once was otherwise. They'd become the goneness of what they'd been, ghosted by what preserved them.

That is how I imagine what the coming of Christianity to European peoples along the dying roots of the Roman Empire would have been, and what it might have meant to them. It was the end of the world that itself would not end. Ending without end. Apocalypse. Oblivion. Eternity, by another name. European peoples in the fading Roman period were awash in dislocation, speaking the tongue of their conquerors, already homeless in their home places, traumatized by culture loss, and the Christian missionaries cannibalized that homelessness, and made it a prime attribute of the soul.

Here's one example. In 601 AD, just as the authorized missionizing of England began, Pope Gregory proposed a programme of pacifying the locals. The face of their spiritual practice would be saved, and the soul of it subverted.

...I have long been considering with myself about the case of the Angli (the English); to wit, that the temples of the idols in that nation should not be destroyed, but that the idols themselves that are in them should be.

—Gregory the Great, in Liuzza

The scene I'll imagine now must have happened over and over in the eight or so European centuries that began with Roman Empire and ended with the mass conversion to Christianity, during which time and by which means "the West" was created. The indigenous peoples would have had their holy places, the looming place of the Gods. There were mountain tops and springs to mark such places, and the boreal peoples would have groves of oak or yew, the seat of the Gods, perhaps the bodies of the Gods, perhaps the Gods themselves, in any case telluric and numinous.

Enter the missionaries. Alert to the power of pageant and the august moment, the prescient among their leaders would have taken the paganry to the sacred grove and reasoned with them as to the clear merit of an only God who ruled over such groves but did not stoop to become them or inhabit them. When it became clear that the draw of the abstracted deity, and the severing of that creator from creation, was lost on the primitive imagination of the simple and intransigent natives, a demonstration of the abstract was in order. In full view of the priests and the elders who pleaded and warned against it, the missionaries proceeded to cut down the trees or foul or fill the springs, probably hauling them away for winter wood or filling their horses' water troughs.

"You warned of the fury and the madness that would be unleashed if these oaks were to fall,"

they may have said,

"and as you can see, we remain healthy and safe, and so do you. There is nothing to your beliefs but superstition and the devil's work."

And the pagan priests may have turned to each other in genuine dread and said:

"It's all much worse than we imagined. Who could have foreseen humans capable of dumb desecration such as these? Their power is madness, and it makes madness as it goes. We feared that madness might be loosed upon the world if we didn't protect this home of the Gods. Now we see from the invaders ways that, indeed, the madness is already loosed somehow, and the thing we feared has already come to pass, and is among us now. We have failed to keep it from the world."

The people most discredited by the act would be those who'd lived with their Gods the longest, and had the depths of their lives bound to them: the medicine people and the elders. And their grandchildren might have told the story in something like this way:

"They say there were trees on the nob of that hill, by the edge of the field where nothing much grows. The people who used to live here believed in tree Gods and all of that old stuff. But the trees died and nothing happened."

That *nothing*, mind you, would be the West.

Come the West

Now it may be too much to say that without Rome there'd be no Christendom, nothing of the kind the world has seen. It may not be too much. I don't know. This much is written in the charter of modernity, though: the early centuries of the common era saw Christian missionaries, themselves Roman citizens for the most part, tracing the dying roots of the Roman Empire, learning its language and its ways, biding their time with syncretism, accommodating their exhortations and imprecations to the not-yet-extinguished seasonal obeisance and sign reading and telluric faith of the locals. Riding the rough road into town, riding the plough into the field, Christianity as it was bought and sold west of Palestine soon and certainly became a religion, and then *the* religion, of settling, sedentary cultivating and trading people, everywhere in Europe the Mediterranean brought it. And as it did so, it took up the responsibilities that come with adjudicating orthodoxy and enforcing the exorcism of paganry and administering civilization.

You were probably taught some version of the history of Western Civilization at school. Very likely, if you were, it was the authorized history you were taught. The river course of time came trickling out of

Mesopotamia, rose in Egypt, flowed freely in Athens, crested in Rome. Europe was the marvelous delta of civility, America its best idea yet. There was the odd reversal, yes, the odd losing of the way, the occasional lapse of rhythm or loss of faith in the old ideals, but those things came and went, and they spawned not much that endured. Personal liberty, charters of rights, numeracy and literacy, democracy, rationality, self determination, church here and state there—all of it the best of civilization and the best of mankind, all of it God's plan, all of it the mercy of heaven.

These details appear in the record, of course, and I for one have the fortune of living in a place and time crafted more or less successfully with many of these ideas in mind. I'm not condemning or complaining. I'm remembering. The unauthorized history of the West also includes church/state collusion. It includes the systemic policy and practice of the enslavement of humans and of the living world. It includes the recurring concentration of fortune among the few. It includes the deification of growth, and the psychologization of the natural world. It includes widespread and ongoing extirpation of local culture. If culture is the modulated achievement I contend it is, tethered to the consequence it visits upon the home place it would be sustained by, then the unauthorized history of the West includes the adamant, systematic war on culture. The West, as the brooding, incarnate, inanimate and ghosted hulk it has become, is post-culture.

I would for the sake of clarity and inclusivity declare that this thing I'm calling the West is not a racial reality, certainly no longer the particular achievement or possession of Europeans or their spawn, or Americans, or anyone else. The marvel of the thing is how affably it swelled out over the banks of its own beginnings, how user-friendly it became and how quickly, how adaptable it was to local conditions, until *local* was central command's idea of local, a new selling feature, an effigy of the history and flair the West is secretly nostalgic for but will not remember. A syndrome masquerading as a culture, the West exported itself effortlessly, and continues to find customers and takers and adherents in every blighted, traumatized place it has had a hand in creating.

One of the first times I taught in Maui a local woman offered to sing, to call in her ancestors and ours to learn and accompany and bless the proceedings. This she did. It was stirring and forceful and utterly present, and practiced. No surprise, it made many there wish they were Hawaiian, or it made them imagine for the duration that they were. Such is the consequence of the appearance of "the real thing" in the West. So many Westerners are ready and willing to throw their mongrel history over the side for the spiritual smooth sailing they imagine comes with imbibing an "intact culture."

At day's end she took me aside to explain a bit more about the song she sang and the cultural boil it came from. Then her voice lowered to conspiratorial, trusting range, and she said to me:

> You know, we have this word, this name for white people: *Haole*. But it doesn't really mean "white person" at all. There's no mention in it of colour or of race. The root word is our word for "breath," or for "spirit," or for "life." Our way of greeting is to touch at the forehead and the nose and let our breath mingle. When the whites started coming, they wanted to shake hands, which to us meant keeping their breath separate from ours, and their spirit and their life separate from ours. It turned out that that was what they wanted. That hasn't changed much, not really. So *Haole* really means something like, "keeps his breath and his spirit to himself."

And then she paused, and in a tone of remarkable sorrow she said:

> "You know, we have a lot of Hawaiian Haoles now."

What this elder seems to have meant is what I mean. The West is not a race anymore, if it ever was. It isn't a people. It isn't a geopolitical sector. It isn't a lifestyle. It is the utter voiding of culture, masquerading as the best of cultures. It is a syndrome—the trauma of ectopia, of ecstasy—masquerading not as a particular culture but as the apotheosis of culture, the essence of culturedness. In that sense of the term then, there are Indian and Chinese Westerners in the hundreds of thousands or millions now. Everywhere is not the West—let it be so—but the West is truly everywhere.

⊰❧⊱

So with that caveat in mind, I come to the Four Horsemen of the Apocalypse who have carried the West to the world. Yes, flagrant language, indicting and accusing language, to be sure. For a few pages, I'd ask that you not decide prematurely as to the accuracy or fairness of the image, but only consider, and extend something of the host's etiquette towards these unruly guests who may even now be tarnishing the furniture and bringing down the tone of the marketplace of ideas.

There are four markers, four cardinal points on the compass of recent history, a history during which we've seen the malignant breaking of the world into colour-coded spheres of influence, a calculation and conjuring by which the West and its ways and means, is recognizable. These four markers are probably more recognizable to whatever outsiders, pagans, and renegades are left than they are to civility's beneficiaries, its crusaders, its pitchmen. Each has been offered up to the world as an achievement of civilized people, though it is probably better to say that each of these things was done to people in order to civilize them, by people to whom it had been done, and so on down the sad line. But *and so on* does not mean "that's how it's always been." That notion, as may become clear, is one of the Four Horsemen.

Each of these markers is part meteor and part crater, part cause and part consequence. For all that, they are spells. By this I mean that what has come to pass for history, for the way it is, is likely a kind of veneer that has been laid over the armature of the verities and particulars of time and place so convincingly that our habits of understanding and preference and the eye are more persuasive than most learning we are subject to. By the four spells of the West, I mean four epistemological and phenomenological habits, four bewildered habits of the mind that have come to "hold space" for the West. These spells—universality, eternality, inevitability, potentiality—are carried on through the generations principally in the habits of our speech.

⤞✦⤝

Now this word *spell* is worthy of being lingered over a while unless, for want of some lingering and some considering, the undisciplined, unlearned approach to the word becomes a spell itself. Etymologically the word *spell* has a history remarkable for its consistency of pronunciation and spelling over many cultures and centuries. Old Saxon, Old Icelandic, Greek and Latvian, Tocharian and Indo-European, all have the word in a form and sound recognizable to us.

Lexigraphically it tends to be so that a consistency in phonetics is accompanied by a consistency in meaning. As a verb *spell* means "to count out," (hence "*tale*" and "*tally*"), or "demark by the articulation of constituent parts." As a noun it means "the employment of those ways of articulation to have influence or consequence upon the proceedings." The meaning of this word is fairly consistent wherever the word appears, not substantially altered over all those centuries and all that cultural and topographic terrain. To track the enormous significance of this, imagine that *sound carries meaning*. In other words, imagine that there is semantic meaning to the sounds you make, that purpose-driven, dictionary-enabled project of being understood by the particular words you choose and how your order them.

And then imagine that, particularly in the minds and mouths of the poets and, alas, of the pitchmen and high-end digital thieves, there is something like onomatopoetic meaning, levels of meaning conjured by making the sounds. It seems likely that language is mimetic—onomatopoeic—*not only in its origins but in its sound*. The sounds that we make in speaking, you could say, may not only be arbitrarily associated with particular meanings. They may be incarnation and conjurer of meaning simultaneously. It may be that we still come to language in some fashion as we did as early hominids, as we do as infants, borne along by the sound of skilled poetry or eulogy or story, our capacity for wonder and for awe conjured by alliteration and rhyme and rhythm and all things arithmetic, a strophe of sound that can reappear and be remembered when that sound is made.

Many cultures have foundation or origin stories in which speech and what is spoken are the means by which things happen and cease happening, by which things are made and unmade. In many cultures, speech is known to be a Godly function shared with humans, to be learned, nurtured, cared for, and practiced with high regard for outcomes intended and otherwise. Such is its volatility and consequence. Many cultures that have coalesced and receded to become the West have retained this understanding of the word *spell* from their old days of oral skill, and have committed it to literacy more recently to help remember this function and this power.

The semantic lineages that hold speech in high regard would have practiced that regard in the act of speaking, at least on their better days. Alertness to the conjuring power of words lies beneath oral cultures and literate cultures, too. They share a fundamental understanding and something approaching an ill-at-easedness about words. To them, words are more than good or bad, kind or unkind. They are of vast and volatile range and consequence.

> In the Quiche Maya creation epic, the Popol Vuh, their Gods say it clearly: "We made humans so that we are called upon and we are recognized. Our recompense is in words." These Mayan Gods are honoured and praised, and paid for the gift of making human life by human speech.

There are, in every profound sense of the terms, neither good nor bad words. There is speech, and it is a powerful, conjuring thing, and on the skilled tongue it does not submit, crimped into domesticated, housebroken categories. For example, though you may never have said aloud what I am about to write, I think intuitively you may have known it to be so and may have lived some aspect of your life accordingly. *Spells are not cast in the mind, in silence. They are cast by the tongue, in speech, aloud.*

We have a word, antique now in English but still compelling elsewhere. It is used to signal pleasure at meeting, but it carries more. We might say with self-conscious flourish and feeling a bit the Elizabethan re-enactor: "Enchanted." Other romance languages employ their equivalent, probably with more skill or suppleness these days. But for all the variance of style, the word comes to one recognizable meaning and confession across all those places where it is spoken. It has the consequence and power of something like, "I have been sung or chanted by you." You might call it *enchantment* if you welcome the spirit arousal and confusion of the thing. You might call it a *spell* if you don't.

The old root of the word comes close to *sing*, but it more so has the tone of *rhythmed murmur*, and it remembers a time when people understood the conjuring power of speech and the elegance and subtlety of heart that conjuring asked for. It employs the means by which spell and incantation are made, and the ways by which they are overturned and undone. The old meaning of *enchanted* is something like this: "I have been conjured and called by you, and consequence and the stuff of life are at hand, and many a thing has come to the light, and just now, having met you, the river of my longing for life knows the shore that gives it its course and reason."

More or less, that's its swath. That is something of what it is to be enchanted, to be called back again into life by the thrum of chance encounter. You won't find that definition in any dictionary, but if you've ever been enchanted, you might recognize the moment there.

An astounding piece of phenomenological witness and wisdom is in the word. *Chanting* is not quite singing, no longer straight speech, but is perhaps the mother of them both. Chanting is something rhythmic and arithmetic, something cadenced and counting, something professing and processing, something the supple human tongue and soft palate were made to serve, the dance of meaning and the servant of meaning.

The chant is mnemonic and mimetic. It has the way of memory and of cognition and recognition, the way by which life lives, the probable beginnings of everything.

You know, involuntarily but intuitively, that your presence and the meaning of your presence and the meaning of your life are granted to you by others. You can overreach yourself in order to manage the means by which you are seen and understood, and like me, surely you have done so from uncertain time to uncertain time. You can see this manipulation of image and impression everywhere you look, and there are people who are paid well to do so on behalf of the buy and the sell. But at day's end, at marriage's end, at life's end, there will be the memory and not the remembered. You know that. Anyone wanting to know anything important in this life of ours can know that.

If you catch the scent of this deep propriety, you become more inclined to proceed as if the meaning of your days is entrusted to others, and something like humility winnows your days. This is achieved by a myriad of skills and gestures, some affectionate and some choreographed by etiquette, but most or all of them are stillborn if they do not, from time to time, overflow as speech. As you speak and are spoken to, so you happen, so you appear, so you mean and are meant.

If the meaning of your days comes to you in the attestation of others, then it can be withheld in the same fashion, by the same skill. In this way you can hear in the sound of the word *enchanted* something like gratitude, like thanksgiving for something like a solemn, subtle substance having come to you through another's willingness and hospitable skill in speaking as if you are *so*. This may seem an immense amount of semantic and existential and spiritual currency to attribute to a phrase, and it is. But many a thing is said in an enchanted way, for the sake of that murmur, and it seems to me that the Lords of Life themselves are enamored of the thing.

❧

I made my living for a time in the death trade. One of the things you can learn there, or be unnerved by there, is how central speech inadvertently is to the palliative project. Regardless of one's specialization or motivation or skill set, the capacity most consistently resorted to and relied upon was speech. Speech was how every professional person cared for every dying person, or failed to care for them. It is astounding to consider that during all my time in the dismal arts, virtually no real and sustained attention was given to the use and misuse of language. Skill was assumed, not established, and certainly not required.

Imagine it. You're dying, and you know it. As your citizenship in the land of the living comes under serious review, as the strained etiquette of polite conversation and society becomes wobbly and indiscrete, as your very existence as a living dying person becomes more and more uncertain, the skills of language by which you could be gathered back into the land of the living for the duration of your dying are less achieved, less practiced, less turned to. You are *disenchanted* by the living who are there to care for you.

Perhaps it was the inadvertent practice of this existential apartheid that prompted those rare, bracing, candid gravestone inscriptions more common in former centuries. This isn't often how they were written on the gravestones, but it carries the tone.

> *Yes, yes. You go on, you hasty bastard, commander-in-chief of your little life. Go ahead and prance through this leafy glade, tithing the odd memory as you go, as any lord might do for underlings, clucking your tongue at the dates, at the shortness of so many of our allotments. You are making your unsuspecting way towards us even so. A word to the wise: soon enough you'll see it all. Soon enough you'll be here. Aye. There it is.*

So, the gift of speech is a big deal, and enchantment is a big deal. And, most especially, spells are a big deal, too. The thing is a mandatory mystery. Spells are broken by the same means by which they are cast. Spells aren't decided and then undecided, meant and then not meant. They are unraveled and undone by taking them back, by speaking otherwise, by taking the very words by which they were cast and redeeming those words. You can read about spell breaking all over, particularly in the burgeoning section of the bookstore called New Age: shamanic, so this isn't really esoteric information. In English we use the verb *to see* as a synonym for "to realize, to understand." The truth is that curers, fixers, therapists, seers and spirit mechanics of all stripes concern themselves more with the unseen that is there under the ordinary, the unspoken that whispers beneath the spoken, and the business of spells is transacted there.

In cultures still informed by these things there is training to quicken and sharpen the eye and the tongue to make them prone to the mercurial and the peripheral, and there is training to coax the unseen towards revelation. There are languages reserved for adults that children overhear everyday but are gently barred from speaking. There are languages only for men and only for women. There are whole languages and hues of nuance and meaning particularly reserved for the deep practitioners of the culture, the elders. And these are all held dear within one culture, one language. Here are a few details of such training.

1. The world is *alive. Alive* means "of consequence." It means "it pushes, it pulls." It means the world is sentient. It does not mean the world is benevolent, as in "tends to benefit or favour or bear me in mind because I mean well." Certainly, no matter how much meditation we achieve, the world doesn't become benign, nor does it become an extension of your "consciousness" or mine.

2. All living things partake of the web of sustenance. In ways neither metaphorical nor uneventful all living things eat and are eaten, sustain and are sustained. The willingness to be subject to and bound by this reciprocity is the animus of life, and that willingness is the means by which humans are recognizable as living things by other living things.

3. The warp and the weft of this web of sustenance is the exercise of radical hospitality, an etiquette binding and abiding, whose gestures extend the aliveness of the world and cast it into high relief, whose etiquette is probably *more alive and enlivening and resorted to* in times of adversity and consternation and deep uncertainty than in times of plenty. The politics of scarcity do not survive the practice of hospitality of this sort.

There are others, but for the purposes of understanding spell breaking, these might do. The skill being taught by these principles is the skill of being on the receiving end of aliveness. It is, in other words, instruction towards animism.

There are spells that seem principally spells for the eye. This means that the eye is bound by the spell. It governs what the eye sees.

> One example: Our verb *to speculate* means something like "to offer up and perhaps to profit from the vagaries of life," but the older meaning is closer to "to observe from a distance, from above." The habit in this case is the practice of keeping some distance from that which you propose to learn, thereby preserving your prejudices and preferences and objectivity. The result is that you forever mistake the way things are for the consequences of staying so far away from them.

The spellbound eye's ways of seeing extend the spell, you could say. But those habits of the eye are subservient to the other kind, the spells for the tongue. This means that the habits of speech (and speech may be amongst the most habit-amenable gifts in human life) and the habits of perception that follow from them perpetuate the spell, particularly by shrouding it in the vernacular of the everyday. Spell casting as a rule is far from spectacular, drawing attention to itself. *In order to bind, spell casting hides in the shadows of habit, principally in the habits of the spellbound tongue.*

The spell is brought to the breaking point not by cleverness or irony or sarcasm (for those are habits themselves, and spell casters), but by skillful articulation of the radical etiquette of ordinary sustenance. If you're a practicing animist, you know that spells are as alive as you are. If you're a practitioner of this deep running, life sustaining etiquette, then you enquire of the spell what it is that sustains it. You do so in a way that already begins the sustaining, the feeding. This requires a ready and learned generosity of speech, generous in scope and volume and in kind. Spell breaking begins with a generous, spoken serving of what has kept the spell alive, in much the same way I described earlier using the conventions of the English language to attempt to disarm them.

It is counterintuitive in the extreme, yes, but a spell breaker is a master practitioner of welcome, not of banishment. He or she is an innkeeper, a publican, not a cop, not a private security wonk or a mercenary. If you are to be a spell breaker, you learn generosity, not parsimony, and you part most heavily from what you have learned. Instead of keeping it for yourself, you spend your learning. That is the radical etiquette of spell breaking. And from this practice and tuition you begin to see the architecture of the spell come into view. It is miserly, retributive, grasping, trafficking in poverty and in hope and hopelessness. It is animated by spiritual penury. Like a Monsanto of the mind and heart, it maintains ownership over what it claims to give away for the benefit of others. It exercises dominion over what it teaches.

You don't starve a spell to death. You feed it to life. Bound as you are to the etiquette of sustenance as an animist, you break the spell of the persistence of "the way it is," by breaking that grinding habit of inevitability that passes for understanding. When you are starved by the sense of irreducible constancy that beggars your life and your speech, you break the monotony of the starved speech by enchantment. You feed what has been starving you. You do so by how you speak. Marvelous power.

Spells are spells more in their consequence, and not so much in their mechanics or in their words. An enchantment is enchanting when it employs the murmur and the arithmetic tongue to recognize the deep-living dignity of each aspect of person and place. A spell is a spell when it employs the Gods-giveness of language to cast a pall over life, to keep its aliveness from it until that aliveness takes on the shape of allegation, concept, theory, symbol. These are all syntaxes of spell casting.

Spells are acts of seduction, a particular brand of theft that masquerades as attention giving and affable regard, all the while employing the gifts of the tongue to withdraw from the reciprocal etiquette of getting and begetting, of nourishing and being nourished, to take and to profit thereby.

Enchantments are acts of courtship, wherein the aliveness of life is recognized and appears in the extension of deep courtesy through achieved speech. In that sense, courtship is an exercise of deep discernment in the service of courtesy, learning what sustains what you propose to court or admire or speak into view.

So, the great act of informed defiance in the face of speech-occluding spells is to craft more speech, finer speech, deeper nourishment, crazy hospitality, reckless expenditure of generosity. You don't seduce a spell into submission. That is more spell casting. Instead, you spill the best wine because the honoured guest, the spell, has appeared. You break the best crystal in its honour. Speech of this kind amounts sometimes to a shower of admiration without approval, affirmation without agreement. The spell of poverty is spoken into existence, nourished by a spoken reciprocity it once abrogated and preyed upon. The spirit geometry of the thing is a marvel. Darkness is brought to light by a diet of what it darkened. The spell is articulated, you could say, or broken, by eloquence. The spell then is a casualty of radical, inclusive generosity of speech and soul. The dangerous storytellers, on their good days, do just that.

A. The Universal

The Christianity that moved west from Rome beginning roughly in the fourth century of the common era seemed more entranced by the Roman example than repelled by it. The Christian missionaries practiced syncretism broadly, accommodating and appropriating indigenous symbols, devotions, practices, and calendrical ceremonies until they were rendered down as precursors of Christ and foretellers of the Christian church and the Kingdom of God on earth. The timing and the temper of Easter (spring planting/death of winter), All Hallows' Eve (harvest/feeding Gods and ancestors) and Christmas (death/birth of the sun) are three examples. But in a subtler way those missionaries were themselves missionized by what preceded them.

The Roman Peace, as I suggested earlier in this chapter, conjured a kind of global citizenship from the ashes of indigenous culture. In this fashion the Peace was a precursor of the Fellowship of All Believers. Both claimed to be catholic in scope, ordained by history, the manifest will of the divine in the world. And this is one of the spells by which the West became itself and one of the means by which it does its dark business in the world.

"Underneath the skin we are all the same. Everyone wants the same things for themselves and their families." These are articles of faith in the West. They underwrite the West's understanding of humanity, its humanism and its free trade. And they have the spiritual octane of a bumper sticker, or a fridge magnet aphorism, or a greeting card. But these are spells. They are perpetrators of cultural disintegration and trauma. Ironically but typically, they are also the consequences of cultural disintegration and trauma. They are cause *and* effect, as most spells are.

Though the reach and breathless certainty of this spell is recognizable in the name I've given it, probably the term *globalization* is more fitting. Think of how many songs of freedom and redemption and struggle you've heard and hummed to yourself that require the utter collapse of real and sustaining diversity as a prerequisite for singing them. "We Are the World," of course, is a cringe-worthy allegation, and there is "One," and many others too disturbing to recall. Of course, there is "Soul Has No Color," and "One God, One World," and there was the famous "I'd Like to Teach the World to Sing." What are these selling?

I don't say that these aren't soothing propositions that cool the churning and calamity of human-on-human violence. I ask only whether we who purvey globalism are certain that all those we mean to include in this Family of Man seek that inclusion and absolution, or welcome it, or even recognize themselves in it. Is it possible that we are spreading our loneliness around, mistaking it for kinship? Are we sure that the kinship we seek is found in this subcutaneous sameness? Are we finding yet that the deepening loneliness that so clearly rises from the eclipse of culture is soothed by the allegation of global citizenry, global culture?

You can tell that I'm not finding that, no, and I'm not sure at all that this is happening. I'm finding during the course of my days that the spell of globalization confounds the sustenance of local culture, in fact, forbids and banishes it. The spell of globalization marks that devastation so skillfully and so obscenely that the particulars of those local cultures still standing look like obdurate, progress-defiant obstacles to us solving our "global problems."

B. The Eternal

> Consider the English word *always*. *All* is not confusing, and "each and every" describes it well. *Ways*, though, ways means something more like "manners" or "tendencies" or "routes." Reassemble the word and you get something more like "what prevails." How has it come to mean "That's how it was, and that's how it will be"?

If things today have the tone of sameness from place to place—like a hotel chain, an amusement park, an airport, a children's menu—the trance this induces is one of inevitability and improvement. Things are getting better when they're easier and more familiar, and things are certainly less different as you move about than they were even a decade ago. And the internet is making just about everything easier and faster, so things must be getting better. The spell is this: people have wanted things to be easier and more familiar to them and better as far back as people go. All the passage of time has done is to make this evident. It has always been as it is now, everywhere. You can count on it.

This is the second spell of the West. The West, as we've come to live it, is principally a trance of order induced by literacy and standardization, sustained by grim appropriations of language. The tone and pitch of the spell is expansive, promising constancy across time and space, but the consequence is constriction. When the West is exported to the world as it has been, when everyone believes what the West believes about "humanity," treasures what the West treasures, and rolls like the West rolls if they only could, It's a Small World After All.

So the momentum of the spell of the Eternal is centripetal. It collapses all the particulars of place and time, collapses that aspect of your mind given to detail, exception, inconstancy, lacunae, mystery. The spell of the Eternal makes time and the passing of time illusions to be ignored or worked through. It has that circular sense about it.

It's ashes to ashes. It's dust to dust. When the eternal moves into the neighbourhood there are no endings, there are no deaths. So, there are no elders either, no particular wisdoms. And since it is death that in all its metabolizing mystery feeds life, there is no life either.

Mystery is not a gap in your knowledge, a snag in the weave of your dominion. Mystery is not something that hasn't been clarified or sorted or brought to heel or made to behave. It isn't something that hasn't happened, or hasn't happened fully. It isn't something that is being kept from you. It enforces ambivalence, the mother skill of inquiry. Consider what *ambivalence* means today and you see the war on mystery that the spell of the Eternal wages. The dominant culture of North America is adrift in the doldrums of information, exercising its right to the infinity of opinion. Opinion is now the right of all, thanks to talk radio. It is also the opioid antidote to humility for a people humiliated by the unknown. But ambivalence in fact is an articulation of human conscience. It is the eclipse of opinion by mystery, and it is a good way of contending with the collapse of discernment that says, *"It's always been this was,"* that says, *"People have always thought that it's always been this way."*

C. The Potential

Chances are that some well-meaning teacher offered this to you, in the name of inspiring you or goading you: "You're not living up to your potential." When you hear this as an older person, it amounts not to inspiration but indictment. Apparently everyone else can see who and what you should be and do with yourself, and how to do it, though the self-evidence is lost on you. Alas, it seems that it may not be in your potential to live up to it. If you hear this as a young student, you are cast adrift on the secret sea of "could be."

Potential means something like "could be, but isn't." Held to a standard of "maybe," young peoples' potential is fated to remain an allegation. Forever in the future, drawing you towards itself, somehow more authentically real than you are—that's your potential.

Well then, what is the potential of whatever history you studied? What is the potential of children who are stillborn? What is the potential of the aged, the played-out, the spent? I know the instinct rises here to placate and to cheerlead, and I feel it myself. But allow the usual understanding of *potential* to run its course, and let the claim of the thing, its self-evidence, weaken as it will, and do you notice how little potential there is in the going, and none in the gone? That's because potential requires a future, because potential is a hope-addled addiction to the virtual, to the fresh and clean, to the promise, to the untainted. To heaven, in other words.

Never mind what's been done, the dross of possibility not quite realized. What's yet to be: *that's* where the best part of us appears. That is as fundamental an article of faith in the West as there is.

But prod this bit of the architecture of hope and faith, and mortar starts to fall away. If the future is the repository of the best part of us—for that is the faith architecture of progress, of evolution—what or who are we now to those who came before? Are we not their future? Are we not the best part of them shimmering into the world, into time? Are we not what they might have been, just as surely as the present is the past's future? Are we not either the incarnation of their potential, or its exhaustion, or both?

If that is who we are, the irretrievable playing out of what they could have been if only…, then is *this* the machinery of progress we've been tinkering with and relying upon for a good while now? Are we the betterment of our forbears? And if *potential* is that perpetual motion machine that grinds the past into raw material for a brave new us, could it be that the spell of potentiality that we labour under is what keeps our ancestors from us?

No, we are not potential *anythings*. We are meant and dreamt *somethings*.

D. The Inevitable

The foregoing three spells conjure the fourth. They wring a cadence out of crisis, a momentum that spirits you away from the inertia that attends, engaging your conscience in a deeply compromised and compromising time such as this one. It is reassuring, isn't it, in a dark sort of way, to be awash in concern and impotent rage at the ethical free fall of this regime and to resort to the kind of new age fundamentalism that lets you tell yourself, "Well, this is what wants to happen." Does it really?

Double, double, toil and trouble. That may on occasion describe your work week, or what daunts you in your meditation class, but some might recognize it as a chant, an invocation, a signature song of Shakespeare's Weird Sisters. It has cadence, it rolls across your tongue as you say it. It gathers as it goes, the way all knowledge does, gaining in sobriety and gravity and import as it does. Rhyme is a discredited thing among us these days, simplifying middling work, clever but not the métier of real merit, tolerated in the context of popular radio or children's literature, set aside otherwise. But alliteration and cadence and rhyme have deep lineage in prayer, in elegy, in litany, and cadence and rhyme are hallmarks of incantatory skill and were so long before Shakespeare's time.

So the witches are witching in Act Four of *Macbeth*. There is the cauldron, and the eye of newt and the rest. Mostly they are speaking in rhythm and rhyme. They are not so much describing what they're doing as doing what they describe, by speaking it. This all occurs in the present tense, both the describing and the conjuring, spoken things. Yet this kind of work is routinely described as "fortune telling the future." In fact, they are attempting to *make* the future, by speaking as they are in the present. Though Macbeth might rely on them to foretell, the Weird Sisters know they are describing. It isn't the future they relate; it is the present. Without their machinations, the future they are attempting isn't a given. It isn't inevitable, not at all.

One contemporary rendering of just this understanding of incantation and its effect on time is a scene from Leslie Marmon Silko's book *Ceremony*. A native man is recently returned from the war against the Japanese in the Pacific, and he bears all the marks of what we call PTSD, what his peers might have called spirit loss. He is haunted by people who have died by his hand or his dereliction of duty. He is taken to see an old medicine man living at the edge of town, a traditionalist and so an outlier, even to his own people. Seeing the haunting going on, the medicine man tells the suffering man a story. It is written down in verse, as if the medicine man is chanting. It is a story told to make witchery—the root cause of the young man's suffering—tangible. The medicine man is a spell breaker, and he speaks witchery into sight, using the same skills witches do.

He describes a witch's coven where a kind of contest has begun to see who can conjure the darkest darkness. All the witches have stood and delivered save one standing in the shadows, unknown to the rest as to tribe or era or gender. This witch resorts to none of the standard hocus pocus.

> *"What I have is a story."*
> *At first they all laughed*
> *but this witch said,*
> *"Okay*
> *go ahead,*
> *laugh if you want to*
> *but as I tell the story*
> *it will begin to happen.*
> *Set in motion now*
> *set in motion by our witchery*
> *to work for us."*

The story goes on to describe very clearly the witchery that made the coming of white people to the Americas, the consequences for the native peoples and for the land. The witch's story ends with a chanted refrain:

> *Whirling*
> *Whirling*
> *Whirling*
> *Whirling*
> *set into motion now,*
> *set into motion.*
>
> *So the other witches said,*
> *"Okay, you win; you take the prize,*

but what you said just now—
it isn't so funny.
It doesn't sound so good.
We are doing okay without it.
We can get along without it
we can get along without that kind of thing.
Take it back.
Call that story back."

But the witch just shook its head
At the others in their stinking animal skins, fur and feathers.
"It's already turned loose.
It's already coming.
It can't be called back."

—Karen Marmon Silko, *Ceremony*

⤜⧊⤛

Consider our word *weird*. This is the modern spelling of the Old English word *wyrd*, which first appears in a written account of the skaldic poem *Beowulf*, dating to somewhere between the sixth and tenth centuries of our era. It has not meant "strange" until fairly recently. It is typically translated by scholars as "fate." This word's Latin root is *fatum*, "a thing spoken by the Gods," past participle of *fari*, "to speak." Again we are brought to the crucible of speech. The thrust of the word is clear and powerful. *Wyrd*, or *fate*, is "the consequence of what is spoken by the Gods." It does not mean "what is going to happen now, come what frigging may." Nor does it mean that the fix is in, inevitable. It wonders what you will do, now that the Gods have spoken.

It has a parallel in its linguistic cousin, Icelandic. There is *geofa,* and *ogeofa,* meaning "good and bad fortune."

> A man's luck is a supernatural being that guards him and may leave him, like the Greek *daemon.* This *geofa* has nothing to do with fate, if you take fate to mean a hostile plan, a beneficent plan, or any plan. The key to this notion is that the word *gaefa* is cognate with the verb *gefa,* "to give." It refers to the good things given to you by nature, circumstances or pure chance. Hence *gaefa* is what you are or should be grateful for in life. You have not earned it, nor do you deserve it. Your *gaefa* is your blessings."
>
> —Thorstein Gylfsson, in *Njal's Saga*

Fate is not a recipe for defeat or depression or despair. Think of the line binding *fate* and *fatal,* and you can see clearly the fundamental shift in the understanding of life in the West since the regime of right/wrong, black/white, true/everything else, dark/light, sin/salvation, human/divine, heaven/hell came to town. It goes from a high regard for the conjuring power of speech to a resigned ordination of defeat and slavish resignation to a dark host of givens, from acute attention to the details of the present moment, to a collapse of the mythic imagination into archetype: Groundhog Day, by another name.

There is nothing inevitable about the strange days we find ourselves in. There is nothing inevitable about the withering of old people and the atrophy of elderhood in our time. The inevitability comes in what you say about it. In speech we share something of the repertoire of the Gods. We are spoken by the Gods. In that sense we are the *wyrd* of the Gods. We are murmured over and dreamt by our ancestors, and we are their latest hope for this world they left to us. What we do with what is granted us, and how we rise on behalf of the troubled time we've been born to, that is the *wyrd* that *we* conjure. That is the means by which we might become the ancestors for others that we'd want for ourselves.

13

THE TRUTH PUT LIKE AN AXE

Would that your last elder dies before your loneliness comes to you.

—Georgian tribal curse

ou may have counted on the stars, the firmament, as it is still often called, to be the fixed point in your whirling life. The night sky has in fact not always been as it is now. Even its centre is not where it once was. The serpent coiled around the pillar of Aesclepius (from whence come the apothecary's sign and, abstracted, the barber's pole), the dragon coiled around the *axis mundi* of creation that soars up into the heavens: these were once observable statutes of human life. The *axis mundi* and its guardian are old, sustaining stories for Northern peoples.

The World Tree

The third millennium BCE was the peak of the climatic optimum, a time of abundance in the boreal northlands. The North Pole was not indicated by the Pole Star, but by the constellation of The Dragon. The processional motion of the polar axis in 2830 BCE brought the star

*Alpha Draconis within ten minutes of arc from the pole.... At the time
the Dragon coiled around the pole at the centre of the night sky ...
Today Polaris is fifty minutes of arc away from the pole.*

Felice Vinci, *The Baltic Origins of Homer's Epic Tales*

The mythic image of the World Tree exists across all the old cultures of
Europe. There are different iterations for different places, but one salient
feature they seem to share is how the World Tree, the *axis mundi*, binds
heaven and earth, the realm of the Gods and the realm of humans. But
in what direction does this binding go? The favoured answer today is
that the World Tree establishes an affectionate and dynamic bond flowing from Gods to humans, proof of divine presence on the scene. The
World Tree is planted and tended by them. The subterranean fret of that
assumption is that humans would otherwise be floating in a meaningless,
Godless night, that the tree is an umbilical tether to survival. That is a
very modern take on the human relation to the divine, and probably the
minority view in the time before the Romans and the Christians.

The older understanding of the World Tree is otherwise. It is, first of
all, not a symbol or a metaphor but *a tree*, and as such, it is something
like a conduit for sustenance, a reciprocal sustenance that mysteriously
goes both ways, hither and yon, photosynthesis and radiant capillary
action, from us to the Gods and from the Gods to us. It is the agent of
mutual care. It is a living incarnation of that indigenous understanding
of sustenance being the currency of ancestry, and it conjures an ancestral kinship between Gods and humans. So the covert understanding
here is that the *Gods have need of humans* in some fashion. The World
Tree carries that need to the lives of humans, and humans translate that
need in their cultured and devotional ways.

And the World Tree keeps Gods and humans at a distance that
grants viability and sanity to the world and to its humans. *Without the
mediating mercy of the World Tree, humans would be undone and driven to
madness or worse by a blistering exposure to the sheer volatility of the Godly
realm.* The World Tree is, to use Nick Cave's evocative term, pushing
the sky away. The World Tree and the distance from the Gods that it

grants is the proof of their love for us. Our willingness to care for it, and to cultivate that distance, is how we love them.

And so it is not a stone pillar of enduring inevitability, not a coaxial cable of eternity, not an impervious universal constant. It is not Heaven and Earth and the crucified Christ in between of the conversion, though it may have been where they got the wooden cross idea from. It is not a symbol of personal meritocracy upon which every judgment from on high turns. It is a living tree, after all, and it can sicken, and it can die. Boreal myths have that theme to them, too. There can and probably there will come a time, they say, when the tree cannot hold, when, through inattention or caprice or hubris or spell or the ministrations of darkness the membrane of sustaining sanity and mediation will wear and tear, and the dragon slumbering at its foot will stir, and the unbearable Godliness will bear down.

The Natural Order of Things

By "the natural order of things" I don't mean only or even primarily the procreative cycle, nor the food chain, nor the getting and begetting. I do not mean the inevitability, the guarantee, the givenness, the inalienable plodding and unwavering nature or essence of things. I mean the current and the disposition of time. I mean the preponderance of things, their valence, the leanings and likelihoods, the story of how it often goes.

Just as you see in the forest floor, and as you saw in the understanding of *dodem* and of the spiral of time, the natural order is rooted in the generative power unsheathed by death, in every metabolic and metaphysical sense that can be meant. *It is emphatically sustained by and articulate of the past.* The natural order of things is the past, through death, claiming kinship with the present moment, through sustenance. The past murmurs the names of its heirs, and that murmur conjures the present, coaxes it up into the light. The animating principle of this architecture is memory, the incarnate recollection of the past whose lived chant is *longing*, whose consequence is *belonging*. So the natural order of things is prone to the past. It is pending. It is in its elegant way not entirely likely, not a given. That is how it charms us into action on its behalf.

The human capacity to have a memory of what we've no lived experience of is the past's ways of longing for life. It is the way by which the natural order of things bears us, how we imbibe the natural order. It is the memory of everything but us, giving us a birthplace in the field of longing, which is known to us as the past. Memory, then, is the generative power of the past, coming on.

Now, many world myths include attempts to account for this mystery: How is it that we have a longing for kinship—a lived kinship—with the Makers of Life when, at best, we seem to be able only to imagine it, not remember it? Is it a generic but ungenerative want, born of being forever a stranger in a strange land? Many of these myths answer,

"No. That longing is the shard of a memory of a time when the Gods *were* your neighbors. This longing is a sign of a memory when the Gods were in the world, before they took their leave. This longing is a memory of us that the Gods have."

Why then do so many of these stories so often tell a story that requires trespass or transgression to make sense of that longing? And why do these stories render the whole thing as loss and rupture and a chronic payback for having blown it? Perhaps this comes from our unwillingness to be God's memory, or God's remembered, and from our insistence—our demand—to remember God instead, *to have what we long for and not to be had by longing.*

"The Gods are loving this world, and death feeding life is that love, and the past comes to humans as the elder of the present."

This is a fair rendering of the spirit of the World Tree myths, and a sign of the natural order of things at work. Now comes the hard part, the grown-up part. The natural order is sustained in a way that is the very articulation of grief. The Gods withhold their hand and don't subvert the natural order in order to save it. The natural order is the Gods remembering, and it seems to include us routinely finding ourselves on the outside looking in on this order. And miracles are not the Gods intruding into and rupturing the natural order long enough to snatch a particularly beloved bit of it from the death-unto-life-unto death of it all. Miracles are, all together, the natural order of things, going on until it doesn't.

Could it be that our grief at imagining something that we do not seem to be able to live—a kinship with the Makers of Life—is the natural order at work, too? And could it be that this longing we have is not a punishment for what we failed or betrayed or transgressed, but the way by which the detail of the natural order that includes us is nourished and sustained? In other words, could it be that our longing for home is the lived chant of the natural order *granting us our present* by murmuring the rosary called by us *the past*?

So it may be that this chronic but far-from-universal sense of being strangers in a strange land, spectacularly not at home, is our end of the deal, the means by which the portion of the natural order that bears us is born. And it may be that it chants our corner of the story into the Story, and in this way makes for us a home. There are places in the world where *the human longing for home*, when it is skillfully learned and practiced, *is home*. This is a mystery of human life that deepens with the living of it.

It might be that *our longing is the Godparent of our belonging*. Our longing is us keeping our end of the covenant wrangled and recalled by the Makers of Life as the World Tree. And it may be that the end of our longing, when it becomes our truth instead, or our possession or our birthright, is us reneging on the covenant we've been the beneficiaries of. *It may be that the end of our longing for the Gods is a spell we call The Truth.*

The Truth

Coifi, the chief of the (English) priests exclaimed to his King (c 760 CE), "For a long time now I have realized that our religion is worthless; for the more diligently I sought the truth in our cult, the less I found it. Now I confess openly that the truth shines out clearly in this teaching which can bestow on us the gift of life, salvation, eternal happiness. Therefore I advise your Majesty that we should promptly abandon and commit to the flames the temples and the altars which we have held sacred without reaping any benefit."

Bede's Ecclesiastical History of the English People

There is this business of "The Truth" to consider. A palpably big deal in philosophical, devotional, and juridical circles for a long time now, you and I know what the truth means. It means the demonstrable *facts*. If you've ever been on the stand, you know that *they* know what it means, too. It means something that is utterly, faithfully "whole and nothing but." It is the opposite of false, of wrong. It means that if you want to know what's up, if you don't want to be led astray, if you want to be with the smart money, you'll find out what's true, what's *so*, which is more important, more fundamental, than finding out what's *right*. When you know what's true, you know what the deal is. In an age high on information (and the quicker the information stream the better) and low on trust of public officials or the standard talking heads, truth counts—as long as it describes *what's really going on*.

Truth for most of us is an unerring, enduring, and timeless constant, an essential, self-contained, and utterly reliable cabal of unconquered attestations going back into the mists. *Truth* disputes the passing of time indisputably. It has no need of age or aging. It serves best by outliving and outlasting whatever it claims to serve. *Truth* inhabits a particular expression or incarnation parasitically, moving on when the expression or incarnation miscarries or wanders or changes or grows inconstant. One example might stand in for all of them:

> The true facts of your misdeeds having been found out and adjudicated, Judgment Day is come, and there is but one more true thing to be established. Though you may pay your debt to society to the fullest, and though your shame might wax and wane, and though you might be outstanding and honest the remaining days of your life, the truth is that *you will always be guilty*. You will continue to be guilty after you die. That is all.

By this measure, there is nothing true about elders. And by this measure, memory is a poor midwife to the truth.

We know how to determine the truth of a declaration or report today. We cross-reference. We verify. We check it for ourselves, if we care enough about it. Many of us turn on a little machine and get square-eyed for hours on end, parsing as we go. We do all of that because *the truth is out there*, sometimes subtle, sometimes savage, but always there to be found and relied upon. Either that, or we've given up, or we came of scholastic age in the reign of deconstructionism and we're now persuaded that there is no such thing as the truth, that there never has been, that it's all convention or convenience or consensus, that it's all story time, what they call *narrative* now, that there's only personal truth.

But these are not opposites, not at all. The second view is but the collapse of the first. Both of them agree that once upon a time there was such a thing as the independent, incontrovertible truth, as an idea, that the quality of truth is a quality that dwelt in the thing itself, the principal attribute of whatever it is that is being sought. Plato saw to it, and he was persuasive on this point.

Well, we have our sense of truth from Plato's Greek heirs, but it has come into the English language explicitly through the Roman conquest of Germania and Britannia. The Romans, who like imperialists everywhere idolized what seemed beyond their ken, so often mimed and mined all things Greek. The Greeks had the word *alethia*, which in its literal and older sense meant something close to "not hidden," as in "not forgetting what makes you human and alive." The Romans translated the word but not the understanding. They called it *veritas*.

One way to get an idea of how deeply the Roman colonization of the Anglo soul has gone is to look at how many commonly used English words contain *ver-*. There are several pages of them in the dictionary. Two will suffice to give you the feel of the thing: *verb*, and *very*. The first is the root of all action in the language, the second is the root adjective, the superlative of everything, and they both derive their meaning from the understanding that there is this thing called *true*, at the bottom of it all, or above it all, that you can count on, out in the mind of the world or the cosmos. That is where the truth is to be found, in the pure forms that lie behind or within the things of the world. This understanding informs everything you've been taught about *metaphor, simile, fable, symbol, image*. There is this truer something, behind or within, that they all allude to. I went to a university that had this one word—and *only* this word—on its coat of arms: *Veritas.* I can tell you that the university's founder and chancellors seemed very serious about their imaginations being properly colonized by the word, about the merit and veracity of the thing, and about passing on the illuminating gifts of the colonization.

> The Romans seconded an Old English word. It struck them as a fair translation of what they meant by *veritas.* The word as we have it today, the sound and the approximate spelling, seems to be as old as Old English is old. In its archaic local dialect forms (West Saxon *triewe,* Mercian *treowe*), which are cognate with its likely even older continental origins (Old Frisian and Old Saxon *triuwi*), the word consistently was used to mean something like "faithful," or "loyal," or "trustworthy," or "authentic," or "vowed upon," or "oathed." The difference between the modern and the old meanings might seem insignificant, as if they are shades of the same colour. But they are not.

The Old English *true* never did mean anything like *veritas.* In the Old English soul, the quality of the true thing derived not from what was being said, or what it was being said about, not from some particular event or object in the world, not from a divine essence dwelling within an illusory form. Theirs was entirely an associative or communal and not an essential understanding of the word. The quality of truth was in the honour and standing in the community held by whoever was decrying it. Now to us today, this might seem like a slender thread indeed to string faith or decision-making upon. But consider that the principal attribute of urban, suburban, and increasingly, of country life is anonymity. You yourself are known by a remarkably small circle of people, and from this small circle comes your renown, your merit, the very meaning of your life. This meaning usually goes no further, and the legions of people you'll never know, never meet, stand there at the edge of the meaning of your days. They are the obdurate limit or end of the meaning of your life. If you say something, you declare something, what's the biggest possible consequence of doing so? Ask yourself what *your word* or *your name* means in the greater scheme, and you get the feel of the poverty of it all now. This goes a long way towards explaining the hankering after celebrity and fame and notoriety. It explains the website mania, the ersatz "community" mining for "hits." They call it "YouTube," though candidly, it should be called "MeTube."

But in a cultural milieu where people in a general way are known to each other, standing in the community is everything. It determines your opportunities, your wealth, your marriage options, your social, intellectual, devotional life. Literally, *your name* comes from your standing. In many places in the world, it is your community that gives you your name to safeguard. Whatever you lend your name to, whatever you put your word to—what you say and what you are called, two functions of speech—there the fullness of your standing in the community is traded upon. If you are willing for all of that to be at stake, then the quality of what you attest to is worthy. And all of that constitutes *true*. The truth of a thing is not its primary attribute. The truth of a thing is not in its nature. The truth of a thing is a consequence, and not a cause. It fans out from lives lived in existential and syntactical proximity to each other. The truth of a thing is the child of a way of life that bears the village mind in mind. Truth is a medium by which village-mindedness dreams, dares, declares, affirms what has granted it its life. It is village-mindedness murmuring to itself, which its members overhear.

These pre-conquest peoples didn't know that they were pre-conversion peoples. They found that out from the missionaries who washed up on their shores a few centuries after the Romans. They knew qualities of reliability, honour-boundness, honesty, the endurance and the power of the oath, qualities that were established over time by the consistent behavior of those trusted and entrusted. Being made by vows, truth was a quality that—something like beauty—required the passing of time for it to be achieved and recognized, to take its place in the life of their communities. By this understanding you could say that *they had no truth. They did, however, have the means of truing.* True was not a particular quality of anything or anyone. It was a way of going about being alive. We have very few manuscripts by which to understand how they might have understood these things, how they understood themselves. They perhaps had not much literature. They may have not had the sense of authority that unerringly comes from what is written. They may not have needed it, likely having a substantial oral tradition instead, being practitioners of the oath, minders of truing, relying upon what is said.

What they did not need was the coming of a foreign language—Latin—and a foreign religion that traded in Latin—Christianity—to bring them the truth. I am no expert in anyone's grammar, much less the grammar of Old English, but I'd wager that for a good while it may have been impossible in that language to craft the phrase "the truth," or to have it do what that phrase does to our mythic and poetic imaginations today. The English language that you and I share now is radiated by the phrase, run through with it. Still, there is that shudder in the translation from *veritas* to *truen*, that possibility that the truth isn't true and hasn't been for a good while.

Imagine then what mayhem of the spirit ensued when a culture practicing truing was conquered by one who owned The Way, The Truth, The Light. Imagine what became of the Gods, the ways. You have before you, in *truen,* what became of the language. Everywhere the Latin language went, The Truth set upon the people and the land. The reciprocal covenant was overturned in favour of the commandment covenant. And the West as we know it now was born. That was The Truth, at work.

The World Tree in Wither

Then an old harrower of the dark
happened to find the hoard open,
the burning one who hunts out barrows,
the thick-skinned dragon, threatening the night sky
with streamers of fire.

Beowulf, ll. 2271–2275

You can see clearly now that whenever The Truth is traded upon as something that is the antidote to ambivalence and the vagaries of diversity, *the antidote to the passing of time itself* and to the pleas of the past, that's when there is no truing to be had. Impermanence is thrown overboard, the unenduring lose their place, memory and name and word are poor, discredited stand-ins for The Truth, and elderhood is decorative nostalgia.

The Truth is not the World Tree withered. The Truth is its withering. Intolerant of time, of any time but the timeless, The Truth makes a symbol of incarnation and empties it, turning it into a mirage and an allegation and an imperfection, the cup and not the wine, the disposable "take out" version of Real Life. But when *trued*, The Truth becomes a chimera, a haunting, the four spells of the West bound into the one true all-in-one. It is shown to be what it is, the belligerents known to us as eternal, universal, potential, inevitable, testimony's end, the village mind's final poverty.

The withering of the World Tree, that architecture that separates and binds the world and the Makers of Life, is the withering of the past that we prompt by forsaking it as fate, or as gone, or lost. Modernity has traded in the past, in favour of the spells wrought by the future and the predictable, the assured, the known. Prayer is traded in for metrics, elders traded in for growth. And the World Tree's protector has become our adversary, threatening the night sky, roused by The Truth to protective fury.

Remember that particularly grim curse that opened this chapter? *Would that your last elder dies before your loneliness comes to you.* It's chilling, at least to me. Unleashed, it would prompt a cultural malaise at least as lethal as any germ warfare might. It may have done just that in the West. As any good spell does, it shows a faithful reckoning of the power of the well-placed word where it meets the place elders hold in the public life and the spirit life of their people. Grim, and properly stricken, it is a curse smelted down in the crucible of tribal enmity and war. It is a thorough curse that understands deeply how mandatory honoured elders are for a living, viable culture. You hear the possibility that the loneliness we have in our throngs now might have come from our elders already having gone missing in action, absent without leave, snafu'd, fubar'd all.

But now cure it of its curse by inflicting it with generosity, by rendering it as a plea, by truing it, and you get this:

> Your elders are your living memory, the presence of the World Tree among you. They are your antidote to that grinding certainty that you've done something terribly wrong sometime, and that's why you've grown hesitant, all full of longing for a better day. They are the better day you are longing for. They are the ones you should remember, they who are doing your remembering for you, those of them left. They are doing your testifying and your truing now. Hold onto them. Make more, if you can, before you forget how. Let your loneliness in this world come to you before their deaths come, before you forget that there are elders yet. Let it sweep you to their doorstep.

⌘

Forsaking what has been for what might be, exercising dominion where being wet-nursed by mystery formerly was found, this is what withers the World Tree. The old among us are regarded—when they are regarded at all—as largely being past and passed by, largely already done. In a culture addicted to potential, the old are potential in collapse, a pile of what could have been and now will never be in the corner, a burden needing upkeep but not sustenance. The tragedy of the thing is that when they are elders *they are sustenance*. They are that which feeds the present. The present is the presence of their memory, the very present the rest of us imagine that *we* are conjuring, the rightful inheritance we dumbfoundingly regard as the future. No, our rightful inheritance is the past.

Older people resenting age and any limit, who've shrugged off the world and the young, who nurse grievance and retirement and Freedom

55 in equal measure, they are the visitation upon their people of the withering of the World Tree. That supreme reluctance, that cranky pausing for the next payday, to find out what's in it for them, that living visitation upon the younger generations of a florid example of a youth unable to die away, a ghost of time passing, the husk of youth tarted up as "being all you can be": these are the wretched encumbrances of an uninitiated greying person whose middle age is failing them. They are the withered and the withering, both.

You recall that important safety announcement? To proceed without safety is in the spirit of the natural order of things. To insist upon it as a human right, as a prerequisite for health and sanity, to engineer an assault on mystery with conviction, with information, with binary oppositionality in your language, *that* withers the World Tree. And this has been thrown into motion by the agency of the four spells of the West. And its wasting creed is inanimism. And its degenerate forbear is bankrupt discredited tradition, Oblivion, Nothing, Non-being.

Elderhood is one stout antidote to the learned insignificance that howls in the heart of those jockeying for recognition. The elder doesn't compensate, doesn't kneel at the altar of the One True Self, doesn't lie about the immensity of the untested merit that others accumulate, or the trued unlikeliness of prevailing. The elder proceeds as if he or she is needed, rarely with any invitation to do so, that lack of invitation being as close to authorization as he or she is likely to get. The elder proceeds as if the sorrowing insignificance of the younger ones is all the prompt that is necessary or likely. That inarticulate sorrow and the poverty that beggars and mutes it is what makes the case for elders in our midst.

14

AT THE FOOT OF THE WORLD TREE

Seamus Heaney remains one of Ireland's fine offerings to the world. A scholar he was, a poet laureate, a master practitioner of being both discerning and troubled aloud at once, an adroit humanist during the Northern troubles, and learned and daring enough to take on the translation of the ur-text of all things Anglo Saxon, *Beowulf,* and to insert a Celtic tone into the proceedings when his scholarly mind was persuaded of its presence, thus earning the rancor of Anglo Saxon precinct minders (some of whom pronounced it "too Irish," the richest of ironies in recent Anglo-Irish relations) and producing a popular bestseller in the bargain.

Mr. Heaney found himself drawn over and over to a series of remarkable archaeological finds made mainly during the nineteenth and twentieth centuries by peat cutters in Denmark and the Baltic region. Wine-coloured bodies reared up out of the peat. They've come to be called Bog People, and Mr. Heaney wrote about them in his poetry. Preserved by the tannic properties of peat bog down to their eyelashes and character lines in their faces and fingerprints and the stitch of their caps, they come to us plum and rust and seeming to slumber. The consensus is that they are late Bronze Age people, but there is uncertainty among the experts as to how they came to lie where they did. Human sacrifice or corporal punishment for some transgression are the main contenders, given the nooses and the wounds they bear. Most of them are on display now in national museums in the area. The most renowned of them was found in an area called Tollund in Denmark, and so he is called Tollund Man today. One of Mr. Heaney's poems is called "The Tollund Man in Springtime," and it is found in his book *District and Circle*. (Consider having the poem open alongside as you read this chapter.)

Mr. Heaney seems to me to have been drawn to writing about the Bog People as he was drawn to his father's farm work. Emboldened by the vigorous patristic example, he cleared himself enough of it to take up what he called a life spent digging with the pen. Given the sectarian violence of his country's recent history, given the torment over what constituted the verities of culture beneath citizenship and prejudice that probably claimed the good minds of the time and place, it isn't hard to imagine what claim those Old People of Europe, looming up intact out of the Old Ground, would make upon the poetic imagination and the soul of the new. It seems to me that, as Mr. Heaney aged and deepened and was resorted to by his fellows, the Bog People whispered to him of the depths of belonging, its obligations and its pull. And so as a person obligated by the past, his voice was lent less and less to self expression as his work went on and was more given over to the timbre of the place that granted it to him. So you might imagine that "The Tollund Man in Springtime" is an aging man's filial piety drawn down in service to the travails of his time and a brace against its trappings and prejudice. I hear the poem to be a stirred up, tragic, longing-begetting and fully achieved meditation on ancestry. It is the murmurings of turf, prompted by the contentions of a very specific life, an utter time. It is the very stuff of elderhood, rendered by an elder. What follows is a meditation on that stuff.

So there is a bog man in a display case in Denmark. He is the colour of old wine. He was put in the ground with violence, and the violence done to him seems meant either to soothe the justice of the time or to feed the ground or its Gods, to feed the grind of seasons. Or both, perhaps. But how was he to do that, in those days? What was their understanding of the architecture of sustenance, that they would kill son or father or grandfather and plant him in the ground? What did they know about the alchemy of ground and God? And who are they to you and me, these long generations after?

The lives of those people at that time and place were largely given over to gathering and rudimentary agriculture and pastoral pursuits, to adorning their material culture, to living the life entrusted to them by their Gods. As cultivators, they must have been keen observers of the ebb and flow of life, the mutual obligation binding them to their home and their Gods, the power of death to grant life. Tollund Man and his ilk were given to the ground, probably with this reciprocity in mind. He was planted like you'd plant a seed, perhaps with some misgivings. You could say that the power to sustain life that was bound up in the strength granted him by his Makers his kinsfolk granted to the earth instead.

This interruption is the defining thing, that and his being interred. Clearly it was not a metaphor, not for him nor his jurors. It shouldn't become one now. We ought not to imagine it his "intention" to be put in the ground nor his death symbolic, a kind of inside joke, the feeding of the ground symbolic, his ground and his Gods symbolic. Desecration is not symbolic, though, and there is much desecration in symbolism. Tollund Man was put under, seed and solace and sustenance all at once, succor for the earth that sustains and not symbol for the sustained. That is how it appears to me.

Seamus Heaney's poem begins with Tollund Man in a display case, having endured preservation, stirring to awareness. There in that case, the museum technicians tore the metabolic rite asunder in the name of learning and preservation. Even before you read the poem, you have looming the question of what suffers preservation, and whether what is displayed *is* preserved, and whether that for which he was planted centuries and centuries ago can survive the preserving, or has, and whether preservation isn't as resolute a gesture of lostness and homelessness made in the name of being at home as there is.

One mark of indigenosity is the lived and dynamic relationship of human language to the spirit of place. Old languages seem to understand themselves to be the sound that their home ground makes. Humans who belong to a particular place have overheard that murmuring, and their language mimes that sound, taking dictation more than miming. So their language itself is a blessing, the tally stick by which their stories of home are remembered and told. To speak the language of your ancestors is to remember and reconstitute your common ground. In that way, through a common language, you could say that the present generation is the dreaming and murmuring of those who've gone before, coming up from the boneyard ground as indigenous speech.

But Tollund Man was pulled from the boneyard, and in the display case in the poem, in horror-movie fashion, Tollund Man awakens, and the dead man rises. Neither dead nor alive now, his preservation begun, his animation suspended, he lurches towards modernity. Disinterred and left to the air he would go to dust. But preserved, he is condemned to wakefulness without life, his dreaming done, and now he has become a stranger. In the poem he walks among modern people now, in the modern world, to find whether we are what his life was taken for. Are modern Europeans his heirs? Are they sustained by his death? And who are we North Americans to him then, so many of us scattered from that ground?

> *Into your virtual city I'll have passed ... neither god nor ghost, not*
> *At odds or at one, but simply lost*
> *To you and yours ...*
>
> *I re-awoke to revel in the spirit*
> *They strengthened when they chose to put me down*
> *For their own good ...*
>
> *I was ... all told, unatrophied.*

We read the poem and we think the thoughts, and it isn't long before something happens. By the stirring of the Tollund Man, and by the sonar of homelessness and vague regret most modern people bring to what we have lapped and lost, and by the sorrowed skill of the skald Mr. Heaney, we become not informed so much or inflamed so much as unignorant of what has anciently preceded or predicted us. It is a different order, something apart from *aware*. *Aware* might have the enabling tone or the power to prompt you toward fidelity or good conduct. But *unignorant* leaves you as *unatrophied* leaves you. Having seen and been drawn nigh, there is nothing further to it. What you might turn towards *now*, and in what spirit, and with what expectation or demand to know and to be sated, *that* is what is up for grabs. It seems to me that Mr. Heaney obliges the reader towards history, and with courage imagines that we modern people have become unignorant of our ancestral histories without necessarily growing conscience.

He gathers proof. Unignorant we remain, unremittingly haunted by the allegation of consequence we did not intend, not yet midwived by the utter mandate and necessity to proceed otherwise and to change our course. It is still hellishly, sluggishly up to us. Almost everything seems still, with so much of the tally taken, up to us. This is the pall of the Anthropocene fallen upon modernity.

And so Tollund Man, *"neither god nor ghost, not at odds or at one, but simply lost to you and yours,"* comes among us. He looms at the edge of the European imagination, heraldic, telluric, poetic, prompting whatever sense of spirit and ancestry still pertains. He becomes famous. Neopagans make pilgrimages. He, killed and planted for the sake of life and the Old Gods, is taken for an Old God. He becomes an article of faith in a faithless age, dowsing rod and magic spring to the modern and the upheaved and the homeless.

And what comes to Tollund Man as he stirs in preservation is what we have done with this garden entrusted to us, this living world. His sixth sense dowses panic in the birds at twilight and at noon, and a difference in the standing water. Water in our time is a sentinel species and a sentient being, credited by Heaney with bearing what he calls the *"clear alteration in the pooling rain,"* the fouling of the water table, groundwater pollution.

The coming again of Tollund Man does not promise what the faith seekers and faith mongers wager it does—continuity through the ages, enduring identity, tribal dignity, and calm. Nor will it. Think on how many of us have lurched without thinking to the conclusion that all before us have wanted what we want, treasured what we on our better days treasure, are as we are, under the passing, illusory skin of time all of us the same, the power and the glory forever, kingdom come, amen? Sepia and nostalgia for the re-enactors and the magic men, Tollund Man and his copper tribe now are taken for our better pre-conversion days come round again, with the distractions and the ignobilities leached out this time.

Tollund Man looks for some sign that his life was properly taken, necessarily taken, that we here, now, bear the marks of betterment that his abbreviated life vowed and was given over to. We are to Tollund Man what might have happened but didn't, what might have been nourished into real sanity by his sacrifice and was not. There is no tincture for this swoon, this modern magical thinking that claims him without learning him. His peat body is on display, far renowned, and no awakenings have come among the living, *"while all that lay in wait still waited."* Can you hear Heaney's countryman, Yeats, presage to all this and coming to his own elderhood, fingering the rosary of the modern world and calling out?

> *…Mere anarchy is loosed upon the world,*
> *The blood-dimmed tide is loosed, and everywhere*
> *The ceremony of innocence is drowned;*
> *The best lack all conviction, while the worst*
> *Are full of passionate intensity.*
>
> *Surely some revelation is at hand;*
> *Surely the Second Coming is at hand.*
> *The Second Coming! Hardly are those words out*
> *When a vast image out of Spiritus Mundi*

Troubles my sight …
The darkness drops again; but now I know
That twenty centuries of stony sleep
Were vexed to nightmare by a rocking cradle,
And what rough beast, its hour come round at last,
Slouches towards Bethlehem to be born?

William Butler Yeats, "The Second Coming"

❧

And so Tollund Man rises. What was it that raised him up? *"I re-awoke,"* he says, meaning to me that Tollund Man understands his killers as having committed him more to sleep than to eternity, a benign take on the noose still lying as a torque round his neck. Sleep, the younger brother of death, so utter when it descends. There can be specters, too, gatherings of the misbegotten, and nightshades, and calmings down, and summons and clarities unsuspected. Maybe his sleep was like our kind of death, haunted after all by purposelessness.

Maybe. That's the best, the most faithful we can be, from here. The rest seems jargon, ranting and fret. Maybe our sleep is practice for our death, and our lives the dreams our ancestors have. But you can hear the slipping in the gear of this benevolent sequence as clearly as I can. What becomes of it all when the transmission is disturbed, when those who came before were left homeless and afraid, when there was no shared understanding any longer that we *receive* our lives, that we live unto those who came before, just as we die unto them, or that it is our willingness to live that way that dreams those to come? What happens when we no longer live as though we are the memory of our heirs?

What do I mean, "What happens?" It isn't fantasy or conjecture. This time of ours, this *is* what has happened. We are what has happened.

I am not the first to write such things down. I am not the first to write them down this morning. If I am proceeding as if any of this were so, then there is every possibility that in this understanding of time passing, of what might bind generations and what might still bind them, of from whence comes our best, I am passing something along that has been passed to me. Any claim of authority is mainly memory that has come, for a little while, to vertigo or free fall, a little amnesia that seems to be the cost of cultivating memory in a sordid, self-made time, rising over and over.

So we inherit the intended, the gold of what has been, yes. And we inherit the misbegotten, the cast aside, the dross. We inherit the conversion and the turning away from ancestors, yes. But we inherit the poverties of ancestry, too. "Ancestor" does not, should not mean "fully achieved," "flawless," "unerringly noble and cool." I wonder if the sacrificial impulse or creed that put Tollund Man in the ground could be a sign not of unsullied ancient genius, but of something already gone profoundly, sordidly wrong by then. Could it be that the practice of human sacrifice—any sacrifice—is a sign of something already gone awry, and not the ceremonial highwater mark of old?

There are parents who routinely remind their children of the sacrifices they have made for their sakes, and so on. You could come into your adulthood thinking *sacrifice* means "what you give up, what you part with, in the name of love, to correct someone and bring them along the good path. And if there's a little guilt that you can trade on later, well, so be it." A little etymology goes a long way, though, when you are wondering about things you thought you knew.

> In poetry, as in life, it is useful sometimes to wonder over the fine print. *Sacrifice* is a word that comes to us from the Roman world, and it exercises the dominion so telling of that time. The first part: *sacrum*. Modernity subjects the word *sacred* to much opinion and edgy declaration. Still, there is some willingness, even in these times of post-belief, to grant that there is some order of life, or some condition, that connotes things "otherworldly," things in the order of mystery and of gravity that have the capacity to confer or alter meaning or consequence in this world. But the adjective *sacred* also

has the tone of something in this world set apart and extraordinary, and so there is the idea of apartness to it. *Something Holy* or *divine*. So far, so good, though a little weighty when you consider it being in the repertoire of contemporary parental instruction and example.

And then we have the remainder of the word, *facere*, from the Latin, meaning "to perform," but also in a simpler form meaning "to make," from which we get our verb "to fashion." Reassemble the word now, and you have something very close to "to make holy," "to make sacred."

And then ask yourself whose job has it been in human history to make holiness, to craft the sacred. And from what? Does this strike you as a human activity? It doesn't strike me that way. Are we authors of the sacred, exercising dominion and authorship over it all, or are we heirs to the sacred, or at least to some understanding that there is such a thing? From whence comes the idea that we have whatever discipline and wisdom and enduring regard for this bright blue world we have been entrusted with that enables us to fashion the sacred? And do all cultures practice sacrifice, or did they?

You know the answer is no. Some cultures did and still do, and they tend to be agricultural and sedentary and acquisitive, and they leave a considerable dent on the world as they go. Some did not, and do not, and their lived relationship with the world around them doesn't seem to have included compensating the world for their presence in it, or making a deal on the installment plan with the Great Overseers to make good on their primordial trespass, their primordial debt, much less taking over the reins and making things sacred.

What event or affliction precedes or prompts sacrifice? Consider the real possibility that *something happened that made sacrifice seem mandatory*. That is worth being troubled by, the idea that something happened in particular times and places and not in the psyche or in the ooze or the philosophical ozone. When cultures or individuals perform sacrifice, they are acknowledging some prior rupture between creation and creator, between life and whatever grants and sustains life, such that the sanctity of things has to be reinstated, reiterated, redeemed, by *them*. Something happened to sacredness, or to peoples' ability and willingness to care for it or observe it or live as if it were so, and sacrifice is the phantom limb of that something, the closest thing sacrificing peoples have to a memory that *it has not always been this way.*

Making sacrifice seems an inadvertent confession that our lived encounter with the sacred is in ongoing disrepair, that we've taken up the work of making sacred, a work that is not ours. We who are on the receiving end, who are beneficiaries of the sacred, we fill and refill a broken place, and in so doing, we lose track over and over of what might have happened, what might still be happening. It may be that every act of sacrifice shrouds the sacred and keeps us from it. Sacrifice is palliative, then, concealing what it pretends to soothe.

Sacrifice is some way of trying to close a gap that has opened between people and their makers, between people and the conditions of their having been made. They are repopulating their silent sacred precinct, redeeming some fallen time or place or action, attempting to craft sacredness from the desecrated. It is the setting up of a shrine in the crater made by a bomb that went off so long ago the crater is mistaken for the valley where God lives. The detonation is God's departure from that place. It isn't an insurance policy securing divine approval. It is a shell game, taking on the power of the divine to restore or conjure or prompt the presence of the divine.

Sacrifice is probably the deification of profanation, practiced by a culture whose creation story is one of fallenness or rupture, or sin, whose religious foundation is anarchy. *Anarchy:* the subliminal fundament undone. So sacrifice seems not to be a practice dictated by the Gods. It seems a practice dictated by their absence, by the rumour and the terror that humans are on their own. It is the flip side of idolatry. Sacrifice might be a consequence of the Gods absconded, a grim scramble to make as if they've never left.

Mr. Heaney tells us that Tollund Man *"reawoke to revel in the spirit they strengthened when they chose to put me down for their good."* This is a declaration of purpose, but it is also fingering the rosary of consequence. I am not sure what "spirit" Tollund Man found strengthened, but his revelry and his strength is a child of sacrifice, as he says, a sacrifice *"they"* perpetrated for *"their own good."* It seems entirely likely that the mythic ancestral past Tollund Man inhabited had already seen the disturbance that prompts sacrifice. Tollund Man himself might have been on the receiving end of the malignant dream that had become in Bronze Age northern Europe a time of sacrifice. And he has awoken to clear alteration in the bog-pooled rain, to smelling in the air *"exhaust fumes, silage reek ... the thickened traffic,"* the chemtrails across *"what was once the inviolable blue sky. The calamitty of it."*

Disembodied is the bracing word Mr. Heaney uses to describe a displayed body, an ancestor that has come to be more artifact than kin. Tollund Man laments the *"faith placed in me"* by modern Europeans, the kind of renown offered up around an artifact by people kinless from conversion, haunted by a kinship disqualified by conversion. And then comes that beautiful sorrowful reversing that is so much Mr. Heaney's skill: "me faithless as a stone." He is faithless and fetishized as "early inhabitant," "sacrificial victim," "remarkably well preserved." Far renowned, but unknown.

> *"In the end I gathered*
> *From the display case peat my staying powers*
> *Told my webbed wrists to be like silver birches,*
> *My callused hands to be like sward ...*
> *These I learned from. My study was the wet."*

And Tollund Man remembers that his spirit was fed or sustained by the peat, placentally. In the ground for millennia he became the northern European Green Man, the terrestrial part of the World Tree, the abiding spirit of place, wrists of silver birch, hands of grass. These particular floras' appearance, placement, and growing habit are all signals of some disturbance: fire, deforestation, clearance, and the like. They signal an event that has come and gone some time before. The birch appears as a liminal species. It signals sylvan regeneration at the edge of a clear cut, at the border of a ploughed field abandoned to fallow or fiscal collapse or a death in the family. The birch is a fringe dweller. It appears where the pagan and the progressive part ways and means and reasons, or where they meet. It certainly marks where they contend. As it happens, the birch marks the reclamation of the field by the forest. And birch is the tree, along with the cedar, that has most served the hyperborean, the Northerner: its skin for clothing, footwear, container, canoe, shelter; its blood for sustenance and spice; its dried flesh malleable for the bend or the arc and friendly to ready fire, sparked to flame by its skin in any weather, hearth maker.

And Tollund Man telling the story of his interment *is* the natural world greening and growing and going down. This is his chant, his death song, his battle cry, his catechism. Tollund Man is restored by recounting the story of generation and regeneration, of demise and rising up, of death feeding life. And he learns. He watches animals abide in the fields of the present day, and as he does so, everything he once knew visits him again in the form of his edgy, discomforted lament.

This is the hedge school of country peoples Mr. Heaney is describing, indigenous learning of the enduring kind, rooted in acute, patient, hours-long attendance to the natural world. Where I live, there is still, floating about, a residual, intuitive version of an old First Nations creation story, whose arc Mr. Heaney is brailing, knowing it or not. I don't remember where or when or from whom I heard it, but as you'll see, the story accounts for that, too.

> The old people say that when the Makers sang the world, they gave everything its song, its mark, its way of being itself. The old people say there were millions of ways of being alive that were sung into the world, and for all of that, there was no confusion. The Makers sang the birch, and that's how birchness came into the world. The song included that magical bark and that sweet sap, and other things. The song also included *birch wisdom*, you could call it, the way by which the birch knew where and how to grow into itself and how to spread its seed.

And the birch never wondered how to do these things, or whether it should, or when. By being a birch, it knew. And it never wished it was that granite stone lying at its root. It did not envy the granite stone its stillness or its firm ability to stay put, which is graniteness in the world. And the granite did not envy deerness in the world as the deer went past, nor did it covet the deer's ability to roam and to eat. Nor did the deer envy the birch's ability to mingle with other trees at a great height or see great distances, though it might have served the deer well to do so. And this was the way the world was made, all these abilities making life.

And they say that people were made in the same way, at the same time, with the same ability to be people as the birch had to be birch, and the granite granite, and the deer deer. It is hard to remember those days, they say, but it is so. People had two things that no other made thing had: they knew how to be people, and they were confused sometimes about how to be people, or when, or why. This was part of people's nature, to forget what all the others knew: how to be themselves.

That's how those things came into the world, through us. We are the original forgetters. And the old people have forgotten all of this more times than anyone else who's around. They are here to remember all that forgetting and to tell this very story when they do, so that we recognize ourselves again and might not fret so much and mistake this as something like sin. And when we do, the remembering happens again, and our ability to be people is restored for a while.

⚜

Tollund Man learns the place he has come to. This learning is him coming to, his restoration articulate. And he learns not the "eternal return," not the enduring "collective unconscious," not the "under the skin we're all the same," nor any of the other spells of universality, constancy, and essentialism by which modern people live and are known elsewhere. Tollund Man's staying powers are only specific and immediate and locally derived. And he sees that things have changed. In a fundamental, irretrievable, incontrovertible way, this very Jutland or northern Europe is not as it was. What he knew, he says, came back to him, and in that moment he knew himself, and his world was not the one he'd awoken to. He'd been buried in swamp, at a lake's edge. But the lake is gone now, and where he died is gone, and with it the reasons for his death.

"Learn that where I am from, and all its whys and ways, are unlearnable," he says. That seems to be his offering to the present order that would claim with him a kinship unlearned and unearned. This is the affirmation that appeared at the poem's beginning.

> "Listen," Tollund Man might have said, "I am neither God nor ghost, not for you or against you, but from all I have seen, you have lived without me, and it seems now that you cannot learn me."

In case you think that all of this is to be found only in mythic time or idle philosophy, I can assure you, as one who laboured for years in the death trade to deliver something like a good death to those who more often than not refused it, that many dying people—most of them—were haunted to the very edge of well-being and lucidity by a question that nothing of their able-bodied lives prepared them to answer: unto whom shall I die?

Without the cultivation of radical, ancestral memory, a cultivation that must proceed, come what may, regardless of motivation or outcome, regardless of what is remembered and what the remembering might to do to the rememberer, regardless of the spells of eternal return, of "nothing new under the sun," of inevitability, life is hollow and death is oblivion. Without the living presence of the past, you cannot know your times. That is the condition in which Tollund Man now lives. He himself has become the allegation of the past, the spectacle of a chance find, renowned but misnamed, renowned but dismembered, displayed and revealed and unlearned.

The poem could have ended there. But this is a poem entrusted to a labouring poet who seems to have been visited and lingered over by the ancients, and he does something else, something that is the very heart of redemption faced with postmodernism and the dissembling religion of the day. There's a shift in voice. The poet seems to enter the poem in the last stanza, subjects himself to what comes to Tollund Man, courts kinship and kenning with the Bog People. He doesn't say how long ago he did so, but Mr. Heaney tells of having gathered Tollund rushes from somewhere close to the old shoreline. He yanked them out of the ground roots and all as Tollund Man was yanked, the rushes clinging to a bit of display-case peat.

At the poet's home in a broom closet in Ireland, the rushes go rank. The poet's own museum case failed to preserve, and he is left with Tollund dust in his hand and nose. This is the moment when the poem could collapse in self hatred or self forgiveness. But again, Mr. Heaney has some trueing about him, and it does not fail him, and he does something else. In faithful memory and imitation of his own working ancestors and people, in line with his chosen work, the poet joins his spit with the Old Ground.

> *Dust in my palm*
> *And in my nostrils dust, should I shake it off ...*
> *As a man would, cutting turf,*
> *I straightened, spat on my hands, felt benefit,*
> *And spirited myself into the street.*

The thrill of ancestral food comes to the poet's body and it is enabling. Learned and spirited, he sets the Fourth Temptation aside and steps into the hurly burly of amnesia's marketplace. It is to me a glorious, indicting, redemptive recitation of ancestral memory, and it is the elder's function Mr. Heaney fulfills. He contends by remembering.

Tollund Man asks whether this modern world and we modern people are who he was sacrificed for. He gets long lines of tourists and a display case for his answer. His question is: Are you my people? Are you what we became? Now I don't say that the poet would agree with me on this thing. He seems to have been more than content with his Catholicism. But the poem reads almost stanza for stanza to be a dirge for ancestors. Better still, for ancestry.

The clear and utter cost of conversion to Roman Christianity for indigenous European tribal peoples was their ancestry. That was the tariff for entering into the Fellowship of All Believers, and into the Kingdom of God. They divided their calendars and their devotional lives by the year of their conversions. Their tradition keepers would likely have been early casualties in the first generations of this struggle for the souls of the people. There aren't many primary sources from the time that tell us how the missionaries went about their work, but here are two pieces which give some idea of the project. The first is written by Alcuin, head of Charlemagne's palace school at Aachen (Charlemagne was the first Holy Roman Emperor, the one who forged Europe's first Christian Kingdom), in 797 CE. In it you can read the severe apartheid against and the utter dismembering of the Old Ways.

Let the Word of God be read at the clergy's meals. There it is proper to hear the reader, not the harpist; the sermons of the Fathers, not the songs of the heathens. What has Ingeld to do with Christ? The house is narrow; it cannot hold them both. The King of heaven will have no fellowship with so-called kings who are pagan and damned ... the pagan laments in Hell.

—in Liuzza, Beowulf

The second, a year-end report of a seventeenth century French Jesuit missionary in Huron Ontario, might well stand for the tone and temper of the undertaking. It seems fairly clear to him that the Hurons were a good stand-in for his own pre-Christian ancestors. Their resemblance activates the spiritual arrogance so mandatory for the missionary project. And you can hear, ten converted centuries later, the haunt of the Old Ones coming round again.

It is so clear and so evident that there is a God who made heaven and earth that our Hurons cannot entirely ignore it. Though their minds are greatly obscured by the shadows of age-old ignorance, by their faults and sins, yet they do grasp something, but their misunderstanding is serious. They have some knowledge of God, but they neither honour Him, nor love Him, nor fittingly serve Him, because they have no places of worship, no priests, nor holy days—in fact no ritual whatsoever.

Some are obstinate, attached to their superstitions and evil ways. This is particularly true of the Elders, because aside from them—and they are not numerous—the rest of the people know nothing of their tribal beliefs.

We have two or three Elders of this kind in our village. I often have arguments with them, in which I "force them into a corner" and make them contradict themselves, so much so that in all simplicity they admit their ignorance while the other people laugh at them. But, still there is no yielding. They resort to the idea that their country is not like ours, that they have a quite different God, different heaven, in a word, different ways.

Another good old man, having fallen sick, would not hear of going to heaven, saying he wanted to be with his ancestors. A few days later he gave in, telling me an amusing tale. "Rejoice," he said, "for I have returned from the land of the souls and I found no one there. They have all gone to heaven." There is nothing useless for salvation; where it pleases God, even dreams can help.

—Jean de Brebeuf, *Huron Relations for 1635/1636*

So powerful were the missionaries that they emptied the land of souls of those they converted. They turned people from their dead, from their traditions. The point here is as simple as it is tragic. Set aside the extraordinary arrogance of the posture, and still you have an outright war on tradition, on indigenosity, and on cultural inheritance. The casualty was anyone who aligned themselves with the waning spirituality and wisdom of conquered places. Converted European Christians seem in a similar way to have turned on their elders by disowning their wisdom. Within a generation or two, they probably turned on the institution of elderhood. It has been in some kind of terminal swoon among their heirs ever since. Ironically or sadly or both, the self-identified pagans now gathering in Europe seem bent on turning from their Christian ancestors as a way of gaining a more desirable ancestry for themselves. They've learned well. And white supremacy might be the unclaimed bastard heir of the same vexed and ancestorless regime.

THE THIRD ACT

15

THE PEOPLE WHO ARE GOING

Sudden

ld people in an uninitiating age can be and so often are sweating out their crumbling diminishment, tracking the indignities, misanthropes without a cause, their grudge match with Fate in full swing. They have an able spokesperson in Roger Bacon, the all-round twelfth century Renaissance man:

> *The Accidents of Age and Old Age are, Grey Hairs, Paleness, Wrinkles of the Skin, Weakness of Faculties and of natural Strength, Diminution of Blood and Spirits, Blearyedness, abundance of rotten Phlegm, filthy Spitting, Shortness of Breath, Anger, Want of Sleep, an unquiet Mind, Hurt of the Instruments....*

> —Georges Minois, *History of Old Age*

But these are not "accidents" or symptoms. They are consequences of inattention for the most part, uninvited visitations of a bit of profligacy. Unwitting homeopaths, claimed by their aging but not by their times, old folks now seek out for succor the disease management arm of that very social order that prescribed diminishment and a fading of the light for their days. They look up as from a daze, awash in the suddenness of it all, dumbfounded that their middle age has abandoned them without notice, that their lives are the nightmare stuff of continuing care institutions.

Sudden: the preferred way for the end of anything to come, that it *happen*, that there be no preamble, no notice. In a culture that doesn't believe in endings, knowing that things are ending—and not the endings themselves—is the real cause of suffering. Oh, you could know of it. You could have known of it all along. There is tuition. There are those who came before, whose ranks you never imagined joining. The endings aren't hidden. They aren't gone, those of them that have occurred, any more than the beginnings are gone. The end is out in the schoolyard of your life, playing in the sun with the other children of your allotment, as cruel and full of honest regard for the world and its lives as the other children are.

Sudden means that "I couldn't have known that it would end." *Of course* it means that. "Let's pretend we're not pretending"—that's what *sudden* means. "Let's make as if we couldn't possibly know what makes us pretend." Pretending doesn't extend out there, beyond the limits of the imagination. Pretending doesn't conjure. It cowers in the corner of the yard, hands over eyes, making as if what can't see can't be seen.

Aging is not a matter of coming to the end by degree or increment. It is not toe testing the river of time for its current or its torrent or its temperature. Everything, including aging, is simpler than that, and so more confounding to many. *You age. You are not aged.* You are not on the receiving end of age, no matter your belligerence or refusal on the matter. The waning of the body: yes, that is what happens to your body, the once-noble conveyance soon enough outworn and not beholden to you or your hankering for more. But you could consider reserving the word *aging* to describe what you may or may not do while your body gathers its growth rings. You could reserve the word to describe something active, and so undertaken, and so determined and decided upon. Not summoned, not controlled. Served.

And by that measure many old people haven't aged. They've lost their tender years, sand through fingers, had their middle years' compromise stretch out into what their lives have come to mean, never really arriving at age, only being thwarted in the practice of their old habits of dexterity.

Some people charge away when the light goes green, and speed towards their doom. That is a fact of urban and suburban life. But they cannot speed towards their age. Their age is not sitting out ahead somewhere, in the future, waiting, like a bus station waiting on a bus, or an apple tree waiting on the killing frost. Their age is in the speeding seat beside them, sitting there while they refuse to age.

Age is a *daemon*. It is a Greek notion, not quite angel, not that benign. Born when you were born, your daemon was, no more agile or alert, no more capable or prescient than you. The particular genius of a daemon is its capacity for fidelity. Your daemon keeps faith with you, whether you keep faith or not. A fugitive capacity in humans rarely sought or practiced until it is missed, fidelity seems like the exercise of failing to be otherwise, of being this-wise, of being you-wise. No longer estranged from the little village of DNA threads winding and wending their ways round each other or from the unbeckoned memory of that which you have no lived experience of, the murmur of ancestry in your blood, and your hankerings and in so much that won't obey, your daemon is more you than you are likely to be. Because you have the illusion of options and the option of illusions afforded you by the competence of your younger, wilder days and by your consumer culture, you *can* be otherwise and *proceed* otherwise, for a while. You can grow tired of yourself. You can sprout disillusionment.

> Consider the word *disillusionment*: to be bereft of illusion is a spiritual practice in other places, as reliable a midwife to the endurance of sanity and the sanity of endurance as you could want. The broken capacity for illusion: it's sworn off here though.

You could veer off in the direction of the Tree of Youth whose boughs are low with potential.

Your daemon, the one born alongside you whose companionship you neither covet, nor condone, nor condemn, wavers not, wanders not. The daemon, wild and not bewilderment, finding you without confounding you much, goes your way, with grace under pressure, and is not inclined to drink too much and follow someone more promising home. It is minder of the clutch of reasons that you were born now, in these times, to this place, attendant at the swinging gate of your coming in and your going out, companion to the tried and the tutored aspects of your days.

Your daemon *is* your aging. It does not suddenly appear. It's been there for years, for decades. The daemon age was by your side, long enough to help you to the unsought understanding that age is something you do—or you don't do, or won't do—and it is not something that happens to you.

This is to say that, yes, it seems possible for you or me not to age. We might refuse to age, forget to age, be truant to the understanding that aging is a skill entrusted to us. We might refuse to come of age in a time and place addled or bereft of culture, where there is no tutelage for *growing old*. To a competence-addicted people, aging is the undoing of competence. It is the sheltered workshop of the compensatory swoon, the sow's ear repurposed by those who can no longer carry lint and spare change. Think of how a mercantile culture enthrones growth and you see quickly that our expression "to grow old" is at best a misnomer, more likely a lie. Growth gathers as it goes, as does youth, and aging demonstrably dispenses. Aging is a pay-as-you-go enterprise. So unless the phrase *grow old* employs "growth" the same way that *grow poor* does, you can lose the scent, the warning signs, the cautionary tale that is aging in this time and place.

⁂

Sudden: this is an attribute of our unwillingness to learn what is there to be learned. When you're willing to learn, you learn the signs, you learn the presences. You practice portent. You divine. The future is what has always been. It is *the present in exhortation*. It is something like the imperative of the present, a prayer the present might have made and might yet become. The elegant English phrase "Would that ..." carries that tone beautifully. It is a prayerful conjuring that is part supplication, part demand. But *sudden* is the confession of an unwillingness to heed the signs, to learn the spoor and sprawl of your days. *Sudden* is the tyranny of the future, the not yet, imagined to be hiding in the spell of potential.

You remember *potential* now. You opened the Book of Supposed To, you did, and you found there a parallel universe taunting the universe you've learned with the allegation that it could all have been otherwise, and so should have been, and so could still be otherwise, if only you get it right this time, before sudden things take it all away and live up to what should have been. *Sudden* is not a condition or an aspect of aging. It is a condition of truancy, especially if you come to the Third Act of your life suddenly.

Now, the elder knows how the Third Act goes, tutored in endings by those who came before and who ended more or less on schedule. In an era when age is not the sage nor desert saint nor camino pilgrim, but the errant mendicant down on his luck and looking for shelter, the elder is the innkeeper. Knowing the likely expense such a guest will incur, the elder puts the ledger away and inquires after age's appetite and thirst, radically hospitable and so a poor accountant.

The work of the elder is determined entirely by what prevails and what ails a people at a given time. A hawker of redemption, the elder is as likely as not to derange the dusty furrow of habits personal and cultural. The elder raises up the possibility of transgression, surfaces the possibility that *transgression is obligation*. That is not violation for the sake of rupture or the jaunty spirit of overthrow. It is not an occasion for self expression. That is the elder function imagined as "unrestrained cavorting" by the uninitiated or the young or the envious. Instead, the elder's mandate is one of keeping a weather eye on the horizon, on the signs, and then changing course, with most everyone else below decks or in the rigging. The elder gives his or her waking hours to the swell below the culture's surface, the one that remembers what has been and what has blown through, wrecked and wrecking and enraged. The elder does so entire and engaged. As the Polynesian steersman ties a fine thread from his genitals to the tiller so as to have the thrum of the wet world run through his body and so as to not lose his way should he slumber, and by this charts his course for the would-that and the yet-to-be, so elders have the rumour and rancor of their days running through them. And from those willingnesses come augury and divination, an acute attention to the days we are granted. Soothsaying, in a word.

So the restoring realization of the thing is that elderhood doesn't reside in personality or character. They may be the horses that elderhood rides into town upon, but elderhood is wrought by occasion, by the needfulness of the times, not by the needs of the elder. If, for example, the times are rife with unexamined and frail allegations about inclusivity, as our reeling democracies are now, the elder's presence asks that the hallowed principle of diversity withstands the presence of those who are deeply hostile to or threatened by diversity in its midst, asks whether it can be *that* diverse, or should be. If the times are enthralled by this phantom of "natural," the elder function is to oblige "natural" to earn its keep by testifying to the undomesticated, uncooperative nature of nature, hard on the citadel and the belief systems as it is.

⌘

Organizational charts and the like tend to treat the office of Chief as naturally occurring as a rock formation, inevitable, solid, meant to be. But it seems that for some tribal peoples at least a chief arises only in the presence of external threat, when the people require the kind of leadership that is best found in practiced, skilled hunters. The chief maintains this position for the duration of the threat, and is tasked with making the job obsolete. Upon successful service, the chief is no longer needed and must go back to hunting. The office is a child of its time. When it accrues to particular personality types over long periods of time, you find that type manufacturing ongoing external or internal threats to legitimize a prolonged stay in office. Real service means the dissolution of the office.

So elderhood, its presence on the scene, is sought almost always only in hindsight, by the medial generations, who are swallowed by swallowing, exercising dominion over the life they haven't yet and may not live. Elderhood is the antidote to The Truth, personal and otherwise, that The Truth will not seek.

⟡

The work of being stilled, quieted when trouble comes: something there has the elder tone. Elders have no debt to torment, or to anything that binds them to a reflex of conscience or to rancour, or that makes them mimes to turbulence. Elders call still water to rise when the people have no memory of thirst.

Elderhood is a visitation of contentious courtesy. It is also the maintenance of courtesy. Rumi advises God's help when coming to the mannerly life, such is the challenge of doing so.

> *Inner gifts*
> *Do not find their way*
> *To creatures without just respect.*
> *If a man or woman flails about, he not only*
> *Smashes his house,*
> *He burns the world down.*
> *Your depression is connected to your insolence*
> *And your refusal to praise.*
>
> —Rumi, "Praising Manners"

And the elder finds the ability to praise—not approve, praise—in the midst of courtesy and knows depression to be a sign of the atrophy of that skill.

Elderhood comes to a body in time. To the extent that you live your body and are claimed by time, you may be moved to elderhood.

Elderhood in our midst is time slowing down long enough, or coalescing enough, that we can see time happen. Our challenge is not that time happens so slowly that it defies observation, but that it happens so quickly that its measure is always slipping from view.

Elderhood in our midst is the willingness of some to testify to the grief and love tangle, to the loving of what has slipped from view, and to the grieving of what has not yet done so, and by learning endings, by being willing to slip from view, and then by ending. The elder's job in a competence-addicted culture is not to prevail or succeed or win. It is to wane, and then to end, and to be good at it. This gives the rest of us a chance to get it right.

Elderhood is learning the work of blessing, and with greater and greater courtesy, seeking it, and by asking for its bestowal—and by bestowing it thereby. Crafty bastards, elders, and all along not letting on, all along not knowing they are. They confer blessing by raising and praising the worthiness of those they seek it from. The alchemy of blessing is known to elders. They know its power to subvert unworthiness and confer merit, and to raise up, raise up enough so that the waning is clear, so that when the time comes, there is a hilltop of earned merit from which to descend. When an elder is buried, they are wrapped in the worn cloaks of their various offices, adorned with the worn names by which they were known in their lives. By the time their people are done with them and they go to the ground, elders have disappeared into the layers of what their lives have meant, all memory remembered.

⌘

Elders are the visitation of time upon the people. By virtue of their willingness to forgo both the follies and the capacities of their younger days, and to be summoned to the feast hall of days, and to answer the summons pilgrim style, seeking the generous host who has included them on the guest list, by practicing with the limits of dexterity and endurance the courtesies age would recognize them by, elders are the mystery days of younger people.

You could go further. You could go crazy and say that elders mediate the Gods of Death and of Time. Without them, without the calming consequence of their presence, the encounter with the Divine would be unbearable, undoing and calamitous. The Gods seem to be subdued in their encounters with humans by the presence of the old, who, I suppose, resemble them in some way. Perhaps elders have a visage or a posture or a composure compelling to the Gods, or familiar to them. Perhaps the Gods go easy on us sometimes, when we're taking care of the elders in our midst. Elders grant to the rest of us the mercy of mediation with the Gods. Elders are the World Tree of the generations.

To take the measure of a time, there is no option but to find people whose ways appear to have forsaken completely the quality of timelessness. Elders are possessed of this skill of specificity and locality as few others are. They are pride of place, the ways particular places and times have of being recognizable to themselves. The elder presence is prismatic, refracting the opacity of his or her times into its spectral parts, revelatory. Like a raku tea cup, elders are their time's deep running artistry, all arrived in one place.

It is in the nature of real places and real times not to spill mercy everywhere and all at once, for example, and so it can be properly said of elders prized by their place and time that they were generous and wise and seem gone too soon to have finished their work. There is the feeling that not quite all of them was poured out, that there was more, or should have been more. So their particular elderhood is that one that bears the changing of the guard, or bears a scanty promise that casts the generosity of the Gods of Death and Time into high relief. No more fortune than a place and time can properly bear, the elder is fortune's merciful way of scarcely, sparingly, haltingly appearing.

Elders are those through whom the rest of us come to know the endurance and upholdingness and understanding of time. They are time having its way, moving and gathering and harrowing and winnowing as it goes. If, as they used to say, kings and queens are the living memory of the days when the Gods conjured us as neighbours, serving by being served, dealing in succor and solace and the solemnities of suffering, then in this way elders are royalty. Their going away from us sorrows us in times of culture sanity, but it does not abandon us.

The People Who Are Gone

The Canadian poet Alden Nowlan wrote a poem called "The People Who Are Gone" sometime in the latter 1960s. In it, a Maliseet elder, whose English name is Peter Little Bear, is telling Mr. Nowlan the story of how his people once brought young boys to the forest for initiation. As a kind of throwaway forethought, Mr. Little Bear delivers two lines of quiet, surgical devastation:

> *Until the white man came we had no history*
> *and now we have nothing else.*

I call it surgical because of the honed edge of the observation, honed so finely by living that the edge barely appears. There is no rancor, no argument in the pronouncement, and it veers precipitously to a confession of a cultural poverty of the deepest kind. Whose cultural poverty, though? Very early in the poem, the catholic scope of conversion, the whitening of indigenous places and people comes into view. Endure the sage indictment, the incorruptible so-ness of the thing, and linger in a shadow whose hot grievance is tempered by cool grief, and something like this realization comes rising: before the appearance of white people in their midst in the sixteenth century, the Maliseet *of course* had language, tradition, culture, devotion, village-mindedness, social order, conflict, intertribal mayhem, ordinary suffering unto death, and all that made them human in a world not wrought in the human image for the singular benefit of humans. They lived, you could say, alongside their Gods. They knew the animals upon whom they relied as their kin (hence Peter's surname). That reliance was the alchemy of kinship. And they carried their dead as they went.

All of this meant many things to them, no doubt. It meant their lives, their social and their spiritual lives, it meant their life ways and their material culture. And in there somewhere, Mr. Little Bear tells us, it meant their understanding of time. I hope this does no injury to his peoples' story to say that "Maliseet time" was the only time there was in those days. There was "now," where they had their lives, and there was the past, alongside which they lived their lives, and the past carried them to those from whom they came. The Maliseet "now," you might say, was a grandchild of the past, and their ancestors dreamed the present, the now, and that dreaming gathered the living in due course to the past. So the current of time moves to the past for them. In that way there is no future, no not-as-yet that everything comes from or goes to, no cache of possibilities that, cobbled together, comes to resemble the never-ending and never-realized pour of potential that so informs the present strivings and posturings and shenanigans of our current regime.

Here's why this strikes me as a mandatory aspect of contemplating elderhood: the Maliseet understanding of time that might have survived Alden Nowlan's recording of Peter Little Bear's remembering, and the grains of memory he deemed it wise or worthy to tell, are utterly redemptive, restorative, and recalling. Their understanding of time gathers their dead to them, and they to their dead, because there is no temporal intolerance that bears only one tense at a time, one order of existence or premonition or remembrance at a time. Their understanding of time is a rolling pageant of the departed. Though the poem is called "The People Who Are Gone," and though Mr. Little Bear seems to have used the word "gone," he was, after all, speaking English, and English is replete with temporal intolerance, and our syntax and meaning-making apparatus requires it, and our understanding of sanity itself relies upon it, and had he been speaking Maliseet instead. Had he been able to call them "the people who are gone" at all. Or if he had been able to, the Maliseet phrase might not have meant what it means in English: utterly lost, absent, without recourse or redress. You see, it appears the Maliseet are their ancestor's dream, and their speech, and their wisdom. The Maliseet "present" was *meant* by their ancestors. The Maliseet "past" was the grandparent of the present, and so they had no history in our sense of the word, no ancestor "gone" or "lost." What they had instead was a longhouse built of ancestral inheritance, where the living lived the lives dreamt by their ancestors and granted by their Gods. That is how I imagine it.

You could say that Peter Little Bear uses Alden Nowlan to notify us that the Maliseet of the time he is speaking of had no ability to lose their dead comparable to our own. They had no linguistic ability, no phenomenological ability, no spiritual ability to lose them. The catastrophe of the white man coming, a catastrophe linguistic and phenomenological and spiritual, included the advent of "history," of goneness, of the past. With forced conversion, the Maliseet became spiritually obliged to lose their dead, to turn away from them. They were subject to moral dismemberment by a temporal order that dictated that everything answer either to the past or the present or the future.

Peter Little Bear and Alden Nowlan are sending us this message from a time where this loss has already occurred, and to some degree, has been lost track of. They have done so in a language that was the principal vector for this calamity. "We have nothing else," Mr. Little Bear says, "but the inheritance of loss." "We are," he may be telling us, "by virtue of knowing your God and speaking your language, as white as you. We have the goneness you have, the ancestorless freedom you have, the museum-quality history you have."

And for all of that, the story, the reportage, sits there on the page, *doing something to you as you read it.* That is the Great Mystery, the *G'chi M'nido*, of the thing. It is a faithful rendering of being rent. That has a consequence that the conversion to English monotheism for some reason cannot contain. In you and me reading, and reading aloud, a couplet of bereavement and ethnic cleansing, the possibility that it was once otherwise is raised up. No longer potential or pre-contact, it is tangible and real and deeply corrosive of the authorized memory entombed in the language-enforced mantra that the past is gone.

How gone can the past be when in talking about the past something happens to this time we occupy now? How lost can the past be when even the whisper that it has not always been as it is now sends up a tendril of memory curling out beyond the weeds of guilt and complicity and compassion fatigue and political correctness? I say this because our encounter with a Maliseet memory in a poem doesn't only reveal a Maliseet encounter with English Reformation monotheism. It rouses a memory, an unbidden memory, that murmurs of the presence of turned-aside-from dead, the ancestors of the white folks reading or hearing that couplet. This, of course, is spell breaking at its most subversive.

To whoever reads this now: how gone can your people be when you can be stirred by a Maliseet man in the mid-twentieth century telling a story to a lapsed Gael whose poetry re-Gaels him and—maybe—some of his so called "non-indigenous" readers. The poem tells of a time of genuine ignominy that itself is not over, not gone, and somewhere in the overhaul of grief rise the ancestors turned away from in the time of forced conversion in northern Europe, which the forced conversions of New Scotland and New Brunswick are late incarnations of.

The ripple of unbidden memory, the murmur of a possibility breaking on the shoal of authority and amnesia: this is as much the presence of an ancestry unsought and unbidden, a redemptive consequence of an unwelcome, inconvenient, grief-encrusted memory that is conjured by the particulars of someone else's story. And this is the elder function, the skald's task—to remember, at great cost, and to testify and bear faithful witness, and to give over whatever skill one has been granted and entrusted with to what is unwelcome. These elders' poetry is the door and the banquet hall both of the mutual life and the village-mindedness called Here, Now. And this is the elder's presence and consequence. They are there to be the end of possibility and fantasy, to articulate the memory that bore "now," to forsake the crazy quilt of all that could have been but never was for the slender thread of what was asked of them, and what they often failed to catch onto, and what they thereby became. And what they became were master practitioners of failure. That is what the elder is, even the elder of a former foe or a former victim. They are redemption, in the form of memory.

16

THE SWEDISH TOTEM POLE

There are, probably, merits to museums of the kind that propose to preserve history and culture. I'm not persuaded that is what they're doing, but the various funders and donors seem persuaded. As is my wont, I do wonder how they are doing this preserving. It is worthwhile knowing that many—nay, most—of what are called the great museums of the Western world began to coalesce in and around the period of empire building. Once secured militarily, these empires—the Spanish, the French, the English and the American, to name four—institutionalized the plunder of cultural patrimony wherever they went and sent the booty home. In good conscience, no one should call these things "collections." This preservation was not entered into for the sake of the peoples and cultures that produced the goods. It was entered into for the sake of the learned, the cultures fate and history had designated as the repository of the civil and the cultured.

If you nose around this practice a bit, one sordid detail emerges. Routinely, it is new cultures ransacking old ones. Overtly this was done in the name of God and country, but covertly it seems compensatory and strangely nostalgic. The military campaigns in question were, at various times, aflame with the righteousness of the One True Religion, and they took deep offence at the "different understanding" that the

Gods of the conquered had offered their peoples. But in the waning days of solving the "native problem" in their respective dominions, each of the vanquishing cultures seem to have entered into a period of something like a subtle, sepia longing for what they had all but obliterated. A strange brew of nostalgia and regret at being obliged to witness the full consequence of what they had put into motion, the wholesale assigning to oblivion of that which had preceded them: this was on the menu at the colonial cafes of Europe and America. It was as if the mantra of monotheism and modernism either exhausted itself in the spectacle of victory or had no stomach for governance and for ordinary life. It reminds me of how my dog is with a squirrel crossing his path. On the very rare occurrence that he brings the rodent to ground, he stares down at it forlornly. The thrill is gone, and he doesn't know what to do with what he's taken the life of.

Imagine an old couple, living alone in the midst of a middle-aged neighbourhood, who are defeated by symptoms and infirmities and are then relegated to assisted living centres by those they appointed to care for them. Picture their house, sitting there, suddenly abandoned and strangely vulnerable. There are early signs of vandalism and plunder, so their families gather to divide the valuables according to preference or sentiment. Some begin to wonder if they didn't act in haste, if something else couldn't have been done instead, if the dissolution wasn't premature or in something like bad taste. And there is *something* that sticks in the throat, which seems inevitable, probably, but not quite right. That *something* begins to loom when the goods are being divided, when the old order that was the *arche* of their younger lives is disassembled and sent to the shelves of memory, or to a yard sale, to strangers for dimes on the dollar. This is something like the underground story of colonial triumphalism, its unauthorized memory.

It is in this veil of vague, unrepentant, involuntary regret for the excesses of modernity that you find the beginnings of anthropology and sociology and museums as we know them. They had the practical problem of making inventory and order of the flotsam of ethnic cleansing, colonial triumphalism, and God-endorsed grave robbing, so appraise and collate and cross-reference they did. As a rule, this first generation of anthropologists fanned out across the desolate fields of victory and superintended the documentation of demise. Most of them kept field notes, and it is there that you find the almost messianic appointment to catalogue and measure and record "before it's all gone." They were in on the utter and inevitable passing from history and from view of primitive peoples. Most were sure that these peoples were through disease and dissolution disappearing forever in that very generation. This nostalgic instinct to dig the bones and collect the patrimony and preserve the memory of what only a few years before they feared and demeaned and made war upon was by then noble, and learned, and civilized, and the least that could be done.

You can read these cantos of propriety in many of the descriptions accompanying the display cases filled with stuff from this period: "Effigy pipe, ninth century BCE, believed by its user to put him or her in the presence of ancestral deities." The key word, of course, is *believed*. *Belief* is anthropologese, and it means that these people were inventive and imaginative, yes, certainly, and, ultimately, poorly informed. It means their seething inner life prevailed, that they were reduced to beliefs, and addled by them in the longer term. And because they had beliefs where the self evidence of gravity, psychology, progress, binary oppositional thinking, and cause/effect efficiency should properly sit, it means they—more or less properly, or inevitably, or both—lost. So they are the preserved, and the West the preserver.

⤫

Modern Western art, and with it the visual and symbolic world we inhabit, is inconceivable without the pillaging I've described. Consider Basquiat and Banksy and street art. Consider Twombley, Lucien Freud and Francis Bacon. Then Rothko, Motherwell. Then Giacometti, Brancusi, Picasso and Braque and Cezanne and Gauguin, and then consider Fauvism and Cubism and tribalism and primitivism. And much of it comes down to the very earliest years of the twentieth century, when the various New Worlds had been brought to heel, as the cauldron of world war was put on the fire to warm. It comes down to a small anthropological museum in Paris called the Trocadéro, full to the Victorian hilt with masks, door posts, statues and ceremonial gear and attire wrested from Polynesia, Africa, Australasia. The younger artists of the time had all but given up on the Louvre. It was the Trocadéro that primed their civilized souls. Then begin to wonder why some of your children are desperate to get "back to the land" they know nothing about, and why they will turn to "native spirituality" a hundred times before they turn to where your great grandparents came from.

I am wondering in all of this whether this instinct to preserve is the modern Western world coming to its senses finally, or whether it is the modern Western world desperately trying to come to someone else's senses instead. I happened upon an upheaving little documentary film some years ago that put this whole business into high relief for me. At the turn of the last century, the native peoples whose lands unto time immemorial were the west coast of this continent and are for the moment known as British Columbia and Alaska and Washington were in ragged, plague-induced disarray. Some of the communities were gone altogether, many had forty to seventy percent of their populations die away without benefit of ceremony then or in the time to follow. Many were forcibly relocated by colonial authorities to places more amenable to administration. It meant that most of the longhouses soon fell into disrepair, and the soon-to-be-famed totem poles were melting into the rainforest.

Enter the fortune hunters, the government surveyors, the amateur anthropologists. The door posts and totem poles were sawn off and spirited away to museums half a world away, the provenance often recorded in lieu of permission sought. The film tracks the pangs of conscience that beset the governance of a European museum that knows two inconvenient things. It knows that the totem pole in their possession was obtained without consultation, permission, or anything similar during this period, and it knows that the people it was taken from didn't die off into oblivion after all, or melt into the background of progress inevitably progressing, casualties of the regrettable but understandable ethical practices of the time, a footnote of "history" and a learning experience for the dominant cultures of the West today. In fact, they are still very much alive, and they are aware of the location of their pole.

Negotiations for repatriation were undertaken. The delicate minuet of current regret for past excesses mingled with professional curatorial practice on the Swedish side, and it made for good tension. But another layer of unexpected turmoil appeared. You might imagine that there was unanimity on the native side, but there wasn't. It happened that the museum required the construction of a climate-controlled exhibition hall in the native community as a condition of repatriation of the totem pole. It was this condition, and not the pole itself, that proved the flash point for some old understandings stirring.

Consider the savage irony. This is a totem pole, a recitation of first ancestors, a tally of sustenance rooted in dying, melting into the ground of nourishment, and the Swedes in their curatorial regalia are requiring the final undoing of the real ancestral function of not lasting forever as the condition for returning ancestral patrimony. Can you hear in this seemingly reasonable and responsible condition the unchecked, unexamined, and unwitting extension of the cultural poverties that still haunt the West so desperately and prompted the looting and the theft and all its justifications in the first place? Well, whether you can or I can, it seems there were people on the reserve who could.

Money was not the problem on the native side. There were government grants and the like that, after much wrangling and application, could fund the building of a hall. The challenge came in the form of a generational split in the native community. It seemed that many of the younger progressive people were all for repatriation of the pole to a new hall on the reserve. The more of their old stuff that came back to them, the better. Some of the older people, mysteriously more inclined towards tradition perhaps, were troubled by the preservationist condition attached to the repatriation. And, according to the slant of the film anyway, it came down to whether it was ever in the manner or the heart of traditional culture for these people to preserve anything, particularly anything carved of wood. In fact, in former days, after lifetimes of ceremonial and daily-life employment, the poles and the buildings went the way of life, melting into the ground from whence they came, the climate itself the molars of ancestry and tradition.

And this is how culture was preserved, by holding none of it above the ground that gave it its life. Far from disappearing, traditional culture was reinstated with each honoured person and thing going to ground. The ground itself was the cache of all things traditional. Younger people with no lived memory of the depth and the abundance of their traditional culture were hard-pressed to agree to a long-lost piece of their proper inheritance, with all the symbolic import it would carry, melting into the rainforest again. It may be that a little of the cultural poverty that produced empire and grave robbing and museums and nostalgia and a free-floating anxiety masquerading as hunger for anything of substance and endurance in a world full of meaning-free eclipse had made its way to the west coast too, no surprise, and it had confused tradition with preservation. All the while it seemed it was the older people of that community, the ones with childhood memories of grandparents' stories of how once it was otherwise, who, by agreeing to forgo the gravitational pull of loss and the faux solution of preservation, and by agreeing to go to ground themselves when their time came and be remembered, not climate controlled or preserved, dug in their traditional elder heels and mysteriously gave their younger relatives a living example of endurance, of grace under pressure.

So this could stand as one example of the notion that elderhood is not a quality or condition of individuals, not an iteration of personality. You could well imagine that elders remain beset and bewildered by all the various character flaws and personal failings known to the rest of us and are not masters of frailty. Nor have they been radiated by the pure light of inexorable wisdom and by virtue of that purity that will never fail you. Their elderhood resides in them having grown a deep familiarity with the slights and slings and sorrows of being human, in having a lot of time-in with the vagaries of nobility, with foible and with folly. Their elderhood is forged by the madnesses, the sadnesses, and the mandates of their time. You could say that elderhood is a kind of homeopathic remedy a culture in desperate straits fashions for itself, a crazy time's dream of well being and sanity.

17

SPILLED WINE, BROKEN CUP

Old Desire

No one drinks old wine and immediately desires to drink new wine; and they do not put new wine into old wineskins, lest they burst, and they do not put old wine into a new wineskin, lest it spoil it.

—Gospel of Thomas, Log. 47

his observation on the finer points of the vintner's trade comes from a collection of sayings, aphorisms, and parables attributed to Jesus, dating from the late second century of the common era, perhaps earlier. Many biblical scholars see the Gospel of Thomas as among the oldest strata of biblical literature, something that was probably relied upon as a source of authentic testimony to Jesus's message and manner by the writers of the synoptic tradition. Whatever light it might cast on the Jesus story, a little exegesis here might go a long way to lending an understanding of the alchemy of old.

Mention the name "Jesus" and a lot of associations or expectations of the "do this/don't do that" variety begin to stir. But if you look to this saying for another commandment, you do so in vain. There are none. You don't find a "should" or a "don't," nor a "maybe" nor a contentious "but." It is a description of what happens, how things tend to go when you slow down and pay attention, nothing more. Prophylactic life lessons are a dime a dozen. But being able to see things as they happen right in front of you: that might be the Kingdom of God Jesus seems to have spoken of so often.

❧

Is it okay to drink wine? It doesn't say. I suppose that if the wine is bad you ought not to do so, for your own sake, but the wine in question here isn't of the good/bad variety. It is old, and its age is not a matter of opinion or debate. So you are in a different realm of life with this little story. Let's allow that they had wine figured out by then, that they had wine culture, too. Aesop didn't tell this one, because this one is for grownups, those for whom life rarely obeys the grim playground etiquette of right and wrong.

If you are lucky enough to have a couple of old bottles around, you are probably saving them for some important occasion. The longer you keep them, the more significant the event that prompts you to open them. Their agedness alone speaks of your esteem for the event and for the company once you open them. If you don't, you are saying something else about the event and the company. So the little story could well have begun: "Well, you know how it is with old wine, ..." because that is the realm you are being invited into. The telling of the story is the opening of a particularly old bottle, you see, and you are the honoured guest whose appearance has prompted it.

So, *No one drinks old wine and immediately does anything*. That is a fair way of reading the story so far. There is something about old wine that, if you are willing, will slow you down a bit. You've had some of the old stuff, and your collegiality is beginning to brew, and your hail-fellow-well-met-ness is starting to rise, and you are inclined to lounge a bit, and the beginnings of table fellowship are at hand. This moment that is at hand, and this company, will more than do.

> *Company: Com* is Latin, meaning "with." And the root word, pan, is "bread." So in its noun and verb forms the word describes "how we are with bread." The real quality of our communion isn't found in how we are with each other, but in how we are with the bread, the time, the world between us. The medium does the trueing. There's something Godless, soulless, about immediacy.

The story gets better: *No one drinks old wine and immediately desires.* There is something about old wine that can prompt a little contemplativeness, a little brooding, a little melancholy perhaps, a little ruminative lull in the proceedings. It is not fuel for desire, for acting on what you want. It doesn't banish desire, or demonize it. It hands your want back to you and asks, "Recognize this? Still interested? Still gotta do it?"

> *Desire:* Lionized, demonized, trivialized, deified, it is the surrogate for love for people on the move. Guarantor of immediacy and sensation, frisson, prelude to courtship when courtship is more of the same, executioner of courtship, more likely, desire has lots of takers. Most things that satisfy desire promise much and ask little, something in the manner of a summer blockbuster. As user-friendly as a consumer culture can bear, desire is. As such, it is also crucial for successful seduction, seduction being best known as a scheme for larceny in which the victim is certain that he or she is in receipt of a rare and mandatory treasure. In an age hooked on catharsis, longing is too often taken for unrequited desire.

> Leonard Cohen as an old man sang: "I'm tired of choosing desire. I've been saved by a blessed fatigue. The gates of commitment unwired, and no one trying to leave." By this I take him to mean:

> Being old has suspended most of the "got to's," including the one that once compelled me to union of any kind at any cost. Without

that particular "got to" in tow, I am mysteriously able to be with someone now. With the freedom from having to be here has come the burden of being able to stay.

In case you think this is a veiled recipe for getting old, remember that in the story, the drinker is of indeterminate age. It is the wine that is old. So, perhaps there is something about old wine that does the aging, that prompts aging in one who partakes, in one who is exposed to its alchemy.

It may be that the wine diminishes in volume as it ages and deepens in its funk. I don't know, but it feels likely. Does wine become old as a consequence of adding more, younger wine to it as it ages? No. This prolongs its middle age. By the time it is old wine there's probably less of it than when it went into the cask. But what's left is all old, all of it the steeped and strong and tempered kind. Maybe *the alchemy of old* suspends the mandate for momentum and success and more when it is invited in. Maybe it unmurmurs the growth mantra.

So maybe that's it: *the aged ages.* It is the agent of age, and it deepens not by acquisition but by diminishment. *Full* doesn't mean limitless, eternal, potential. *Full* only comes with limit. It means that everything is possible, and that most of those things aren't likely. It means being visited by limit and by reduction and by waning, for the duration. That is a parabolic declaration, an anarchic achievement. It doesn't reverse the order of the cards. It drops the deck all over the floor. And we're only halfway through the first line of the story. We're not chugging here. We're sipping. We're going slowly because the story is the old wine the story is talking about. You hearing it is you drinking it.

No one drinks old wine and immediately desires to drink new wine. That's just the way things go, the story says. There is something about the old stuff. It ruins you for the new stuff. Oh, Beaujolais is fine, more than fine. It's rambunctious, but it's thin, in a way. At least, it's thin as soon as the old stuff comes out. There's a time and proper place for the new, sure, but that place is made by the subtle, slowing presence of the old. You don't sneer at the new thing, once you've tasted the old. If you do, the ennobling of it has been entirely lost on you. Instead, you can understand now that the new wine is something that might yet turn to beauty, should age have its way with it. This is the way that the old wine began, after all, as new wine. You see this with age's eyes. You are readied for beauty.

⌘

I remember only the bare bones of this story. I don't have its origin, but I do have something of its spirit. There was a call that came in one day to the studio of a painter of some renown in the West. She picked up the phone and amidst long-distance cellular static, she made out a very formal greeting in an English heavily leaning to Japanese inflection. This man was calling her on behalf of a Zen Buddhist monastery. The monastery was in the midst of finishing a new meditation hall, the first new construction in many years on the grounds. His duty was to inquire about her willingness to accept a commission to decorate the ceiling of the hall. Complimented and stymied at once, she asked how her name had come forward. The spokesman didn't know. Was this a competition? No, he said, she was the only artist considered for the project. Did they know that she had no background in things Japanese or Buddhist? He didn't know, but he guessed that yes, this was understood.

She asked what kind of design they had in mind. This was entirely up to her, he said. Were there particular images that should be included? Excluded? None that he knew of, he said, though perhaps the standard religious imagery of the West might be set aside. Okay, she asked, then was she to submit a model, scale drawings? Or some kind of proposal? Oh, he told her, no proposal was necessary. She had already been chosen, and her design would suffice. So, there was nothing to guide her design, nothing preferred or forbidden, nothing to approve or improve?

"That is correct."

he said.

"So the first time any of you see the design is when I do the work in the new hall?"

she asked.

"That is correct."

he said,

Unnerved by the lack of constraint or direction, the artist then objected.

"But this is crazy!"

she said.

"So much time and money involved, no guidance, all this risk, and I just come and do it, and you've already decided that is as it should be?"

"That is correct."

he responded.

"But what if I do the whole thing, you people come to see it, and somebody doesn't like it?"

she said.

"Somebody doesn't like it? Oh,"

he said,

"this is guaranteed. In the way you mean it, nobody will like your design. This is just as it will be."

"That nobody likes it?"

she said.

"Yes, madam,"

he said.

"But all the money, all the time it takes! Its madness!"

she objected.

And he replied,

Not so much madness, madam, but novelty. That is what is assured. You see, for the abbot and for the monks, and for the country still, beauty is not possible right away. You must make the design, and it will be new, and because of that, it will not be beautiful. It will be many other things, they are assured of that, but it will not be beautiful. It cannot be. But perhaps, after some generations in the presence of meditating monks and incense and the light coming and going from the hall, perhaps the beauty begins. Perhaps it grows some beauty as the time goes along. It finds its way among us. We come and go. In days to come, it will be a part of the world, but we won't see that happen. No, neither you nor I nor the ones who decided upon you for this design will see its beauty, but that is not our responsibility. Our responsibility is to govern ourselves as if its beauty might appear some day, as if there will be a time that will rely on us proceeding accordingly. And we do this because the faithful, awkward novelty of former times has become our beauty now, you see. Unlike your people, we are the heirs of beauty, and not its creators. This is our understanding. Age is our teacher in the matter of beauty. Anything not showing its age is still young, and patience is required.

There are many cultures, usually cultures that have been in their home places for millennia, for which the young of anything is many things: vibrant, able, promissory, and the rest. But it is not beautiful. Whether it is a tree in the forest or the forest itself, whether it is the work of art or the ceiling of the meditation hall or the glance across a crowded room, the youth of anything is, for the moment, free of beauty. No young thing has been around long enough to achieve beauty. For these cultures, beauty comes with testing and trying and tempering. It comes with the stoop and the patina of age. There is no "age before beauty," not for them. There is aged beauty, and the beauty that seems only to come with having been around. "Age before beauty," they might say about our little epithet, is a crime against nature.

Legions of kids are coming downtown from the North American suburbs looking for OxyContin, looking for Fentanyl. These are prescription drugs. They are not mood alterers per se. They aren't hallucinogens. They are morphine's grim offspring. They are analgesics. They are pain relievers, and they are one of the more pernicious prompters of addiction, and their manufacturers know it. And young people, in droves, from the most materially prosperous culture on earth are at demonstrable risk to themselves, at this moment, self-medicating for pain, a pain not many anaesthesiologists would countenance. The manufacturers know that, too.

> Then consider the etymology of *anaesthetic*. There is the negating prefix, and then there is *aesthetic:* pertaining to beauty, to the capacity to make beauty and to recognize and be informed by beauty. So the sum consequence of being anaesthetized is to be disabled where beauty is concerned, to be unable to make beauty or to know beauty or to perceive beauty.

So, who treats themselves for beauty? The beauty-bereft, that's who. These kids aren't out on the corner looking for beauty in their lives. They've given up on beauty. They've lived its absence long enough. They're awash in the new and improved, the Version 9.6 of Everything, and many of them can't take it anymore. They've been obliged to proceed minus the presence of ratifying human agedness. They're twenty-five-year-olds in competition with fifty-five-years-olds for the same music, the same clothes, the same girl/boyfriend, the same payday, the same enlightenment. They are bereft of elders. Their solution is to disable that part of them that longs for that kind of human beauty, the time-sanctioned, the time-honored kind. They've tried swearing off the stuff, but it doesn't work. The longing for aged beauty is involuntary, and it's too strong. It takes strong medicine indeed to get by without it, to make as if it doesn't matter anymore.

⚜

And they do not put new wine into old wineskins, lest they burst. People who are under the influence of the aged don't go doing that, so the story goes. The tutelage of age runs through them, much as the warmth of the old wine does. The story doesn't say they shouldn't. It says they don't, which is a beautiful reversal on the shaming that so often passes for teaching. This is fermentation science, and this is the soul's life speaking.

New wine's volatility is its mania for sweetness. Still consuming, still on the take, still growing and molten and utterly persuaded of the Multiplier Effect, it will by the off-gassing of fermentation break apart whatever crucible contains it. *For now.* Under the influence of the old wine, you'll give the new one its due. The new wine doesn't know this, but that's its job, to grow itself towards stillness, until the harsh, acidic sweetness has been tempered by time, and the febrile frailty of "new" is soothed into reducedness and depth.

The next time you are in a personal development seminar and you see boomers everywhere, still with a taste for the Beaujolais, appetite unchanged from youth, trying to acquire a Sanskrit name or Lakota name or two and to grow at their age, consider recommending to them the Gospel of Thomas. When are you allowed to stop growing, and take up the exemplary, care-worn work of being grown? When are you ever allowed to look like old wineskins in this culture? "You don't look your age." From the mouth of youth and envy, this is a compliment. From the mouth of age, though, this is a lament.

So you drink the old wine, and the warmth comes on, and the tannins are doing their work, and there stirs something like an unsought capacity and willingness to know the world and all its ends for what they mean for you when it's your turn, and to know beauty, and to be on beauty's receiving end, and to not wish otherwise. You don't know what it is exactly, and it doesn't mean doing anything immediately, but you do begin to feel as though one of the keys to the kingdom might be coursing through your veins. This is not mood altering. This is the end of mood. This is something like wisdom coming on, what Leonard Cohen called "Johnny Walker wisdom."

And they do not put old wine into a new wineskin, lest it spoil it. This is a little more fermentation science for your consideration, masquerading as a bible story. The new wineskin—probably goat or lamb—has a rawness from the contents of the gut that hasn't been tempered and will continue the digestive mandate of life, consuming and converting to energy as it goes. The dynamic ambiance of the new wineskin can seduce the old wine to volatility again, to becoming "young at heart." Old wine is not immune to the draw of the sweet and the young, just as drinkers of old wine are not. They're not Teflon, and they're not bullet proof. They are not on the other side of it all.

The crafting of port, or fortified wine, shows this so very well. Port was an invention of the Age of Discovery, and the necessity of controlling spoilage and scurvy was its mother. If you want the old stuff to last across the Middle Passage of the Atlantic or of life, you have to slow its aging. And you do this by adding—what else?—sugars. That makes port, and port's middle age can last for a century or more. Drink enough of that stuff and you begin mistaking sweetness for age, and easy drinking for good enough, and ease for medicine. That's the work of that spoonful of sugar. But the wild alchemy of old wine is a powerful thing. It turns out that it is the bitterness—the bitterness of sweetness passing as time passes—that is old wine's medicine. It isn't the antidote to life; it is life itself, rolling on, gathering you up as it goes.

The beauty of this old musing about old wine is to me also its grief-measured wisdom. It isn't creed or screed. It is a tempered murmur. It has noticed that, under the influence, age will stop growing and, as a holy trade-off, start deepening. The old of anything no longer has its hand out in expectation or in supplication for whatever comes next. It has its hand out in greeting and in benediction. It is time spiraling, bringing the old wisdom back, in full view of the stilled tippler, blessing the young of anything with an example—and a chance—of enduring beauty.

Chalice of Old

There are times in your life that seem to be crafted just so you can do the right thing. It isn't likely that there are times set aside just for this reason, and perhaps it is as unlikely that the right thing announces itself with a clarity that leaves little doubt, but it is a useful conceit, a kind of fable that can refract the light of mercy into the particulars, where you can catch a glimpse of what is at stake. These moments seem to show themselves more in the rearview mirror than the windshield. But still, they are there.

In the early days of my time working in the death trade, it seemed I had already begun to appear as an outlier, as someone deeply under-persuaded—troubled, more so—by the status quo. The odd interview had begun to appear, one in particular calling me in caps in the header THE ANGEL OF DEATH, so the rustle of temporary notoriety had begun. When you are anointed THE ANGEL OF DEATH in print, at least two things can happen. You can become, pardon the vernacular again, a shit magnet, thanks to the instant access granted by the internet, drawing inconceivable attack or claims of unfounded kinship. Or, people recognize some kind of lucid hurt that has come their way in this phrase, and risk their isolation, and contact you somehow. Something contrary showed in the name, apparently, so people similarly troubled tended to seek me out, sometimes to air grievances against the medical establishment or against the family status quo when someone was dying at home.

There was a man whose sweetheart had recently died, and her family had boxed him out of attending the official mourning for various reasons that seemed compelling to them then at the time, but perhaps are regretted by some of them by now. You'd think that the death of someone close to you is one of those moments tailored for deep decorum, when the best of you trumps the rest of you. It isn't necessarily so.

This young man's plan was to have me accompany him on a prolonged road trip to a remote location in the northwest corner of the province, and in some ceremonial fashion consign the last of her things in his possession to the flames on an island they had camped on years before.

The route brought us through a few of the northern midwestern American states at a time when the convening of men's conferences in that area had begun in earnest. These events had been brought to my attention the year before. They seemed to have a tent revival tone to them, fraternal and redemptive and mournful and tribal, and a number of men whose ways I knew and respected found the ideas compelling and recommended them to me. On the way back east from the ashen sorrow of the island ceremony, the young man and I attended one of these conferences.

As it happened, the list of teachers included a few emerging luminaries whose names would become shorthand for "men's work" in the years to come. I had read some of their work. The whole business was by turns bewildering, enchanting, intimidating, and at times, deeply inspiring. One of the last evenings was given over to a kind of culminating feast woven from what appeared to me to be threads of Carl Jung and Joseph Campbell and Bread and Puppet Theatre and Sufism and a kind of pan-African catechism and pan-Indian funky quotient, to name a few.

As it went along, there was a spirit of rabid irreverence that began to claim the proceedings. The theatrics included some kind of barely rehearsed play that held the teachers up to a consideration that went from lampoon to ridicule, depending, probably, on how crowd pleasing a given teacher had been during the week, or on how seriously he took his teaching assignment. This was where things flirted with anarchy and with cruelty, frankly, and a kind of group mind began to assert itself, whose project seemed to include what the English call "taking the piss," bringing down every raised-up person and idea, killing every Buddha met on the road. It is a volatile proposition to raise to a spiritual practice among a generation of men who, many of them, had deeply ambivalent relationships with cruel or remote fathers and with men in authority, in a culture long on the entitlements of youth and privilege. It is certainly an idea that has enjoyed quick uptake in the West generally, and I've no doubt that its popularity can be traced easily to the deep resentment heaped upon older people for getting what they could and cashing in early, leaving the rest awash in indecision, in the particular tyranny of being leaderless.

James Hillman was among the teachers that night. He was reedy and a Yankee, and conservative looking and brilliant in insight and speech. He was, all in all, a necessary but anomalous presence in an event that was heavier on catharsis and tribalism and ecstasy than on the labours of learning. His was what should be called a deeply achieved mind, but this had begun to put him at a distance and a bit at odds with many of the younger men and men his age in attendance, men who probably had enough of feeling unequal to accomplished men well before they got to the conference. He was admired in a way, yes, but largely because the titular head of the event clearly favoured Hillman's presence there. So you could say he was tolerated and attended to and envied and inveighed against perhaps in equal measure.

One of the principal fault lines running through the men's work communities at that time was this deep unnerving uncertainty about elders, about what might constitute elderhood, about whether there could be such a thing any longer, about whether older men could be turned to and trusted, about whether old men were elders because they were old. If you recall the sixties' mantra about not trusting anyone over thirty, you have some sense of the lineage of this misgiving. It was certainly talked about and conscious to some degree, but it also lurked in the emotional wings, sullen and snarling and seeking its time. And the generational fault line cracked open that night.

One of the lampooning actors snuck up behind James Hillman and poured red wine over his head, enough to run down his shirt and pants. What I saw wash across his face in that moment was acute anger at what seemed to him to be extraordinary indignity, a spooked recognition of the aggressiveness that suddenly was swirling around him, and an equal recognition that this "calling down the mighty" was in the cards, set loose by the disabling grief illiteracy of the times. He was in the crosshairs of hurt right then, and he knew it. I sat maybe twenty feet from him, but all of that was legible from that distance. For a second, the group mind hesitated, wondering if it went a bit too far in this treatment of an older man. But the general hilarity continued, the play went on, Hillman was handed a towel. He stood where he was, shrugged, and with a frozen smile cleaned himself off as best he could. In his demeanor he went along with the tribe, but in his eyes he was adrift in indignation.

It was a moment of frank, disfiguring shame. It had happened so fast that there was no interfering with it. What did present itself to me in that wine-drenched minute or so afterwards, was the possibility of going to James Hillman, of helping him dry off, of offering to fetch him a clean shirt, and of standing with him and apologizing. I did feel all of that run through me. I am deeply unproud to say that I did none of these things. I hesitated, as unsure as some others must have been about whether this public shaming was somehow in the cards and part of the deal and mandatory for the Movement. I was ashamed to have been a witness to the thing, but in some fashion, not ashamed enough. Too young and too foreign-feeling, and not wanting to stand apart from this tribal jazz I had sought out, and not courageous enough, I froze. And the moment passed.

Years went by, as they do, and my life gained its few accomplishments, as it can do. I didn't think about that moment much at all. But I did get a bit older. You don't know you're getting older, as a rule, though people around you seem to know that you are. Some invitations come in that are persuasive of the rumour of standing, or notoriety, and they add to the evidence that time is gathering you as it goes. One invitation stood out for its mysteriousness. I was asked to attend a biennial meeting of the Jungian Congress, as a presenter. I was to join a panel discussion, the panel's title something like, "Jungian Analysts Meeting Indigenous Healers." At the time I was neither. I am still neither. I asked the organizers what position they imagined me assuming in this discussion, given that I could find myself nowhere in the title. I was told,

"Oh, we know you don't belong in either group. As an outsider, you might be able to say the things they can't say."

So the unlikely thing went ahead, was well attended and seemingly pretty successful. At the end of the second day, the idea was floated to head into the city for a celebratory dinner. We assembled in the busy foyer of the hotel. Most of my party had begun making their way to the taxi stand outside in the cold, but I was delayed in one of those revolving doors, caught behind a slow shuffling, mostly bald old man. I saw them signaling me to hurry, and I signaled back that the shuffler in front of me made it impossible for me to hurry over to my important life. Eventually he got clear of the door, and I came out behind him. Striding to my rendezvous, my taxi door open and one foot inside, I glanced over at my obstacle, leaning on a cane, taking his place in the taxi line twenty feet from me. I'd seen him once in my life, but I knew him instantly: James Hillman, now bent over and like the ancient of days, surrounded by handlers and luminaries, at the conference for a special study session devoted to his life's work. It's the kind of accolade usually reserved for people who appear to be at the tail end of their professional productivity, or their lucidity. I was cold, I was spent from talking and contending all day, I was being told to get in and shut the door, I was awash in that memory from twenty-five years before. I hesitated for a second.

You can think a hundred thoughts in a second, it seems, or be host to a hundred have-to's. Time slows down, but not in any way that helps. It doesn't make more things possible. It just makes more things legible. But seconds obey the passing of time more faithfully than we do, it seems, and they make their way through the revolving door of our attention span and come out the other side, over. We do the lingering.

I wish I could say that that moment was redemption, that the memory overcame my awkwardness in crowds, that I knew what twenty-five years ago asked of me, that I told the others to go ahead without me, that I elbowed my way towards him and caught his ebbing attention and told him about the spilled wine and the ignominy, about how I should have stood for him, because he was an older man and a wise man, because he deserved better. I wish I could say that he remembered, and thanked me for the consideration and the moment, and that his handlers then whisked him into the cab and into his deeply achieved life, and that I watched the cab pull into traffic, some wrong made better by finally doing the right thing by an old man.

But I was in the taxi and out into traffic before I knew it. I looked back, and I couldn't see him. So in the midst of a very expensive dinner in a very proper restaurant, I stopped the general conversation, and I told that story of the wine spilled. I told it because of the memory, wishing I'd done the right thing, maybe hoping that telling it was the next right thing, or the next best. I for one grew up with very few old people around me, and fewer elders. I had no training in the thing, in the particular skill of having elders. During the unsteady course of my days, that has showed. I read a few months later that he was dead.

18

WE'LL BOTH BE OLD MEN

Let them call it "your life" when they talk about you, if they do. But you know better. You know by now that it is barely your life, such is the implacable mystery of the thing. Better, you could say that the fiction called "your life" is a fiction not because there is a question as to whether you're alive or not. It is a fiction because it is neither yours nor is it a hireling dedicated to your transport. Nor is it that to which you are a mentor or a husband or steward, nor that which is entrusted to you, and so on. The jangling mystery of the thing is that this "your life" is *conjured* by having been entrusted to you. This "you" or "me" comes about because this aliveness constellates for a time in a place, and all that time and place turns into this fiction called "your life" or "my life." *Fiction*: from the Latin "to devise, to fashion or shape." So, when they propose to talk about you, if they do, they might consider talking about this life that made you instead. And you appearing in their midst will be recounted in time to come as part of the life that made them.

As I've suggested elsewhere in this book, the point at which *fiction* took upon itself the attribution of "falsehood," "allegation," "feint," is the point at which the fiction, the allegation we now call *fact* or *truth* mauled the indigenous European imagination, creating or conjuring the idea that there are things and beings of the eternal and universal kind that have always been. The fact that they endure—which is to resist change and the current of time, to disobey the obligations of place, to thwart and refute all this—is to a truth-addicted person or culture what makes them true. By that measure, anything that gives way to time and the vagaries of place and incarnation does so *because* it is a *fiction*. It is ephemeral, inconstant and unreliable because it is made by life.

But if you are willing, consider that every made thing is the maker's song and sign and stamp, the thumbprint and attestation and avowal, the makers' way of being themselves, and that we ourselves are made, then we and our many truths, and our many ways of truing, are one of the fictions (and nothing more, and nothing less) by which time and place appear, as mandatory as each made something in this living world appears to be.

Anyway, this fiction that is the life and days granted to me remains mysterious—in fact, gains in mystery—as it lopes along. And my temporary entanglement with other fictions as I go deepens the mystery by concealing so very little and prompting into notice so very much. Not everything is revealed, quite, for which I render some gratitude. If we work backwards from the evident, we might come to the sorrowful mercy of this mysterious, human life. That portion of the mystery of life that comes to us as something understood, manifest, given and clear and trued is often already of such a degree of ramshackling and dishevelment that the Gods hold "the rest" in escrow. What we don't understand isn't a gap in our understanding. It is kept from us for a while, sometimes for longer, pending our capacity to see and to carry a little more. This architecture, what we so often mistake for the blind spot, the dark zone, the place beyond all hope, is the love and deep regard by which we are beheld by what causes us. The threshold of our understanding is that little betrayal we rail we rail against for a while. We claim for ourselves—that little fiction, our "self"—the right and the general capacity to endure revelation and to know it all, eventually. But, mercifully, mystery prevails, and we have shards of the big story and little more, that those to come might inherit from us.

And so it was that I found myself in a place I sought not: Iceland. Even for a person to the north born, the name of the place alone persuades me to search elsewhere for comfort, particularly in winter. It is, by most measures, an uncommonly accurate name for a country. But I was in Iceland in summer, at the summer's navel in fact, by kind invitation of someone willing to organize a teaching event for me there. Now, I have grown accustomed to and fond of the particular regimen of seasons, all four of them. And my metabolics and my mind seem governed by them. The ending of seasons I find reassuring and melancholy-making all at once, and it makes a place in the heaven of affect for the brooding and the gloomy, the pending shadow and the rest. I recognize my fellows from northern climes by this proclivity for drawing their heads down between their shoulders, instinctively obeying wind and the particular seasonal finalities. When we travel south, we are so clearly "come from away." You would think that the further north you go, the more likely it is that you'd be seasonally adroit and be yourself subject to calendrical change without notice. But this is not the case. As you approach the extremes of pole or equator these changes blur, soften, cease. It is only in the intermediate places, those on the border of extremes, that the subtlety of calendrical endings prevails. Iceland is, as we'd say, "up there," and as much consequence as visitation of the blue grey palate, visually, emotionally, phonetically.

So being there at the summer solstice had me giving myself up to a night that was more like endless, boundless, relentless dawn. The sun never quite reared up, or set, depending on how you felt about it, and for an enormous part of the day the succor and penumbra of night was gone. You had to decide that it was night, since there were no signs save your flagging energy or attention to detail or the behaviour of the locals. Imagine *deciding* on what had been for your life an eternal verity. Imagine the arbitrariness of the thing, an arbitrariness that seemed to border on idolatry, elevating fatigue and flagging attention span to the echelon of a deity, a calendrical deity at that. That's the Land of the Midnight Sun for you, a parlour car on the Mystery Train.

I was teaching a few things there, up in the north of the country, making a few allegations, making a case for a kind of regal sorrow that personal sorrow can't rule. This session was a little about the state of the world, a little about the mandatory limits of translation and about the God-givenness of culture and diversity, and the like. In the mornings and evenings we met in a little village hall that had a small stage at one end that put me in mind of a primary school gymnasium. Local people provided the food from the menu that sustained them daily, and they honoured us.

Today the place is going through the disfigurements of tourism, and lately that is combined with the grievous insult of a pastoral way of life based on shepherding and fishing swooning and passing away. The local kids want the internet and the city, and so farms that have been farms for a thousand years threaten to become hobby farms for dot-com guys from town, or escapes and the like, or airbnb destinations, all versions of the living death which is globalization. The spectre of resource extraction has come to take the place of the local Gods, in the form of a hydroelectric dam.

But when I was there, it was still a living place, with a sense of itself that included knowing full well that its most vital days were, for the moment, well behind it. My host wanted to give me some understanding of how things had been here for many scores of generations, and part of the education included sitting me down to watch a documentary film made in the 70s about that very area and its two villages. The film focused on a robust farmer and his family, still making a go of it at the edge of the world. There were a few sheep, a self-made fishing boat at the self-made dock, a half dozen shacks drawn from driftwood in states of melting back into the ground, the main house leaning away from the wind and still mainly upright. There was a scene in the kitchen, where the old woman worked over a steaming pot on the little electric stove, and a couple of teenage boys lingered awkwardly at the edge of camera range. The old man had just come in from a hard day on the sea, aglow and awry. Alive and safely in his kitchen once more, he did what he'd probably done for decades. He slid across the bench built into the wall behind the table, leaned into the corner in exactly the same spot, decades of practice, and rested his head on the same place stained with hair grease, a brown smudge on a wall painted enamel emerald green. The posture looked as though it might be hard on his neck, but he looked thoroughly content and fully at home, and all was belonging.

This is not something we see often in daily life in the West. We see exercises in propriety, all manner of us exercising ourselves out on the edge of dominion. We see all the signs of self-assuredness, not always accompanied by the abilities that grant it. We see preemptive and pre-mature allegations of selfhood, but we rarely see—or I rarely see—someone engaged wholly in the inflections of being entirely at home, not waiting or wanting to be elsewhere, whose presence is not pitted headlong towards the not-yet or the could-be or The Plan. Fatigue, I'm sure, helped the old man ease himself onto his bench, and having done the same thing scores of times before would have put him in the manner of it, but what this scene pictured was a skillfulness any achieved human being from any era probably would have recognized. This man was someone affable and arrived, whose entire life and its ways were caught up in attending the moment, who could reach across the table to serve his ancestors their due, who could know around and below him the Gods of his place, who could gather strangers into the abundance of his allotment of days, who could mete out rough elegance, and mead from the flask, and smoky salty mutton leg of last fall's slaughter, and fermented shark, and kindness. All of this was in the incline of his day's end, of his leaning in his kitchen.

That is what I saw, anyhow—a picture of so much consequence from so little striving. I suppose it was the uncommonness of the thing in my days that claimed so much of my attention and my admiration. And it must have been that detailed devotion to his place that placed him so squarely in my notice. This magnified by many times the feel of fate and mystery and fortune that attended me on a trip the next day to that very fjord, to that very farm, to those same ramshackle buildings

with forty more years of melting into the turf and leaning off the wind
and still somehow upright.

The road we followed clung to the shore's edge, and the shore was
a fjord, which meant that we were forever driving in the shape of a "v"
in order to cover a short as-the-crow-flies distance, which meant that
the drive was constant and it was slow. With the pace and the progress and the meander, the trip had a tone of the processional about it.
Once past the defunct fish plant, it was clear that the road we were on,
fitful and fissured, hadn't been there for centuries, perhaps not even for
decades. Before it, there was probably a two-wheeled path, ground out
by wagons, and before that, a footpath of sorts for those who wouldn't
go over those high hills that are the backdrop to everything coastal in
Iceland. And before that, and still, there was the sea.

When you're told that the farm you are visiting is a thousand years
old, you look for the signs. You look for the old foundations, the signs
of people come and gone, of failed farms along the way, of the detritus of a
civilization in search of civility. In Iceland you seek these signs in vain
once out of the main cities. I suppose there are old timers, or archeol-
ogists (which is what modernity has to replace old timers) who could
point to the subtlest heave in a patch of ground and help you see what
remains of the turf house of yore. What you can see is the restraint that
climate and economy and Lutheran severity has obliged the people to
over the centuries. And it shows in what is not there. People in the
countryside live, it seems, in the bracket, in the kenning of those who
went before them. I don't say they seem content to do so. I only say that
they seem willing to be drawn along by the mutterings of Old Ones, as
if those Old Ones had already fingered the edges of the cloth of growth,
of more, and had passed along the tested and tried wisdom that what
is possible isn't likely. The wisdom of the shoreline, and the heaving
horizon, and the fierce beauty of a place unadorned: by these you Braille
your way along a shore-hugging scent of a road to a thousand-year-old
farm that looks maybe fifty years old.

Of course the farm dog knew of our approach before we'd rounded
the last hillock and the sloping, grassy place came into view. I suppose the

gravelly warning of the wheels was enough, or the engine whining along. It is a fine thing to get done with a long drive and have the greeting of an animal without reason for fear, whose days seem clearly and properly to include your visit. My dogs leave, among other signs for the visitor, a disregarded femur from the butchering, its schmeck long gone, a deer head with the nose gnawed up to the eyes half buried in the snow. But they are roused by the appearance of something unfamiliar that walks upright, such is their breeding, and they are vocal without the hackles up and the teeth shown, such is their training. Much like a new parent who swears off the example of his parents and promptly proclaims the hackneyed parental things that once galled him, I find myself assuring would-be visitors with the line I once thought to be reckless and indefensible: "They only sound fierce. They're friendly, really." But this Icelandic dog regarded us as she did the wind. We'd come in from elsewhere, would linger in the eaves and the grasses, then would be gone into the wide world.

Her welcome stirred the old farmer, who'd been pulling at a pile of scrap metal with his young nephew. He straightened up, wiped his hands on his work pants without effect, and came over to the car. A fine greeting ensued, but you wouldn't call it warm. "Warm" would have been premature, inconsiderate of the mandatory distance that strangers cover in order to meet. We had some social ground to cover to make our way to "warm." I recognize this country practice where I live too. It's what people from the city mistake for standoffishness. It's understandable. Uncovered social ground in the urban world is like undeveloped land: either a threat, or waste.

The old farmer I think felt honoured a bit that we'd come to visit. He walked us around for a while, probably to get the drive out of our bones. We stopped in a field by a mossy outbuilding. The old man nodded to the remains of the old dock we'd seen in the film the night before, the same one the old man's father heaved nets upon once his son had tied off the boat. A bit of a story came out. He warmed to the telling of the washing ashore of a few land mines the Germans had left in the North Sea, years after the end of the war, when he was a child. They were still live when they came up on the beach we were standing on. His father, using the standard wiles of the farming life, figured out how to defuse them eventually, but as it happened, one went off during a storm. Years later our host was driving sheep on the mountain behind us, a half-mile up, and found there, wedged between two rocks, a tire-sized piece of the mine. He spoke of it even then with wonder. He knew how the metal got on the mountain, but he was still happening upon it as he told the story, still mystified by the strange, ordinary things that made up his days.

Though it was the summer solstice, this being Iceland, the breeze could be cooling. So soon enough we were invited indoors. Now, in the film of the night before, there were many shots of the men working and the sea slashing ashore, but there were few of the buildings, which looked as unspectacular and unlikely now as then, as unworthy somehow of a thousand-year-old homestead now as then I supposed, and so it wasn't clear to me that we were headed into the same house as the one that the old man had grown up in, the one his father had taken his ease at day's end in.

Shoes off, a new bottle of Crown Royal in its purple tote bag given over as greeting and peace, we crowded into the bit of hallway and down into the centre of every worthy house, the hearth room. The kitchen had table enough for six fit close. The table had seen as much work as it had food. There were a few unmatched tube steel chairs, spent calendars on the wall ... and there was the wall, that same glossy emerald enamel. So I was in the same house, the same room where the old man's old man took his ease at day's end.

The old man didn't look at me hard or long when we were introduced. It was more as if he took in the coming and goings of my face in a second or two, and the next few minutes he took to wonder about what he saw, and what it meant that I'd come, and such things, and who I might yet be. It was an old time kind of greeting, all inquiry and wonder, no analysis or postures reminiscent of domain or flairs of virility, as can happen when men strange to one another meet in a place long on material sophistication and short on civility.

Eagle Mask was his name. Any thousand-year-old people that can give their boy children names like Eagle Mask, and have that be the name they take to school, meet the parents of a prospective sweetheart with, hold down a job with, and loads of other endurings of life that claim a person long before they age, surely such people don't wonder when and if they might yet be a culture. Imagine toting such a potent load of a name around with you as you learn the nickel and dime of being a man and a human being. And his brother's name was God Man. So he wasn't unusual in this, even in his own house. And his father's name was Christian. So you wonder how the Gods worked out their various claims upon such a place and people.

Well, Christian was long dead by the time I met this old man Eagle Mask who was his son. But he was not gone. I thought that the aged son bore something of his father's elfin manner, especially in the eyes. But men are marked by their mother's look more often, and I suppose she was doing most of the gesturing as Eagle Mask bade us sit down and be at home. The place had enough, maybe more than enough of the look that places get when there seem to be only men to attend them. To say that Eagle Mask was handy would discredit his abilities, and the house worked, yes, and everything that needed its fixing seemed well fixed, but there wasn't the tone of a place lingered over and tended to, which is another order of "fixed." And it was as if the kitchen was not quite anyone's domain any more.

As the mismatched cups were brought out to give the Crown Royal and our arrival their due, Eagle Mask made some subtle and brief comment to the lady who'd brought me, and she turned to me quite pleased and said that the old man had the strange and welcome feeling that he was suddenly younger by some considerable years, since I bore such a powerful resemblance to Christian, his father, whose like he hadn't seen for quite a while. I took it as a compliment, and it might have been a thing of wonder to Eagle Mask to have the shade of his father sitting there in the emerald kitchen again with him.

Through the interpreting lady, we were able to go on together without the long pauses between strangers generally given over to producing new things to say, and soon enough we were wondering on the resemblance, a resemblance the lady corroborated. I'd seen it with my own eyes in the film the night before. I had no ancestral traipsing that included Iceland or Scandinavia that I knew of. England yes, some, and Ireland. When I was about to commence a teaching session in Kilkenny once, I was pegged by a number of older women in the room as one come back to his kin, clearly Irish once. I asked them how they knew such a thing, and one of them said, "Well, just look at yer 'ead," and they all concurred. Ancestrally, that was as close as I could get to Iceland, so far as I knew.

Its well-known in that country that Eagle Mask's family and all their kind had left their mark all down the length of Iceland's past, testified to in the *Landnámabók*, which remembers the first generations of settlement in the ninth century, the Norwegian diaspora, and who begat who thereafter. It's also well-known that they were want to sail and pillage, and the piratical deeds of his ancestors are to be found in several other country's old histories across the north of Europe.

Now it had become clear to me on this trip that kind and earnest Icelanders were proud of the fact that their ancestors conquered no one and displaced no one in the founding of their country, and in fact had themselves been obliged to flee from royal chicanery and the like in Norway, and so were on the right side of history, and could look anyone in the eye and stand by the story of their beginnings. But it seems forever thus, that there is authorized history and there is the other stuff, the inelegant and forsaken stories. And it may be in one of Iceland's somewhat forsaken stories that they did the work of clearing and breaking their ground with slaves taken from the Shetlands and the Hebrides and particularly from Ireland.

And it was in this rend in the official cloth that Eagle Mask and I found our common ancestor, the one from whom we claim the disposition of our eye, our frame, our colour. She was probably a young girl, probably stolen from her family and from Ireland to work the household and the new land. And work and begetting she did, and her mark marks both Eagle Mask and me now maybe eight hundred, maybe a thousand years later. And sitting there in the kitchen, we remembered that woman, and we remembered how mysterious and how close is our conjuring.

There was a seat of honour in the kitchen, of course, so far as I could see it. There were all those chairs, and then there was that bench in the corner, the stigmata of paterfamilias on the wall above marking the place. The young nephew was seated there playing a video game on his phone. I was fairly sure he had no idea how hallowed a place it was. As luminous and numinous as it was, I likely could never have taken that seat, even if it was offered to me. It was enough that I bore the look of Eagle Mask's father, and it would have been more than enough should I have come from away to sit in his place again. So it seemed to me. I was content enough to drink to the old Gods of Maybe that had gathered us, and to the raveling, unsought camaraderie and kinship that had gathered us, too.

There are moments in life so incandescent that the normal day can scarce contain them without breaking to bits, perhaps in the same way that there are moments in a life so large that they threaten the ribcage and the sternum that grant them a temporary home, and do all but break apart the bone house with their amen and their air of "a mystery here among us come from away."

As you might guess, this was one of those afternoons. They bring all those in attendance to the edge of the ordinary and remind each again of his or her mandatory home in the usual days, and they stir themselves towards their own endings. So it was coming onto the dinner hour. Our meeting was deep and proper and unlikely, and it was coming to its proper end. We put our glasses in the sink, gathered shoes at the door. The farm dog welcomed our departure as she had done our arrival, and we all made our way to the car left by the farm gate in the wind.

There is not much to say beyond "God to your way" or the like at a time like that. We all knew that we had truly met. So there was no awkward vow to gather again, or to remember this day, or each other. The whiskey was kind that way. I was awash in its kindness, so I could not make out Eagle Mask's parting words, which sounded a bit clumsy in translation. My hand in his, the wind ruffling the tall grass and the sea lapping the stony shore as it had done forever, Eagle Mask said:

"You look I see to be an old man."

There was a strained silence after my guide relayed his words. In truth, though I look every one of my years by now, I probably don't quite qualify for "old man" status yet. I certainly don't proceed as if it were inevitable, given the cardiac inheritance I bear.

So he looked to the translating lady, and it was clear in his look that he knew the rudiments of English, and he knew that her translation was off somehow. Whatever he said, he said again, still looking at me steadily.

"Ah no, no,"

she said.

"Eagle Mask says to you: 'We'll both be old men.'"

And he put his hand on my shoulder, and I did the same, and we nodded the only farewell left to us. He may have been an old Lutheran, and he probably was, but this was old school, wicked paganry, Druidical divination and nothing less, put to the good use of blessing my days for me, all of them left. We'll inhabit this wild world a little while yet, he said. Together, he said.

Let me say to you now that I don't believe that any of us should get old enough that the kinship of old people seems forgone and unremarkable. If there is such a threshold, where the mark of age is no longer a mystery come to gather us mysteriously, I myself hope not to get that old. It is in the gaze and the grip of an old person that you can appear suddenly whole and foretold, your life attested to and looking back at you with something like calm and a fondness for you, now that you've come this far. That is how it was at least for me that day. There was an old man, his father looking at him through my eyes, granting me my days, blessing me with an endurance he's already seen. He gathered me into his line, foretold our greying and sitting quietly at the table, the imprimatur of our days on the wall above our murmurings, a sign that the world is mysterious but not foreign, and kind, and that time will not forget us.

19

NOT THE BUDDHA

I was in yet another bookstore in yet another airport a half year ago. It isn't the best place to buy a book to while away the transcontinental hours, but the whole enterprise can get you to thinking. Really, they're not even bookstores. They are grottoes of grim fascination with technology, and they are selling gizmos that promise to enhance the reading experience but are clearly helping to make books—the paper kind, what they call now the bricks-and-mortar of the trade—a nostalgic memory. This is something that is happening in your lifetime. *Nostalgia* sells well (the word means "the return of pain"), and it is a halfway house on the road to oblivion.

I don't know by what criteria books are chosen for inclusion in airport shops. As I've scanned the pointless isles, I've been stymied by it. There are the usual items appealing to the business class, star elite, gold and platinum partners, and so on. They are clever for the first couple of pages but seem to burn out beginning with the witty titles. There are the deeply misanthropic items that feature profanity in the title with one letter starred out, coy and mockingly clever slanders of modern peoples' ways. There are all manner of self-esteem and self-help offerings, of course. There are biographies of people you'd not be likely to inquire after, and some cookbooks. Always cookbooks. Not much in the way of literature, I've noticed, unless it has been discounted to retail oblivion. Taken as a whole, the range of titles suggest that the people who choose this stuff credit the travelling public with little or no attention span, contemplative chops, or general give-a-shit. I know this: I've written two books that made it to the marketplace, and I've never seen either of them in the airports I've passed through. I don't know what that means, marketability-wise, for what I've done. It may be a compliment, and it may not be.

Regardless, I was in one of those shops, trolling, thinking that I've lived long enough to see reams of books about the zeitgeist of the times with the mark of ephemera all about them. One promised a brief history of mankind. Now, provided you haven't caved into misanthropy entirely and you still imagine humanity as something like a worthy subject and a worthy audience, why would you settle for a brief history of *anything*? Imagine what gets left out. Imagine that a good story might take at least as long to tell as it did to happen. Isn't the enterprise of learning something of how things have come to be as they are worth the time it might take to learn it? When did learning become cruel and unusual punishment? Yes, I know that not everyone will read the Loeb classics in their wondrous bilingual splendor, in their scores. Almost no one will. Still, when did the value and merit of the hours of your life come down to a matter of how easy they'll make it for you as you go along? Old school is what I've become on this and other matters. Not *old school* as in vintage leather jackets and 33 rpm stereo sound—not cool that way—more like *old school* as in stuck and left behind by the thrum of the next new thing. I suppose I'd never be accepted into the kumbaya congregation of The Church of What's Happening Now. Too late for that.

I myself don't while away hours. A protestant-in-manner to the death, though largely lapsed now, I am prone to working. Not droning. Working, by which I mean giving myself to something, hopefully to something like the highest, noblest bidder. There is, of course, the problem of fetishizing activities that are not much more than dithering. If you don't find the highest bidder for your attention and your skills, and still you are fond of working, and you obey the fondness to a fault, you could, in time, resemble someone on the subtle end of the autism spectrum, full of involuntary getting on with your life, life probably going the other way. But if you work at it, and the reason for your birth comes into view, work can be good for you. So it has gone for me, anyway.

The indignities can mount as you go along. They truly can. I do not mean the long list of dissemblance that becomes your body in time. Books that catalogue "infirmity" as synonymous with geezerdom are out there now, playing their part in discrediting elderhood by discrediting age, though they'd never own up to it. Being left out of the time parade: *that* would be undignified. You'd be a freak of nature. Give in to that kind of lunatic cheerleading, and then do the existential math of the thing. You see that you are sentencing subsequent generations to navigate this veil of tears utterly bereft of the venerable signs of time making its way, of time leaving its maker's mark upon you. You discredit whatever cooperates with time as a losing proposition, as a failure of the will. How is anyone to come of age when *age* has become "too much sun," "too much stress," "too much"?

No, by *indignities* I mean the laurel of vague regard bestowed upon the greying head by the peak-income-generating boors racing to their deaths. I mean the graceless approval heaped upon whatever they mean by *timeless*. I mean those cantos of crafty delusion and secret dread sung for change, for novelty, for the newest shiny thing. It leaches dignity from the bones of our mutual life for people who are old enough to know better to line up for a better deal than still being here. Though they might no longer remember what they wish they could or are glad they can't, they themselves are memory for people half their age. They are living testimony, living witness to the vagaries, to the unleavened mercy that comes with not being, in the mortal and enduring and utterly faithful words of the patron saint of the Orphan Wisdom

School, "in full command of every plan you wrecked." Bail out of the age parade and you betray those unwittingly seeking sustenance from your creaky presence on the scene. That is not a right. It's not truancy, and it's not a day off. That is dereliction of duty.

I've been teaching about this fractious phantom called elderhood for maybe half a dozen years, and over the last year I've begun to make some preliminary gatherings of my take on it all. Happily I've found that there was some willingness out there in the world to consider this very thing. I'd begun to call the sessions "Meditations from the World Tree, Withered." I'd intended to use that as the subtitle for this book, but I'm fairly sure that every focus group in the hemisphere would pooh-pooh it as hopelessly long and confounding. It doesn't give itself away in seconds, and in that way is not pornographic, and so it has no seat in the marketplace of book cover designs. But people seem to figure that elderhood is the preliminary phase of dying, so at first blush, those who figure I am The Death Guy might go along with it.

Years ago, sometime after the release of a documentary film about my time in the death trade called *Griefwalker*, I was approached by the online arm of a Buddhist magazine. They had a kind of movie study group, and they asked me to participate in a month-long online discussion forum. I reluctantly agreed. I say *reluctantly* because 1) I wasn't a Buddhist, as far as I could tell; 2) the film wasn't Buddhist, as far as I could tell; and 3) I didn't really know how to do an online anything, never mind going back and forth with unknown people about a film in which I appeared. But I was persuaded that this was something the film, otherwise not very well promoted, might deserve.

I was on the road teaching at the time, and I awoke one particularly bright morning in New Mexico with three new companions. I had bronchitis; I realized that I'd utterly forgotten to check in with the discussion group; and I discovered that the allotted month for doing so was already half over. Awash in feeling irresponsible and breathless at the same time, hoping that my silence would be forgiven or, failing that, overlooked, I had my host guide me through the Byzantine machinery of gaining online access to the group. Surprisingly, people had been weighing in on the film, and they'd been weighing in on me, too.

I'd somehow counted on the reviews having a particular Buddhist bent to them, meaning that I imagined they would be gentle in some fashion, of the inquiring kind, flirting with benevolence, maybe innocently but welcomingly bright-sided. I imagined that the group had committed to something like a spiritual equivalent of the Hippocratic Oath. All of which is to say that I knew very little about the on-the-ground realities of North American Buddhism, obviously. These were my fantasies, not theirs, and they can't be defended, and shouldn't be tried at home.

So I was a bit chagrined when I read through the reviews. Though it was advertised that I would participate in the discussion, very little of it was directed towards me. It was largely about me instead, as if I was in a room of people who knew I could hear them but seemed unrestrained by that, as if I were a ghost who hadn't gotten the word yet that I was dead, that my time was over. One particular thread of the discussion centered on an apparent gap between what I was "preaching" and what I was "practicing," always a ripe killing ground when anonymity prevails. A variety of my shortcomings were explored, their causes revealed. There were attempts to defend me—half hearted, I thought—by pointing out that it didn't really matter what kind of person I was, that the teaching could rise or fall on its own impersonal merits. And then came the coup de grâce, the murderous denouement. In a gesture of equal parts dismissal and forgiveness, someone ventured that I was to be offered a pass on my shortcomings, since I obviously wasn't the Buddha.

And that was the one that stung. What was so obvious about it? I wondered. Was it so glaring as to deserve this dismissal from the Pantheon of Worthies? Was *the Buddha* so obviously the Buddha at the time? Is anyone? It was dismaying that it was so obvious from the film that Buddhahood had escaped me utterly. It was a proverbial chicken bone in the spiritual throat, at the time. But I remembered Hesse's Siddhartha, which is the extent of my formal study of Buddhism. I remembered that scene from his early life of luxury and comfort and parental design, when he clambered over the garden wall and dropped into the world. Out in the street he saw age, saw its fate, saw what it meant for him and his future, and was gutted by it. He saw suffering, and the rest, and that seems to be all he saw, at least for a while. I don't know for sure, but it may be that the religion that fanned out from him had some element of that moment in it for a while, too.

Maybe *that* is a young person's take on aging, no longer restricted to young persons: diminishment, depletion, demise, then the deep end. Maybe that take on aging is a rookie mistake, entered into as if it is no mistake at all, as if the mists have lifted and heaven and earth have conspired to bring all to this noble truth, that aging is suffering, and that's all that it is, or almost all. I know that there's more to it than that, that Buddhism in all its flower is more elaborate on the subject than that. I know that Buddhism's scholars and practitioners have this whole business of suffering sorted in ways that have escaped me. I know there is attachment involved in the arrangement. Maybe, though, that "suffering from age" is oracular degeneration. Maybe that suffering is the unclaimed bastard child—or one of them—of refusing to age, refusing to fess up to being able to hear time murmuring your name, refusing the deal that was so nobly struck early on. Maybe all of this, and the awareness of all of this, is to be surrendered with greater and greater grace, now that you are coming of age, now that you are singing your grief song of gratitude, now that you are able to stand on the street corner of your life in the dusky light and see it all, finally, and wish the whole thing farewell. Not the Buddha, really, not by then. The witness.

20

MY MOTHER'S FATHER

My mother's father was something of a titan. I don't remember him being tall. He had no girth. He didn't have a mane of hair, no gypsy moustache, no musk to him, no flourish in his accent. He wore glasses, combed his hair straight back, kept it there with hair cream. He seemed to dress for business, kept a long pea and flower garden beside his house. He hadn't a tooth in his head that was his, all of them long ago pulled in favour of dentures top and bottom, operable props when he was feeling rascally, left in salt water in a glass when he lay down at night. He listened to the radio at breakfast, worked in the town tannery as a young man, knew his neighbours, had a workbench he knew how to use. His wife, bless her, was possessed of a class consciousness come direct from the old country. Though she herself came over as an infant, she imagined somehow she was marrying up when she married him. He came home from the leather trade each day with the alum and the abattoire funk in his hair instead. From what I could tell, she never quite overcame the disappointment.

My mother's father won the national amateur hockey championship two years running with that small-town team, and probably parlayed that local notoriety into a steady arena job. Eventually he became the manager of the place, and as such, he was lord of mythic terrain in small-town Ontario around the time between the two world wars. Everyone seemed to know him, but he carried his authority with a light touch. He knew every subterranean corner of his domain. He booked in dangerous tattooed wrestlers who I got to meet, and fiddle bands, oversaw town hockey and the figure skating clubs. He programmed music for roller skating in the summer when the ice was out. He asked me once about a song that came on the radio that he knew at once was good for public skating—"Paint It Black," by The Rolling Stones—and made me feel the prince when I knew the song and could tell him who sang it. He let me in on the magic kingdom of older men. They would drop in midday, when the arena was quiet, and in the blue smoke they'd trade war stories, some rough language, easy camaraderie. He would offer to shake my hand, then squeeze it so tight that the outside knuckles were brought together in a painful circle that made me writhe and whimper, an act of pure grandfatherly love for a grandson, whatever you who weren't there might think of it. He listened carefully when other older men spoke. He was of the last generation that seemed to believe in grace when among strangers. He tipped his hat to ladies, and he was in a small-town way all elegance as far as I could see. And I sat it on these lessons in age.

Somewhere around this time I was taken to a family reunion. I didn't know what those things were, which tells you something about the stringent understanding of family that hovered around me in those days. There were scads of people I didn't know. Among them were seven of the wildest, unhousebroken older men I'd ever seen. Nicotine fingers, slicked back hair, shirts half unbuttoned, missing the odd tooth, loud. I'd have called them gypsies had I known the word. But things turned out better than that. I was told in a hushed way that these were something called great uncles, and they were *my* great uncles, my grandmother's brothers. My grandmother, who wouldn't profane the moment if she had reasons beyond reason, who had English propriety as house furniture, she had the wildest brothers, marvels of raw splendor, dangerous types, and they were mine somehow. But she was so embarrassed by their manner that she'd all but disowned them years before, and I'd been raised without so much as a mention of them. They were the uncharted treasure of my childhood, and they were forbidden, and I never saw them again, a sacrifice to her marrying up. To my grandfather, they were characters, but in the name of domestic peace he didn't keep up contact, and all those little poverties turned into inheritances.

I say that my grandfather knew how to be an older man, but the truth is more likely that he had some of that forced upon him, too, as many men do. The labour laws of the time dictated that when he turned sixty-five, he was retired, and that's what the town did to him, right around his birthday. He and his family were piped out to centre ice in front of the town, speeches were made, he was gifted for a lifetime of public work with one of those black leather easy-boy recliners that are more suited to people with a few wheezy months of life left to them than to a man who was vibrant and alive and filled with purpose on his last Friday of work. He was roundly praised, and then his experience was surrendered with his massive key ring, and the show was over, and we all went back to his house.

On his first Monday morning as a man of leisure he was lost, and he was never found, I don't think. His wife obliged him to drape a handkerchief on the head rest of his recliner, so as not to stain the leather with his hair cream, and I don't believe he ever took to the thing, or to that little slight on his manhood that the handkerchief must have been.

I don't know how much longer my grandfather lasted after forced retirement, but he didn't live to see seventy, I don't believe. Within a year, maybe two, he had a stroke, then another. He came back from each one, but diminished, unsteady, and hollowed. Then one came on, and he didn't come home from the hospital. I was too young to know what it meant for him to be moved to an old folks' home across the street instead of to his house, though I know it well enough now. The last time I saw him was from the sidewalk in front of that "home" one frozen winter morning, him all stiffened on one side, his face a grimace, his wife holding his sleeve and wagging his right arm up and down in facsimile of a wave of goodbye. Everything I knew of the man had been taken away from him, maybe he was crying there on the other side of the plate glass, if he could still cry by then, and his one arm being waved for him, a robot's farewell.

And for all of that, there is still a memory I have of him that hovers over and haunts most of the others, particularly now that I am a few years short of his life span, particularly because it has the last words we shared before that last stroke that took his speech. His daughter, my mother, found herself alone raising two young kids at a time when that was a rare thing, a disfiguring thing, and she turned her entire life over to getting her children raised sane and respectful. Respect was currency in that house, and it is tested in single motherhood when the oldest is the only boy. The stirrings of adolescence were bringing all of that to a pitch of brooding, and uncertain etiquette. During that time, I was out at the edge of being respectful and had a wretched unwillingness to know the difficulties of my mother's travail on our behalf.

Somewhere in there my grandparents came to stay for the weekend, to help out in a troubled time. I could see that my mother loved her father, and that her mother's presence tested her somehow. There arose some incident. Maybe I was asked to do something I thought beneath me at the time. Whatever it was, I objected. I more than objected. I was openly dismissive, probably, or worse. A few silent seconds went by. It was then that my grandfather beckoned me over to him. I was still full of myself, and I stood stiffly in front of him. In that moment he looked at me very coolly, as if from a great distance, in a way he had never done before. He lifted up his right hand, and he was pointing at my chest. He made as if to tap on my sternum, and in a voice full of formal, alien rigour he said to me,

"Don't let me hear you talk to my daughter that way again. Not ever."

That's all he said. It was part warning, part manifesto of fatherhood. All of it is what an older man, grandfather or not, owes to someone wayward and slouching on adolescence's threshold. Of course, I was slayed by the trespass, by the betrayal, by him going over to the other side, another parent voice in a siren choir of parent voices. My adoration for the man had naïveté in it, maybe more naïveté than love. So I was especially, exquisitely, ruthlessly and permanently betrayed by him when he suddenly became someone's father.

It is, for all that, a treasure, that memory, the grandfather I was granted sitting alongside the granduncles I met once, all of them giving me people to come from, all in their fashion the treasure hoard for the Third Act of my life. My grandfather in that moment stepped out beyond the long shadow of comfort and familiarity, and became an elder to me. Lost as a souvenir of my childhood, he returned to me the duties of fidelity, and he became an old man, caring for who he loved. And I wish he'd lasted long enough for me to get it, to sit beside him one time, both of us men, so that I could have atoned for speaking so poorly to one he had borne into the world.

21

MAKING CHIPS

Young Man

I suppose you could get through all your days and call them complete and worthy, without ever having carved a bit of wood or stone. I suppose you could, but I wouldn't wish it on you. You could read paeans of praise to the thing, but it won't be raising you to break bread with the Michaelangelos and the other dusty brooders if you do. You could YouTube the subject until you can't see, and then imagine trying it out on an odd piece from the woodpile, but you won't slip the feel that you're just Watching Yourself Being the Woodsman. The truth is that none of this will make up for taking a small piece of the world in your hands, and pleading for precision, and asking for help, and making a mark.

⁓

As it happened, I came into a little notoriety, and certain invitations to attend and to perform and to solve and absolve came in, and I took them, most of them, and headed away into the din and glare of the road. A portion of that became The Mankiller Tour 2015, which granted me leave to show a book I'd written to that portion of the world that would have me. The following year saw not much respite from the invitations or the travel, surprisingly, and so the tour became my days, mostly. Wonder of wonders, I got a band, and we did concerts steeped in grief and mystery. Whether the tour has lived up to the name I know it by is yet to be seen, or at least yet to be seen by me.

With this work came a fitful but good living wage. I'd toyed with the desperate enterprise of a new building to house a proper school many times over a couple of years, to get me off the punishing road for a while. But I put the idea away again just as often, having built several houses and the like in my time and having a good memory of the ordeals they became, and having sworn I would never do that again to myself. But this time seemed different. There were a few young men around who, together, seemed to strike a note of capacity and willing-ness, and they needed the work, from what I could tell. And I'd slept a night in a turf house reconstruction of Eric the Red's childhood home on a fjord in Iceland that same year, so there was that ancestral pull and example in the mix. And the northern soul in me had settled in for the duration now, and as much as I could be taken in by a stone courtyard in Bali and other genius human designs in the temperate world, all the possibilities of my climate and land and ancestral thread dictated a post-and-beam teaching house, a solid thing with walls and heat and a proper roof.

The decision to go with those young men as the makers of this shelter for the dream of a better day that has claimed me came down to one quick interview. I don't think anyone, myself included, knew it was an interview at the time. We were just talking. I was rolling the thing back and forth across the threshold of sanity, seeing if it favoured one side over the other. Idly I asked whether any of them had done anything like what I had in mind before. No, they answered, no one ever had. They wanted to, every now and then, but they didn't know anyone with enough money to pull the trigger on such a thing. I asked whether any of them felt that, standing there that day, they thought they could do it. No, they answered, none of them was able to do the building as I had described it. Their candor a compensation for their inexperience, I figured this was probably the right crew for the task. I didn't have anyone else in mind, but it didn't seem to matter. They were rattled by the possibility, and afraid of it, but they couldn't turn away. And that struck me as noble, more a qualification for such a thing than prior experience. We'd see in the coming months if I was right, if their prodigal lives had indeed driven them to that empty hilltop in late spring, stakes in the ground, the strings between them the sole allegation of this hall that shone in my mind, the giddy likelihood of failure all around us.

⋰✠⋱

You too may have found that, just as in life, it is proper and proven that the tools for a carpentry job be well stropped and shining. Your building and your life begin there. You could dream of the hall for nights on end, as I did, and imagine Eric the Red himself is sending you the building plans (I didn't really do that), but the truth is that your every dream for the hall lives or dies in how the timbers are squared and trued, and that this is the lion's share of a life's work, too, the truing of what it will take. Everything else, whatever raucous or romantic or redolent thing you manage in the banquet hall of your life, follows upon how these early days and ways are taken up. And as someone who has been obliged by the blessed fatigue to surrender to patience (which is to say that I am considerably older than I was, and older than these four young men, and so more easily winded than I remember myself to be), I've come to see that there are *only* preliminaries. There's only the trying and truing, as you yourself may have been tried and trued and then released from youth. And that is when it is done, when the dice are cast. Every new thing bears the marks of its early days. Those marks stay for a long time, testifying to how you came to what you claimed to hold dear. The lighting of the tallow candles and the setting of the trestle table in the feast hall of your days are good and welcome things, but yet

I suppose you could more properly think of them as the aftershocks of attending well to the beginnings.

And this is just what the young men did. They had found a cache of rusty tools given over by an old timber man whose back had years before foreclosed upon his love of the wood, and these were just the kind of tools needed for a job of this scale. So they took these scarred, chipped blades, and they hovered over them and bore down upon them and honed them into life again. Oiled and sandpapered and whetted over and over until the blades fairly sang in the shafts of sunlight coming down to the shop floor, their edges were honed sharp as to be both lethal and just, as the smith had intended. And the young men sang too, and murmured the kinds of love songs men of renown reserve for what they rely upon most. And Scullery Royalty prepared the soups and stews and breads that preserved them as they worked. And I had the blessing of seeing all of this gather. It took days of attending to those edges to redeem them from tireless rust and neglect. I got antsy for the work to commence, until somewhere in the second day I saw that it *had* commenced. The young men themselves needed honing and stropping and truing. They became, out on that hilltop, an undeclared medieval craft guild, claimed by discipline and devotion, and by the fellowship of the wood. And by the likelihood of failure they were anointed into an upright, employed, worthy manhood.

And so it was that during those days—most of the summer's days and many of its evenings—of truing the wood, I found myself astir in old memories of the life I had lived as a carver of stone almost three decades before. I saw the posts for the teaching hall lying there in their dozens, scored and mitered, and the old longing in my hands began to rise. I watched the young men clamber over the pile. I remembered then the handmade life I'd once had.

I was a goner. In the posts and the beams I began to see the old hieroglyphs, the Old Gods and the Rough Gods, the Dusty Rafter Dwellers and the Ancients of Days, the Worthies and the Wastrels, all of the jangle of ancestors and kin over there in Old Country, before the days of the Middle Passage. They were fingering my memory for its edge and hone, seeing if I was willing to give them a seat there in the hall that was yet to be made. And I figured then that this is what I'd done all of that learning in my carving days and lost my hearing for. I would heave to, one more time. I would strop my old chisels, coax off the rust of neglect. And then I was in the privileged moment where I and the square wood began speaking together again after the long quiet of making a living and having a family had come between us.

⌘

Imagine that you are a certain age, no longer what you might have thought of as young and so no longer enjoying the various out-clauses that allowed you to behave badly when you were feeling awkward. They granted you years of untethered flailing while you fully exercised whatever freedom from deep belonging the culture granted. But it has occurred to you by now that most of that freedom is a safety valve provided generations before. Its purpose was to buy off your discontent, sell it back to you as adolescent imprecision, tolerate the acting out that ensued, sell it back to you a few years later as "legitimate compromise," something you could live with. Imagine now that all of that has dwindled, its power to soothe you gone for good.

So, you are there, at some kind of crossroads. Heading off in one direction is most every example you've seen of deep morality, or what you hoped was deep morality, now in disarray and engaged in the passion play of getting by. In the other, the weeded over trail through the underbrush of the reason you may have been born. More than "what you're good at," more than "what you want," the reason you have been born hints at design and mandate and a purposeful presence granted to you at birth. It hints at something greater than what you could come up with on your own. It hints at the possibility that this something is not so far away.

And, for that moment, that's all you have. You are enjoying the avails of freedom, as the order you've been born to understands them. It's all you have because the obvious enticements of potential, of "be all you can be" the blandishments of personal style, they've all begun to take on water. It's all you have because you are operating in an elder-free zone of self determination, with something less than the bare minimum of tuition and example in anything beyond enlightened self interest, and you've been doing so for years. So, it's "Over to you."

Though it wasn't entirely clear then, I stood at that very crossroads in my early thirties. It was a bit late for the "what am I doing here?" contemplation, and it wasn't for the first time, and I knew the territory somewhat. Recently married, recently graduated, recently entered into fatherhood, it was another of those beginnings you wouldn't go looking for. Fortune had granted me a bit of breathing room in the form of "marrying up," and the chance presented itself of assembling enough of the tools of the trade to begin practicing what I'd for some years imagined I might yet love: stone carving, of all things, an antique and antiquated endeavor that had, at the outset, the signs of a life's work, without the means or manners of such a thing.

Working with stone is an enormous privilege. At least, that is how it came to me. Stone is stern, stoic, grave, enduring. Stone has all the hallmarks of time, too. It has a tangible but subtle grain or current, an inextinguishable memory reaching into the mists and coming up with fossils, with sand grains perhaps from the earth's mantle itself. Stone always struck me as time slowed enough to become visible, agreeing to be at hand, willing for a while to be known.

After flailing on my own for a time and growing weary of myself and my self-administered inability to do the stone justice, it occurred to me that if I was to honour the noble marbles that I'd imported at considerable expense from Pietrasanta in Italy, I should learn those things that lay out beyond where my excitement and imagination ended. That's where much of the learning seems to live. For a time I, in a technically efficient sort of way, imitated the work of the luminaries whose work I admired at the time. The limits loomed up before me again. I set out to find a living, local practitioner, whom I imagined to be waiting for the likes of an acolyte like me. It wasn't easy.

Whoever had done this before me had long since figured out there was no money to be made, that there was little demand for the work here in the tradition-free New World. I no longer remember how I found Mr. Cox. Maybe it was stumbling across a number of style-dated full-sized Greek myth carvings tucked away from the Ferris wheels and carny barkers on a brief expanse of lawn in the exhibition grounds of the city I lived in.

Here was someone who'd done the work, evidently for decades, who was in retirement but still alive. So, without for a second wondering what it may have done to him to watch his life's work collapsed into "quaint," into "craft," eclipsed by the Chinese knock-off and come to a time when anything once carved in stone no longer was, I called Mr. Cox.

It was a rough encounter. Excruciating. He wasn't getting old. In his eighties by then, he *was* old, and he'd been old for some time. My opening gambit was an undignified faux pas so bald and unreflective that I wince even now to recall it. After the standard introduction I told him that I did the same kind of work as he, and that I hoped it would be okay if I dropped by and got some pointers that would deliver some similar kind of success. Clearly I was banking on him recognizing a brother in arms, someone worthy of his musing and ministration. Clearly, he didn't. There was a frosty silence.

He then said,

"Same kind of work, eh?"

and I probably equivocated a bit and acknowledged that I was still in the formative stages. I hope I did. More silence, always instructive in hindsight. He let out an exhale of low-grade torment, and then asked me this:

"Do you work every day?"

Scrambling now, because I knew the right but not the honest answer to be "yes," I said:

"Well, I do think about it every day."

"Do you?"

he said. Thinking I was over the threshold and into the initiates' chamber, I told him I did.

"Well, maybe you call me when you work every day."

And the phone clicked off, and I held the receiver, and I probably made the following pronouncement over the proceedings and over the receded hairline of this old man from whom I proposed to take something of his life's learning, who by virtue of calling him I had acknowledged as factotum of all things sculptural: "Asshole." I don't remember doing so, but probably I did.

And how did I carry him down into this purgatorial half-life reserved for the deeply discredited and the disquieting? Well, he failed to go along with my relentlessly naïve project of getting for myself what I didn't know how to learn, and he failed to reward me quid pro quo for calling by opening the hoard of his technical knowledge, savvy, and connections. Of course he was an asshole. Of course he was. We weren't even in the realm of the Two Betrayals yet, and I—knowing next to nothing about stone or sculpture or what it cost to have a life's work—already had him figured out.

Well, I was gored by a dilemma. I hadn't entirely given up on Mr. Cox, though he'd slipped down a few rungs in the Pantheon of Worthies I imagined joining. I had his phone number, and I had this Gordian knot. How much time had to elapse for me to qualify for this audience? How many days of work amounted to *working every day*? Anyone who has obtained the phone number of someone he or she wants to get to know better has been there. There are two possibilities that appear in the midst of your striving and your plans. Either you call too soon, which is a sure sign of desperation, which will wither any worthiness or comeliness you might have enjoyed until that moment. Or you call too late, a sure sign that you are too cool, way too aloof, and generally not worth the trouble.

I didn't know any way of untying this knot then, and I don't know it now either, but after about two weeks of working every day I was disconcerted enough to call, figuring I would never be more qualified to do so, no matter how many more "every days" I racked up. He picked up the phone. I began to introduce myself, and he cut me short.

He sighed,

"I know who it is."

"Well, okay,"

I said.

"I know it hasn't been too long since we spoke, and I could have waited and kept working every day, and I will, but for what it's worth, I'm serious, and I hope that's good enough to come over."

"Two weeks, eh?"

he said, and I just had no response that would do. After a long pause, he said,

"Okay. But there's a condition. If you agree to it now and renege on it after I die, I will figure out how to haunt your ass to kingdom come, and I will do it. Okay?"

I said,

"Okay."

"Right then,"

he said.

"It goes like this. You come here in a week, and I'll tell you everything I know. It won't take too long, probably not as long as you're hoping it will. I don't know that it will help you, but that's up to you. In exchange, you will keep absolutely none of it to yourself. None of it. If you do, well, I'll find you."

"Alright,"

I said.

There were many stories that came out of that meeting. We were out in his backyard, and I was admiring the obvious merits of a life's work in the gardens and the ponds, and I admired it aloud. After a minute of quiet—he was probably weighing the merits of telling me something I was unlikely to understand for another thirty years, at least—he summed up the whole thing. He said:

> "Yep. I've been lucky. Very lucky. When we broke up, my wife didn't turn the kids against me. I got just about everything I ever asked for in this life, and I don't know many that describes. But I never asked for love, not really. I went along with it, but I never asked for it. And I never got it."

That's an old man's story.

The other one amounts to an etymology lesson, one I've told many times but I don't think I ever wrote down. The stone carving life has, of course, gone on for many, many centuries. The Romans, and then the Italians, developed a lot of the technical savvy that turned it from a craft into an industry. Along the way, they developed a taste for certain kinds of stone. The preferred stone for statuary work has come to be called, no surprise, *statuario* marble. I've had a few choice pieces in my time. This kind of marble is graced with a crystalline structure so fine that it will take the subtlest, most articulate detail and hold it, and it is priced accordingly. There is a poor man's marble with a resonant name but a dappled utility, called *travertine* marble. Travertine is coarsely grained, probably younger in geological time, often with holes that make subtle work all but impossible.

But human ingenuity is not absent in the stone trade, and many years ago, carvers figured out how to take bees wax and tint it with travertine dust and fill the holes so adroitly that from a distance, to an untrained eye, the marble looked whole and flawless. You have probably been in a good many lobbies of apartment or office buildings clad in floor-to-ceiling sheets of travertine marble with nary a hole showing, such is the skill of the trade, without you wondering how they got sheets of stone that large and perfect out of the ground.

Now, the Latin word for wax is *cera*. We have borrowed a Latin prefix and it appears often in English: *sin,* meaning "without." Though the word has probably been used for centuries now as a synonym for "honest," "faithful," "pure," and the like and has been used to evoke an inner quality of intent, the simplicity of the thing, courtesy of the stone trade, is this: *sincere* has a less abstract meaning, and always has. It means "without wax." It means, "Alas, the holes show." And this quality isn't held in particularly high esteem in a time and place where the standard is, "Don't let them see you sweat," where "You don't look your age at all" is offered up as high praise, and where authenticity is sacrificed for marketability time and time again.

And it may be that sincerity is a signal feature of elderhood, where looking your age took the best part of a lifetime to get right. Everyone younger than you can get their bearings as to where in their lives they are from your willingness to be deeply on the receiving end of yours. You are an elder. You neither lead nor mislead. You live unto your days instead. That is what Mr. Cox did for me. At least, that's what he showed me, a willingness to be whole in a way that the sorrows and the misdeeds appeared. From what I can tell, he hasn't taken to haunting me, not yet.

And so it can happen in that carving work that there is the first flush of taking dictation from the Great Beyond, or so it seems. There are bits of story waiting on the telling blade, or you hope there are. As you draw and erase on the stone or wood you lay claim to a lucidity that gathers Old Gods to you and nothing less. Without that temerity you are unlikely—and maybe unworthy—to strike when the time comes.

The problem is, you don't know what to do. You linger over the pencil lines. You plead them towards a story, because this is not the time for self-expression. There are acres and ages of good stone or wood under your hands. Ruination and waste are just there at the edge of your ideas. There is plenty of room for faltering. But if you rely on the pencil for certainty you'll never carve. And so, after pomp and prayer and a breath on the blade, she bites. Too late to think more, the work's begun. "Making chips" is what the carving men call it. It steals your nerve. It ruins your confidence, and it dares you to strike the chisel and make your mark on this piece of the world that is on loan to you for a time.

So, there I stood, among the beams and posts, and make chips I did. I ran my hands on down the length of the wood, and bore down and cleaved away. As the flush subsided and the excitement left me, the scale of the mess came clear. I was too far in now, there was no way to leave it. Acres of chips were waiting to be cleared so the dream image could appear. I went through the particulars of the creative hell of workmanship. Strike after strike, blow after blow, and the hours and days gone, and there was nothing to show. The whole enterprise, the whole design was as flat as a cartoon. It was worse than going into the forest and drawing on a tree. Worse, there was the feeling of transgressing the grain and that solid, singular gesture of the planned, trued post those young men entrusted to me. Nothing of merit added, only little habit spasms where the hands are remembering what they can't form any longer. It'd been too long, I thought, too many years since I'd done it, and now I have this caprice to answer for. And those young men are watching.

And this is the bulk of carving when you are trying to court it back to you after decades of neglect. The great acres of time between starting again and whatever the reason might be for you to do so have appeared. You can't wait, not for inspiration or assurance or a sign of progress or providence. You have to work, with nothing to show, until that magic moment when the light glances just so, and there's a movement in the wood like a deer behind the bushes, and something comes forward and something recedes, and there is the life that was always there and always willing to show itself. You sweep up the chips, and you have proof for now that for a time you were willing again. And in four months time you will take the winter's sting from your fingers and the tools and the cold in the new hall by feeding these chips to the woodstove, the proper end for all your willingnesses, aflame and temporary and ebbing. You are now deep in the Second Act of your allotment. You've seen more of life at this stage than you will ever see again. All your errors are earned. All the victories are grace. Most of the story of you, almost all of it, has been told and duly noted somewhere. And if there's luck, you have a few young men there, watching, and somewhere in there is the art of the thing. And when one of the young asks what you meant by it all, you might say, pointing to the carving, "Something like that."

I commend that to you.

This Curl of Life

Storytelling, it seems to me, is the oldest of the conjuring arts. It has dabbled in the bright lights, veered towards the sunny side of life in the last centuries, and is often afforded a flat in the ghetto of "children's entertainment" today. But for all of that, we ignore at our peril the example of those cultures who know it to be so that the world was spoken or told into being, that speech is one of those noble verities we are entrusted with by the Ancients of Days and by the Gods to help them do their work here. I am asked from time to time where whatever skill I might have for the language came from, and my ready answer is that I was read to, certainly from birth, probably while in the womb. So story is in my hearing. That is the way the world comes to me, as a storied being wrought by story, telling humans again and again into being. The arc of human life, the warp and the weft of the thing, is a story's arc. I trust that arc. I trust the sound and cadence and arithmetic tally of story. And it seems that story trusts me, in some fashion I don't command. At least, story seems to bear me in mind from time to time, and I take that for a summons.

I have heard the story I'm going to tell only once, and it must have been several decades ago. It strikes me as a trued story. It also strikes me as something that happens. In storytelling, as in life, this is a good distinction to make. There are things that happen, factoids of a kind, whose occurrence may not bring much with them, and so probably they are awaiting something like truing. And there are trued things that our troubled scene in this mystery play of human life have yet to see and learn and be brought to stillness by. Because it shares both shades, I tell this story now in the way that seems to do honour to it and to your willingness to consider it, though it isn't much like the way I heard it. Probably better to say that I will tell you the story according to what it does to me to remember it.

Like so many of the good ones are, this story is apocryphal, no doubt, by which I mean that it probably arises in as many places as it is needed, and so it seems to come from Somewhere Else. It remains for our time an entirely accurate story, one in which we could recognize things that have so far loped out just ahead of our understanding.

⌘

There was a young man, and his heart was for the wood, and for carpentry. The young man's father wanted other things for him, better things, so the father thought, and so he disapproved.

Now, without the disapproval you'd have a fable, a little checklist of rights and wrongs by which you could navigate a grief-free life. But this is a story, and stories use fables for kindling to keep them warm when they are on the darkening road heading out of town, far from home, the road we're on, the road the story makes for us.

This may be Japan, or Indonesia, or the Black Forest, or anywhere carpentry was an achieved thing, a deep-running craft curated and credited by the culture and not the skill in search of a reason that it has generally become in the West. For all that, this story seems probably to date to a time when handwork was not something someone with aspirations pursued so much anymore. So there is upheaval in the story's background, and the culture's travail finds its way to the personal life, as it does in life.

This may have been a place and time when the quiet endorsement of an older person was held in some esteem. The endorsement isn't approval, and it isn't rooted in the attitudes or opinions of an elder either. You'd imagine that elders have plenty of both. I imagine it, too, but the working life of an elder doesn't trade on those things. It trades on the trials and the times, on what is needed and not so much on what is needy. Endorsement from an elder is like a summons from the Gods. It is all the sign you're likely to get that you must proceed and that you can. It trades in fidelity to the time-tested, world-serving depths of the culture. It recognizes authenticity, and real merit.

Generally, it doesn't encourage. If anything, it requires courage to attend to the attention an elder bestows upon you, and to proceed as if you have been recognized, even though the merit they've recognized has, for the moment, entirely escaped you. The esteem of an older person in a place that has regard for age is tested and honed and tempered by the ragged facts. One ragged fact is that the old person was young once, and that young person wanted something, and so had confusion. Elders remember those days and have a secret regard for them, especially now that those days have come back again in the form of a younger person full of want and confusion.

There is the rankling disapproval by a father of the desires and designs of a son. It is not the abiding encounter with the impersonal wisdom of an elder we have here, that's true. But *the encounter with the story*: that might be where the elder's voice comes in. And it may be in the magic of the story that a father's disapproval drives the son to the elder's stoop.

So, perhaps the father and his approval was of that kind of fact. Perhaps not. It is, after all, a mark of wisdom and culture to be willing to keep separate the strategies of parenthood from the regard of elderhood. But the son chafed under his father's disapproval, so much so that he went to the considerable risk of leaving his family and their home and striking off in the direction of the wood. And he was gone for years, incommunicado.

Years went by in the quiet house. By then that the father's disapproval had the sepia of regret about it, too. Time, and visiting that little altar of regrets that is kept out behind the house, can temper your lordship. He may have been less the elder by then than he once thought himself to be before, and more the wayward father. He may have been freer with his approval by that time. He may have begun to bestow it upon others, in covert recompense for the old miscalculations of fatherhood. I hope he did. Fatherhood has a lot of old miscalculations. It can't be otherwise, it seems. Deep into his middle age he may, by then, have been willing to trade all his precious paternal approval outright for some sign of his son's prodigious arc back towards him, or some sign that the wood was unexpectedly kind to him after all. The father may have found himself in that place fathers can find themselves when the dust of difference settles, wishing or hoping or willing to have been wrong. But the quiet of the son's goneness settled on the house and on the father's years. That quiet was one of the few signs left that the aging man was once a father.

The mail didn't come often to that house in the country in those days, so when it did, the mailman probably had some sort of rhyme to chant coming upon the gate, so as to draw auspicious attention to what he bore. One particular day that rhyme plucked the father from his regrets. There was the mailman at the gate, and there he was with a small package. The father, he took the package into the house. Unwrapped, it was small enough to fit easily in the palm of his hand. It was that kind of well-wrought wooden box that nobody makes anymore. The profit margins prohibit the work now, and only idleness or patronage or the wiles of craftsmanship prompt that beauty into the world.

It was held together neither by screw or glue but by joinery, crafted to the scale of dollhouse furniture. It was a wonder. The top slid back smoothly, and inside the father found only a single curl of wood shaving, maybe an arm's length. There was no note, no return address, no inscription of any kind. Only the box, immaculate, and this curl of wood.

This is a kind of shaving that can only really happen by the time-trued marriage of a woodsman's well-timed felling of the tree, to the careful curing of the tree to dryness over a decade or more, to a well-made plane, to a well-forged blade, to a well-honed edge, to a masterful balance that rolls the craftsman's weight from the ball of the foot to the heel as he draws the plane over the wood's face and raises what looks to be sea foam, or mist rolling in from the shore of another world. And the shaving can, given all of that skill, be many feet long, curling back upon itself as a spring would, curling back over the plane, round the wrist of the carpenter. Anyone who's seen one knows that curl to be the quiet voice of the old craft master showing again how it is done. It is an unscrolling miracle, with the discipline and obedience of the craft written there. Mastery is what coaxes some willingness in the shaving to be lifted a few hair's breadths at a time from the old tree. This curl was translucent, gossamer, the very godparent or godchild of the seed that bore the seedling that bore the first true leaf that bore the stem that bore the tree.

And that was the message the prodigal carpenter sent his father. Raising his hand, he testified. He learned the craft that called him, yes. But somehow, in the days since his hasty, inelegant departure he learned his father, a little. And so he sent the scroll.

The story doesn't dwell on the son's part in all this. It stops abruptly, with the arrival of the little package, with the curl of wood in the father's hand. That's because it isn't another prodigal son story. Instead, the story walks you along the path that can so painfully, so mercifully part the father from his fathering. That partition, and whatever other departures prompt it, that is the beginning of the rumour of elderhood swirling.

The father will always be father to his son. He'll always be the night sky and the constellations of his son's days. There's nothing to be done there. But this departure means the ending of his fathering days. He'll not father his son again, and he's beginning to see it. He'll not be a father again, not to any other generation. These are endings of the utter kind. These are the endings that kindle elderhood. They are elderhood's parturition. They are how middle age's chrysalis is broken. No longer parenting a few, you can now be elder to many. Endings are what lay the ground for the deeper, approval-free endorsement of life that bewilders and beguiles the life of an elder. Those are the same endings that befuddle and bestow merit of the enduring kind upon younger people. Those younger people, someone else's kids, pass through the pollen trail of an elder's attention, and that claims them for a life of service to what has served them all along.

⌘

And it seems to me that as you get older, you might bear down upon your life and give it the quiet consideration it deserves. Do so, and you could catch glimpses of the shoreline that guides it and contains it and won't let it go on forever. It's mournful, and it's trued. Many's a time I've been asked in interviews whether, having seen so much of the deaths of others, I'm finally "good" with my death, all resigned and accepting, my desire for life left in the parking lot of demise, the keys left inside. As if that's what I'd want, after all that.

I tell you this: from the glimpse of my death I've drawn down a great longing for life.

> We have this word, *belong*. We use it to mean "being a part of." But the old English prefix *be-* has the semantic consequence of intensifying as it goes. So *belonging* means something closer to "the deepening of longing."

That's how you belong—not by finally arriving, but by having the longing for arrival quickened, by being willing to long after life by living. That's how I belong, anyway. I find that being alive is habit form-ing. I'm deeply fond of the thing now, irrevocably fond of it, properly wrinkled as we both have become.

So, catch a glimpse of the end of what you hold dear, even of your ability and your willingness to hold someone or something dear. Don't blink. There are all the unbidden memories of things that were good and things that were otherwise and never made quite right now come, all of it trued and trustworthy now, the edges honed and mercifully sharp. Your life curls back towards you in some way just then. Great lengths of it are raised by the hone of your faithful witness to the full weight and the full wreckage of your allotment, what you did with what was entrusted to you. Your life finally, for a while, is something like you now, legible in the curl. The dispensation of age can settle upon you. The light of these older days of your allotment can pass through the curl of your memories undisturbing, undisturbed.

Held up to the window in the unforgiven light of judgement and regret, that curl of memory might melt away altogether into the dust it is anyhow. But it is aligned for the moment instead, by whatever tempered discernment you can manage and by your love for that which you won't live long enough to see. So it is bound into something sinuous and fragile and precious and elegant. And there is your life, mysteriously, mercifully sent back to you in the small, labored-over pressure-fitted box of what you could not concede.

Your children and mine were born into a troubled time. Among a host of other things, that is something we did to them, unawares probably. And if we put our shoulder to the mournful wheel of this living world, and proceed as if they are here among us, and if we are wrecked on schedule and get good at that, we will end up being thieves of a kind. We will take from them their chance to go on as if those who came before bore them in mind not at all. They will have their poverties, yes, but they will not inherit that one from us. They'll have to find other reasons for not being able to go on, for giving up on it all. They'll have to find their own misanthropy, different prized possessions. They deserve less than we had, less of that poverty, not more.

Would that hearing this story does something like that to your day, unsettling you in that strangely welcome way that leaves nothing as it was and prompts grace and gratefulness thereby. Maybe a story about a father and a son, curling, then uncurling in just that way, *is* the elder, for now, for however long the story seems needed and useful, going as the elder goes, bound soon enough for the quiet corner, the end of its days.

22

NEVER BE A POET

Should the first half of your life be given over to some cyphering as to the reasons for your birth and the particulars of its time and place, and then be given to acting on those discoveries, then regardless of your success with the purpose of the first, the second half of your life is to find those among whom you might live out those reasons to live. You might call it "finding your people."

As it happened, I did not find myself in such a place. In the dominant culture of North America, knowing who your people are is not a given, and certainly not a necessity. But against that heavy weather, I claim that it is a significant aspect of your life's work—and I recall very little for myself in the way of training or example in this matter—to find your people and to make them, in equal measure. This isn't a matter of finding people who are like you so much as finding people who are *simpatico* enough that your life appears when you are among them. Seniors' centres are a woeful approximation. Maybe seniors' centres are what happen when people don't get the memo announcing that they are indeed in the second half of their lives and don't do its work.

I received my memo in the bank in town a few years ago, which was as good as place as any to discover where in my life I was. I was certainly well into the Second Act by then, so you could say it was more of a confirmation memo. On reflection, it was more of a sign that the Third and Final Act was in the wings.

I'm sure you've seen the computer terminals tellers use that now adjudicate all of your transactions. That is, if you are still antique enough to go to a bank, bypass the machine out front, and have an experience with a person, as I do. This particular day, the teller was sorting through my business, and prompted I'm now sure by some automatic notice on her screen, she assumed a casual tone to inform me that the bank would soon be sending me a special offer in the mail. This was unprecedented, so far as I could remember.

"Really?" I said, "What for?"

"Oh, they're just going to offer you things."

The repetition made me instantly suspicious that something was up. It doesn't take much banking to get me to this point, as the manager of the branch who has, on occasion, gently suggested various investment strategies well knows.

"But what kind of things?"

I asked.

"Oh, just discounts and things,"

she said.

Trying to sound intrigued and not cornered, I asked what was to be discounted.

"Oh, transactions. Things like that."

Up until then I'd been penalized with transaction fees for coming into the bank in person and taking up the teller's time. These are strange days in the customer service sector. This seemed an enlightened move on their part. Still, there was this nagging sense of the hand inside the puppet offer. There was something I wasn't being told. I smelled it.

"Well, that's very good, but why am I getting this offer now?"
I said.

"Oh, because you've been a good customer of the bank,"
she answered.

Well, I'd been a customer for as long as I'd lived in the area, a good while, and there'd been no discount in sight all that time. Something wasn't quite right.

"Yes, that's true. But why am I suddenly getting this attention?"
I said.

She stopped what she was doing. She folded her hands. She looked down at her desktop, and she didn't move. And that's when it hit me: my sixtieth birthday was looming. All of the birthdays that end in zero have become noteworthy events these days, but this was one of the Big Ones on the old odometer of life. The special offer was prompted by the Big Six O, and she was prompted by her terminal to mark the occasion.

But she wouldn't say why. It was like being in the doctor's office, the doctor now young enough to be your son or daughter, always a disconcerting development, the test results in code lying on the desk between you, you trying to read the tea leaves of his or her voice or vocabulary or body language in a vain effort to find out what is to become of you.

So *I* said it. I asked her,

"I'm about to get the geezer discount, aren't I? That's what's coming."

And there was a long silence, when she wouldn't look up. It was as if she'd been in a well-intended connivance that had been spoiled, and now she was forced to fess up. It wasn't the word she would have chosen, probably, but the jig was up. There was no use continuing to be discreet.

She looked at me finally with equal parts pity and pain, as if I was asking for it, and in as even a voice as she could manage she said it:

"Yes. Yes, you are."

So, that's how I got my memo.

⸎

It is a neat scheme, and perhaps it is true. It is tempting to imagine the second half of your life as a reduced version of the first, or as a tamed version, a disconsolate version, or an unnerved version. The culture that I was born into champions vitality and novelty so adamantly that the second half of anyone's life suffers in comparison to the first—unless the second is one long payday. The prejudice that favours momentum over moment is one that often rises when the two tasks are confused, when younger people trade indecision about the reasons for their lives for a companionship unencumbered by purpose, when older people forgo the tether of community for the freedom of self-actualization. But there is merit to a second half of life not free from but *steeped in the labour of the first*. It isn't reward. It is more like employment, of the radical kind.

Here is a story that may assist with the first project, or with the second. At the very least it may help with figuring out in which half you might linger, perhaps unawares, awaiting your memo, or where the threshold that binds one to the other is to be found.

Should life deliver to you for safekeeping a child, and should that child and those who sent him or her to you keep to the arrangement beyond the tender years, and should that child come to his or her majority lucid and possessed of memory and mysteriously amenable to you, it may come to pass that the child is still talking to you, and saying things of consequence or intrigue or solace, or supplication. There is nothing in this that is guaranteed, and so it may come to you as some sort of wonder that the odds did not foretell, especially when you consider how it may have been with you and your parents, or when you consider the stories you are hearing these days about how angry young people are with older people. It may incline you to gratitude of the deep running kind, and interrupt the recitation of the cantos of grievance and general decline that can gather together and gain a voice there in the Second Act of your allotment.

And so it came to pass that my daughter was fourteen or so and we were just done with our dinner, and it came to me in that moment that she and I were in a time that might not be repeated, when the claims of whatever life awaited her were not yet there, when the bones of my days were clear and upright enough to bear their weight, when each of us was limber enough of body and mind to go out on the wander. And so I asked her where she would like to go.

"Where do you mean?"

she asked, and I answered her:

"Anywhere."

When she realized that I didn't mean somewhere in the neighbourhood, she said,

"In the world?"

"Yes, in the world. If you wanted to go anywhere with me, soon, where would it be?"

I said.

It only took her a few seconds, but the answer was sure:

"Ireland,"

she said. And within a week, that's where we were.

It was her first time to anywhere in Europe. It was my first time there as a grown up with kids and responsibilities. It was also the first time I was driving with some powerful jetlag on the wrong side of the car on the wrong side of the road in the dark without a map or a plan. The first roundabout we came to almost undid us, and that was without any traffic to speak of. By grace alone we found accommodation, a former manor house turned out for tourists. By first light we looked out the window and saw just beyond a wire fence a Bronze Age tumulus, the carved curb stones poking through the grass, cows grazing the place. It was one of three such mounds in the area, another of which was the rebuilt Newgrange.

The feel of augury was in the air. Later that day I met a maker of coracles by the side of the road, and we compared notes on boat making for an hour. By dusk the next day, we were born along by enchantment, which is to say we were in our first pub, with a proper pub dinner before us, in Sligo Town, and there I learned the mysteries and the merits of Guinness. It's a fabled thing, fully warranted, and there's nothing I can add, except to say that I'm not much of a drinker and never have been. So the cumulative effects of all this magic landed, and at night's end I handed my daughter the keys, and over her protest I entrusted her with our well-being.

The first time driving standard is always tricky, but the challenges swell when you are fourteen and stalling and staggering your way across a kind of barely two lane levee in a blowing storm in the dark, with the darker Atlantic on either side, waiting, your father awash in the grog and the glories of life in the seat beside you, temporarily useless for authority or problem solving. Mysteriously, we made it to our hotel. She wasn't impressed with being put in that position I don't think, but she must have been proud when she lurched into the parking lot and we were safely still.

The next morning down at breakfast we were greeted by the owner, an ex-priest with the redolence of authority and the residue of a priestly demeanor and a keenness to chat up visitors. During one of the coffee refills he gave us his take on the state of the nation. These were the days of the Celtic Tiger, when Ireland was Europe's Silicon Valley and the money was pouring in like never before. He himself was perturbed by the willingness of his neighbours to go into massive unprecedented debt for the sake of owning holiday villas in Tunisia and the like, but more so by the as-yet-unpublicized spate of suicides of young men in the midst of all this promise of prosperity. He called it an epidemic, and he was in some way confiding in me.

We commiserated, and we witnessed to the sorry thing, and the lacey dining room at mid-morning took on the iron amber hue of the strange wide world beyond. By this time I was working full time in the death trade at home, up to the chin in endings of all kinds that were not my own, and the synchronous encounter with grief and mystery on this side of the Atlantic had my daughter looking at me in some way as if we'd just met. These are powerful moments, when your parent is taken up by the Mystery Play of Life before your eyes, no longer mostly your parent, his or her ways now indistinct from the murmuring of the Big Story, your neat version of the thing now adrift across the fields at last light.

An hour later the two of us were driving down the main street of Sligo. We passed a small building on our right that might just as well have reached out and grabbed the wheel from me and rerouted the day. I didn't see the place, but the seizing was unmistakable to anyone who'd had some of this burdening his feel of the purpose of his days on and off for many years. The one-way traffic pushed us along until we could find off-road parking. We doubled back on foot, looking for something, my daughter now persuaded enough by these mysterious days to go along with me.

It turned out to be a storefront in lime green enamel tile, a butcher shop, or a former butcher shop. For there, in the window, beneath the rails and the meat hooks, where the cuts of meat were once offered, were scores of wood carvings. I myself had been a carver of keen endeavor years before. There was enough synchrony afoot to oblige me through the door. The proprietor was on his side of the counter chatting with a customer, so we toured the place, which was filled with more carvings. Mercifully, they were not little bits of free-form amorphous self-expression. They were, from what little I knew, characters and stories from Irish myth and lore, which is to say that they were denizens of the place, and they loomed in the shadows, the place all linseed and wood dust.

Soon enough the customer left, and I began speaking with this butcher-turned-carver. He seemed glad to have someone visit who knew something of the craft, and we talked shop, and my daughter looked on. I admired the work, and the dedication evident in the place. There was on the counter between us a half-carved piece of considerable girth, the biggest in the shop, and I enquired after it. It was, he said, a temporary grave marker, and gravity came into his voice when after a moment's pause he let on that it was of his making. And that it was for his son. He had died a fortnight ago, he said, so it was fresh in every way, and the full weight of the thing settled upon us all. Another long pause, and the man said:

"It was by his own hand he died."

Quieter we all grew, the sudden candor and quickening of the moment probably a surprise to us all. And it deepened again:

"T'was his right."

the carver said, the benediction firm and the sorrow in the room complete.

"This world was too hard a place for him."

And no doubt it was. What this asks of a parent I would never want to learn too closely. What this asks of a witness was something I was not a stranger to. Whomever leaned closer to whom I don't remember, but we were arms on each other's shoulders then, him weeping and me feeling the tears and the whiskers of another man's face on my cheek for the first time in many years. We'd been speaking for all of twenty minutes by then, but we were parents and we were older men, and we'd seen what life can do, and it was enough.

Well, where to go from there? What is there to say that won't scatter what wonder has gathered you into? But we spoke for a while anyway, about the carving life and about life too. I must tell you that such a time beggars any ability you might still have to be casual, or it can. It did, that early afternoon. And still, though you can't find a good reason to do so, incandescent as such moment are, you must leave the shop, and you will, though you'll have to pretend for a while that you have to. Life has had its wary way with you again, and just outside the butcher shop door on Wine Street in Sligo life awaits whatever you'll make of it having come to you as it has, all brine and sweetness and human-scaled mystery, with your child on the cusp of her days of alertness, looking on, no longer sure whether you are the same man who took out the garbage and then went to work and came home again, and you no longer sure.

However we made it to the door I don't recall, but we did, reluctant. I'd my hand on the knob, but I couldn't make myself pull it open, and the butcher turned woodcarver saw it. So he said something, which I know now was his way of coming round the counter and blessing my departure.

He said,

"Son. A bit of advice?"

And without turning to him I said,

"Yes, sure."

And he said, all clarion and oracle,

"Never harm a poet."

Who would do so, such that a caveat was needed to vouchsafe them? Still, if poetry and poets are troubled and trouble, as in any sedate society they are, the plea to spare them harm belongs. I didn't try to translate, not then, but without knowing what it would ask I did take up the oath.

"No. I won't," I said.

Still, I didn't move, or I wouldn't.

And he in his generous way saw this, and so he said,

"Well, alright then. A second: Never love a poet neither."

As if this would get me out the door and into the fray. I faced the door still, and I said to him no, I wouldn't love a poet, though I didn't know how hard or how easy that might be, or whether I'd be able to, or whether I'd already failed to, or whether I'd done so unawares. Or all of it. You can hear in this the chicanery of the poet in full effect, practicing upon you what he would warn you away from, a proper subversion of whatever tendency you might still have to be okay.

Now so much of life's wet-nursing of us comes in threes, the way jokes of the cosmic kind tend to do. So you know that I was at the door yet, stilled but not waiting, and you know he saw this, too, and you know he said the next thing, probably the only thing left to say to get us to the other shore of our meeting. It was mercy unbound and unstrained.

He said,

"Alright then. A third, and you'll be off. Never *be* a poet."

And I said all that was left to say. I said,

"Well, Michael, it's too late."

I don't know where that came from, looking back on it now. It sounds too braggadocious, something a poet might never say. But I believed it to be so then, and the intervening years seem to have born me out. By that afternoon it was certainly too late to be untried, untempered, above the fray and a foreigner to the shambles. The woodcarver must have lifted his crozier then, and summoned the saints, and blessed my steps, for he gathered me into the mead hall of the Ancients of Days.

He said,

"Yes son. It's too late for the both of us."

Well, I suppose that we were both right that day. I myself was dazzled and done for and strode out into the hurl and sway of the street and into my days, my daughter my only witness then and now to all of this.

Of course your life laps your memory. And amnesia's stepchild, nostalgia, can make sepia of your drastic days. So years went by, some of them conducted as if such a thing never happened at all, as if the words were museum pieces and not marching orders. And then it was a decade. My daughter and I grew older.

And then I found myself in the poetry section of a used bookstore. Such places should have warning signs over the stacks: *Here be treasure, and the sunken ark.* I saw a book title: *Daddy Daddy*, and the poet's name, Paul Durcan, unknown to me then but an Irishman, the jacket said, and so perhaps the maker of something considerable. The Irish not only saved civilization, they tell us, but they raised conversation to something approaching an art form. It is an unnerving place from which to accept a teaching gig—I've done it several times—but it does crank out its poets. The book turned out to be steeped in the latter years and in the death of Durcan's *da*, and so I bought it.

A few days later I found a poem called "Antwerp, 1984," an account of a train trip he took with his aging, Parkinson's-agitated father, retired from the bench and, as the poem tells you, five years from his death. It seems the poet found his father to be slipping away from him even then. Whatever it was that gave him his sudden tender devotion, regardless of whatever rancor had sired their younger days together, Mr. Durcan began to make an oath to the old man, what he'd do with him when he died, what he'd do with his body, in particular.

And I pledge that when they fell you,
While they will sell you for firewood,
I will give logs of you
To a woodcarver in Sligo,
Michael Quirke of Wine Street,
Butcher turned woodcarver,
Out of which to magic statuettes
Of the gods and goddesses of Ireland,
The Celtic Deities.
I will wash your body
In linseed oil and turpentine.
I will put you in the window
Of his butcher's shop in Wine Street.
I will call you by your proper name,
Mac Dhuarcain,
Son of the Melancholy One....

Life wonders after us, it surely does. It goes on with us, then without us. A few more years went along, and I made for myself and my concerns a school, a setting off place for whatever skills I now possessed for being troubled aloud about the current regime. And, wonder of wonders, a few years into it, my daughter decided to join the school, letting me outgrow what she took for her father. And in the last morning of the first meeting of her class I told that story, wild and entire and weepy. And she told me later that yes, though she'd little memory of it until that morning, she remembered it now. The whole thing now clearly has happened again, she said, just I told it, just as it was.

FINALE

I am, in my fashion, a farmer in a dwindling water hole of farmers at the edge of provincial legislative neglect, where the local governing brain trust would just as soon see the whole works turned over to recreational development and are taxing accordingly. I oversee my fields as they withdraw from decades of hard drugs. Most of the farms that flirt with solvency here are those abetted by ever-more-relentless Big Agriculture. Many of the younger farmers (and given the lands' costs now, younger farmers are themselves something miraculous) are going green and going it alone, for the most part, and their weekends at the farmer's markets are probably only distracting them from the other ten months of income-free activity. When idle conversation turns towards farms and their future, sooner or later some of the young farmers will cast a dark eye on those employing chemical help.

I understand the sense of grievance of the farmers and the activists and those others well down the food chain, those at the buying and eating end who have to rely on ingredient stickers, provenance stamps, and the chicanery of "food safety regulations" that are routinely gelded by lobbyists who have already turned "organic" into another feature of GMOs. The truth is that, though I am troubled by the Roundup readiness and the GMO complicity of my neighbours, I can't turn on them, certainly not when their backs are turned. Their self-reliance is turning on them, and that's plenty.

There is something about being in on a hard time that doesn't require hardness of heart to weather the thing. We are in a time of extraordinary turbulence and devious misrepresentation and governing wisdom gone AWOL. I leave it to others to imagine the better world they know is out there waiting. I hope they're right. My job here has been to articulate some sense of how things got to be as they are, aging-wise. Those older people who've never had an elder-blessed time of life are in the same line-up for the same emotional and spiritual paydays as their children and, soon enough, their grandchildren. Some of them have thrown in the towel. They're waiting it out.

But I do not turn on them either. I don't know how they could do otherwise, given everything. I've been pleading throughout these proceedings for older people to give up being old long enough to consider elderhood as something they could help nurse into our midst. Looking to be rubberstamped into elderhood by other old people: that's not elder work, and it's not culture. That's the activities room at an old folks' home.

> I was interviewed for a kind of "elder radio" programme. The hosts were three older people who frequently referred to themselves as elders. I asked how they got to be elders. "Oh", one of them said, "we decided that's what we are. We just call each other that. Nobody else does."

The fact seems to be that the greater skill in a troubled time is not figuring out how you can be an elder after all and get the gold watch to prove it, while the give-a-shit is still registering and the creakiness permits. The greater skill in an elder-bereft time, the more village-minded skill, *is to craft the ability to have elders in your midst.* Do what you can to cobble together the ability to recognize the elder function when it appears, to give voice to the recognition, to praise it without understanding it, or approving of it or trying to get in on it, knowing the benefit that might come to those much younger than you if you do so.

> I was in a bar one night in Oaxaca. Idle and earnest chatter being the currency when expats and mescal meet, a thirty-something woman asked me what I did. I mentioned working on this book about elderhood. "Why?" she asked. I said, "Well, I figure something happened to wisdom and to age." "Oh, I know what happened," she said. "Wisdom abandoned people your age. We've got it now."

But I don't think the wisdom of age free floats like that cosmic dust, waiting to anoint the damp wings of an untutored generation, abandoning the old. That's a solution to the atrophy of elderhood that bears the seed of what begat the atrophy.

The ones who conjure elders are not the ones who are seeking out their own elderhood. The ones who conjure elders are the ones who seek out an elder's heartbroken willingness to testify for the sake of a better day, who corroborate that sorrow, who are willing to be wrong about older people and their truancy. My plan, such as it is, is that *young people begin to awaken to the understanding that it is their search for elders*—sometimes grievance-driven, sometimes tried—*that conjures elderhood in a troubled time.* Young people drive whatever chance the sentinel species of elder has of coming back from the brink of tired, retired, redundant despair in the Anthropocene. When the human image, the human psyche and its penchant for habit are themselves taken for the template for life and for the world, it is no surprise that any proposal that doesn't enthrone human centeredness—say, in the manner that hope does—would be called bitter, or sour, or cynical, bordering on misanthropic. Well, I'm not cynical, and I'm not hopeful, and this coming of age is neither. Coming of age in a time such as ours is an enterprise entirely free of hope. Young peoples' search for elders might seem hopeless to the rest of us. But at its best it is free of hope too. Their search for elders is what call elders out.

An elder's job is surely to proceed as if that day might come, to ready themselves when those two clenched fists are held to them, all plea and dare and despair. Sometimes an elder's job is to prompt that day, by planting in young people the rumour that there is yet such a thing as elderhood.

I once was asked by a public school teacher to deliver the "native studies" part of the curriculum.

"That's crazy. You should find a native person to do it,"

I said.

"I don't know any native people, and it has to be done the day after tomorrow."

I thought that that was crazy, too, but finally I agreed to bring in a few things and talk about them, in lieu of a native person. The morning arrived, and I was escorted to a classroom of twelve-year-olds. I sized up the situation, did my best to figure out who the likely adversary would be. The prime suspect was already refusing to look in my direction. He was also the one most likely to be hitting puberty any minute. I knew I had one shot to gain their attention, one gambit. I began by asking the class what they'd been doing at 5:45 a.m. that very morning. The keen girls at the front jockeyed to answer.

"I was sleeping,"

one of them said.

"Getting my beauty sleep,"

said another.

"Doing the homework I didn't do yesterday,"

said a third.

All the while I was making my way through the rows to the hard-to-impress fellow. When I got there I leaned in fairly close, until it was hard for him to make as if I wasn't in the room, and I leaned on his desk.

"How about you?"

I said.

"How about me what?"

he sneered.

"What were you doing at quarter to six this morning?"

I said brightly.

"What?"

he sneered again.

"I know you heard me. Give it a try. It's a simple question."

"F-f-f-fine,"

he taunted me,

"I was sleeping, okay?"

He looked away. But I was thinking about his life twenty years from that morning. I didn't go on to the next student. Instead, I said to him,

"Okay, great. Now ask me."

"Ask you what?"

He was running out of room, and both of us knew it.

"Ask me what I was doing and quarter to six this morning."

"Oh, man."

he said.

"Okay mister question: What were you do—"

And that's when I cut in. It wasn't my best moment, decorum-wise, but I was out on a limb, everybody including the teacher in the back of the room wondering what this had to do with native studies. I wasn't sure myself, but I didn't let him finish.

In the best *basso profundo* I could manage, with a little extra emphasis on the last two words, I said,

"I was praying for your *mortal soul*."

Which was what I was doing that morning. All the heads in the room snapped up, teacher included. Public schools aren't keen on praying these days, and I don't guess they are keen on the soul, mortal or otherwise. But I was twenty years out in front of that kid that morning, without much to go on, and I wanted him to go into his adolescence with that sound of *pray* and *mortal* and *soul* and some older man's give-a-damn somewhere inside him. I don't know that he did. Could be, though, that he's made an elder or two since then.

❧

Here's one last fable for the road. In my earliest farming days there was no barn, and there was no house. There was, though, a tipi, the cheapest, easiest, don't-need-a-permit thing we could do. If you've never lain there deep into the night, the fire down to coals and smoke and darkness rising, your companions deep into their dreams, and looked up through the nest of poles and through that smoke hole, which seems for all the world to be like the first amniotic glimpse we all may have had of this blue whirling home of ours, and followed the smoke and the odd spark up to the sky and the constellations beyond, and heard the general assent in the night out on the other side of everything you know…. Well, there's still time. It is one of the cardinal points on the compass of simple pleasures there to have their way with you. Even if none of that appeals to you, seeming either too hard or too easy, see if you can manage such a night before the ground and the chill and your waning forbid it.

I'm commending it to you because I think one of the keys to the kingdom of mercy and ministration is there in the architecture.

There is the cooking fire, called into life by a bow drill and some younger person's devotion to learning that old conjuring, the arcanum of the thing almost as old as dirt. There's sweat and friction and praying to particular Gods to spark into our little fray, and so far they've agreed to do it. All of that is work.

There is the flat hearth stone and the necklace of round stones, a small bit of the earth's bone washed up by the flood melt that made this corner of the world the *tramore*, the sandy shore that it is, ten thousand years ago, of which the River of Abundance and Time just there on the other side of that field is a faithful memory.

There is the clay cooking pot, dirt and spit, the ash of ancestors and the weepiness that comes from remembering them soothed and smoothed into shape, and fired into a crucible to hold what sustains you. That's more fire yet, isn't it, and more taking? There's wood burned to drive out the damp of the desire for more and firm the clay into a pot, so the children can eat from their ancestors' dust, and so you, awakened to it all, don't lose track of the wake fanning out into the world from everything you claim for your life's needs.

The cooking pot of your ancestral line hangs from a tripod. That is the trinity, each of your parents and whatever it was that brought them together for a time to grant you this life of yours.

Above you, the brace of poles, none of whom came into the world to hold up the shelter for your little life and yet, for now, there they are, cinched together and bowed a little from the weight of holding, leaning on each other like heads on shoulders.

That place where they meet above you, that is the village-mindedness that bore all of this in mind, that knows how to be a pagan, a human, and grants you a place to remember all this. That is the place of assaying and testifying, where names are granted, not made. That is the place where the Dusty Worthies and the errant Rafter Dwellers come to nest for a while like cranky old birds and peer down through the cooking smoke at their heirs and brag about them and upbraid them and claim them.

That all of this—the mantle of stones and the ancestral cooking pot and the sweated-over fire and the tripod of this little life of ours and the towering limbs of this bit of the world leaning together for a while—*meets at all*, though, *that* is the Gods in our midst, or us in theirs. The World Tree, the one elders imitate. Or so it seems to me.

⁌

We have a word: *catastrophe.* Today it is another thing the world doesn't seem to need, taken by many as another sign that we're getting close to The Big One. *Catastrophe* is the very thing that shouldn't be, another irredeemable affront, the caprice of the universe bearing down. Well, no surprise by now, that is only the most recent meaning. As a farewell, allow me to trouble you with one more etymological stone to put in your wandering shoes, to remember all of this by.

We have the prefix *kata*, from Greek. It is a preposition, and so it carries the volatility, the direction, the thrust and purpose of that part of speech. It answers the question, "Where?" The standard definition usually given is "down." But the tone of the word is not a plummet, not a freefall in thrall to physical or existential gravitas. That is an answer that, frankly, has the inferno and hell below. But in the days before hell, when *below* meant something like "beneath what we're ordinarily granted to see," this kind of descent had a purpose dictated by the Mysteries, the *arche* that stands under your life. So a more apt answer to the question, "Where?" might be "down, and then in." Sometimes it meant, "A lot of down, and finally in." Other times it meant, "Not down enough long enough, and so not in, for now." The prefix *kata* in our word means, "A descent to achieve diminishment, so that when the threshold of mystery presents itself, you are spare and spry enough to cross it and enter."

And then the root word: *strophe*. This is a word that swims towards us from the ancestral mists shrouding the Indo-European linguistic homelands. Today it is often used as a technical term designating a form of poetry or song. But its older meaning suggests "a thing braided or woven or gathered in pattern and strategy." When the word enjoys its reunion, its fulsome meaning is something closer to this: "That rope or road that was fashioned for you in the Time Before, by those you will not meet, to give you a way of going down against your plans and good sense, to give you a way down and into the Mysteries of this life, the Mysteries granted you that you would not choose for yourself, the Mysteries that would yet make of you a human worthy of those coming after."

⬥

You can hear in the current meaning of *catastrophe* the contemporary prejudice against descent of any kind, against hiddenness and mystery and being obliged to do anything that contravenes the vagaries of the will, that doesn't cash out, that doesn't seem to serve. It is a word that comes from the devotional life, from the life of discipline and prolonged inquiry into the Big Things. It describes a time in history and in life when your life's path was made for you, not by you nor by the unseen mastermind of the universe, but by the peregrine footfall of ancestors. It is the authentic antidote to the allegation that you're in it alone, that there's nothing trued and tried you can count on anymore. Walk that path alone. The time will come when there'll be others forlorn or seeking, and you'll be one of those they'll remember, though they'll never meet you. They'll find themselves on the road you made by walking.

Elders are the axis mundi of our mutual life, giving the Gods a way of murmuring their dreams of life to us, keeping them far enough away and close enough that we might live. Unslaked, the dreams of the Gods are catastrophic. But elders temper the love the Gods have for this world, by pleading on our behalf for their schemes and their lives to include us after all. And, by being the World Tree that they are.

Elders are heretics in the gilded chapel of self-determination, and they are servants of their elders now dead in times of trouble, and *catastrophe* is their word. We practice how to have time passing through us, and how to have ancestors, by how we are with our elders.

Catastrophe means that, yes, your descent unto the Mysteries will be a solitary one, and yes, you will have companions nonetheless. Please befriend the possibility that the way down *is* the companionship you seek. The path itself is a sign—the only sign you'll probably get or need—that you've been dreamt of, and imagined, and chanted into life by those old ones who came before you.

Catastrophe is the job description of an elder. Be a catastrophe for this age.

SOURCE LIST

Beowulf. Translated by Seamus Heaney. New York: Farrar, Straus and Giroux, 2000.

Bede's Ecclesiastical History of the English People. ed./trans. Colgrave, Bertram, and Mynors. Oxford: Oxford University Press 1969.

Bowen, Thorleif. *Hebrew Thought Compared with Greek.* New York: Norton & Company, 1960.

Cohen, Leonard. "Boogie Street." On *Ten New Songs.*

———. "Closing Time." On *The Future.*

———. "The Flood." In *The Book of Longing.* Toronto: McClelland and Stewart, 2006.

———. "The Future." On *The Future.*

———. "Going Home." On *Old Ideas.*

———. "Slow." On *Popular Problems.*

———. "Tower of Song." On *I'm Your Man.*

de Brebeuf, Jean. *Huron Relations for 1635/1636.* ed. Lucien Campeau, S.J., trans. William Lonc. Toronto: Hammerberg Productions, 2002.

Durcan, Paul. "Antwerp, 1984." In *Daddy, Daddy.* Belfast: The Blackstaff Press 1990.

Heaney, Seamus. "The Tollund Man in Springtime." In *District and Circle.* London: Faber and Faber Ltd., 2006.

Liuzza, R.M. *Beowulf: A New Verse Translation.* Peterborough, ON: Broadview Press, 2000.

Minois, Georges. *History of Old Age.* Chicago: University of Chicago Press, 1987.

Njal's Saga. Edited and Translated by Carl Beyerschmidt, et al., Herfordshire: Wordsmith Editions, 1998.

Nowlan, Alden. "An Exchange of Gifts." In *The Mysterious Naked Man.* Toronto: Clarke, Irwin and Co. 1969.

———— "The People Who Are Gone." In *The Mysterious Naked Man.* Toronto: Clarke, Irwin and Co. 1969.

Popol Vuh. Translated by Dennis Tedlock. New York: Touchstone Books, 1996.

Rilke, Rainer M. "I Live My Life." In *Selected Poems of Rainer Maria Rilke*, ed./trans. Robert Bly. New York: Harper Perennial 1981.

————. "Sometimes a Man Stands Up." In *Selected Poems of Rainer Maria Rilke*. ed./trans. Robert Bly. New York: Harper Perennial 1981.

Rumi. "Praising Manners." In *The Soul Is Here for Its Own Joy*. ed. Robert Bly. New York: Ecco Press. 1999.

Silko, Karen Marmon. *Ceremony*. New York: Penguin Group. 2006.

Stafford, William. "Waiting in Line." In *The Way It Is: New and Selected Poems*. St. Paul, MN: Gray Wolf Press 1998.

Vinci, Felice. *The Baltic Origins of Homer's Epic Tales*. Rochester, VT: Inner Traditions, 2006.

Yeats, William Butler. "The Second Coming." In *The Collected Poems of W. B. Yeats,* London: Wordsworth Editions, Ltd., 1994. 1921.

INDEX

E

foundation stories, 234
four (tetra), etymology of words related to
test, attest, try, 126–127
Four Horsemen of the Apocalypse
carrying West to the world, 232–233
eternality, 243–244
inevitability, 245–246
potentiality, 244–245
universality, 241–243
Fourth Temptation, staying in the wilderness,
164, 184, 186
frailty
costs of aging, 132
slowing down as a grace, 46–47
threats facing the retired, 17
freedom, 351
Freud, 49–50
full, 310
future
bias of potentiality, 244–245
elders are future in present form,
153–154
your whole life is ahead of you, 141

G

gadgetry, 38
generational difference
burden of aging population and, 6
competition between generations,
17–18, 21
glut of old people in North America and
Europe, 211–212
having a talk with a teenager, 83–85
in men's group conference, 319–320
young people in danger of receiving
diminished world, 7
generations
effects of an interruption in "indigenous
savvy," 209–210
elders as World tree of generations, 293
inheritance from (in Jung), 207–208
task of discernment and translation, 209
generosity, of spell breakers, 240
getting it, times of clarity and simplicity,
24–25
give-a-shit/give-a-damn
airport books not conducive to, 336

exercising while it still registers, 380
praying for the mortal soul of a
disinterested adolescent, 384
shifting life claims on attention, 74
globalization
contemporary trends, 20
English as lingua franca of, 28
history and meaning of languages
and, 123
interrupting "indigenous savvy," 210
GMOs, grievances of the small farmer, 379
Gnosticism, 51
God/Gods
animism and, 51
attuned/or unattuned, 156–157
endings and, 44
Gods of Death and of Time, 293
Gods of Harangue, 71–72
Gods of Reorganization. see Gods of
Reorganization
human memory as workshop of, 128
longing for time when they were our
neighbors, 254–255
marketplace as Clever Gods and Rough
Gods, 37
Menial Gods of Scribble and Screed, 71
Old Gods of noble speech vs. One God
of fact and information, 123
One God religions as single-parent
family, 203
parental view of relationship to God,
179–180, 197–199
personal growth as monotheism without
God, 53
pleading for continuance of life, 95–96
repetition as finger print of God, 148
role of elders in tempering the
catastrophic, 387–388
Roman agriculture as war on local
Gods, 216
speech entrusted to humans, 359
spirits of place and time, 208–210
in teachings of Paul, 224
Tollund Man taken as an Old God, 269
transmission preferences of the Great
Beyond, 80
visitation of the Old Gods, 162
where do grandparents fit in parent/child
view of God, 199–200

H

M

S

W

ABOUT THE AUTHOR

STEPHEN JENKINSON, MTS, MSW is an activist, teacher, author, and farmer. He has a master's degree in theology from Harvard University and a master's degree in social work from the University of Toronto. He is a former programme director and medical-school assistant professor. He is the subject of the National Film Board of Canada documentary film, *Griefwalker*. He teaches internationally. With Nathalie Roy, Jenkinson founded the Orphan Wisdom School in 2010, which convenes in Tramore, Canada and in various places in northern Europe. He is the author of *How It All Could Be* (now translated into four languages), *Money and the Soul's Desires,* and *Die Wise.*

www.orphanwisdom.com

ALSO BY STEPHEN JENKINSON

available from North Atlantic Books

Die Wise
978-1-58394-973-3

North Atlantic Books
www.northatlanticbooks.com

North Atlantic Books is an independent, nonprofit publisher committed to a bold exploration of the relationships between mind, body, spirit, and nature.

About North Atlantic Books

North Atlantic Books (NAB) is an independent, nonprofit publisher committed to a bold exploration of the relationships between mind, body, spirit, and nature. Founded in 1974, NAB aims to nurture a holistic view of the arts, sciences, humanities, and healing. To make a donation or to learn more about our books, authors, events, and newsletter, please visit www.northatlanticbooks.com.

North Atlantic Books is the publishing arm of the Society for the Study of Native Arts and Sciences, a 501(c)(3) nonprofit educational organization that promotes cross-cultural perspectives linking scientific, social, and artistic fields. To learn how you can support us, please visit our website.